Founded in 1841, the *Jewish Chronicle* is the oldest continuously published Jewish newspaper in the world. A force for change, a forum for debate and a shaper of Jewish identity, it has played a central part in the development of modern Anglo-Jewry. More than just a mirror of Anglo-Jewish mores, registering waves of immigration and social change, the *JC* has been an active player in historical events. Its editors have intervened decisively in communal history and debated with British statesmen. No historian can understand the inner life of British Jews without looking at the social reports, the sports column, the arts and cultural coverage and the advertising that the paper has carried. This book, written by a noted British Jewish historian, gives an insight into the working of a newspaper, the struggles between editors and directors, and the boardroom politics. It is the story of a publishing adventure that became an institution and helped to shape the destiny of an entire community.

The *Jewish Chronicle* and Anglo-Jewry, 1841–1991

The *Jewish Chronicle*
and
Anglo-Jewry, 1841–1991

David Cesarani

CAMBRIDGE
UNIVERSITY PRESS

CAMBRIDGE UNIVERSITY PRESS
Cambridge, New York, Melbourne, Madrid, Cape Town, Singapore, São Paulo

Cambridge University Press
The Edinburgh Building, Cambridge CB2 2RU, UK

Published in the United States of America by Cambridge University Press, New York

www.cambridge.org
Information on this title: www.cambridge.org/9780521434348

First published 1994
Reprinted 1995
This digitally printed first paperback version 2005

A catalogue record for this publication is available from the British Library

Library of Congress Cataloguing in Publication data

Cesarani, David.
The Jewish Chronicle and Anglo-Jewry, 1841–1991 / David Cesarani.
  p. cm.
Includes bibliographical references and index.
ISBN 0 521 43434 3 (hardback)
1. *Jewish Chronicle* (London, England: 1841)   2. Jews – Great Britain –
historiography.   I. Title.
PN5650.C47   1994
072'.1'089924–dc20   92–43753   CIP

ISBN-13 978-0-521-43434-8 hardback
ISBN-10 0-521-43434-3 hardback

ISBN-13 978-0-521-01913-2 paperback
ISBN-10 0-521-01913-3 paperback

Contents

Preface

For long stretches of its one hundred and fifty year history, the *Jewish Chronicle* held a monopoly of the Jewish press in Great Britain. Even when it faced competition it remained pre-eminent and lived up to its title 'The Organ of Anglo-Jewry', a position of privilege that carried with it the burden of public duty. The paper provided an indispensable medium between British Jews and the wider society, interpreting matters of Jewish interest (as understood by the paper), and offering a response that amounted, virtually, to the view of Anglo-Jewry. If a significant portion of Jewish opinion dissented from its news coverage or interpretation of events, this was usually reflected by the letters page or in opinion pieces. Barring a few extraordinary episodes in its history the *Jewish Chronicle* succeeded in maintaining a consensual position, and it was this which gave it such commanding authority. It is a testament to the paper's influence that critics and opponents have made repeated attempts to undermine it by setting up rivals or buying it outright. Such was its weight, and so great its responsibility, that one editor was removed by the paper's directors for fear of the damage which his editorials were doing to the reputation of British Jews.

By interpreting the world to the Jews in Britain and representing them to the majority society, the *Jewish Chronicle* played a fundamental role in shaping Anglo-Jewish identity. It defined the parameters for debate on communal and other issues; it gave Jews in Britain an awareness of what was happening to Jews in other countries; it offered them a digest of Jewish cultural activity; and it functioned as a forum for the discussion of Judaism. This volume deals with an institution which was both a part of Anglo-Jewish history and a medium through which it was refracted. It is the story of a newspaper, its place in Jewish communal life and its influence on the growth and development of Anglo-Jewry.

Much of the drama of newspaper history comes from the interchanges between proprietors, editors, journalists and business managers. There is the tension of circulation wars and the excitement of technological innovation. At the most exalted level, newspaper histories give an insight into high politics where proprietors, editors, politicians and statesmen mingle. In the struggle for influence over public opinion, newspaper history becomes part of national history.

Proprietors and editors of the *Jewish Chronicle* only occasionally interacted with political figures on the national or international stage, although when they did these tended to be fateful encounters – such as the breakfast rendezvous between Abraham Benisch and William Gladstone or Asher Myers's disputatious meeting with Theodor Herzl. Their interventions in Anglo-Jewish affairs were more frequent and were always invested with gravity. The editorial influence of the *Jewish Chronicle* was cardinal in the formation of the Board of Guardians, the United Synagogue, the Anglo-Jewish Association, The Maccabaeans and the Jewish Historical Society of England. It constantly addressed itself to the affairs of the Board of Deputies and amplified the debates which took place there. Several editors and proprietors played a role in the founding or conduct of these communal institutions.

On a few momentous occasions Jewish, British and international history intersected through the medium of the *Jewish Chronicle* or the actions of those connected with it. The paper was the first to publish Herzl's blueprint for the modern Zionist Movement and was hugely influential, first as an opponent of Zionism and later as its supporter. By 1917 it had assumed such a pivotal role that publication of the Balfour Declaration was delayed until it could be revealed to the world through the paper's columns. For the next thirty years, while Britain dominated the fate of Palestine, the *Jewish Chronicle* was a vital intermediary between Jewish opinion and the British Government.

Sadly, in view of its importance, the historian of the *Jewish Chronicle* is faced with a frustrating absence of sources. The primary material relating to the first century of its existence was lost during the blitz when the paper's offices in Moor Lane, in the City of London, were totally destroyed in a German air raid on 29 December 1940. For this reason, the weekly editions of the *Jewish Chronicle* itself are the chief source on which this history relies for much of its information about the paper. However, significant documents have been unearthed in other archives in this country and in Israel which shed light on the story up to 1940. Using these sources, supplemented by the recollections of individuals which carry back to the mid 1930s, I have attempted to reconstruct the internal workings of the paper, encompassing technological and commercial developments as well as changes in the foremost personnel.

The centenary volume written by Cecil Roth and others, and published in 1949, contains a wealth of detail on the earlier period, although it is frequently anecdotal and unsourced. I have leaned heavily on this work for the earlier period and its existence has made it possible to avoid repetition of much technical data about the publication of the paper in its first century. In other respects, this volume differs greatly from the earlier one in terms of approach and emphasis.

The references to the *Jewish Chronicle* are confined largely to leading articles or editorial notes. These offered a considered response to the chief news items of the week and were intended to shape Jewish opinion or address the wider society. Often they were the vehicle for particular campaigns or hobby-horses. While readership of leading articles in the general press and the Jewish press has tailed off since the 1950s, they were once a crucial element of public debate and repay close attention. Another reason for dwelling on them is the knowledge of who their authors were: the identity of correspondents and reporters prior to 1940 is almost completely unknown. To minimise the number of notes, the date of a leading article is embodied in the text where convenient; the location of the editorial in the paper is easy to find. Otherwise, date and page references to all printed articles are in the notes at the end of the book.

While it is impossible to write the history of Anglo-Jewry relying solely on the *Jewish Chronicle*, it is equally impractical to try writing Anglo-Jewish history without it. The bulk of this work deals with what the *Jewish Chronicle* said about key issues in Anglo-Jewish and world Jewish affairs and why. It also provides a narrative of the paper's inner life, the role of its owners, directors and editors in shaping the editorial outlook and news coverage. The technological and commercial aspects of running the paper are indispensable elements of the story, but they form the backdrop. As distinct from the concerns of newspaper historians alone, for those interested in the history of the Jews in Britain since 1841, a knowledge of where the *Jewish Chronicle* stood at any one time on any particular subject is crucial. This book sets out to meet that need.

Acknowledgements

Many people contributed to the making of this volume. I would like to thank William Frankel, His Hon. Israel Finestein, QC and David Kessler for the sensitive way they managed its genesis on behalf of the *Jewish Chronicle*. They shared with me their thoughts about the paper's history, read every draft of the book and made numerous helpful comments. In combination they provided an awe-inspiring repository of historical knowledge about Anglo-Jewry and a profound experience of newspaper publishing. I also benefited enormously from extended interviews with David Kessler, William Frankel, Sidney Moss, Geoffrey Paul and Ned Temko. David Kessler was most kind and tolerant in answering every sort of inquiry, ferreting out documents and undergoing three prolonged interviews. I would also like to thank Isidore 'Izzy' Bernstein and Maurice Goldsmith for giving me their memories of working on the paper. In the course of my research I visited several archives, and I would like to acknowledge the assistance of Dalia Trasz at the Jewish Studies Library (formerly Mocatta Library), University College London; Simone Mace and the staff of the Rothschild Archive, London; David Massel, who presides over the Board of Deputies Archive, London; Charles Tucker, archivist of the United Synagogue, London; Yoram Mayorek and the staff of the Central Zionist Archive, Jerusalem; Tania Grosz and the staff of the Jabotinsky Institute, Tel Aviv; Dr Tony Kushner and the staff of the Parkes Library, Southampton University, where the Anglo-Jewish Archives now reside; Renée Waale of the Jewish Historical Museum, Amsterdam; and, especially, Linda Greenlick and the staff of the Jewish Chronicle Library. I am grateful to Lionel Simmonds, a former staff member, for his careful editorial attention to an early version of the manuscript. Sections and chapters of the book were read in draft form by Mr Richard Bolchover, Dr Bryan Cheyette, Dr Tony Kushner and Dr Mark Levene. I must thank them for their many useful observations and corrections, although I bear the burden of any mistakes which remain in the final text and the opinions it contains.

The *Jewish Chronicle and Anglo-Jewry, 1841–1991* is dedicated to

Dawn: she has lived with it and with me for almost the same period of time, and both the author and the book would have been immeasurably the poorer without her intelligence, hard work, patience and love.

Introduction

In the late eighteenth century, the press in England was limited to a few London dailies and evening papers that appeared two or three times a week, along with a vibrant provincial weekly press. However, the decades between 1780 and 1820 saw a sudden spurt of publishing activity. In 1781, there were 76 newspapers in England and Wales; by 1821 the number had risen to 267, and it had almost doubled again to reach 563 thirty years later.[1] This expansion followed advances in popular education and the increasing urbanisation of English society. The towns and cities that burgeoned in the course of the Industrial Revolution created a large market for periodicals as well as demand for the advertising necessary to make journals viable.[2]

The growth of the press was also facilitated by technological developments such as the Stanhope press in 1800, the Koenig steam press in 1814 and the rotary cylinder press from the 1850s onwards, which made it possible to print more copies faster at a reduced cost. In addition, the distribution and marketing of newspapers was steadily improved by the use of mail coaches and then the railways. However, machinery was enormously expensive, and newspapers had heavy overheads due to the cost of paper, telegraphy and large, expensive teams of reporters. The taxes on paper, advertising and newspapers added to the difficulties of making them profitable. While circulation could be increased by printing more copies, the increased profit might be only marginal because of the tax on the individual sheets of paper and on the advertisements that they carried.[3]

The financial viability of newspapers was transformed by the relaxation of fiscal controls over newspaper publishing. In 1836 the notorious stamp duty – 'the tax on knowledge' – was cut from 4d. to 1d. The tax on advertising was reduced in 1833 (it had already been halved for supplements in 1825) and abolished in 1853. Two years later, the newspaper tax was finally abandoned. Meanwhile, the excise duty on paper was reduced from 3d. to $1\frac{1}{2}$d. per pound in 1836 and phased out in 1861, adding to the savings that resulted from the falling price of paper itself. All this enabled newspapers to be larger in size, appear more frequently, be printed in greater numbers and sold at a lower price – while earning more through advertising.[4]

From the 1840s, periodical literature in Victorian England flourished. Monthly commentaries on world affairs, literary journals, comic magazines and trade papers as well as a full range of newspapers proliferated. This abundance was attributable to various forces, not least to the political parties which had always had a hand in the development of the press. National and local politicians seized on newspapers and journals to influence an electorate that had been widened by the Great Reform Act of 1832. The profitable ownership of newspapers and their use as tools to influence voters was a pleasing combination.[5]

A similar process was visible in the spread of publications serving pressure groups and religious denominations. Religious periodicals had first appeared in the mid seventeenth century, but the fervid atmosphere of the 1820s proved to be a hot-house for religious publishing. New religious movements, notably the Evangelicals, promoted themselves through the press and stimulated a reaction from non-Evangelical bodies. Dissenters used the press to champion their right to civil equality, while the established church fought back.[6] By founding a newspaper, a minority group enhanced its public status. A journal supplied news from within the group as well as informing its members of events in the wider world, interpreted according to their own sectional point of view and interests. Newspapers were also a useful tool for fundraising and often acted as clearing houses for appeals. Finally, 'the Victorian religious periodical acted for subscribers themselves as a symbol, as something by which the subscriber could define his personal position within the bewildering fluidity of Victorian religion'.[7]

During the 1840s, political controversy and denominational rivalry, aided by the reduction of taxes and duties, encouraged the mushroom growth of the religious press. The Catholic *Tablet* first published on 16 May 1840, and the *Nonconformist*, which appeared on 14 April 1841, were committed to 'principles of tolerance and justice' and dedicated to the campaign against the remaining impositions on Dissenters. Unitarians likewise founded the *Inquirer* in July 1842. Meanwhile, the tensions within the Church of England and the Catholic Church resulted in a flurry of periodicals representing one faction or another. The re-establishment of the Catholic hierarchy in 1850–1, the 'Awakening' at the end of the decade and the possibilities of a cheap, instructional press continued to swell the number of titles well into the 1860s.[8]

The religious press set out to edify its readers, to improve their knowledge of doctrine and to reinforce their faith. There were pages of polemic against schismatic groups or other denominations, and news of missionary work abroad. The staple secular content included reports on parliamentary affairs, foreign news and commercial intelligence. Political news concentrated on the battles for or against civic equality, the abolition of church rates, disestablishment and the range of other issues where religion and politics intersected. Unabashed in their advocacy of a particular cause, the papers also reported electoral activity and lobbying. In addition, there were book reviews, cultural notes, some creative writing and much correspondence. Advertising reflected the social composition of the denomination in question.[9]

The Anglo-Jewish press of the nineteenth century emerged in this context, but its origins cannot be isolated from the prior evolution of a distinctive Jewish press on the Continent. It was greatly influenced by its Continental forebears, indirectly through using the European Jewish press as a model and a source of material, and directly through the employment of Jews born and educated in central Europe. They brought with them the outlook of the Jewish enlightenment or *Haskalah*, intended to disseminate modern European culture among Jews, and injected its ideas into indigenous Anglo-Jewish journalism.

Newsletters in Yiddish had been published in Holland as early as the 1680s, but they were ephemeral. The Jewish periodical press was really a creation of the *Haskalah* Movement. Its proponents, the *maskilim*, believed that the civic standing of the Jews would be improved only by showing the non-Jewish world that Judaism was in harmony with contemporary religious thought and that Jews, still largely confined to ghettos, could fit usefully into contemporary society. To achieve this transformation they set about disseminating a new civic morality among the Jews and encouraged the reform of Judaism. These intentions underlay the publication of the literary monthly *Ha-measef*, the Harvester, in Germany in the 1780s and 1790s. However, the use of Hebrew limited its appeal to an educated minority, and despite its enormous influence, the journal could not be sustained.[10]

The convictions which animated *Ha-measef* were embodied in the more successful monthly *Sulamith*, published regularly in Leipzig between 1806 and 1825 (and intermittently thereafter) by David Frankel (1779–1865). *Sulamith* conveyed to a German-reading Jewish public the importance of moral education, civic rectitude and diversification away from traditional, and despised, Jewish occupations. It asserted that Jews deserved acceptance as equals by their fellow Germans, but advised that social and political equality had to be earned. An integral part of this emancipationist ideology was the demonstration of deep loyalty to the German states in which the Jews lived and a love of German culture. At the same time, *Sulamith* contributed to the construction of a 'public sphere' for German Jews. In its pages they could address one another as Jews, on Jewish matters, and so reconstitute the sense of community that was lost with emancipation and the dissolution of self-contained Jewish communal structures.[11]

Sulamith faded in the late 1820s, and was succeeded by the far more durable *Allgemeine Zeitung des Judentums* (*AZdJ*), arguably the first proper Jewish newspaper. The *AZdJ* was launched on 15 March 1837 in Leipzig by Ludwig Philippson (1811–89). It promoted the ideology of emancipation and transmitted the social values of *Bildung* – education, self-improvement and civic betterment. The paper was also a vehicle enabling Jews to keep in touch with one another and debate their mutual interests. To this extent, the *AZdJ* was a medium for creating a distinctive, ethnic Jewish community.[12]

The same process was evident in France. The French Jewish press may have proclaimed that Jews were merely individual citizens of a particular denomination, but it grew out of collective and trans-national Jewish concerns. In 1840 Jews in Damascus had been falsely accused of abducting and killing a local Christian; members of the community were tortured and the whole of Syrian Jewry faced a catastrophe. The Damascus Affair caused outrage throughout the Jewish world and led to an internationally co-ordinated rescue mission. Out of these efforts came the founding of a Jewish press to publicise the Jewish cause. The *Archives Israélites* was established in 1840, followed by the *Univers Israélite* in 1844. Besides supplying a framework for the expression of Jewish unity throughout the world, as in Germany the Jewish press crystallised the ethnic solidarity of French Jews.[13]

Efforts to found a Jewish press in London were made as early as January 1823 with the publication of the *Hebrew Intelligencer*. This monthly, priced at 6d. (but distributed free), was produced by a group of young men about whom little is known. The four-page paper carried mundane news of communal gatherings and gossip about well-to-do Jews in west and north London. In a more serious vein it allied itself to the cause of communal charities and in its opening statement threatened to be merciless in exposing 'those who, by their actions, shall lay themselves open to observation and censure'. Probably because of this attitude, the paper ran for only three issues before it was obliged to cease publication. A wealthy London Jew who apparently objected to its irreverent tone offered monetary inducements to the printer, J. Wertheimer, to cease publication. Since he depended on other Jews for business, Wertheimer surrendered to these blandishments.[14]

At this stage, the lack of a sufficiently large or geographically dispersed population did not make a newspaper an urgent necessity. Most communal business was transacted formally or informally within the precincts of the synagogue around which communal affairs revolved. Since the mass of middle-class and wealthy Jews in London belonged to one of the four tightly clustered City synagogues, a newspaper was hardly an urgent requirement.[15] It is also likely that Anglo-Jewry did not feel the need for an organ of opinion while there was theological homogeneity. Indeed, if the critical stimuli to religious publishing were an evangelical spirit and schism, they were absent from Anglo-Jewry until the late 1830s. But, at that point, the campaign for Jewish emancipation took hold. Schism, emancipation and the dispersion of London Jewry, combined with the technical and financial developments in the production of newspapers, made a Jewish press not only desirable, but practicable.[16]

The Jewish population of England in the 1840s numbered around 30,000–40,000, over half of which was concentrated in London. The rest were scattered in small clusters around coastal and market towns, as well as burgeoning industrial cities like Birmingham, Manchester, Liverpool and Leeds. They were predominantly artisans, shopkeepers and small manufacturers, often in very humble circumstances, with a small élite of international merchants, factory owners and bankers.[17] Jewish immigration from the Continent had been interrupted during the Napoleonic Wars, but after 1815 the number of poor foreign Jews had begun to climb. In every centre of Jewish settlement there was a large body of pedlars, hawkers and artisans who were barely making a living. Added to this were the old and the infirm who fell into poverty.[18]

The broad trend in mid-century, however, was towards prosperity. Street traders and migrant salesmen were being squeezed out of the economy by fixed retail outlets serving the growing urban industrial workforce and middle classes. Larger numbers of Jews than ever before were moving into the upper reaches of retail, wholesale and international trade. A few pioneers were even penetrating into the free professions, a gradual process that depended on changes in the Jews' legal status. English Jews could not graduate from an English university until the establishment of University College London, in 1827. They were not free to trade in the City until 1830 and were not permitted to practise at the Bar until 1833.[19]

Despite the advance in their social status and wealth, Jews were still denied full civic equality. As a legacy of the bitter struggles between Catholics, Protestant sects and the Church of England over the previous three hundred years, those who dissented from the established church laboured under civil and legal disabilities. By the 1820s the fact that Dissenters were denied access to municipal office or election to Parliament had become an offence to liberal opinion, which increasingly set the mood for the country as a whole. In 1828, after a sustained agitation, the majority of Protestant Dissenters were relieved from such restrictions by the repeal of the Test and Corporation Acts. Following continued pressure, Roman Catholics were emancipated in 1829 under the Roman Catholic Relief Act. However, the Relief Acts replaced the requirement to take the sacrament and give oaths not to injure the established church or assist pretenders to the throne, with a declaration using the formula 'on the true faith of a Christian'. These words effectively – and deliberately – excluded Jews (and some Protestant sects such as Quakers and Moravians) from the benefit of the Acts.[20]

Exclusion from municipal offices and election to Parliament was not simply an indignity. To wealthy financiers and merchants, political influence was a valuable adjunct to business activity and an important mark of status. In Victorian society municipal offices conferred enormous prestige on their holders and the sect or calling from which they originated. It was galling to the social élite in Jewish society to find itself barred from power and honour. Worse, exclusion appeared to confirm the deeply held prejudices within a large part of English society, that Judaism was an inferior creed, and that Jews were not fit to participate in the affairs of a Christian nation.[21]

In 1830, leading figures within London Jewry initiated a campaign for the relief of Jewish disabilities. They pressed their case for ten years without success because, although the House of Commons accepted it in principle in 1833, the House of Lords continued to resist. Opponents of Jewish emancipation argued that the Jews were an alien nation that just happened to reside in England, owing loyalty to their own people and aspiring to return to Palestine. It was said that Jewish doctrine encouraged hostility towards Christians and Christianity, and that Jews deliberately remained aloof from the rest of the population. Jews were held responsible for the death of Jesus, for which some Christians felt they should still be punished by their exclusion from the privileges of citizenship. In some quarters it was considered unthinkable for Jews to enter the legislature of a Christian country where they could influence the conduct of the state church. These arguments were bolstered by prejudices relating to Jewish economic activity: Jews were widely portrayed as hucksters or money-lenders, uninterested in culture and obsessed with money.[22]

In the course of the campaign for emancipation its proponents engaged in fierce polemics in the defence of Judaism. They also practised a form of social engineering on the Jewish population in order to eliminate the features which seemed obnoxious to non-Jews and tried to mould Jewish society more closely to the contours of respectable English society.[23] This process touched on religious practice, too. In 1836, members of the Spanish and Portuguese Synagogue petitioned the heads of the synagogue for alterations in the service so as to eliminate some of the hubbub which accompanied prayers, shorten the duration of the services and add a choir. The petitioners also wanted sermons in English to provide moral instruction for English Jews in a language they could understand. These demands merged with a separate request to establish a branch-synagogue in the West End to serve the growing number of Jews who had moved there from the eastern fringes of the City.[24]

In the spring of 1840, the dissidents from the Spanish and Portuguese Synagogue seceded and combined with a group of like-minded Ashkenazi Jews to establish a separate congregation. They took the opportunity to introduce into the service several changes which were inspired by the Reform Movement in Germany. These reforms aroused a storm of controversy, and in 1841 the rebel congregation was placed under a *cherem*, ban or excommunication, by the Chief Rabbi, Solomon Hirschell. At a time when the Jews of England were pleading for toleration, this was a deep embarrassment.[25]

The Jewish press came into being against this background. Its founders were closely involved in the conflicts of the day. They saw newspapers serving their aspirations for the development of Jewish society in England, notably emancipation. While they differed amongst themselves in terms of emphasis, they followed in the pattern of Continental Jewry. The press was envisaged as a force for moral and cultural improvement, working alongside schools and colleges. The founders called for reforms in the synagogue and sought a greater degree of harmony between Jewish and English modes of worship. As educated, cultured men, they encouraged talent and took a keen interest in literature and historical studies. All of these goals were linked by the urge to improve, to enlighten and to flourish as patriotic Englishmen.

1   Origins and pioneers, 1841–1855

Jacob Franklin and Isaac Vallentine, 1841–1844

Two figures dominate the first years of the Jewish press in Britain, Jacob Franklin (1809–77) and Isaac Vallentine (1793–1868). Although Franklin was born and educated in England while Vallentine was from the Low Countries, both men were typical offshoots of the Jewish enlightenment and combined a deep knowledge of Judaism with a fascination for secular learning. They brought to their involvement in Jewish affairs the outlook of the educated English middle classes, blending the early nineteenth-century belief in reason and progress with the traditional values of Judaism. Their separate, and at times conflicting, ventures into publishing were the outstanding product of this fusion.

Jacob Franklin is usually regarded as the 'father' of the Jewish press in England, even though it was not he who founded the *Jewish Chronicle*. The paper launched by Franklin in September 1841 was called the *Voice of Jacob*, and it actually pre-empted the publication of the *Jewish Chronicle* by several weeks. The two journals co-existed uneasily for six months, before the *Jewish Chronicle* was merged with the *Voice of Jacob*. The latter then held a monopoly position for nearly two years, until the *Jewish Chronicle* was revived, and continued to appear until 1848. Franklin thus presided over the birth of the first Jewish newspaper in England to achieve more than transient success. Many years later, long after the demise of his own publication, he stepped in to save the *Jewish Chronicle* when it was stricken by crisis. It was not without reason that subsequent editors of the paper cherished his memory and paid tribute to his founding genius.[1]

Franklin was born in Portsmouth in 1809 and grew up in Liverpool, where his father was a communal functionary. His upbringing was rigidly Orthodox, but he enjoyed a solid secular education and from an early age taught general subjects to other students. By training he was an optician; however, he won acclaim as a professional actuary. Throughout his life he was interested in education. Inspired by the doctrine of improvement and progress through rational instruction, he was involved in setting up schools in Lancashire and London and was the founder and director of the Mechanics' Institute in Manchester.

Alarmed by what he saw as the erosion of Judaism in England, Franklin decided to set up a Jewish newspaper that would help to combat religious indifference, ignorance and the pursuit of worldly goals over spiritual ones. In 1846 he recalled to his readers that he intended it to fortify every young Jewish Englishman against the attractions of 'a world in which the liberalism of the day was teaching him to covet social equality, than to maintain the spiritual rank assigned to him by Providence'. The immediate conditions which made it conceivable to launch a Jewish journal were supplied by the Damascus Affair, which deeply affected Jews and made them aware of the paramount need for an organ of self-defence and communication.[2]

In the course of 1840, Franklin arranged a meeting of communal activists and intellectuals in London to discuss the founding of a Jewish journal. He invited Dr Morris J. Raphall (1798–1868), Sampson Samuel (1806–68), David Aron de Sola (1796–1860) and Dr Abraham Benisch (1811–78). Raphall worked as secretary to the Chief Rabbi and went on to become minister of the Birmingham Hebrew Congregation. In 1834, he had brought out a Jewish literary periodical, *The Hebrew Review and Magazine of Rabbinical Literature*, which lasted for two years. This monthly was closely modelled on the instructional Jewish press in Europe, and it gave Raphall the editorial experience which the others lacked. Samuel was active in philanthropic work and later served as solicitor and secretary to the Board of Deputies; de Sola was the foreign-born *chazan*, reader, at the Spanish and Portuguese Synagogue; Benisch was a typical enlightened Jew from central Europe, a *maskil*, who had only recently arrived in the country.[3]

Franklin planned to fund the paper while de Sola and Raphall edited it. However, de Sola was barred by his employers from taking up the offer, and Raphall was called to serve the Jews of Birmingham. Consequently, Franklin combined the business side with editorial duties until he was joined by his brother, Ellis Franklin, who took over the commercial work. Jacob Franklin initially collected the money required to start the paper from prominent London Jews including Sir Moses Montefiore, Baron Lionel de Rothschild and Baron Anthony de Rothschild. He also canvassed for subscribers, but succeeded only in achieving a regular circulation of around 300 in the first twelve months. The idea of a newspaper was not universally well received. Franklin later said that he encountered active opposition from 'that class' of men who managed the public affairs of English Jews. They resented the idea of public criticism, while their paid functionaries were afraid of coming under general scrutiny.[4]

When the *Voice of Jacob* was launched on 16 September 1841, it mirrored the agenda of the Continental Jewish press and the religious press in England. In the first issue, the editor avowed 'a bias for what is established and recognised, as contra distinguished from what is speculative or unauthorised'. This was a clear statement of hostility to the Reform congregation: to Franklin change could be admitted only under the auspices, and with the approval of, authorities grounded in tradition. Reconciliation between the rebels and the establishment was possible, but he made it clear who he thought needed to repent as a precondition for this to come about.

The early content of the *Voice of Jacob* owed much to the aftershocks of the Damascus Affair. In the first issue, Abraham Benisch ('A Foreigner') dwelt on the role that English Jews could play in the assistance of their less fortunate brethren abroad. Tobias Theodores (1808–86), writing as 'T. T.', contributed a powerful attack on the blood libel, the allegation that Jews murdered Christians to obtain their blood for Passover and other rituals.[5] Addressing domestic issues, the *Voice of Jacob* championed the establishment of a college for training ministers in England which, it was hoped, would eliminate dependence on immigrant rabbis and ensure that homilies and sermons could be delivered in the vernacular. This cause was one aspect of the drive for moral improvement and was closely linked to the emancipation campaign.[6]

On 26 October 1841, a small item in the *Voice of Jacob* grudgingly noted the arrival of a second Jewish paper, the *Jewish Chronicle*. Its founder, Isaac Vallentine, was typical of the proprietors of the religious press in England. According to his colourful autobiography, Vallentine was born in Belgium and had an Orthodox upbringing. His father was a religious functionary who eventually became the reader at the Hambro Synagogue in the City of London, where he resided with his family. Isaac was apprenticed as a watchmaker, but after various adventures settled down to conduct the bookselling business which his father ran in addition to his duties at the Hambro. From 1837 he branched out into the publication of almanacs, including the Hebrew–English almanacs used by immigrant Jews who tramped the country as pedlars. The production of these calendars was closely allied to the world of periodical publishing, and Vallentine had acquired a good deal of experience in this field before he took the next step of starting a newspaper.

Like Franklin, Vallentine took a keen interest in education and enlightenment. He helped to set up the Jewish Association for the Diffusion of Religious Knowledge in 1828, and the Jews' Orphans Asylum in Mile End in 1831. He was involved in the evening classes at Sussex Hall promoted by London Jews for poor Jewish artisans, a sort of Jewish

Mechanics' Institute. This predilection for educational work reflected the concerns of an enlightened European Jew, but it was also intended to counter the activities of Christian missionaries preying on poor Jews in London. Like most Jews, and pressmen, at this time, he was a Liberal by political conviction.[7]

In the summer of 1840, after Franklin had resolved to start a paper (and possibly in ignorance of this initiative until too late in the day to avoid a collision), Vallentine approached two talented young men to produce the *Jewish Chronicle*. He picked David Meldola (1797–1853), the minister at the Spanish and Portuguese Synagogue, and Moses Angel (1819–98), a graduate of University College London who was a teacher at Jews' Free School.[8] Although Vallentine successfully recruited his editorial team, he experienced trouble securing the necessary finance for the project. A prospectus was produced and circulated, but in the end he was his own printer and publisher – a not uncommon way of achieving economies. The delay of several months meant that the *Voice of Jacob* appeared first, which must have placed the *Jewish Chronicle* at a severe disadvantage.[9]

The *Jewish Chronicle*'s layout was similar to that of other titles in the religious press, although it was smaller, with four pages, and cheaper than *The Tablet* and the *Nonconformist*. The first issue carried a list of agents from whom the paper could be obtained which corresponded closely to the areas of Jewish settlement in London and beyond: one agent in the Strand, three in and around the City, one in Soho and one each in Manchester, Liverpool, Birmingham, Cheltenham and Bristol. It was claimed that copies could be purchased through booksellers anywhere, but there were soon complaints that the *Jewish Chronicle* was unobtainable in many districts. This led Vallentine to get a proportion of the sheets on which it was printed stamped so that they could be distributed at no further cost through the mail. This measure followed a series of articles on Jewish settlements in outlying areas of London and the Home Counties that may have been a ploy to increase interest – and circulation – outside the metropolis.[10]

Vallentine also secured revenue through an advertising supplement which was issued irregularly with the paper. It was more economical to gather paid notices and advertisements together and issue them this way since the duty on supplements had been halved in 1825. At the same time as he was going after a wider circulation, in March 1842 Vallentine offered a special cut-price advertising rate in an attempt to boost the volume of advertisements. His strategy did not succeed, and the paper lost money. Whereas the rival *Voice of Jacob* also failed as a commercial proposition, Franklin had sufficient resources and patronage to keep it going for seven years.[11]

The editors of the *Jewish Chronicle* declared in their statement of aims that 'Our creed is peace to all mankind – opposition to none, and love of God.' But this was not necessarily an olive branch to the Reform seceders. In the paper's very first feature 'On the Law', the author declared that 'The law may be regarded as being divine, perfect and eternal ... It is the pilot that alone can guide us safely o'er the troubled waters of the world.' In a later essay on Jewish ceremony and prayer, 'J. D.' delivered a trenchant defence of traditional forms of prayer. He declared that to make changes in Judaism was to risk danger: 'Public worship would become utter confusion, if all men were deemed sufficiently qualified either to add to, or expunge from the formula prescribed by a duly established authority.'[12]

In its second issue the *Jewish Chronicle* claimed with pride that Sir Moses Montefiore and his wife were subscribers, and it was careful not to offend their sensibilities regarding the Reform congregation. Angel and Meldola never defied the dominant mood of London Jewry on the question of the schism. However, if the young *Jewish Chronicle* sided with the communal establishment on the split among London Jews, this did not preclude a progressive social outlook on other issues. As was to be expected from a journal edited by a school-master, the paper reported frequently on educational developments. There were articles on the Jewish school in Liverpool, Jews' Free School in London and other pedagogic institutions. Like its rival, the *Jewish Chronicle* was enthusiastic about a 'Hebrew College'. On 7 January 1842 there was a lively report of the first meeting of the friends of the college, including a long quotation from a Mr Joseph Mitchell – who would one day emerge as the paper's proprietor.

Angel and Meldola did see the need for some improvement of synagogue services. They published a letter from 'P. A.' calling for sermons in English and dismissing those who once regarded its use as 'a profanation'.[13] More significant, on 21 January 1842, they printed a lengthy account of a turbulent debate at the Western Synagogue in which Charles Salaman proposed a resolution for improving punctuality and decorum during services. But, when the decisive confrontation between the established synagogues and the Reform congregation finally arrived, they aligned themselves emphatically on the side of tradition and the establishment. On 28 January 1842, the paper carried the letter from Sir Moses Montefiore, President of the Board of Deputies, to the wardens of all the London synagogues conveying the resolutions of a meeting of the Board, synagogue wardens and the Chief Rabbi held on 9 November 1841. The resolution ordered the reading of the *cherem* promulgated by the Chief Rabbi, and, since Meldola was a signatory to the subsequent letter, it is hard to see how the *Jewish Chronicle* could have taken a position other than of uncompromising hostility to the Reformers.[14]

Under the terms of the *cherem* faithful Jews were obliged to avoid any contact with the seceders. Angel and Meldola took this injunction so seriously that they declined to attend the opening of the West London Synagogue of British Jews even to report the event. The editors explained that the account of the opening carried in their paper was extracted from the *Morning Chronicle*. Indeed, they considered the new synagogue to be 'the consequence of the obdurate determination of persons calling themselves "British Jews", to make alterations in our ritual and forms of prayer not sanctioned by the principles of our faith, nor the ecclesiastical authorities of the religion, and of their pertinacious rejection of the authority of the oral law'.[15]

Although it reported a few dissenting voices the paper was overwhelmingly hostile to the Reform congregation. In the last of a series of three vituperative articles headed 'The British Jews', the anonymous author declared: 'That the new sect of British Jews must either become the distinct representatives of a nondescript form of religion, or otherwise revert to their former position and belief has been our unchallengeable opinion from the commencement of their visionary and chimerical schemes of modern refinement.'[16]

For the rest of its short duration, the first series of the *Jewish Chronicle* reported the debates and sometimes violent scenes which punctuated the early history of the Reform Movement in England. Such conflict and controversy was customarily meat and drink to a newspaper proprietor, but it seems to have done nothing to assist the fortunes of the *Jewish Chronicle*. This could not have been the result of narrow-mindedness towards the new congregation in contrast to the attitude of the *Voice of Jacob*. If anything, the two papers competed in their shrill denunciation of the secessionists.

Relations between the *Voice of Jacob* and the *Jewish Chronicle* were coming to a head. Both were losing money, and it was clear that there was not a sufficient market for two Anglo-Jewish journals. Franklin proposed a merger with the *Jewish Chronicle*, but was at first rebuffed by Vallentine. Meanwhile, the *mahamad*, the governing body of the Spanish and Portuguese Synagogue, forced Meldola to give up his journalistic career since they considered it to be beneath his standing and offensive to the dignity of their congregation. Franklin then succeeded in persuading Angel to join him on the *Voice of Jacob*. Deserted by his aides, Vallentine now came under considerable communal pressure for a 'consolidation of the Jewish press'. Not long afterwards he suspended publication of the

Jewish Chronicle. For the next thirty months, the *Voice of Jacob* was in a monopoly position.[17]

Left in possession of the field, Franklin could now turn his mind to a cherished project: the founding of an instructional monthly journal for the Jewish population. Even though the finances of the *Voice of Jacob* were parlous, in the course of 1844 Franklin entered into co-operation with some unnamed businessmen with an eye to bringing out a monthly magazine.[18] However, at the end of August 1844, the *Voice of Jacob* carried an angry statement that since 'the objects of the real projectors and guaranteeing supporters of the proposed magazine do not admit a union compatible with our notions of a religiously safe, or an independent and impartial editorship, we declare, that if that magazine appear, it is likely to be rather antagonistic to the existing Anglo-Jewish press, than in concert with it'. The *Voice of Jacob* alleged that the new publication was directly connected with the Reform congregation.[19]

At around this time, advertisements promoting a new series of the *Jewish Chronicle* were placed in the general press, including *The Times*. The pre-publicity promised a greater openness and tolerance on all matters, including religion: the columns of the *Jewish Chronicle* would be 'thrown open to all creeds for discussion of these highly interesting subjects, not being the organ of any party or sect, but striving for truth and justice'. A little over a month later, the *Jewish Chronicle and Working Man's Friend* appeared.[20]

Joseph Mitchell and Marcus Bresslau, 1844–1855

The new proprietor of the *Jewish Chronicle* was Joseph Mitchell, a lively character and, one suspects, something of a rogue. A self-made man who was outspokenly Liberal in his politics, he conformed closely to the model of newspaper proprietors in mid-nineteenth-century Britain. Little is known about his origins: it is not even clear when he was born or where. He is said to have been '"a rough diamond"... who was sadly in need of polishing', and he certainly liked to describe himself as a member of the 'working classes'. When he revived the *Jewish Chronicle* he amended the title to the *Jewish Chronicle and Working Man's Friend*, so capitalising on the democratic mood cultivated by the Chartist Movement and flaunting his supposed affiliations.[21]

Whatever his true origins Mitchell had acquired a modest degree of wealth, although how he came by it is not clear. For many years he was the honorary secretary of the Widows' Home Asylum and a patron of the National Friendly Association for the Manufacture of Passover Bread. He was active in discussions about setting up a refuge for destitute foreign Jews and was so involved in charity work that, in 1853, he chaired a committee of representatives of Jewish charities to consider the implications of the Charitable Trust Bill.[22]

In spite of his philanthropic activity, he does not seem to have been accepted by the Jewish élite. While there are hints that the *Jewish Chronicle* was receiving subventions from the Rothschild family, Mitchell was repeatedly at loggerheads with them in the fight for emancipation. In general he was critical of the influence of wealth in Anglo-Jewry.[23] His reputation would not have been enhanced by the circumstances of his death: he got into financial difficulties and shot himself in Houndsditch in June 1854. Mitchell's own paper carried no obituary of its late proprietor.[24]

Yet Joseph Mitchell was a dynamic figure, and he played a not insignificant part in the long battle for Jewish emancipation in England. In 1847 he inaugurated and presided over the Jewish Association for the Removal of Civil and Religious Disabilities, one of the few popular organisations campaigning for Jewish civic emancipation. It was an important vehicle for demonstrating that the cause had broad support and was not simply the concern of a few wealthy families.[25] Mitchell may have been a 'rough diamond', but he knew the importance of education and culture in the struggle of Jews for social and political acceptance. For example, after a stinging attack by Samuel 'Soapy Sam' Wilberforce, Bishop of Oxford, asserting that Jews were money-grubbing and had no interest in culture, Mitchell offered a £10 prize for an essay on Hebrew literature.[26] He was an early supporter of the Jews' and General Literary and Scientific Institute and used the *Jewish Chronicle* to parade the Institute's merits before the Jewish public, on whom it was largely dependent for funding.[27]

His approach to religion appears to have been pragmatic. In August 1843, he delivered a lengthy oration at a meeting of the Association for Preserving Inviolate the Ancient Rites and Ceremonies of Israel, an avowedly anti-Reform body. Yet, in 1846, the *Voice of Jacob* accused the *Jewish Chronicle* of advocating 'liberal principles' and serving the interests of the Reform congregation. Jacob Franklin mocked the *Jewish Chronicle*, calling it a 'chameleon' that dropped its interest in Orthodoxy when it had a chance to gain support from the Reformers.[28] It was certainly true that the *Jewish Chronicle* displayed more tolerance of the Reform Synagogue than Franklin's zealous organ. However, a close reading of the paper reveals how far the claim that Mitchell was a committed supporter of Reform Judaism is an over-simplification.[29]

Mitchell procured the services of Marcus Hyman Bresslau as his editor. Born in Hamburg and brought up in England, Bresslau had held positions at the Western Synagogue and worked as a Hebrew teacher both privately and at the Westminster Jews' Free School. During the late 1830s he was involved in the production of the *Hebrew Review*, which gave him some experience of the press. Bresslau was a scholarly man who brought to Anglo-Jewish journalism a knowledge of Hebrew texts, literature and history. His Continental origins enabled him to remain *au courant* with intellectual developments among European Jews, and he imported into England many ideas of the *maskilim*.[30]

He was, however, a touchy personality and frequently quarrelled with his employer. Bresslau worked with Mitchell from October 1844 to July 1848, then left the paper for two months after a dispute. He returned as editor around September 1848, staying this time for two years. In October 1851, Mitchell told readers that he had been bringing out the paper single-handed for twelve months. Bresslau later joined the rival *Hebrew Observer*, of which more will be heard.[31]

When Mitchell and Bresslau relaunched the *Jewish Chronicle* on 18 October 1844, they proclaimed a belief in the power of reasoned opinion and the free play of argument that was characteristic of the liberal press of mid-Victorian Britain.[32] While not explicitly endorsing the standpoint of the Reform Movement, the *Jewish Chronicle* defended the right to publish differing points of view. Notwithstanding the fact that it advocated the strengthening of Jewish religious life and Jewish education, it was generally felt that that the new Jewish paper was going to be more broad-minded than its competitor. The *Morning Advertiser* remarked that 'It advocates liberal principles in religion, and is calculated to diffuse enlightened notions on those subjects in which there has been much bigotry among the Jews.'[33]

In fact, owner and editor seemed determined to restore the authority of the rabbinate and to curb the presumptuousness of the laymen, a development which, in their eyes, had led to the split in Anglo-Jewry. They wanted to see Jewish education strengthened to avoid the drift towards trimming Judaism to suit the times. All this would depend on the creation of a progressively minded rabbinate competent in secular matters and worthy of wide respect. These objectives were linked to civil emancipation since, to win acceptance, the Jews had to improve both their image and their actions, a process in which the rabbinate and the synagogues had a part to play.[34]

For these reasons, the *Jewish Chronicle* vigorously opposed the idea of an election to fill the office of Chief Rabbi, left vacant since the death of Solomon Hirschell. This 'campaign', the first run by the paper, was not motivated by élitism or meritocracy. Since the franchise for the election was confined to the free members of the synagogues, who purchased their seats for life, and excluded the regular seat holders, who rented theirs more cheaply, the editors of the *Jewish Chronicle* feared that too much influence lay with the wealthy and powerful upper crust of London Jewry as against the 'virtuous' middle classes. The successful candidate was Rabbi Dr Nathan Marcus Adler, whom the *Jewish Chronicle* had considered to be 'comparatively unknown'.[35]

In fact, Adler (1803–90) proved to be a formidable Chief Rabbi, although like many later incumbents at first he received rough treatment from the *Jewish Chronicle*.[36] The paper hoped that Adler would spread liberal principles of enlightenment and do his utmost to heal the split with the Reform congregation in Burton Street. This did not necessarily entail making concessions: the *Jewish Chronicle* thought he should 'point out to that body the errors in its material and immaterial devotions'.[37] But when the Chief Rabbi eventually issued a circular outlining his programme, the *Jewish Chronicle* commented ruefully on the absence of any suggested improvements in liturgy or ritual. In 1846, the paper was dismayed when Adler continued his predecessor's policy towards the break-away synagogue: it argued that such an attitude would not assist calls for civic justice from Christians.[38]

The call for improvements in the synagogue and rapprochement with the seceders did not mean that Mitchell and Bresslau embraced Reform Judaism. On the contrary: they feared the inroads it was making into a Jewish population increasingly ignorant about the basic tenets of Judaism, materialistic in outlook and poorly led. In their eyes Reform Judaism was the symptom of decline, but it could not be stemmed by diehard conservatism. In a series of leading articles in 1846, entitled 'Devotion in the Synagogue', the *Jewish Chronicle* urged Dr Adler to examine some of the less attractive features of synagogue worship in England. In particular, it drew attention to the very long Sabbath service, the payment for *mitzvot*, honours, by those called to the reading of the Law, the lack of decorum during services and the rarity of sermons in English. The motive behind the leading articles was not to express sympathy with Burton Street, but the opposite. Diehards opposing change were warned that 'Recent events in England and Germany are undeniable witnesses to the fact that the refusal to accede to *necessary* improvements, which the spirit of the age loudly demands, is as dangerous as the indiscriminate agitation for reform. If you obstinately refuse necessary reforms, these applicants will take the reins into their own hands, and will then go further and more rashly than you expected, and than they themselves originally intended to go.'[39]

To gauge the paper's attitude towards Reform Judaism, it is necessary to examine its coverage of Judaism in Germany. After the assembly of rabbis at Frankfurt in 1845, the paper ran a series of leading articles on the

Reform Movement in Germany in which it deprecated the suggestion of many German rabbis that Hebrew be abandoned in favour of the vernacular. It was appalled at the resolution put forward by radicals in 1846, recommending that the Sabbath be transferred to Sunday. Instead, the paper welcomed the call by Rabbi Zacharia Frankel for a conference of conservative rabbis.[40]

The Jews of England were the real target for these animadversions. While 'moderate and judicious' reform was on the agenda elsewhere, 'the Jews of England, of the most civilised country in Europe, appear be to be sunk in lethargy, apathy and indifference to what passes around them ... we almost despair ... of obtaining any improvement as long as the monied interest of the leaders of our congregations rules over both layman and ecclesiastic'. Moderate and controlled change was necessary to pre-empt worse disruptions. The example of German Reform was always held up to illustrate where the line must be drawn.[41]

All the same, the campaign for emancipation led the *Jewish Chronicle* to take a critical view of communal institutions such as the Chief Rabbinate and the Beth Din, the rabbinical court. Its intention was clear: 'We claim justice for, and equalization with, our brethren of another creed ... It is for us, then, to substantiate and render ourselves deserving of them, by instituting such reforms in our national establishments as alone permanently secure to us the privileges which we now enjoy, and hope to enjoy throughout generations.' The paper bemoaned the continuing neglect of preaching and education. In despair, it commented in 1853 that 'We may shut our synagogues, unless we provide for useful pulpit instruction.'[42]

Mitchell was consequently excited to learn, in December 1851, that the Chief Rabbi had issued a circular dealing with the need to train a native ministry and proposing the establishment in London of a day school for the children of middle-class Jewish families. The *Jewish Chronicle* warmly welcomed the initiative: 'With such an institution we need no longer be ashamed to come forward as the champions of civil liberty and the advocates of moral improvement.'[43] In the event, it was four years before Jews' College opened, a delay anxiously remarked upon at regular intervals by the *Jewish Chronicle*. Over this period the paper did much to create a climate of opinion favourable to the College and its intended work, not least by connecting this with the struggle for full civil rights.[44]

Almost every issue of the *Jewish Chronicle* carried news of the emancipation campaign, reports of public meetings and petitions in favour of civic equality for the Jews. It printed comprehensive accounts of the debates in both Houses of Parliament and gave detailed analysis of the political manoeuvres behind them. To refute the arguments against emancipation, the paper printed long articles, often spread over several issues. Thus it became a vital auxiliary to the Jews' struggle and a leading participant in the campaign itself.[45]

It was also necessary to placate the misgivings and even outright opposition of certain Orthodox Jews, notably Rabbi Joseph Crooll, who rejected the need for emancipation because it ran counter to the messianic promise of the return to Zion.[46] Nor could the editor ignore the fact that some prominent lay leaders, particularly Sir Moses Montefiore, were uneasy at the potential cost of emancipation, fearing that it would entail unacceptable compromises of faith and ritual. Despite his commitment to the campaign, Mitchell was true to his word that the *Jewish Chronicle* would reflect all shades of opinion. On 17 January 1845, for example, it printed a powerful statement by 'Judaeus' stating the *Jewish* case against embracing full civil rights.

Frequently the paper reproduced articles from other journals extolling Jewish emancipation. These presented the arguments, sometimes with a new twist, but they were more important as illustrations of the breadth of support for emancipation in the majority society. Several important newspapers and journals were, by contrast, unsympathetic to the Jewish cause. The *Jewish Chronicle*, in its leaders or in articles, tried to answer as many of them as possible. Tobias Theodores was one of the most persistent and effective Jewish polemicists and did not quail at taking on the influential, high-Tory *Standard* or *Blackwood's Magazine* after they suggested that the Jews were unfit to enter Parliament.[47]

The campaign was agonisingly prolonged and marked by heartbreaking setbacks. Divisions within the Jewish camp provided ammunition for the opponents of equality, led to duplicated initiatives and paralysed communal bodies that ought to have been prominent in the fight. The *Jewish Chronicle* was critical of the meagre efforts made by the Board of Deputies. It deplored the divisive exclusion of the Reform Synagogue from the Board as 'foreign to the spirit of the times in which we live'.[48]

In 1847, a new phase of the emancipation struggle opened. Jews now stood for election to Parliament in the hope that victory at the polls would not only be an indicator of public opinion, but also oblige Parliament to change the oath which prevented Jews from taking their seats. Mitchell was personally active, chairing meetings of the Jewish Association for the Removal of Civil and Religious Disabilities which rallied Jewish and non-Jewish voters in the City of London. This was a crucial constituency since Lord John Russell, a leading advocate of emancipation, and Baron Lionel de Rothschild were amongst the Liberal candidates. In the run-up to polling in 1847, the paper carried regular leading articles calling on Jews to agitate for emancipation and to canvass on behalf of Jewish candidates and the Liberal Party. When the Whigs won the election and Rothschild was returned, the *Jewish Chronicle* was beside itself: 'Jews! We are now free.'[49]

When Parliament reassembled, Russell introduced a bill to remove the disabilities on the Jews and so enable Rothschild to take his seat. The bill's passage was followed so keenly by the Jewish population that the *Jewish Chronicle* brought out a special edition on Saturday evening to report the outcome of the vote.[50] However, at this sensitive moment events on the wider political scene upset progress. In 1848, Chartism, the movement for the extension of the franchise to working men, reached its climax in England at the same moment that revolutions broke out in the capitals of several European states. The spectre of Chartism at home and political upheavals abroad tainted measures for constitutional reform, placing Jewish emancipation in jeopardy. Undeterred – or perhaps even inspired – by the mood of radicalism the Jewish Association for the Relief of Civil and Religious Disabilities reconvened at the end of January 1848, with Mitchell again in the chair. He did this even though Rothschild had written to him in October 1847, making it clear that he did not want to be associated with further public agitation while the issue was under discussion in Parliament.[51]

Mitchell and Bresslau thought at first that the Jews had more to gain than to lose from the radical temper. In a pugnacious leader on 19 May 1848 the paper warned the upper house that 'Their Lordships have before them the opinion of Europe distinctly announced and unhesitatingly proclaimed.' But the Lords threw out Russell's Oaths Bill. Anticipating a different result, the *Jewish Chronicle* delayed publication to carry this disappointing news. In a special issue the leader writer was scathing: 'Is this 1848?... And is it true, that an Assembly of English Peers have come to the conclusion, that a Jew cannot be admitted to Parliament because he looks forward to the advent of the Messiah?' The Jews were 'deeply wounded', but as Englishmen, not as Jews. 'Their Lordships have, by their decision, exposed our country and our constitution to the ridicule of the nations around us.'[52] It was all very well to rattle the sabre of revolution, but the *Jewish Chronicle* had to admit that events in Europe had exerted the opposite effect: 'The voice of the people, which at the beginning of the session, spoke loudly in our favour, has now been hushed into silence by the thunders of the revolutionary Continent.'[53]

Jewish aspirations received another blow in September 1850 when the re-establishment of the Roman Catholic hierarchy provoked an outburst of anti-Catholicism led by Lord John Russell and *The Times*. In February 1851, Russell introduced a bill to regulate the assumption of ecclesiastical titles which was intended to curb the aspirations of the Roman Catholics in England. The Act and the accompanying rhetoric fomented an atmosphere of intolerance. 'Papal aggression' gave a boost to the 'Church in Danger' brigade, which associated Jewish emancipation with the threat to Anglicanism. It created a heightened awareness of England as a Christian country and reinforced the identification of Englishness with Protestantism, over and against 'foreign' creeds. The fear of ultra-montanism that dogged Catholic aspirations was equally inimical to the Jews, who were likewise accused of overseas allegiance – to Palestine.[54]

At first, the *Jewish Chronicle* held aloof from the controversy. Then, in a move which may have been genuine or opportunistic, it jumped on to the bandwagon of popular Protestant anti-Catholicism. The paper reprinted articles from the French Jewish press on the plight of Jews in the Rome ghetto. At the time of the debate on the Ecclesiastical Titles Bill, it insinuated that Roman Catholics in England owed a dual loyalty and concluded that 'the introduction of the Roman Catholic hierarchy into this country is a deliberate violation of the rights and liberties of *every class* of British subjects'. The *Jewish Chronicle* thus joined the hue and cry against ultramontanism as a convenient way to prove the loyalty of Jews to the state. This was a paradoxical situation since the paper now found itself aligned with an intolerant movement dominated by Evangelical Protestants who, alongside their animus towards Roman Catholicism, sought the conversion of the Jews.[55]

The prospect of a General Election in July 1852 offered an opportunity to revive the flagging emancipation campaign. The paper encouraged Jews to lobby their candidates, focusing most heavily on the Liberal slate in the City of London, where Russell was again running with Rothschild. Throughout the period from May to July letters and paid notices appealing to Jews to support various candidates appeared frequently in its columns; for the first time, the paper was regarded as a sure way to reach a large Jewish audience and a valuable weapon in electoral contests. In addition it reported every act of lobbying that came to its notice, and repeatedly pointed out that inactivity would be taken by non-Jews to signal lack of interest. On the eve of the poll, the editorial counselled that Jews everywhere should publicly seek assurances that the candidates would support Jewish emancipation; where there were sufficient numbers, Jews should form committees to canvass candidates.[56]

In the election, Baron Rothschild was successfully returned, although David Salomons lost the seat which he had won earlier in a by-election in Greenwich. Notwithstanding it was a Conservative ministry, elected amidst a great deal of 'Church in Danger' propaganda, the paper hoped that it would press on with emancipation and called on Jews to continue the agitation. But another Oaths Bill, introduced by Lord Aberdeen, was again lost in the Lords.[57] The outbreak of the Crimean War then pushed

Jewish emancipation well down the political agenda of both parties, where it was to languish for several more years.[58]

One of the most frequently heard arguments that helped to hold back emancipation was the allegation that Jews lacked civilised values and were unwilling to participate in the culture of the majority society. The advocates of emancipation consequently believed it was necessary to prove that the Jews were, in fact, a cultured people and that they were more than willing to enrich the learning and arts of England. In Germany, the blending of self-improvement with emancipation was distilled in the concept of *Bildung*. The similarity of the process in England can be seen in the explicit comparisons that the *Jewish Chronicle* made between English Jewry and Jews on the Continent.[59]

In March 1847, a leading article on 'Jewish Education in England and Germany' praised the social advancement of Jews in England, but added that 'we are, on the other hand, bound to take a lesson, as to the means of *securing* our privileges, from the plan which they adopt to *obtain* their privileges. To disarm their opponents, they are daily making rapid strides in *self-emancipation*.' The leader concluded: 'Our readers must confess, that, in every one of these three tasks which our German brethren have set themselves, we are also open to improvement; so that, by perfecting the system of our education, by morally purifying the occupation of our youths, and by dispelling the spirit of intolerance from among ourselves, we may secure the boon of emancipation, for which we have so long sighed and struggled, and which will be incomplete and insecure without self-emancipation.'[60]

The perceived connection between improvement and emancipation explains the paper's consistent interest in, and patronage of, Jewish secular education at all levels. When the Jews' and General Literary and Scientific Institution was opened at Sussex Hall, 52 Leadenhall Street, in January 1845, the *Jewish Chronicle* saw it as a great opportunity 'to convince our Christian neighbours that Israel also does not start in the rear of that great cause ... Education'.[61] The paper regularly reported on the state of the Jews' Free School. It gave extensive coverage to examinations and prize days as well as to the annual fund-raising event, often with a clear message: '[W]e would also remind those who spend large sums for the acquisition of our complete emancipation, that much will depend on the progress we make in knowledge, sacred and profane, and the promotion of *Jewish* talent by *Jews*.'[62]

Sussex Hall was dogged by underfunding and never attracted the hoped-for response. Indeed, the dearth of Jewish cultural creativity hampered attempts to counter accusations of parochialism and educational backwardness. In a leading article on 13 November 1846, the *Jewish Chronicle* had to admit that 'The cultivation of literature and science has not, to the present day, been the favourite pursuit of English Jews.' To remedy this, during March and May 1849, the paper published research by Leopold Dukes on ancient Jewish texts in the Bodleian Library, Oxford. In March 1850, the paper offered a prize for a study of Hebrew literature.

Efforts to raise the standing of the Jewish population in the eyes of English society were hamstrung by the persistence of the Jewish poor, who had become a veritable symbol of ignorance and uncouthness. Derogatory remarks in the general press reinforced in Jewish minds the linkage between philanthropy, public reputation and emancipation. Yet the *Jewish Chronicle*'s urgent calls for action in this sphere were vitiated by the unwillingness of most Jewish people to discuss the subject openly and the general tendency to dismiss adverse comment as the result of prejudice. The paper responded boldly that 'This mistaken delicacy, and this imaginary dread of exposure ... have ever been the bane of Jewish society.'[63]

The need for publicity about the Jewish poor and calls for charity arose from the residential division between the affluent and the impoverished. From the late 1840s, the *Jewish Chronicle* noted anxiously that the westwards migration of the richer Jews sundered the Jewish population of London, leaving the poor Jews remote and forgotten. The paper considered it to be a duty to 'undeceive the wealthy' in the West End and alert them to the condition of their co-religionists in the East End – where Mitchell and Bresslau still lived. During winter, when unemployment in the casual trades and bad weather exacerbated the suffering of the indigent, it was the paper's custom to carry an editorial bringing their plight to public notice. Sometimes, the subject was treated in the form of a homily on the theme of the poor in the Bible.[64]

Amongst the growing corps of letter writers who now looked to the *Jewish Chronicle* as a platform from which to air their opinions, the immigration of foreign 'pauper Jews' from Germany, Russian Poland and Romania was one of the most popular explanations for the recurrence of Jewish poverty. Unlike these impatient correspondents, Mitchell advocated a humane policy towards poor immigrants. The *Jewish Chronicle* preferred to regard them as refugees who were often well trained and usually hard working.[65] Indeed, in leading articles it tackled some of the underlying and specific causes of Jewish unemployment in a forthright manner.

During the early 1850s, lowly correspondents frequently wrote to the paper complaining that it was hard for Orthodox Jewish boys to get apprenticeships with Jewish employers. Given the absence of facilities for vocational training this was a serious charge, but the *Jewish Chronicle* concurred that Jewish mendicancy, and the bunching of Jews in 'un-savoury' occupations such as peddling, hawking and market-trading, stemmed largely from the reluctance of Jewish employers to train or hire Jewish youths. The paper pleaded with its co-religionists: 'Let us diminish the numbers of paupers, pedlars, etcetera by accepting the services of those of our brethren ...'[66]

The *Jewish Chronicle* also tried to educate the Jewish public about the need for a more comprehensive system of charity. Mitchell backed Joshua Van Oven's proposals for a free medical service and published moving reports on the work of the new Jewish Soup Kitchen. Each year an editorial reviewed the state of Jewish charities and called for a central board, uniting the synagogues, with a regular body of subscribers. These clearly echoed Henry Faudel's 1844 scheme for a Jewish board of guardians. The paper recommended a combination of traditional notions of *tzedakah*, charity, with Benthamite ideas: 'the principle of utility ought to be the guiding one of this board'.[67]

Behind the discussions of the education and relief of the poor lay the question of class relations. Residential segregation had broken traditional patterns of philanthropy; habits of deference which used to be reinforced by constant interaction between rich and poor were eroded. The mid Victorian middle classes hoped that the visiting system, the scientific monitoring of welfare, would re-establish contact between the classes and shore up the structure of deference. The *Jewish Chronicle* shared and propagated this conviction. An editorial praising female visiting committees reassured the practitioners, 'let them not fear the contact with a class lower than themselves in the social scale; it is this very commingling of sentiment, and the interchange of good deeds and words among individuals rendered almost antagonistic by the present false state of society, that works all the good'.[68]

A more drastic solution to poverty lay in emigration. This panacea was strongly canvassed by the *Jewish Chronicle* in the 1850s, particularly in the case of superabundant young Jewish women. Mitchell believed that the gold rush in Australia had drawn in numbers of Jewish men who urgently needed a wife or a maidservant. A campaign was got up to make unattached Jewish women aware of the golden opportunities awaiting them in the antipodes and to organise suitable means of getting them there. Mitchell was pleased by the success of his campaign. However, a few weeks later he sounded more cautious. Information about the less than glamorous life-style of the Australian gold-prospectors prompted a re-evaluation of female emigration. Some time later, he printed a letter from an émigré English Jew confirming the worst: 'Melbourne is the last place I should pick to send a lot of virtuous Jewish girls to.'[69]

In most other respects the *Jewish Chronicle* of this era paid scant attention to the problems and interests of Jewish women. It advocated greater efforts to provide a religious education for Jewish women who would otherwise be a weak link in the transmission of religious tradition, but there were few women's voices in the paper or models of female public attainment. The exception was Grace Aguilar, who was lionised both as an exemplary Jewish woman and as a champion of her people. Publication of her book *Women of Israel* (1845) was lauded by the *Jewish Chronicle*, and she received lavish tributes from the paper on her death soon afterwards.[70]

On social and political issues Mitchell remained a populist, a middle-class radical who was always willing to take up the cudgels against privilege. As a Jew, he also fought within the Jewish social and political milieu, and he was not afraid of conflict with the powerful ruling interests in Anglo-Jewry. At the height of the Chartist Movement in 1848, the *Jewish Chronicle* took up calls for the democratisation of synagogue governance.[71] Under Mitchell's direction the paper frequently chided the Board of Deputies and the communal magnates who dominated it. Despite its claim to represent English Jews and its semi-statutory powers, the Board was ignored by most of the Jewish population, its meetings were poorly attended and the elections for deputies greeted with apathy. Mitchell ascribed this to the Board's secretive behaviour, exemplified by the exclusion of the press, and its refusal to grapple with the issues of the day, particularly emancipation.[72]

He was caustic about the Board's official attitude towards the West London Synagogue of British Jews. Soon after he took over the paper, it condemned the 'system of petty persecution' of the Reform Synagogue.[73] However, in the following years the Board actually strove to increase the isolation of the Reform congregation. In 1852, the *Jewish Chronicle* exposed to public scrutiny a disquieting example of this intemperance. The Board's honorary officers took advantage of a parliamentary bill to provide funds for voluntary schools to propose a clause effectively excluding institutions operating under the auspices of Reform Jews. The publicity which the paper gave to this affair and the large amount of correspondence it carried was valuable in laying bare the perpetuation of intolerance, even if it had little effect on the outcome.[74]

In the hope of achieving change from within, the paper trumpeted the reforms advocated by a group of liberal deputies: admission of the press, the collection of statistics on Jewish society, regular sessions, the formation of an executive, the promotion of education, and greater concern with Parliamentary affairs. During the last burst of Chartist activism Mitchell's editorials flared with democratic ardour: the choice was 'reform or revolution'. Threatening to back a secession or an alternative to the Board, the *Jewish Chronicle* warned that 'If the Board of Deputies will not listen to these loud demands for reforms, those reforms will, nevertheless, be ushered into existence; and private associations will be formed to conduct the re-organisation so much needed.'[75]

In the run-up to the Board's elections in March 1853, another spate of editorials championed democratisation. By now the idea of reform had taken hold more widely, and several deputies who were advocates of change were elected. With some excitement, the *Jewish Chronicle* anticipated that when the new Board convened, the recently elected liberal members would challenge Clause 18 of the by-laws which perpetuated the Board's monopoly over the certification of marriage secretaries and was used to deny representation to the Reform Synagogue. In fact, business was dominated by the contentious election of four members of the Reform congregation – a development that was to become the focal point of a long-drawn-out and acrimonious test of strength between the advocates of liberalisation and the conservatives.[76]

Mitchell threw his weight behind the new members in a strong editorial on 29 July. When conservative, Orthodox deputies later rallied to exclude the liberal deputies the paper pointedly carried a leader on 'Toleration'. However, in the course of two stormy meetings the liberal cause was thwarted. Efforts to reach a compromise were defeated, largely because of the intransigence of Sir Moses Montefiore, the president. Until this time the *Jewish Chronicle* had obtained its information from friendly parties inside the Board, but it now used the furore to press its own claims against exclusion. After an exchange of letters between the proprietor/editor and the Board's officers, the Jewish press was finally admitted. A week later, Mitchell brought out a special issue on 'The Crisis'. The paper took a strong line. Admission of the four deputies was characterised as an issue of religious liberty, in which the Orthodox deputies represented a Jewish version of the reactionary parliamentarians who insisted on the exclusion of the Jews from Parliament.[77]

The dispute dragged on all through the autumn, despite editorial pleas for compromise. Week after week, the paper printed vitriolic correspondence from representatives of the contending parties. It now played such a significant role as a forum for debate that on 30 September 1853 Mitchell issued a special four-page supplement to carry all the letters that were arriving at his office. In the eyes of the *Jewish Chronicle* the crisis was ruining Jewish hopes for emancipation. To let it go on 'would be political suicide'. However, at a decisive meeting of the Board in December 1853, Montefiore used his casting vote to tip the balance in favour of excluding members of the West London Synagogue on the grounds that they were not 'Jews'. The paper then suggested that the four excluded deputies should resign and refight their seats. But the protagonists were fed up with the Board. The liberal caucus faded, and the revolt was crushed.[78]

Although the conservative forces had triumphed, the struggle was in many ways a turning point in the internal affairs of Anglo-Jewry. On one side were ranged the liberal deputies, led by such illustrious figures as David Salomons, whose language and tactics were more in accord with the spirit of the times than were those of their opponents. The progressive bloc understood the importance of public opinion and ensured that the debate was conducted in the open, something which Sir Moses Montefiore found distinctly uncomfortable. The use of the Jewish press as a platform and an instrument for the mobilisation of Jewish opinion was a considerable step towards the democratisation of the Board's affairs. For a long time to come this process would be halting and incomplete, but the admission of the *Jewish Chronicle* was an irrevocable development crucial to every future campaign for the reform of communal governance.[79]

The Board of Deputies met too infrequently to cope with the important work of anti-defamation, and its modus operandi was, at best, lethargic. For this reason a weekly newspaper was a vital instrument of communal defence. A journal could legitimately take on other journals; it could constantly monitor the press and respond to speeches in Parliament or statements from the magistrates' bench; above all, it could react quickly to an insult and defend Jewish pride and prestige. The *Jewish Chronicle* had to respond almost every week to caricatures and negative stereotypes of the Jews, and its pages form a weary catalogue of literary offences.

Several newspapers and journals were notorious: *Punch*, the *Standard*, the *Morning Herald*, *Chambers's Journal* and *Family Herald*. Hurt was most often caused by descriptions of the poor quarters of Whitechapel and accusations of a Jewish proclivity for 'base' activities such as usury. In reply the editor pointed out, frequently in signed letters to the offending publication, that the stereotype was a false representation of *all* Jewish people and that, if some appeared to fit the bill, Christian society was culpable for this moral degradation. Regardless of such protests, in his accounts of poor Jews Henry Mayhew, who was responsible for the *Morning Chronicle*'s series on London labour and the London poor in 1848–50, engendered misery, while Charles Dickens's *Household Words* was another source of discomfort.[80]

The editors also devoted an extraordinary amount of energy to anti-conversionist polemics. On more than one occasion they made dramatic personal interventions at obnoxious missionary meetings.[81] Every May, at Exeter Hall, the conversion societies met to hawk their wares and discuss their activites. And, every May to July, the *Jewish Chronicle* pilloried them for their pains. The scope of the missionaries' work extended to Palestine, and the *Jewish Chronicle* commented anxiously on their initiative in setting up a hospital for poor Jews in Jerusalem.[82]

By 1854, the correspondence columns indicate that the paper was fulfilling the role of a communal arena. This was acknowledged by no less a person than Sir David Salomons when he proposed the toast to the Jewish press – itself a significant innovation – at an anniversary dinner at the New Synagogue. Salomons commented that 'its impartiality during a recent controversy [the exclusion of the four deputies from the Board] reflected much credit on its conductors'. He added, significantly, that 'he was afraid that it had not been supported as its merits deserved ... The Jewish press should be enabled to be independent; and this could only be by its being supported commercially; we should send it advertisements, and take care that it was distributed.'[83]

Admission to the Board set a vital benchmark. When the central institutions of Anglo-Jewry were created in the course of the mid-century, public scrutiny in the *Jewish Chronicle* was accepted as a matter of course. The press acted as a second chamber for communal debate and a court of appeal to public opinion. In the process, it assisted in the creation of the 'public sphere' in which Jews defined mutual interests and interacted in new ways. The paper made other, subtle contributions to the development of modern Anglo-Jewry. By 1851, it regularly carried announcements of forthcoming marriages and personal notices, while advertisements directed at a Jewish market filled the entire back page. The *Jewish Chronicle* was already en route to becoming a vital part of Jewish social and economic life.

Foreign intelligence, 1841–1855

Before the invention of the telegraph and the widespread use of the cable, newspapers depended on intelligence supplied by merchants, foreign exiles domiciled in England and the foreign press. British diplomats at home and overseas were another important source of information. For decades only *The Times* could afford resident correspondents abroad, and few other papers could finance special correspondents to cover foreign stories. Consequently, foreign news was highly selective and was subject to interpretation by editors at home according to their political leanings. The religious press reflected both denominational and political preferences in its selection and analysis of news from overseas.[84]

In the first few years of its existence, the *Jewish Chronicle* relied almost exclusively on the Continental Jewish press for news of Jewish life in Europe. It quoted extensively from the *Allgemeine Zeitung des Judentums* and the *Archives Israélites*. Later it utilised American Jewish papers such as the *Orient* and *American Israelite* for reports on Jewish centres in North

America. The paper was sold in the West Indies from an early stage and often carried letters from readers describing the Jews of Kingston, Jamaica and other Jewish settlements in the Caribbean.

The scope of its coverage was predetermined by the global distribution of the Jewish population. In the mid nineteenth century, the bulk of world Jewry lived in the Russian Empire, where it was afflicted doubly by the backward state of the economy and by discriminatory legislation. When, in 1846, Sir Moses Montefiore set out on a mission to intercede between Tsar Nicholas I (1825–55) and his Jewish subjects, the *Jewish Chronicle* drew on the *Allgemeine Zeitung des Judentums* to report his progress weekly and devoted great space to his homecoming.[85]

The next largest concentration of Jews was in central Europe in the German states and the various territories of the Habsburg Empire, including Austria, northern Italy, Hungary and Galicia. The Jews of Prussia and the other German states always figured largely in the pages of the *Jewish Chronicle* because of the availability of news via the German Jewish press, and also because German Jewry was such an intellectual and cultural power-house. Significantly, the *Jewish Chronicle*'s first foreign correspondent was based in Berlin. English Jews closely watched emancipation in the German states, sometimes apprehensively lest it outstrip and embarrass their own meagre achievements. Speeches and articles by leading figures in the emancipation campaign, such as Gabriel Reisser, were regularly translated for English readers.[86]

The struggle for civic equality dominated coverage of Jewish life in the German-speaking world and the territories controlled by Prussia and Austria. In 1848, it came to a head during the revolutions which swept over Europe, beginning in Paris in February 1848, with the overthrow of Louis-Philippe. Between March and May, insurrections occurred in Milan and Rome, Vienna and Prague, Budapest and Berlin: the ancien régime toppled, constitutions were granted or promised, and power was seized by liberals and nationalists. In the course of these revolutions, Jews were granted civic equality in the German states, Austria and Hungary. On 7 April 1848 the *Jewish Chronicle* cheered the liberal movements, proclaiming that 'The cause of liberty has ever been *our* cause; its triumphs have ever advanced our interests, and it is only in the bright rays of its illuminating sun that our rights can attain to full maturity.'[87]

In the autumn of 1848, the conservative forces rallied. The revolutionary tide was reversed in France, Germany, Austria and Italy. In Hungary, the liberal nationalists under Kossuth fought desperately against the Austrian and Russian armies to preserve their independence. Kossuth had assumed heroic status in the eyes of Jews after he had abolished all discriminatory laws; thousands of Jews fought in his army. Consequently, the *Jewish*

Chronicle viewed the Hungarians' fight as a battle between 'liberty and civilization' on one side and 'despotism and tyranny' on the other. It kept readers abreast of developments by means of letters from correspondents in Hungary and commentary by Hungarian émigrés in London.[88]

The suppression of the revolutionary movements led to an influx of exiles into England, amongst whom were many Jews. Marcus Bresslau joined with one of the Hungarian Jewish refugees, Dr Schiller-Szinessy, to set up a relief fund for emigrants from Austria. Schiller-Szinessy, a scholar and rabbi from Budapest, later settled in Manchester, where he was appointed minister to the Old Hebrew Congregation. Soon after his arrival in London, he contributed a series of articles to the *Jewish Chronicle* on the Jews of Hungary, including his vivid recollections of the recent débâcle.[89]

Outside Europe and America, the next largest grouping of Jews was in the Ottoman Empire. This vast and ramshackle domain was disintegrating steadily from the mid nineteenth century onwards, a process which affected the Jews in crucial ways. Local movements for self-rule were ambivalent about their Jewish populations, and the emerging independent states, particularly in the Balkans, frequently maltreated their Jewish subjects. The *Jewish Chronicle*'s attitude towards the Turkish Empire varied, although on the whole it was regarded from the Jewish point of view as a case of benevolent neglect. Anti-Jewish prejudice among the Christian peoples who emancipated themselves from Turkish rule, especially the Greeks and Romanians, confirmed the paper's warmth towards the Ottomans. This preference was buttressed by the rivalry between Turkey and Russia and the support which Russia gave to the Slav national movements in the Balkans.[90]

Palestine, which was part of the Ottoman Empire, naturally bulked large in the paper's foreign coverage. As early as November 1844, the paper carried news of a mission to Palestine undertaken by a London Jew who wanted to introduce modern techniques of agriculture to the Jews of the Holy Land. It wished him well on his 'patriotic mission'. Articles on Palestine were published with regularity, as well as letters from Europeans living there.[91] Moses Montefiore was particularly active in promoting the development of Palestine and assisting the Jewish population. The *Jewish Chronicle* supported his various enterprises and assiduously reported his 1849 visit to the country.[92]

Mitchell and Bresslau gave much coverage to early attempts at restoring the Jews to Palestine. The first proto-Zionist of this period was the American Judge Mordecai Manuel Noah. On 19 January 1849, the *Jewish Chronicle* printed his famous proposal for the return of the Jewish people to their ancestral land. Although it paid deference to Orthodox Jewish views that only the Messiah could restore the Jews to Palestine, it praised

Noah's initiative: '[W]e do sympathise with our transatlantic patriot in the theory that the hand of man must commence the good work, and the success must be left to Providence.'[93] His death was front-page news on 11 April 1851. Concern about Palestine was heightened by the activity of missionaries which had grown relentlessly since the creation of the Anglican Bishopric of Jerusalem in 1841 as an instrument for conversionist endeavour.[94]

In 1851–2 the Serbian Rabbi Yehuda Alkalai toured the capitals of Europe to win support for his plan to restore the Jews to Palestine. Alkalai spent some time in London during 1852, and the publication of his pamphlet, 'The Harbinger of Good Tidings: An Address to the Jewish Nation', provoked a flurry of letters in the *Jewish Chronicle*. Solomon Sequerra, acting under Alkalai's inspiration, set up the short-lived Association for Encouraging Jewish Settlements in Palestine. On 24 December 1852, the *Jewish Chronicle* published the manifesto of the Association with a map of Palestine, its first venture into graphic printing. Editorials endorsed the proposals to establish agricultural settlements for Jews in Palestine.

Exotic Jewries attracted perennial attention, although the timing of their appearance in the paper was usually the result of British expansion overseas. It was almost a rule of Anglo-Jewish journalism that articles, like trade, followed the flag. The paper carried a letter to the editor about the Jews of Australia as early as 6 December 1844, when there were only eleven Jewish families in Melbourne. British trade with China and the Opium War, 1839–42, created interest in the Far East and led to the discovery of Jews at Kai-fung. Early reports from Christian missionaries were reprinted in the *Jewish Chronicle* and always excited interest. British expansion in India resulted in the uncovering of long-forgotten communities of Jews in Cochin as well as increased contact with the well-established Jews of Bombay. Interest was accentuated by the Indian Mutiny and the focus on Indian affairs in the general press. The Black Jews of Ethiopia, the Falashas or Beta Israel, were likewise a source of perennial curiosity. In November 1849, the paper printed a letter from a correspondent who had interviewed M. D'Abbadie, who brought news of the Falashas to Europe, during a short stay in London.[95]

By linking Jews around the world and defining their common concerns, the Jewish press played a primary role in the evolution of a modern form of Jewish solidarity and ethnic identity. At the same time as embracing the imperatives of emancipation, which required the loyalty of Jews to the countries in which they lived, English Jews did not abandon their obligations to, or interest in, the Jews of other lands. The *Jewish Chronicle* was both a facilitator and an expression of this process.[96]

2 Defining an identity: the *Jewish Chronicle* and mid-Victorian Anglo-Jewry, 1855–1878

Abraham Benisch, 1855–1868

In January 1853 a new Jewish newspaper, the *Hebrew Observer*, appeared. It was founded by Abraham Pierpoint Shaw, about whom almost nothing is known. However, it was edited by Abraham Benisch, who had come to prominence as a co-editor of the *Voice of Jacob*. A year later Benisch bought the *Hebrew Observer* from its founding proprietor. As early as March 1853, Marcus Bresslau, who had deserted Joseph Mitchell and the *Jewish Chronicle* in the autumn of 1851, was a regular contributor.[1] He and Benisch thereby became associates, but after Mitchell's demise Bresslau returned to the *Jewish Chronicle* and tried to run it on his own. The market could not sustain two Jewish newspapers, and early in 1855 Benisch initiated a merger of the two journals. The new series was called the *Jewish Chronicle and Hebrew Observer*, a title which was retained until 1868. Change did not stop there. Once Benisch was installed in the *Jewish Chronicle* office, it was not long before he ousted Bresslau. From February 1855, Benisch was the sole editor and proprietor of the older paper.[2]

Abraham Benisch was born in Bohemia in 1811, studied surgery in Prague around 1836, and later attended Vienna University. While in Prague he became friendly with Moritz Steinschneider, the great bibliographer of Hebraica, and helped to found a Jewish students' association devoted to the idea of restoring Jewish Palestine. Through his alliance with Steinschneider, Benisch became one of the small group of Jewish intellectuals, including Josef Salvador, S. D. Luzatto and Heinrich Graetz, who proposed a national solution to the 'Jewish Question'. In Vienna, Benisch was at the centre of a covert group of Jewish nationalists and corresponded with Adolph Cremieux, the French Jewish statesman who had played a decisive role in the Damascus Affair.[3]

The Vienna group included Albert Loewy, who subsequently took up a post in London as minister to the Reform Synagogue. In 1841 Benisch followed Loewy to London, where he intended to capitalise on the interest which English statesmen were showing in Palestine. He also hoped to secure the support of English Jews like Sir Moses Montefiore. Benisch made little progress with the restoration project, but he found employment as the secretary of the committee for the election of the new Chief Rabbi and subsequently as co-editor of the *Voice of Jacob*. Between 1848 and 1853, he made his living as an author and a tutor. His publications included a Hebrew primer and a new English translation of the Old Testament.[4]

When he took over the *Jewish Chronicle*, it was in a sorry state. Of the 1,000 'subscribers' only 500 were actually paying for their copies, and hundreds were sent out each week without evidence of payment or any monitoring. This meant that each issue was produced at a hefty loss which had to be covered partly by advertising revenue and partly through 'extraneous support'. Mitchell and Bresslau had, apparently, been accepting subventions from prominent London Jews, and Benisch later hinted that this had compromised the paper's independence.[5]

He was able to balance the books only by combining the roles of proprietor, printer, publisher, editor and reporter. For many years, his sole assistant was his wife, Henrietta, perhaps the first woman journalist in Anglo-Jewish press history. In issue after issue, he implored readers to subscribe and begged Jewish businessmen and traders to advertise in the paper. Within about twelve months the *Jewish Chronicle* had achieved a circulation of around 800 copies; a further 200 were sold through casual trade. This gave Benisch an income of £9 5s. per issue at a production cost of £12, so he needed another 200 subscribers to break even on the cover-price. In the absence of an expanded circulation, the deficit was made up through advertising revenue. This earned an average of £6 over the year, although it was highly seasonal. Major Jewish charity appeals and lists of donors in the winter months could boost income by as much as £10, but in the summer months, earnings through advertising fell to £2 per issue.[6]

Through stringent economies, and thanks to the fortunate reduction of the duties on advertising and paper, by January 1858 Benisch was able to bring the *Jewish Chronicle* into profit. The number of subscribers rose steadily until it reached nearly 2,000 at the start of the 1860s. Advertising revenue was boosted by paid publicity for the wave of company flotations following the reform of company law in 1856 and 1862, which made it easier to form joint-stock companies. For the first time the Anglo-Jewish press was placed on a stable, profitable basis.[7]

An ardent follower of the Liberal Party, Benisch applied the principles of English liberalism to the unreformed, archaic Jewish communal organisations. Since the events of 1853–4, the Board of Deputies had suffered a grave loss of standing. Benisch displayed a marked hostility towards the continuing autocratic rule of Sir Moses Montefiore, and championed calls for the Board's democratisation. He briefly took hope from plans to rewrite its constitution and secure a reconciliation with the West London Synagogue while Sir Moses was out of the country for part of 1855. But the attempt failed miserably. Benisch deprecated the 'absolutism' prevailing at the Board, reviled the 'orthodox party' for its opposition, and complained that its members were creatures of Montefiore.[8]

He opposed proposals in 1856 to make the Board more 'orderly' by reducing the number of deputies through the disenfranchisement of smaller congregations. These, he maintained, elected men of humble means but ample talent. The problem was not the size of the Board, but the way its business was handled. In April 1857, after Sir Moses temporarily relinquished the Presidency, Benisch sarcastically noted that 'with the appointment of a president from the popular ranks, the Board evinces an independence, and elasticity of mind, and boldness of action, which prove that if leadership of an aristocratic chief may flatter the vanity of those marshalled under him, his absence restores something to the ranks which fully compensates for the want of the halo missed in the body'.[9]

His liberalism was reflected also in his social commentaries. The mid nineteenth century was a period of major change for the Anglo-Jewish population, particularly in London. Jewish families moved from the East End northwards and westwards as new suburbs developed in Bayswater and Maida Vale. With the departure of most well-off Jews from the East End, by the 1860s it was almost uniformly poverty-stricken. The *Jewish Chronicle* assumed the vital function of reminding the Jews of Belgravia and Bayswater that they had less fortunate co-religionists in Spitalfields, Whitechapel and St George's-in-the-East.[10] Benisch printed views from the underside of London Jewish life: the world of street traders, illegal hawkers and strike-breakers. He tentatively broached the evidence of a Jewish woman who fell into low company, probably involving prostitution.[11]

A plethora of Jewish charitable bodies in London attempted to cope with the embarrassment and the burden of indigent Jews. Benisch was fully aware of the anguished debate on this question. In his influential editorials he pressed for the amalgamation, consolidation and rationalisation of philanthropic institutions. 'Our whole system of dispensing charity is wrong', he declaimed. 'We obey, in our benefactions, impulse more than principle. It is not the sound laws of economy which we observe, but those of stagnant routine.'[12] He was clearly influenced by the arguments of mid-century 'scientific philanthropy'. In one editorial after another the *Jewish Chronicle* preached the need for a central board to provide emergency relief and simultaneously put clients in touch with long-term aid bodies. These ideas, which helped to shape discussion of how to deal with Jewish poverty, eventually crystallised with the creation of the Jewish Board of Guardians in 1859.[13]

The Board of Guardians was one of the first Anglo-Jewish institutions to which the *Jewish Chronicle* acted as midwife and preceptor. It informed readers of every stage in its creation and provided a unique forum for the exchange of views. Ephraim Alex (1800–82) and Lionel Louis Cohen (1832–87), the energetic and gifted communal workers who were the driving force behind the scheme, made full use of the *Jewish Chronicle* to address London Jews and reply to doubters. They could count on strong support from the editor. The Board of Guardians was formally inaugurated in March 1859, and Benisch later noted with pride that the paper had encouraged its formation for many a day.[14]

Over the succeeding years, the *Jewish Chronicle* gave readers informative, first-hand descriptions of the Guardians' work. Alex and Cohen allowed Benisch full access to its operations, and he, in turn, wrote accounts that were calculated to impress the public and inspire donations or subscriptions. His regular editorials on its annual reports were hymns of praise for current theories of poverty which held the poor responsible for their own plight and turned destitution into a moral issue. 'The Board of Guardians in its operations', he wrote, 'evidently proceeds on the correct view – that mendicancy is only a symptom ... of a deeply seated moral disease, with which it is in vain to battle while the disease is not removed.'[15]

The affection in which Benisch held the Liberals was reinforced by the final stages of the emancipation campaign. When he took over the *Jewish Chronicle*, political concern about emancipation had been obliterated by the urgencies of the Crimean War. But the war had a beneficial effect. The aristocracy was blamed for the numerous military blunders, and Benisch was able to appeal to a widespread discontent with the landed interest which had, for so long, obstructed emancipation. After a Private Member's Bill to amend the parliamentary oath was defeated, Benisch thundered that 'The opposition threatened to the measure by the peers may be traced to two distinct causes. The first may be found in the stagnant toryism which objects to everything that is new ... It is of a piece with the corrupt taste which delights in meat in an advanced state of putrefaction.'[16]

In the General Election of March 1857, Benisch brazenly used the *Jewish Chronicle* to mobilise the Jewish vote in favour of candidates supporting emancipation. On 20 March the paper proclaimed 'Let every Jew employ to the utmost the influence which he may possess for promoting the return of members favourable to the removal of Jewish disabilities.' A leading article the following week, devoted to a letter from the business committee of the Liberal Registration Association, explained why Jewish electors should again support Baron Lionel de Rothschild in the City constituency.[17] The election was a triumph for the Liberals, and Benisch looked forward to a speedy victory for Jewish emancipation. However, a new bill that passed through the Commons foundered in the Lords under the weight of opposition from the Tory front bench. Benisch suggested audaciously that the time had come to reform the upper house.[18]

When the Lords emasculated Lord John Russell's next Oaths Bill in 1858, a constitutional crisis ensued. Russell persuaded the lower house to reject the Lords' amendment, and neither side would budge. A committee of both houses was set up to resolve the difference, and eventually it was resolved that each house should decide on the form of the oath for its own members. Benisch was initially unhappy with this compromise solution. In a leading article on 11 June 1858 he pronounced gravely that a 'great contest is worthy [of] a solemn issue. Nothing but a solemn deed insuring the wronged Jews the restitution [*sic*] of the rights withheld from them, signed, sealed and delivered by both houses in the presence of the whole world can satisfy the demands of justice.' Until August 1860, Jews could take their seats in the lower house only on an affirmative resolution by a majority of MPs and not by constitutional right. Benisch thought that the interim arrangement had the effect of 'making the appearance of the Jew in the House marked, as though he were still wearing the yellow patch which, during the Middle Ages, singled him out for universal scorn'.[19]

Notwithstanding the extensive celebrations, marked by a special four page supplement of the *Jewish Chronicle* on 30 July 1858, the initially equivocal form taken by emancipation meant that English Jewry still felt itself to be on trial. Even after the impartial confirmation of full civil rights under the Parliamentary Oaths Act of 1866, the relationship between Jews and the state caused heart-searching. Precisely because Jews were now complete citizens a fresh set of challenges emerged, revolving around the competing demands of Jewish tradition and English citizenship.

The essence of this dilemma was revealed in heated exchanges in the *Jewish Chronicle* during 1859–60, after a war-scare in England led to volunteers being summoned to repel a possible French invasion. Jewish enrolment in the Volunteer Movement was small, precipitating adverse comment even though Jews pointed out that the volunteer units drilled on a Saturday. Benisch favoured the formation of a Jewish unit that would drill on weekdays or Sundays, but there were vehement objections by those who argued that Jews should be fully integrated into English society and share civic duties equally with other citizens.[20]

At the same time as full citizenship posed new challenges Jews, along with Protestant Nonconformists, were still compelled to fight a series of battles in the cause of equality. Both groups stood united in their resentment of compulsory support of the state church through the rates.

Benisch argued that 'To be consistent, the state must either support church and synagogue, as in France, or altogether exempt Jews from church-rates, as in Austria.' He daringly counselled Jewish MPs to vote for the abolition of church rates.[21] Jews and Protestant Nonconformists lobbied jointly for the legalisation of marriage to a deceased wife's sister. Probably with a Dissenter readership in mind, Benisch asserted in a leading article on 12 April 1861 that the prohibition was 'an emanation from the corrupt papal system, devised for the purpose of enslaving the laity'. The newspapers of Protestant Dissenters, Roman Catholics and Jews also combined forces to end the denominational exclusivity of the ancient universities.[22]

Religion and politics intersected again in sabbatarianism. The campaign against work on Sunday, which threated to cut down the working week of Orthodox Jews to five days, had been an irritant to the Jews for many years. However, the burgeoning of Evangelicalism gave new urgency to the question, not least because of the growing support it enjoyed in Parliament. Following the introduction of a Sunday Trading Bill in 1855, Benisch found himself in the difficult position of urging political co-operation between Jews and Protestant Dissenters while it was precisely the most extreme Protestant sects that promoted strict Sabbath observance.[23]

The Sunday Question regained momentum in the mid 1860s, notably in Scotland. Jews were especially irked because Scottish sabbatarians claimed the authority of Jewish tradition for abstinence from work on the Sabbath and so brought the obloquy of the anti-sabbatarians on to their heads. At the start of 1866, Benisch devoted four consecutive editorials to combating Scottish sabbatarianism. They were of considerable significance since the *Jewish Chronicle* was widely read by Protestant clergymen, particularly in the North. What irritated him most was the use of the Jews as a scapegoat by the anti-sabbatarians. In the fourth editorial, published on 23 February 1866, he protested: 'If the controversy on the Sabbath is to be continued, let the disputants either altogether abstain from unnecessarily dragging in Jews and Judaism, or, if references to them be deemed expedient, let them be represented in their true light.' Benisch was so persuasive that R. M. Morrell, the Honorary Secretary of the National Sunday League (which fought sabbatarianism) asked if the League could republish his editorials, as it had done with an earlier polemic which appeared in the paper on 21 December 1855.[24]

Sabbatarianism cut across the previously cordial relations between Jews and Protestant Nonconformists. This discord was partly responsible for changing the attitude of the *Jewish Chronicle* towards the Church of England. In the great disestablishment debates of the mid nineteenth century, the paper became a stout defender of the Anglican Church. For all his sympathy with Dissenters, Benisch argued that the connection with the state guaranteed stability to the church and prevented it from falling into the hands of extreme Protestants. When the Nonconformists renewed their battle against church rates in the late 1860s, the paper held aloof. It lauded the state church as 'an invaluble protection to so weak a community as the Jews, sure to be the first to be attacked in religious commotion'.[25] Friction with the Protestant Nonconformists, who were the backbone of the Liberal Party, contributed to the political realignment of Anglo-Jewry in the 1860s.

For most of the first period in which Benisch was editor of the *Jewish Chronicle* the paper, like Anglo-Jewry, was firmly in the Liberal camp. Benisch was not afraid to put his paper to work for the Liberals, and he made no apology either for the election appeals his paper carried or for his partisan editorials.[26] Benisch actually characterised Judaism as a precursor to and embodiment of Liberal ideology. In an editorial on 15 February 1867 setting out the reasons why, in his opinion, most Jews would support the Liberal Party he wrote:

This liberalism springs from within. It is not only a product of a feeling of gratitude for the triumph which the Liberal Party has achieved for the Jewish cause, but also the firm conviction that it is the vital principle upon which rests the Revelation of Sinai and the indispensable condition of all progress. The Jew feels instinctively that, politically, he is nothing if he is not a Liberal; and the reflecting Hebrew, moreover, is conscious that the special religious mission entrusted to him from on high cannot be discharged unless the principle of Liberalism prevail generally.

This strategy of reading Judaism into Liberalism appeared at the moment when Jewish political loyalties were beginning to unhinge. Benisch possibly realised that, after a decade, gratitude to the Liberals for emancipation was waning. As far as the Jews were concerned, pragmatically speaking, there was now little difference between the Liberals and the Conservatives.

In the aftermath of the 1865 General Election, in which six Jews were returned to Parliament, all as Liberals, Lionel Louis Cohen objected to Benisch's assumption that Jews were automatically inclined towards the Liberal camp or obliged to support Jewish candidates. He argued that Jews should vote from conviction, for the Conservatives if that was how their opinions tended. To vote a Jew into office *qua* Jew was to defy the basis of emancipation which eliminated religion as an active factor. Cohen was one of the first Jews to challenge the hegemony of the Liberals over Jewish political allegiances, and the *Jewish Chronicle* provided the most influential platform from which to broadcast his message.[27]

The formation of a Tory Government in June 1866 and turmoil over the Reform Bill caused Benisch to reflect more cautiously on the *Jewish Chronicle*'s stance towards the Conservative Party. It now observed that, while in office, the Tories had also passed measures to the benefit of Jews.

The November 1868 General Election was the first to reveal all the elements that were to fissure the alliance of Jews and Liberals. From the moment Disraeli became the Prime Minister in February 1868, the Liberal press indulged in anti-Jewish innuendo against him. Henry de Worms, the first professing Jewish Conservative parliamentary candidate, selected for Sandwich, was the object of shameful attacks by the local Liberal press and Liberal Party candidate. Benisch dutifully reported such occurrences of prejudice and commented ruefully that: 'These zealous friends have injured the Liberal cause far more than its avowed enemies.'[28]

More damage was done when the Liberals in Tower Hamlets selected a converted Jew, Joseph d'Aguilar Samuda, to stand as their candidate. Tower Hamlets had a large Jewish population which was the constant focus of missionary work; against this background the choice of an apostate was a grotesque miscalculation. The *Jewish Chronicle* carried indignant letters urging Jews to reject Samuda, and it was rumoured that the paper was advising Jews not to vote for him, an insight into the authority it already commanded.[29] Lionel de Rothschild was drafted in to assist Samuda, but this may only have damaged his own candidacy. Although Benisch did his best to whip up Jewish support in Rothschild's City constituency, a sizeable proportion of its Jewish electorate voted Tory and contributed to Rothschild's defeat.[30]

Benisch, as a loyal Liberal, must have been torn by the Samuda affair. Each May when the Protestant societies rallied at Exeter Hall in the City the *Jewish Chronicle* published polemics against their trade in souls. It was an annual ritual which Benisch tackled with gusto, regularly producing serial editorials that ran to several thousand words, finding new arguments and never tiring of old ones. His tone was unapologetic and his editorials were unsparing in their mockery of Christian beliefs and conversionist tactics. They were pervaded by a rock-like conviction that Judaism was correct in all its elements and that, one day, this would be recognised by erring Christians.[31]

The paper played an equally vigorous part in the unceasing fight against defamation. It remained habitual for local and national newspapers to identify as Jews criminals who happened to be Jewish, and to associate Jews with mendicancy. Whenever the editor came across an egregious case he would protest, yet the practice continued, as evidenced by the regular rebuttals carried in the Jewish press.[32] The writings of literary and cultural figures such as Thackeray, Ruskin and Dickens fuelled popular prejudice, but however illustrious they were the paper did not shy away from upbraiding them. When the blood libel appeared in *Chambers's Journal*, *Blackwood's Magazine* and *Punch* at the same time, Benisch exploded in fury at the 'do nothing policy' of the Jewish organisations.[33]

Benisch does not conform to the image of the meek, anglicised Victorian Jew. He refused to become an apologist for Jewish criminality and battered any journalist who insinuated that there was an intrinsic linkage between Judaism and venal behaviour. At the centre of his concern was the image of the Jew. With great acuity he compared the effect of this barrage of negative stereotypes with the ability of the newly evolving art of advertising to influence attitudes.[34] A pressman to his marrow, conscious of the power of the popular newspaper and used to wielding it to form opinion, he was ever sensitive to the appalling consequences that would follow if the term 'Jew' was constantly hitched to wrong-doing or alleged evils.

Foreign coverage, the Mortara Affair and Palestine, 1855–1868

Most of the *Jewish Chronicle*'s overseas information still came from the foreign press and Continental Jewish newspapers, although these were now more numerous and varied. When Russian Jewish journals were founded in the 1860s, the German Jewish press translated and reprinted articles which Benisch was then able to use for first-hand reports on Russian and Polish Jewry. Benisch's coverage of Jewish affairs in eastern Europe was heavily influenced by his optimistic, Liberal outlook. He projected on to the Russian, Austrian and Turkish Empires the whiggish version of progress that seemed to be the lesson of Jewish history in England. The *Jewish Chronicle* identified with 'liberal' forces and railed against 'reactionaries' – both within the governing regimes and within Jewish society.

The hated Tsar Nicholas I died soon after Benisch became editor and was succeeded by Tsar Alexander II (1855–81), who came to the throne with a reputation for enlightenment. Benisch looked on Alexander as a 'liberal' and showed much sympathy for the task the Russian Government faced in handling its Jewish population. Like many enlightened, western Jews he held the bulk of Russian Jewry in low esteem. In an editorial on 11 April 1856, he wrote that:

We feel by no means called upon to become blind apologists of our Russian co-religionists, nor are we disposed to view the Russian legislation with regard to the Jews as the emanation of a wild fanaticism aiming at the gradual destruction of Jewish existence, as reported by some who have watched and discussed the series of ukases [decrees] concerning the Jews which were issued during the reign of the last Czar. We admit, to our great sorrow and mortification, that the Russian Jews are far behind their Western brethren in civilisation and general knowledge – that many of them are characterised by habits and peculiarities which convert them into disagreeable companions or neighbours, by a perversity of judgement which often renders them inaccessible to the most powerful arguments, and by a low standard of morality which calls for particular caution in dealing with them.

The paper excitedly reported the lifting of restrictions on Jewish residence and occupations outside the Pale of Settlement, measures which were regarded as necessary incentives for the Jews to improve their educational standards.[35] The mood of optimism inside Russia was reflected in the establishment of a Russian Jewish press advocating self-improvement and civic equality. The first major paper, *Razsvet*, edited by Osip Rabinovich and Joachim Tarnopol, was welcomed heartily by Benisch as a 'harbinger of happier days for Russian Jewry'.[36]

The nationalist insurrection in Poland in 1863 provoked mixed feelings amongst English Jews. Benisch followed it with rapture, identifying the rebels as liberal nationalists and anticipating that their success would lead to the emancipation of Polish Jewry. The paper argued that it was the patriotic duty of Jewish Poles to throw in their lot with their fellow countrymen, but hesitated to endorse the principle of revolution.[37] Not everyone in Anglo-Jewry shared this view, and many were suspicious of Polish intentions towards the Jews. While Sir Francis Goldsmid, MP favoured active support for the Poles, Lionel de Rothschild, MP counselled that it would be unwise to antagonise the Russians. Through the summer of 1863, debate between the contending parties raged in the letter columns of the *Jewish Chronicle*. Several Polish correspondents saw the paper as a way to influence Anglo-Jewish opinion directly and paid for the insertion of letters pleading that Jewish and Christian Poles had a common cause. On 23 October 1863, the paper virtually endorsed the doomed rebel cause: 'A free and independent Poland could not but be Liberal.'

Along with his Liberal politics, Benisch's foreign commentary was guided by his hostility to Roman Catholicism and the temporal power of the Papacy. This antagonism stemmed from the bitterness which Jews felt towards the Roman Catholic Church after centuries of oppression under its aegis. But like his projection of English liberalism abroad, it was also a mark of how far he identified with English policy and dominant attitudes. For Protestant politicians the Papacy symbolised superstition, reaction and despotism: Rome was represented as the very antithesis of English liberty. This animosity was kept alive by a cluster of politically active, militant Protestant bodies including the Evangelical Alliance, the Protestant Reformation Society, the National Protestant Society and the Society for the Propagation of Christian Knowledge.[38]

When it was revealed, in 1858, that a Jewish boy had been abducted in Rome and baptised under duress, the story was seized upon as further evidence of Catholic iniquity and Roman barbarism. The case of Edgar Mortara was subsequently woven into English domestic politics and diplomacy. For English Jews this meant that the Mortara Affair received huge publicity, comparable with the Damascus Affair of 1840–1. It also entailed co-operation with Protestant organisations, largely founded upon a shared antagonism to ultramontane Roman Catholicism.[39]

The *Jewish Chronicle* first brought the Mortara case to public attention early in September 1858, when it was already under the desultory consideration of the Board of Deputies. Benisch was all for a more aggressive approach. He addressed a personal appeal to Cardinal Wiseman and English Catholics, whom he characterised as liberal-minded, as distinct from Vatican officials and ultramontanists on the Continent, who he asserted were the real villains. The officers of the Board of Deputies meanwhile made representations to the Foreign Office as well as various MPs, and in October published an appeal in *The Times* which was also circulated to Catholic clergymen.[40]

By now the Evangelical Alliance had taken up the cause, and it was receiving wide attention in the Protestant press. This was welcomed by the *Jewish Chronicle*, but with significant reservations. In a leading article on 12 November 1858, Benisch commented that the Evangelical Alliance objected less to the principle of forced baptism than to the fact that it was Catholicism which had claimed Mortara. Nevertheless, the Alliance held out the promise of influential assistance, and this led Benisch to stress what he saw as the affinities between Jewish and Protestant Nonconformity. In two editorials on 3 and 10 December, he developed the argument that the Reformation had promoted religious toleration and moved Protestants closer to the Jews, since both religions stressed the importance of Old Testament scriptures: 'It is the Bible which is the religion of the Protestants, and it is the Jews who preserved it for them at the risk of their lives, and taught it them in due time.'

The Jewish–Protestant alliance, which Benisch had helped to construct, bore fruit on 19 October 1859 when a statement decrying the abduction of Mortara was published in *The Times* signed by a host of Protestant clergymen and MPs. It was, wrote Benisch in the next issue of the *Jewish Chronicle*, an apology of British Christianity to Judaism for a wrong that Christianity had perpetrated upon the Jews. A few weeks later, an impressive deputation from the protest committee waited upon Lord John Russell, the Foreign Secretary. It asked the Government to see that the treatment of the Jews be included in the deliberations of the proposed congress to settle the fate of northern Italy. Encouraged by these movements, Benisch urged the Board of Deputies towards greater co-operation with the Evangelical Alliance.[41]

Meanwhile, the Mortara Affair had been overtaken by war. In February 1859, Piedmont, with French backing, invaded Austrian and Papal territories in northern Italy with the object of creating a unified Italian nation state. The fate of the Vatican was decided when Garibaldi descended on Sicily and proceeded up the Italian peninsula, conquering the land remaining under Roman rule. The *Jewish Chronicle* viewed the collapse of Papal authority with undisguised pleasure: 'The Papacy has served its turn. Like seedcorn in the ground, it has been converted into a hideous mass of putrefaction, after having germinated and sprouted forth.'[42]

Hostility to Roman Catholicism and pro-Protestantism continued to colour the paper's editorial line and coverage of foreign affairs well beyond the Mortara Affair.[43] The pattern was reinforced by the behaviour of the newly emergent Christian states in the Balkans. In Wallachia and Moldavia (united to form Romania in 1862) discrimination, riots and blood libels recurred monotonously between 1859 and 1867. Editorials in the *Jewish Chronicle* called on the Western Powers to intervene when anti-Jewish rioting again erupted in Romania, and on 22 May 1868 it even urged the British Government to send a gunboat.[44]

American Jewry presented a happier prospect, but the picture was not all rosy. While the *Jewish Chronicle* marvelled at the rapid growth of the American Jewish population during the late 1850s and early 1860s, it was an inchoate mass with no centre of gravity or single representative body. During 1859–60, the editor condescendingly advised American Jews to form an organisation like the Board of Deputies which would also enable them to do more on behalf of their less fortunate brethren in parts of Europe. He was glad to see the formation of a Board of Delegates and reviewed its progress with benevolent, if patronising, interest. Unfortunately this new institution was soon disrupted by the Civil War. The paper covered the Jewish angle of the conflict by extracting reports from the American Jewish press. In a leading article on 1 February 1861, Benisch nailed his flag to the mast when he ascribed the persistence of slavery (and the war) to 'the failure of Christianity'.

Benisch's liberalism, his belief in education and the superiority of western Europe, found an ideal vehicle in the Alliance Israélite Universelle (AIU). The impetus for the formation of the Alliance came from the Mortara Affair, when it was felt throughout the Jewish world that a standing organisation was needed to meet such crises. The AIU was formally inaugurated in the summer of 1860, although setting up a Jewish body with international Jewish concerns was not without complications. Apart from the practical difficulties, the founders had to overcome the ideological obstacle posed by the emancipation ideal that Jews were primarily the citizens of their country of domicile, different from other citizens only in respect to their creed.[45]

Benisch anticipated Jewish opposition to the new organisation, but the *Jewish Chronicle* declared that 'The Association [sic] possesses our full sympathy, and we shall be happy to promote its efforts in any way we can give it.' A lively debate took place within Anglo-Jewry, largely conducted in the pages of the paper, over whether the Board of Deputies should affiliate to the AIU. Benisch was disappointed when the Board declined to do so, though subsequently his enthusiasm for the Alliance dimmed because it seemed to him overly subordinate to French interests.[46]

Palestine continued to bulk large amongst the subjects which animated Benisch, and he has sometimes been treated as a proto-Zionist. But a careful reading of his editorials on the Holy Land reveals a more complex attitude. He never shrugged off the aversion which Orthodox Jews felt towards plans for the re-establishment of a Jewish nation. His policy towards Palestine was more a projection of Victorian philanthropy on to the impoverished Jewish population there, spurred on by annoyance at the activities of Christian missionaries.[47]

The *Jewish Chronicle* gave extensive coverage to Montefiore's 1855 mission to Palestine, although Benisch courageously dissented from the way in which the great man operated. He thought that relief funds should be disbursed by an accountable public committee, with priority given to projects designed to make Palestinian Jews more self-sufficient. Otherwise, the paper warned, western aid was likely to become a dole attracting hapless Jews to Palestine.[48] These caveats recurred during the famine relief operation in April 1860, when Benisch even suggested that no help be given to a Jew in Palestine unless he had been resident there for five years, a qualification that was even more stringent than those applied by the Jewish Board of Guardians in London.

The *Jewish Chronicle* gave wide publicity to the numerous Christian advocates of restoration, such as the Revd John Mills, Sir Culling Eardly and James Finn. But Benisch was not personally enthusiastic about their plans. He resented the missionary zeal underlying this interest in Palestine, and in 1862 complained bitterly that Finn, the British Consul in Jerusalem, routinely abused his powers of protection over local Jews.[49] Yet, whether inspired by Jews or Gentiles, restoration schemes were always accorded a full airing. On 30 October 1857, the *Jewish Chronicle* published a translation of a second appeal by Rabbi Alkalai. Writing under the nom de plume of 'Gossip' in 1864, Benisch engaged in an exchange with a Jewish group based in Frankfurt-am-Oder that proposed a settlement plan. He treated their project with enormous scepticism, provoking an aggrieved reaction from several correspondents in Europe, including Rabbi Kalischer, the early exponent of religious Zionism.[50]

Benisch familiarised English readers, Jews and non-Jews, with the intricacies of the Holy Land. But his abiding concern for Palestine was tempered by traditional reservations and cool-headed pragmatism. In a typical comment on 4 January 1867 he wrote, 'If Jewish colonies are to be formed in the Holy land, let them spring up spontaneously. Let them be a natural, indigenous, and not an artificial exotic plant. And if it be the design of the Divine Providence that these colonies should form the nucleus of a national restoration, political combinations such as we can at present not foresee will arise and remove the external obstacles, which in the present state of affairs appear to us to be insuperable.'

Jews, religion and culture in mid-Victorian Britain

Today, a reader perusing the *Jewish Chronicle* of the late 1850s and 1860s might be forgiven for expressing surprise, even dismay, at the repetitive and prolix essays on Christianity which occupied the editorial space. Yet these dense excursions into theology were a central part of the paper's raison d'être and are essential to appreciating how middle-class, educated and cultured Jews in England understood their place in English society. The *Jewish Chronicle* helped the literate, thoughtful members of Anglo-Jewry in mid-Victorian Britain to orientate themselves as Jews in relation to the dominant culture; it provided them with a Jewish gloss on the major intellectual developments of the day and formulated a response which they could adopt. To the good fortune of Anglo-Jewry Abraham Benisch was able to act as interpreter, interlocutor and interrogator. He edited the *Jewish Chronicle* at a crucial moment when political and theological debate commingled, when the internal workings and external relations of the Church of England were a public issue and several major controversies exploded within the church, rocking the foundations of Anglicanism.[51]

In *Essays and Reviews*, published in 1860, seven leading thinkers in the Church of England attempted to harmonise Christian doctrine with contemporary scholarship, particularly the 'Higher Criticism' emanating from Germany. This involved jettisoning such impedimenta as miracles and reinterpreting much of the biblical story of Jesus as parable or myth. Most controversial was the vindication of the truths of Christianity not by revelation – miracles, prophecy – but according to their moral validity for humankind. By overturning the traditional interpretation of scripture the authors provoked outrage from Church of England clergymen. During 1861–2, the church indicted *Essays and Reviews* in a series of ecclesiastical and civil court actions. In June 1862, the Dean of Arches, Stephen Lushington, found the two most prominent culprits, Rowland Williams and H. B. Wilson, guilty of violating the sixth of the Thirty-Nine Articles, which affirmed faith in the supernatural inspiration of the Bible, but granted the permissibility of questioning scripture in the most far-reaching way. The verdict was contested unsuccessfully in the Privy Council and, although it was condemned by Convocation, the damage was done.[52]

Benisch devoted a number of leading articles to the debates in Convocation and the prosecution for heresy that was later brought against H. B. Wilson. He argued that the dissident authors were being tried for questioning notions which the Jews had long rejected, so that a victory for them would be a vindication of Judaism. Such was the interest amongst Jews that Roland Williams's letter of defence and his response to Lushington's judgment were carried in the *Jewish Chronicle* the following week. On 15 July 1864, following the Privy Council's ultimate decision, Benisch pronounced that: 'Henceforth a Jew beset by conversionists need no longer confine himself to his rabbis, but may appeal to the evidence of orthodox Christian divines for the correctness of his views, and cut short all controversy by showing that in the Church itself the messianic character of Jesus, so far as the scriptures are concerned, is an open question.'

However, the next crisis to shake the church proved to be potentially devastating for the Jews as well. Biblical criticism since Voltaire, while intent on undermining Christianity, inevitably involved an assault on the foundations of the Jewish faith.[53] In *The Pentateuch and the Book of Joshua Critically Examined* (1862), Bishop John William Colenso of Natal subjected the Old Testament to a bruising, rationalistic critique. He demonstrated by an impressive, if not always accurate, array of arithmetic, geography, philology and history that the biblical record was historically incoherent. Far from having a single divinely inspired author, it was, in fact, the work of many hands. Colenso also ridiculed and condemned the stories they told. He found elements of the narrative describing the activities of the Hebrews to be immoral and barbaric. Consequently, it was necessary to recast the truths of Christianity and detach them from the Old Testament. This was too much for many Anglican clerics, who called on Colenso to retract or resign: his case rumbled on in London and South Africa until the end of the decade.[54]

At first Benisch was dismissive towards Colenso's tome. He pointed out that it contained nothing about the Five Books of Moses that rationalistic authors within the Jewish canon had not already said. More seriously, to his mind, it was based on a faulty translation, was full of errors and was powered by a prejudice against Jews and Judaism. However, he then subjected it to a critical examination that ran over no fewer than fourteen editorials. This massive exegesis must hold the record for the longest, most opaque leading article in the history of journalism. It is questionable whether it was even an adequate reply. Benisch became bogged down in minutiae as he systematically worked through every solecism and mis-calculation. Only twice did he deal with Colenso's vituperative philo-sophical and moral objections to the Old Testament. Despite his familiarity with the Higher Criticism and pride in his own rationalism, Benisch fell into the trap of defending the historicity of the Old Testament.[55]

The Colenso Affair placed Benisch in a quandary. He did not want to help the Anglican establishment close the door to free inquiry that might lead to a re-evaluation of the Gospels and diminish the messianic stature of Jesus; but nor did he want to foster destructive reviews of the Old Testament. Overall he appears to have been convinced that the Jews had more to gain from openness and relentless scholarship. Surveying the agitation within the Anglican communion he told readers on 21 June 1867 that divine providence was at work, loosening the grip of Christian dogma through the work of scientists and scholars. Eventually this would lead to a fairer reading of the Old Testament, with an eye to its true message.

Benisch was not content to rebut allegations against Judaism or to indulge in simple apologetics. He believed that Judaism was inherently superior to Christianity and that, sooner or later, the world would recognise the fact.[56] His belief in the superiority of Judaism could attain exalted heights. In the course of reflecting on the work of missionaries, he wrote in the weekly gossip column on 16 September 1864 that, 'It is morally certain that the gross heathen mind is incapable of at once grasping the sublime Jewish verities. A state of transition is absolutely necessary for it. The abyss yawning between spiritual Judaism and material pragmatism has to be bridged over. Christianity is that bridge ... It is for this purpose that providence allowed Christianity to come into existence, inserting it between paganism and Mosaism.'

This confident tone was typical of the style in which all the denominations in England vied for public support. Furthermore, Benisch was buoyed up by the knowledge that, for once, Christian doctrine was on the defensive. He proclaimed repeatedly that Christianity was moving into a period of profound reformation that would leave it closer to Judaism, if not merged with it entirely. Yet his cheery commentaries tended to insulate Jewish readers from the radical implications of secular thought for Jewish beliefs, too. He maintained that whereas Christianity was vulnerable to scientific discoveries because it was founded on irrational beliefs, Judaism and rationalism were compatible. But argument by assertion was not always going to satisfy the increasing numbers of public-school- and university-educated members of the Jewish middle classes.[57]

The long struggle for emancipation, and the Jews' sense that acceptance was to some extent conditional, contributed powerfully to reshaping the nature of Jewishness and Judaism. Jews responded by minimising that which, aside from their creed, set them apart. As a result, by mid-century, voices were raised in apprehension of a new and puzzling phenomenon that was conceived as 'de-Judaisation', although it would be better understood today as assimilation. Benisch sometimes described the process as anglicisation. It was a trend which he viewed with deep misgivings.

Benisch saw anglicisation, which he attributed to education in non-Jewish schools, eroding Jewish attachments at both ends of the social spectrum. An editorial on the Jewish poor on 15 August 1856 observed that: 'Home influences, early associations, and strong Jewish feelings bound the illiterate to his people and his faith with ties strong enough to resist the most powerful shocks. Can we anticipate the same result from a generation exposed to the operation of other principles, actuated by motives unknown to their fathers, and accustomed to consider matters from a different point of view?' The same processes affected the middle classes. Indeed, the erosion of Jewish conviction amongst the scions of the élite was most worrying: 'Our synagogues are but rarely visited by this enlightened generation ... Most of them stand altogether aloof as if a superior education absolved them from the duties which each individual especially owes to the body among which he received his existence ... What the home only neglected the school altogether rejected.'[58]

The unprecedented importance of Jewish women, as mothers and homemakers, to the continuity of Judaism and Jewish tradition did not escape Benisch. For this reason he considered that the education of Jewish females was possibly even more significant than the work of Jews' College. His purview extended to Jewish working-class women. The *Jewish Chronicle* dared to publish reports that they were often to be found in 'casinos, dancing salons, and low places of amusement' for lack of a Jewish recreational milieu.[59] The paper's letter columns carried a lively, sometimes angry, discussion of these issues. In August 1861 a particularly vigorous exchange followed the assertion of one correspondent that Jewish women were to blame for the decline of the Jewish family because a Jewish wife was so expensive to maintain that Jewish men preferred to remain single.

The improvement of Jewish education, the ministry and synagogue services were all seen as means to stem the tide of defaulters. Benisch enthusiastically threw the paper behind Jews' College, which opened in August 1855, and swept aside the reservations of those like David Salomons who deplored separate Jewish educational institutions. He hoped that the college would soon supply Anglo-Jewry with English-born ministers who could relate to the new generation. On 23 November 1855 he looked forward to Jewish clerics 'whose ardour of enthusiasm will break forth and rouse and kindle with Shakespearean vigour and Miltonian sweetness'. Continuing the tradition of questioning established religious practices and advocating cautious reforms, Benisch opened the columns of the *Jewish Chronicle* to debate on Jewish ritual and prayer. Orthodox fears that the paper was in sympathy with Reform Judaism, as embodied in Germany or the United States, were groundless. The paper's hostility to 'the Berlin apostasy' did not abate.[60]

Coverage of cultural affairs was not confined to theology, the school or the synagogue. Benisch encouraged the publication of Jewish history and literature and tried to stimulate interest in Hebrew. In October 1865 the paper arranged for the translation and publication of extracts from Heinrich Graetz's path-breaking *History of the Jews*. The 1860s saw the emergence of Benjamin Farjoen, a fiction writer who was to acquire a national reputation in the following decade with novels on Jewish themes. From an early stage in his career he was lionised by the *Jewish Chronicle*.[61]

By dint of hard work and its monopoly position, circulation continued to rise throughout the 1860s. Advertising burgeoned in line with national trends for class papers, and in his yearly reflection on the conduct of the *Jewish Chronicle*, Benisch delightedly informed readers that it was in profit.[62] This happy situation rested partly on the income derived from the dozens of company prospectuses which were printed on the advertising pages between 1862 and 1867. Benisch was caught up in the feverish speculation himself and 'puffed' several companies in the editorial columns during 1863–4. However, when the economy went into recession and share prices collapsed, the profitability of the *Jewish Chronicle* was badly damaged. Benisch was personally left in financial difficulty.[63]

At this moment of vulnerability a new rival appeared. The *Jewish Recorder* copied the lively style of the 'new journalism' pioneered by the *Daily Telegraph* as well as its revolutionary price of 1d. undercutting the *Jewish Chronicle* by 2d. To fight off the *Jewish Record* Benisch overhauled the style, content and size of the *Jewish Chronicle* and reduced the cover-price to 1d. He diversified the coverage of the paper along the lines of the old *Hebrew Observer* and attempted to provide general as well as Jewish news. Finally, he started bringing out a one-penny and a three-penny edition, probably losing money on both. It was a disastrous experiment.[64]

On the initiative of Jacob Franklin, three leading members of London Jewry combined to buy the paper and pay off its debts. The group comprised Lionel Louis Cohen; Samuel Montagu (1832–1911), Cohen's brother-in-law, who founded Samuel Montagu & Co., foreign exchange bankers; and Lionel Van Oven (1829–1905), a descendant of a family which had been prominent in the emancipation struggle and charitable work amongst London Jews. Van Oven was a friend of the assistant editor, Michael Henry, and was in partnership with his brother in a jewellery and diamond business. When ill-health and financial problems meant that Benisch was no longer able to run the paper, its new proprietors turned to his second-in-command.[65]

Henry had come to the editor's attention with a letter on Jewish charities, published in the *Jewish Chronicle* on 1 April 1864. He subsequently returned to the columns of the paper as the author of a leading article on Jews and poverty. Over the next three years, he wrote many other editorials and assisted Benisch in various capacities. In an editorial on 5 April 1872, he recalled that when he finally took the helm it was 'under conditions of serious and critical difficulty'.

Michael Henry and the perils of Liberalism, 1868–1875

Michael Henry (1830–75) was born in Kennington, south London, the youngest son of a merchant. His mother, née Emma Lyon, was an educated woman who had grown up in the home of a Jewish minister who taught Hebrew in Oxford and Cambridge. The Henry family moved to Ramsgate, where Michael grew up. He was a precocious child and composed poems and prayers before he was ten years old. After his father died in 1840 his mother took the family back to London. Henry then spent four years as a scholar at the City of London School before being sent to Paris, where one of his sisters lived, to learn book-keeping in a counting-house. After a short time he travelled back to London and found employment in a patent office. One of his jobs there was to sub-edit the *Mechanics' Magazine*. Over the next few years Henry also wrote for the *Mining Journal* and edited the *Investors' Almanak*. In 1857, he set up his own business as a patent agent, which he continued until his death in 1875.[66]

From an early age, Henry was active in general philanthropic and Jewish communal affairs. He founded a charity in 1847, served on the council of Jews' College and represented Sheffield Jewry at the Board of Deputies. Education was a passion, and he was deeply involved with the Stepney Jewish Schools and the Jewish Society for the Diffusion of Religious Knowledge. He wrote tracts for the Society, addressed meetings of Jewish working men and regularly attended the prize-giving ceremonies at the Stepney Jewish Schools. In addition to these interests, he had several other hobby-horses. He was an enthusiastic supporter of the Life Boat Fund (perhaps because of his early years on the coast) and energetically advocated the use of hymns, choirs and congregational singing in the synagogue.[67]

In the range and origin of his interests, Henry was a 'typical Victorian Englishman' of the mid nineteenth century. He was aware of contemporary developments in the Anglican Church, and his belief in the virtues of collective singing may have found their inspiration in movements there. His creed of self-help for the poor and his interest in the Charity

Organisation Society (COS) likewise underline the extent to which he had absorbed contemporary English social thought.[68] Henry loved England deeply; during the Crimean War he wrote a patriotic ode that was published in the *Weekly Dispatch*. Yet his Jewishness impinged on his general outlook in ways that provoked self-examination and forced him to explain, as well as justify, how he was not quite a 'typical Victorian Englishman'.

Despite the eclipse of the proprietor-publisher-editor, the *Jewish Chronicle* did not lose its independence. Cohen and Montagu, the dominant figures in the consortium, represented opposite poles of opinion on almost every Jewish and non-Jewish issue of the day. In 1885, both were elected to Parliament, Cohen as a Tory MP, Montagu as a Liberal. Cohen was the founding genius of the United Synagogue in 1870; Montagu established the alternative Federation of Synagogues in 1887.

Moreover, Cohen believed in the value of publicity in communal affairs and urged Henry to be fearless in exposing the faults of communal organisations. He regularly wrote letters to the paper under the signature 'Lambda' and sometimes contributed editorials.[69] He was mortified when, in a leading article on 13 October 1871, Henry wrote that 'we will never degrade ourselves by admitting into our columns expressions of opinion foreign to our mission, adverse to the interests of the community, offensive to individuals, detrimental to Jewish institutions'. In a letter which appeared two weeks afterwards, 'Lambda' criticised the assumption that 'delicacy' was a requirement of a Jewish journalist. 'Give me', he wrote, 'instead of delicacy, advocacy and good feelings – courage, neutrality and Spartan vigour. Bring the community inexorably face to face with its foibles or its merits.'

Henry's own sense of his function as editor reflected the changed status of journalism as a profession. Prior to the 1850s, the newspaper writer was a despised species of humanity and the press was regarded largely as a corrupt institution in the thrall (and the pay) of politicians or vested interests. The concept of the Fourth Estate as an articulator of public opinion, a vital adjunct to popular education and an instrument of control over government emerged from the role of the press, especially *The Times*, during the Crimean War. Emboldened by this transformation, Henry asserted that 'Never was there a nobler vocation than that of the Press writer. Never has there been a greater, more exalted evidence of the power of human intellect and the influence of the best instincts of the human heart than the evidence embodied in the Press of England.'[70]

The new editor had a further cause for confidence and belief in his independence. The early 1870s were prosperous years for the nation. Advertising revenue boomed along with consumer manufacturing industries. Patent medicines, brand-name household commodities (particularly washing powders and soaps), foodstuffs, beverages and tobacco, alongside consumer durables such as ready-to-wear clothing and home furnishings were heavily promoted in the press. The personal notices marking births, forthcoming marriages and deaths grew spectacularly, until they filled more than an entire column on the front page.[71] It was also notable that the paper's geographical horizons were broadened. During the early 1870s, the news about Jewish centres beyond London became more detailed and regular. This in turn generated more advertising.

The paper also benefited from the publication of appeals and subscription lists which were virtually a guaranteed income from communal organisations. By the mid 1870s, four of the 16–20 pages in any issue could be taken up by advertisements and paid notices. Such was the paper's prosperity that it was enlarged in 1872 to 16 pages as a standard issue. Even so, by 1873 it was necessary to use small print in some sections to accommodate all the news, and it became customary to issue supplements for the overflow.

New names appeared in the burgeoning correspondence columns and as contributors, most prominently 'Nemo', the pen-name of the Revd Aaron Levy Green, the minister of the Central Synagogue. The paper was filled with verbatim reports on the proceedings of communal bodies so that it was an indispensable adjunct to communal governance, akin almost to the parliamentary Hansard. Its advertising capacity, its function as a communal noticeboard and its popularity as a medium for social and personal announcements all indicate its popular appeal and development as an Anglo-Jewish institution.

Henry's extensive connections and personal popularity suggest that he was a sensitive and accurate spokesman for middle-class Anglo-Jewish opinion. His editorials and commentaries reflected, and reinforced, the identity of Jews whose families had been settled in England for several generations and acquired a distinctive set of Anglo-Jewish attitudes. Perhaps because he was native-born, unlike Benisch, Henry gloried in being English. He was also fiercely proud of being a Jew. Much of his writing was an attempt to reconcile these two identities and to harmonise the obligations which they brought in their train. Being English-born may also have sensitised Henry to the insidious effects of acculturation to the point of assimilation. Two questions – how to prevent complete assimilation and how to be a good English citizen, spurning separatism – often formed the polarities between which his editorial comment moved and shaped the paper's policy on domestic affairs, foreign issues and Palestine.

The ambivalences within Anglo-Jewish identity were expressed vividly by the tension between pride in the degree of acculturation of English Jews and panic at incipient signs of complete assimilation. 'There is scarcely a distinctive feature of England that is not a distinctive feature of Judaism', Henry wrote proudly in an editorial on 25 November 1870. Yet in the same issue, he protested against allowing Jewish children to act in school pantomimes, a quintessentially English institution, since they took place on the Sabbath and were 'the first step on the road to vicious excitement'. The synthesis of Judaism and Englishness stopped well short of intermarriage. On 29 March 1878, 'Notes of the Week' grieved over the wedding of Hannah de Rothschild and Lord Rosebery: 'Alas! What degeneracy do we behold.'[72] Henry rounded on English Jews who permitted their children to be educated in non-Jewish schools. To his mind, mixed-denomination schooling resulted in 'a tendency to a perilous amalgamation with communities differing essentially, vitally from our own'.[73] He seemed oblivious to the conflict between such declarations of exclusivity and his profession of complete identity with England and the (Christian) English.

The contradictions between Jewish particularity and the mores of the majority were increasingly highlighted by state intervention. Mid-Victorian liberalism was premised on reason and universalism, often crudely summarised in utilitarian terms as the greatest good for the greatest number. But this frequently boiled down to majoritarianism and post facto rationalisation. The heart of the matter lay in the tendency of the Christian majority to disguise its preferences as 'universalism', rendering the opposition of the Jewish minority 'particularistic'.[74]

Collectivism, or state intervention, thus placed Jews in an uncomfortable situation. Writing in an editorial on 3 November 1871, Henry explained that 'all we desire to maintain is this: that it is not sensible or advisable to imagine that our community stands on the same footing as other denominations; or that arrangements which can be readily adapted to those can be as easily adapted, or in some cases adapted at all, to our Anglo-Jewish body... We trust that in all we have said we have not manifested any ungracious consideration of the indulgence shewn our community by parliament and by the administration of parliamentary statutes; but it is natural that we should be anxious for the intact maintenance of Jewish requirements, even more than of Jewish material interests.'

For these reasons, Henry viewed with apprehension the trend towards state intervention under the Liberal Government between 1868 and 1874. Anglo-Jewry found itself faced with a multiplicity of statutes which threatened to draw attention to Jewish differences. The reform of popular education in the 1870s made the question of particularism acutely difficult.

Henry vehemently objected to the idea that Jewish schools should be placed under state supervision. Worse still was the prospect of compulsory mixed schooling: 'The blending of Jewish children of the lower and lower-middle classes with Christian children of the same social calibre is dangerous – frightfully, fatally dangerous.'[75]

The tension in Henry's position was exposed graphically in an extraordinary editorial on 18 November 1870, in which he addressed the parents of Jewish school-age children. 'We urge them', he wrote, 'before it is too late, to shun the government schools, to shun government interference, and to manage and support their own schools just as they manage and support their own synagogues and their own burial grounds. If they do otherwise they will regret their decision. The Jews are essentially, irrefutably, inevitably divided from their Christian fellow-countrymen in the sphere of juvenile instruction.'

The *Jewish Chronicle* prodded the Board of Deputies to lobby the Government and Jewish MPs to ensure the independence of Jewish schools. But who would pay for them? In a leading article on 29 April 1870, Henry used the arguments of liberal universalism to the benefit of the Jews, maintaining that since Protestant and Roman Catholic schools were state aided, Jews should benefit from state funding, too. If the state would not pay for Jewish schools, then, as he suggested above, the Jews themselves would have to do so. It was only much later that Henry began to suggest ways of operating within the terms of the 1870 Education Act and improving the sort of supplementary Jewish education that could be given to Jewish children in Board schools.

Factory legislation, framed without consideration of Jewish specificity, was no less egregious. The extension of the 1853 Factory Act in 1867 brought under its scope workshops employing over fifty people. Small workshops, including tailoring establishments, were now obliged to close on a Sunday. Consequently, observant Jews would have to shut their premises for two whole days or risk prosecution. Henry compared the effect of the Act to the penal legislation against trade unions introduced by Castlereagh, and in 1869 called for its amendment.[76]

Many 'old Liberals' who owned or edited newspapers were alienated by Gladstone's reforming Government of 1868–74. To the extent that collectivism impinged even more worrisomely on English Jews it corroded their traditional party political allegiances. Under Henry's influence, the *Jewish Chronicle* acquired a Conservative tinge for the first time. His warmth towards the Conservatives was partly a reaction to the ambitious legislative projects mooted and implemented by the Liberals. It was reinforced by the repeated onslaughts which the Nonconformists in the Liberal Party made against the Church of England.[77]

The departure from the fiery Liberalism of the Benisch years is symbolised by a leading article on 12 January 1872 inquiring into the best forms of government. It argued that the Bible favoured aristocracy and monarchy and concluded that Judaism was 'the foe of despotism, priestcraft, and timocracy on the one hand; and of communism, ultra-republicanism and socialism on the other'. When Gladstone asserted in the course of the 1874 election campaign that Jews in the City endorsed the Liberal Party, the *Jewish Chronicle* insisted that there were no Jewish issues at stake and, consequently, no party could lay claim to their votes as Jews.[78]

As well as helping to reshape Jewish political allegiances, the *Jewish Chronicle* had a formative impact on Anglo-Jewish communal life, most notably in the creation of the United Synagogue. As early as 27 April 1866, Henry had used the paper's editorial column to set out the blueprint for a centralised organisation, on the model of the French Consistoire or the Protestant Evangelical Alliance. The new body should also make membership accessible to the humbler members of the middle classes and foster their participation in synagogue affairs. His reasoning coincided with the determination of Lionel Cohen to rationalise and unify Anglo-Jewry by establishing a 'united synagogue'.[79]

While Cohen conducted the gruelling, three-year-long negotiations to win agreement for the new body, Henry contributed several compelling editorials and a pamphlet to the cause of congregational unity.[80] In April 1868 he personally pleaded its case during a debate at the Hambro Synagogue, of which he was a member. The implementation of the scheme required an Act of Parliament and was terribly protracted, but Henry kept the project before the Jewish public during 1869 by publishing a series of leading articles on synagogue improvement.

From the outset, the paper was admitted to the meetings of the United Synagogue council and played its share in the discussions which guided it over the ensuing years. In his favourite medium of the serial editorial (four or five on one subject were not unusual), Henry discussed reform of the liturgy, improvements in decorum, synagogue finance and training the clergy. This was a conscious effort to educate the Jewish public to the benefits of the United Synagogue and stimulate support for its work. Each year he promoted interest in the elections to the council, and lamented the popular apathy which they usually revealed.[81]

The creation of the United Synagogue highlighted the need for an adequate supply of trained ministers. Henry was a member of the council of Jews' College, and he reiterated how important it ought to be in this respect. In editorials he laboured to counteract the derogatory view of the ministry that retarded the provision of adequate training facilities.[82]

The question of liturgical reform also came to the fore. No less a person than Dr Asher Asher, the secretary of the Great Synagogue and first secretary of the United Synagogue, wrote to the *Jewish Chronicle* in April 1869, as 'Aliquis', to propose a 'synod' to discuss how far and in what ways improvements could be made. Henry, by contrast, stood firmly by clerical authority. He wanted changes that would harmonise Judaism with the spirit of the age, but he orientated himself according to the ritualism and ceremony that was becoming fashionable in the Anglican Church. There was more than an echo of the Royal Commission on Ritual, 1867–70, in the *Jewish Chronicle*'s pronouncements on the desirability of introducing sermons, choirs, congregational singing and organs.[83]

Nor did the Board of Deputies escape his critical gaze. 'The most moderate man amongst us', he observed on 27 August 1869, 'must admit that the Jewish public is not completely satisfied with its communal government, and that from defects in organisation, difficulties occur and dangers threaten.' Unlike those who argued that the presence of Jews in Parliament made the Board redundant, Henry maintained that it still had a role to play. He was aware, however, that the Board was crippled as long as the Reform Jews were unrepresented, and so worked hard for a reconciliation. The intransigence of the Board in this respect influenced his attitude towards the formation of a new representative institution, the Anglo-Jewish Association.

The Alliance Israélite Universelle of Paris was fatally disrupted by the Franco-Prussian War of 1870–1, and some sort of replacement was badly needed. In a letter to the *Jewish Chronicle*, published on 17 March 1871, Abraham Benisch urged English Jews to fill the gap. His call was endorsed by Henry. A group of Jewish notables subsequently met at Benisch's home and established a committee to collect funds for this initiative. Benisch reported for the *Jewish Chronicle* on progress and eventually announced in its pages the formation of an Anglo-Jewish Association (AJA) to be linked with the AIU.[84]

The AJA encountered strong communal opposition, expressed in a series of sharp exchanges in the *Jewish Chronicle* correspondence columns. Lionel Cohen considered the new Association to be 'unnecessary, useless, and impolitic', no more than a ploy by the Reform congregation to undermine the Board from which they were barred. The dispute raged into the autumn. Henry was so deeply involved that he intervened at a meeting held in September 1871 to resolve the tension between the Board and the AJA. In his eyes while the Board excluded foreign affairs from its scope and remained unrepresentative of all English Jews, there was, sadly, need for another body.[85]

From 1870, Henry was increasingly preoccupied by Jewish immigration and the foreign poor. Since most middle-class Jews lived far outside the East End, the depiction of the immigrant 'problem' in the *Jewish Chronicle* was vital in shaping their attitudes. Indeed, the range of views on this troubled subject was defined well before the mass immigration that began in the 1880s. Commenting on the foreign Jews' quarter in Spitalfields in 1872, Henry wrote that 'we admit at once that we feel ashamed of it'. The *Jewish Chronicle* complained about the practice in Germany of sending poor Jews on to England – Jews who were 'too idle "to work, yet not ashamed to beg"', who deserted their wives and children in England when they moved on to America. The following year, the paper noted from the annual report of the Board of Guardians that the bulk of new applicants for support were foreign-born. It commented that 'We confess we cannot understand, if we may be pardoned such a remark on a serious subject, why these *magnetic* Poles are *attracted* to our shores.'[86]

The religiosity of the immigrants was considered equally off-putting, as evidenced by Henry's comments on the consecration of an immigrant synagogue in Fashion Street. A *klezmer* band, a musical troupe specialising in ceremonial events, accompanied a parade through the streets of east London as the scroll of the Law was taken in procession from a house in Commercial Street to the new synagogue. Inside there was music and gaiety, with the women in the gallery throwing raisins and nuts to the children down below. The *Jewish Chronicle* commented with disapproval: 'To English eyes the subsequent dancing, shouting, and clapping of hands which took place in the synagogue, appeared somewhat out of character in a religious ceremony ... We unhesitatingly condemn the public procession, as religious processions are not politic and perhaps illegal. Surely such parades are scarcely respectful to religion, and they are certainly undignified.'[87] To be fair, Spitalfields was close to a district which had seen church ritual riots in 1859–60 and which was notoriously prone to public disturbance, so this was not wholly unmitigated snobbery.

A year later, the *Jewish Chronicle* took issue with another immigrant practice – *tashlich*. During the Jewish New Year, a crowd of Orthodox Jews assembled at Custom House Quay to perform the ritual in which breadcrumbs are thrown into the water to symbolise the casting out of sin. It was a picturesque scene, but Henry objected that: 'Our foreign brethren ... must not bring discredit on their generous and free-born British brethren by their unpleasant vagaries [*sic*].'[88]

Henry insisted that the immigrants could be reformed if they were brought into close touch with English Jews. He deprecated the establishment of *chevrahs*, small backroom prayer houses, in the East End, arguing that they preserved the immigrants' sense of separateness and removed them from the reach of English-born Jews. In taking this line, the

Jewish Chronicle followed Lionel Cohen, who condemned the attempts of east London Jews to raise money for small establishments such as that in Artillery Lane.[89]

One solution was for the United Synagogue to build a large synagogue in east London, through which English Jews could exercise a vicarious influence. When the growing Jewish community in Stepney and Mile End appealed for funds to build a prestigious synagogue, Henry acted as an intermediary between the United Synagogue and Stepney Jews.[90] Another strategy lay in the provision of 'improving' facilities for the Jews of east London. In 1869, Henry helped to found the Association for Providing Free Lectures to Jewish Working Men and their Families. The *Jewish Chronicle* claimed credit for the idea of the Jews' Free Reading Room, opened three years later. Henry was also an enthusiastic supporter of the Jewish Working Men's Club, inaugurated in 1874 under West End supervision. He distrusted 'self-culture' and insisted on élite control of the club's proceedings.[91]

Henry's ambivalence towards the newcomers was laid bare by an embarrassing episode which also raised questions about the self-censorship practised on occasions by the *Jewish Chronicle*. In March 1872, at a sub-committee of the London School Board, Moses Angel, headmaster of the Jews' Free School, described immigrant Jews as 'the refuse population of the worst parts of Europe'. His words came to light through a report in the *School Board Chronicle* and led to murmurings of disquiet throughout London Jewry. The *Jewish Chronicle* had chosen not to record the original incident since 'We were unwilling to give, through our columns, additional publicity to a statement of a prejudicial nature.' Henry condemned the particular remark, but broadly defended Angel. This angered many readers, one of whom complained that the *Jewish Chronicle* 'threw rose water over Mr Angel's evidence and expunged from its report' the offensive words.[92]

In his editorials on poverty, Henry marked himself out as a convert to the 'scientific philanthropy' championed by Edward Denison in the mid 1860s and brought to fruition in the Charity Organisation Society (COS) by Charles Loch and Samuel Barnett. During the 1870s he applied its ideas to Jewish charities, advocating rationalisation and urging the careful selection and scrutiny of beneficiaries.[93] He also called for a programme of industrial training and apprenticeships with Jewish manufacturers to take working-class Jews out of the unstable manual trades into which they crowded. But the power of the Jewish press had its limits: it was several years before the Board of Guardians responded to these promptings.[94]

The problem of conversionism was allied to that of Jewish poverty, since missionaries preyed upon luckless Jews. While Henry was editor of the

Jewish Chronicle, it faced one of the most scandalous cases of conversionist activity ever recorded in England: the abduction of a Jewish girl in Cardiff. This case went to the High Court, where the family of the girl lost the argument that she should be returned to their care. Henry did not conceal his distaste for the proceedings, but he dutifully set about disputation with Christians in a spirit of hurly-burly, which sometimes upset his readers.[95]

In a more positive spirit he engaged in a long, complex exchange with the Revd Charles Voysey, who was expelled from the Anglican communion for heresy and founded the Theistic Church in 1871. Voysey fascinated Henry because his concept of Christianity seemed so close to Judaism as to make a mockery of conversionism. In fact, the opposite occurred and Jews were drawn towards Theism.[96] Whereas Benisch entered into polemics with the certainty that Judaism was immune to the ravages of the Higher Criticism and science, Henry struggled to reconcile science and religion. 'Darwinism, it must be admitted, is opposed to the Biblical account of creation', he wrote in 1871, but manfully found arguments to defend traditional Jewish beliefs.[97]

Possibly because of the waning influence of religion, Henry turned to Jewish history and literature as a vehicle for Jewish identity. In an editorial for Benisch on 17 May 1867 he had protested at 'the sorry fact that this great community presents the rare and undignified spectacle of a people apathetic as to its ancient glories; contemptuous as to its national greatness'. As editor, Henry tried to rectify this by the publication in serial form of James Picciotto's *Sketches of Anglo-Jewish History*, beginning on 15 August 1873. These essays were a breakthrough in Anglo-Jewish historiography and became part of the edifice of Anglo-Jewish identity. Picciotto's biographies of communal figures and accounts of communal institutions gave Victorian Anglo-Jewry a knowledge of itself, instilling pride in its origins and all that had been achieved since the resettlement.[98]

Foreign coverage continued to be influenced by hostility to Roman Catholicism. At the time of the uproar caused by the 1874 Vatican Decrees, Henry cited Gladstone's polemic against the Vatican and remarked of the relations between Judaism and Roman Catholicism that 'These creeds are at opposite poles of the religious system of the civilized world.'[99] The paper sided with Otto von Bismarck, the Prussian Chancellor, in the *Kulturkampf* which Henry interpreted as resistance to 'Jesuitical aggression against the German Empire' and 'the great uprising of Protestantism against Ultramontane Catholicism'. Again he praised Protestantism as the most tolerant and beneficent milieu for the Jews.[100]

Romania remained a thorn in the side of western Jewry. During Easter 1872, anti-Jewish outrages there prompted the AJA to organise a protest meeting at the Mansion House, followed by a deputation to the Foreign

Office. A special correspondent for the *Jewish Chronicle* attended the subsequent conference of Jewish leaders, including Sir Francis Goldsmid, Crémieux, Bleichroder and Bischoffen, held in Brussels in November. In February 1873, Henry brought out a supplement to include the report of the Romania Committee. It was equally a celebration of the security and international stature of Anglo-Jewry, which felt able to make such a confident intervention.

Reportage of American Jewish affairs increased markedly during the late 1860s and early 1870s. Henry introduced a regular column from New York and a running feature on Judaism in America. Again, the selection of subject matter was influenced by domestic preoccupations. America took the place of Germany as the paradigm of religious laxity and dissolution. American Jews were held up as a warning to English Jews of what might happen if there were too much or too little reform.

Henry's attitude towards Palestine was paradoxical. He decried the practice by Reform Jews of deleting references to the restoration of Zion from their prayers for fear of incurring the accusation of dual loyalty. But for him Palestine was primarily a symbol of Jewish unity and faith. Although his attachment to Palestine was sentimental, he was nevertheless capable of astute geo-political judgments and predicted that the Suez Canal would have a major impact on the development of the region. The *Jewish Chronicle* continued to carry reports and comment on Gentiles and Jews who advocated a restoration of the Jews in their ancient homeland. Henry was keenly interested in the agricultural school at Mikveh Israel set up by the Alliance Israélite Universelle. The *Jewish Chronicle* published Benisch's special translation of the original proposal by Charles Netter on 29 October 1869 and monitored its subsequent development. In 1873 Henry started a regular column from Jerusalem.[101]

In June 1875, Anglo-Jewry was stunned by the news of Henry's premature death. His clothing mysteriously caught fire late one evening while he was at home. Although he escaped major burns, he suffered severe shock and died twenty-four hours later. His loss deeply affected English Jews since he had been active in so many fields and was so well-liked. Tributes flowed in sermons and obituaries, and several Michael Henry charitable funds were established to preserve his memory. One was used to purchase a lifeboat, the only sea-going vessel to bear the name of an editor of the *Jewish Chronicle*.[102]

Benisch redivivus and the Eastern Question, 1875–1878

After Henry's death, Benisch resumed the editorship of the *Jewish Chronicle* by agreement with its owners. On his return he made a few changes in the layout and introduced a number of new features including a column, written by himself, entitled 'Notes of the Week'. These 'notes' became an important vehicle for his social, literary and political commentary. He devoted more space to European Jewish affairs and instituted an irregular feature on 'Jews of the Continent'. During 1876 he ran a series of European-style feuilletons and started a section on 'Notes and Queries' in Judaica.

The editorial line shifted noticeably. Benisch took a more positive view of state education than Henry had done. There was less criticism of communal organisations and less stress on 'scientific philanthropy'. The prolix, serial leaders on Christianity and missionaries returned, and Palestine featured heavily. However, Benisch's second editorship was dominated by the Eastern Question and the Bulgarian Agitation, the most prolonged and serious anti-Jewish agitation since the 1753 Jew Bill.[103]

The uneven experience of the Jews in the newly independent Christian states of the Balkans predisposed western Jewish opinion to favour Turkey whenever its empire was faced by external aggression or insurrection amongst its subject nationalities.[104] When the Christian population of Herzegovina and Bosnia revolted against the Turks in August 1875, Benisch lightly dismissed the news as the latest 'swindle of nationalities'. But the events in Bosnia triggered an insurrection by the Christian population in Bulgaria, whereupon Turkish troops sent to suppress the nationalist forces massacred thousands of innocent Christians. When the *Daily News* transmitted this story to England, there was uproar. It was an issue which was bound to take a religious form, and it placed English Jews in an appalling dilemma.[105]

Benisch had to justify continued support for Turkey at a time when English Christian opinion was aflame with anti-Muslim feeling. His first attempts were feeble. He told readers in his 'Notes of the Week' on 28 July 1876 that 'The horrors committed upon the Bulgars are merely incidental to the mode of warfare in those regions', where slavery and massacre were common. 'We are not apologizing for Mohametan atrocities', he wrote; 'We wish only for matters to be placed in the proper light.' Benisch repeated that he and all other Jews felt repulsion at the spectre of massacred Christians, but he refused to condone the Slav cause and forcefully maintained that its supporters were helping into power a national movement that was as intolerant as the foreign rule it was fighting to overturn. He confessed a week later that 'It is not without hesitation that we have given expression to these views. Not that we believe we are wrong, but we fear we may be judged wrongly. It is not pleasant to go against the stream. But we have a duty to perform to the thousands of brethren-in-faith scattered all over the dominions of the Crescent.'

Benisch placed himself in an even more awkward position when he urged those who supported the Bulgarians to do so for reasons other than religious feeling. This was clearly at odds with the *Jewish Chronicle*'s own position, which was based on the pre-eminence of Jewish allegiances. By the beginning of September, he had given up any pretence of universalist motives: 'Blood is thicker than water', he declared in the first of a series on 'The Eastern Christians'. 'And if the sympathy of the Northern Sclavs [*sic*] with their Southern kinsmen is justified simply because they are of the same race, surely the Jews in the free countries of the West have a right to espouse the cause of their down-trodden coreligionists in the countries of the East.'

Others did not see things in the same light. Gladstone came out of semi-retirement from politics to lead a crusade on behalf of the eastern Christians. This set him on a collision course with Disraeli's Conservative Government and its pro-Turkish policy. Gladstone's pamphlet *The Bulgarian Horrors and the Question of the East* (published in September 1876) ensured that religion, politics and attitudes towards Disraeli would be irretrievably, explosively mixed.[106]

It was Gladstone's stated belief that because of their loyalty to foreign Jews, English Jews were anti-Slav and tolerated the massacre of Christians. Gladstone was convinced that Disraeli's Jewish origins were an influence on his conduct of policy. In a letter to Leopold Gluckstein, reprinted in the *Jewish Chronicle* on 13 October 1876, Gladstone explained that 'I have always had occasion to admire the conduct of the English Jews in the discharge of their civil duties; but I deeply deplore the manner in which, what I may call Judaic sympathies, beyond as well as within the circle of professed Judaism, are now acting on the question of the East; while I am aware that as regards the Jews themselves, there may be much to account for it.' Gladstone was joined in the war of words by A. E. Freeman, a prominent Oxford historian and fellow Liberal. Letters filled the columns of the *Daily News* and *The Times*, asserting the merits of Christian government. Many were abusive towards the Jews and attributed their sympathies to alleged investments in Turkey.[107]

The agitation left Benisch in a double dilemma, as a Jew who was both an Englishman and a Liberal. Worried that the Liberal Party was alienating Jewish support, on 18 October 1876 he wrote to Gladstone explaining Jewish motives. He pleaded with the Liberal leader to issue a condemnation of Christian atrocities against the Jews to balance his rousing calls to support oppressed Christians. The two men met a few days later. In the course of the interview, Gladstone said he believed that the Jews should have equal rights under Christian rule; but he reiterated his critique of 'Judaic sympathies'.[108]

In May 1877, Benisch again corresponded with Gladstone to elicit a message of support for Jewish claims against the insurgent Bulgarians and their allies. The two men met on 3 May, but Gladstone remained unmoved. He wrote to Benisch, in a letter published in the paper on 11 May, that 'I cannot disguise from myself the fact that of the Jews, apparently a large majority are among the supporters of Turkey and the opponents of effectual relief to Christians. The Christians will be delivered and at no very distant date ... If I am alive, and in politics, I shall strongly plead for their allowing free equality of civil rights to the Jews. But I cannot do this upon the grounds that the conduct of the Jews has deserved their gratitude.' This was hardly encouraging, and the following week Benisch described it as a 'semi-angry utterance'. He commented charitably that 'The extreme humanity of Mr Gladstone which impels him to espouse with such ardour the cause of the oppressed Sclavs in Turkey, prompts him to be unjust and uncharitable to the Jews.'[109]

The accusation that Jews, from Disraeli downwards, were motivated by dual loyalty gained in volume. In *The Ottoman Power in Europe* (1877) and numerous articles A. E. Freeman attributed Disraeli's policy to his Jewish and 'Asian' origins. The Eastern Question thus revived the arguments about Jewish emancipation which had been widespread only twenty years previously. Benisch was mortified by the double standards of Liberal parliamentarians and the Liberal press. In an editorial entitled 'Epidemic Fanaticism' he attributed the vehemence of the opposition to 'religious antipathy'. While English Christians expressed solidarity with Bulgarian Christians, 'they yet undisguisedly blame the Jews in semi-mercenary language, because the majority of these, impelled both by the ties of community, race, as well as faith, sympathise more with the Turks, the protectors of the Eastern Jews, than the Eastern Christians, the persecutors of their people, and demand from the Hebrews of the West an abnegation of which they themselves fail to set an example'.[110]

Traditional Jewish support for the Liberal Party was now haemor-rhaging under the impact of the controversy. In November 1877 Serjeant Simon, a prominent Liberal Jewish MP, tried to rescue the situation by reproaching Gladstone and calling on him to issue a statement of sympathy for the Jewish cause. The *Jewish Chronicle* gave a good deal of publicity to the overture and offered Gladstone a perfect opportunity for a rapproche-ment, a point which Benisch drove home in his editorial comment. But, possibly under the malign influence of the pro-Russian publicist Madame Novikiff, Gladstone remained silent.[111]

Benisch was further dismayed when Goldwin Smith, the former Regius Professor of history at Oxford University and a well-known Liberal, launched an explicit attack on the Jews in the course of an article in the

Contemporary Review. Smith held that the Eastern Question exposed the political tendencies of the Jews and showed emancipation to have been a mistake. Jews were not like other Nonconformists: theirs was a primitive religion in which tribal exclusivity and race mixed with religion. The 'nobler part' of the ancient Hebrews had become Christians: the rest wandered the earth where they excelled at money making. Jews gained control of the press and exploited the guilt which Christians felt towards them because of their earlier oppression. Yet it was now plain that they could not be good patriots: 'their only country is their race; which is one with their religion'.[112]

This outburst astonished Benisch as much by its origin as its vehemence: how could such a great exponent of Liberalism be so illiberal in his attitude towards the Jews? He could not believe that Gladstone countenanced such propaganda, but the Liberal leader did nothing to remove himself from such company. In an article in *Nineteenth Century*, he actually reiterated his opinion that the majority of Jews were pro-Turk. Benisch was now very disturbed at Gladstone's reiterated position: 'The pertinacity with which he clings to this erroneous view is truly deplorable.' However, as much as Benisch might accuse Gladstone of 'illogical reasoning', there was truth in the latter's assertions. Benisch wanted to have his cake and eat it: he wanted to defend the right of Jews to have a special sympathy for fellow Jews abroad while rejecting any criticism of that right, and he wanted to trumpet Jewish solidarity, then claim that it did not really exist.[113]

The Eastern Question had internal repercussions for Anglo-Jewish institutions in which the *Jewish Chronicle* was also embroiled. As a founder member and a vice-president of the Anglo-Jewish Association, Benisch was furious that the Board of Deputies declined to send a representative to an international meeting in Paris on the Balkan situation. Henry de Worms attended on behalf of the AJA, but the Board of Deputies, jealous of its prerogatives and resentful of the AJA's activity, passed on its own views to the Foreign Office and added that it was the only channel for communication between English Jews and the Government. This prompted Benisch to write his most outspoken editorial assault on the Board so far: it was isolationist, arrogant and, above all, ineffective.[114] There was an angry exchange of correspondence in the paper between de Worms and Lionel Cohen, while Samuel Montagu, speaking at the Board of Deputies, suggested that the importance of the AJA was inflated by the *Jewish Chronicle* because of the connections of its editor.[115]

Although the overseas crisis dominated these years, domestic matters were not neglected. Benisch differed from Henry in taking a more relaxed attitude towards the foreign Jewish poor. True, he maintained that it was necessary to 'rid them as soon as possible of all those externals not rarely repugnant to English feeling and to imbue them with English sentiments'. But, in general, he viewed the immigrants sypathetically as refugees from persecution who were fundamentally good-hearted and, above all, devout. Before most others, he appreciated the institutions which they themselves set up. In his 'Notes of the Week', he made the revolutionary proposal that the *chevrahs* could be adapted to the purposes of anglicisation. To encourage a more positive view of them, during 1876 he began to publish letters and articles giving details of their history and internal workings.[116]

Benisch was back in the editorial seat at just the moment when Britain acquired the majority shareholding in the Suez Canal. He commented, prophetically, in 'Notes of the Week' on 3 December 1875, that 'Unintentionally, and incidentally – England has thereby materially become more interested in the fate of Palestine, than she was before.' Soon the *Jewish Chronicle* was urging that Britain obtain control over the land routes to India too. Benisch did not disclaim a particular Jewish interest in this, but argued that Jewish and English objectives were one. With uncanny accuracy, on 4 February 1876 he wrote in an editorial, 'if ISRAEL's [*sic*] highest aspirations are to be realised, we fain believe that it would be the English to which the glorious call would go forth'.

Not long afterwards, George Eliot's *Daniel Deronda* appeared, giving rise to yet more speculation in the paper on the prospects for resurrecting the Jewish state. The *Jewish Chronicle* accorded the novel a rapturous reception because it hoped that its sympathetic portrayal of Jews would help to eliminate anti-Jewish prejudice. Eliot's achievement dented Farjoen's reputation. His 1877 novel *Solomon Isaac* was slated for the 'innate vulgarity of both subject and treatment'.[117]

In these years, the profitability and reputation of the *Jewish Chronicle* waxed. There was no shortage of advertisers: Benisch maintained the trend in display advertising so that by the late 1870s, the paper carried up to eight pages of advertisements, including half-page advertisements for consumer goods such as clothing or furniture. In July 1878, he started a Professional and Trades Directory listing Jewish traders serving the Jewish population who could not afford paid publicity.

Accounts of the second period of Benisch's editorship, until his death in 1878, have depicted him as a sort of lame-duck. In fact, during this time he furthered the consolidation of the *Jewish Chronicle* and promoted its emergence as the dominant arena for communal discussion. The Eastern Crisis showed that it was a vital medium for debate with non-Jews, and a considerable weapon in the defence of Jewish interests. In turn the paper's standing accurately reflected the position of Anglo-Jewry: well anchored in Victorian society, British Jews boldly entered the fray at home and in international affairs. With the central institutions of the community established and working effectively, it was possible to indulge in self-congratulation and self-criticism. The paper was a vehicle for both, and it became natural for English Jews to resort to it when they felt the need to express their opinions and feelings. This symbiosis made it a superb mirror of Anglo-Jewish life in the mid-Victorian years, and a chief element in the process which formed the outlook of modern Anglo-Jewry.

3 The era of Asher Myers and Israel Davis, 1878–1906

Asher Myers, the Russian Crisis and the immigration debate

In his will Benisch left the *Jewish Chronicle* to the Anglo-Jewish Association which he had helped to found. However, the new owners had no desire to run a newspaper and quickly looked for a buyer. It was subsequently acquired by Israel Davis (1847–1927), a barrister, and Sydney Montagu Samuel (1848–84), a wealthy scion of the Samuel Montagu family, who combined business in the City with an active interest in the world of letters. Benisch also stipulated that Asher Myers should be made the 'manager' of the paper. Davis and Montagu accordingly appointed Myers editor and made him a partner even though he contributed no capital to the purchase.

The son of a synagogue official and bookseller, Asher Myers (1848–1902) had received a private education followed by commercial training in Moses, Son and Davis, wholesale clothiers. In 1868 he was involved in the publication of the *Jewish Record*, although his participation ceased after twelve months and he seems to have lost the money he had invested in it. For six months in 1870, he was employed as the principal officer of the Board of Guardians, a position which gave him a valuable insight into the workings of Jewish philanthropy. He eventually joined the staff of the *Jewish Chronicle* with responsibility for its business affairs, although his duties broadened after Benisch returned to the editorial chair. According to Israel Davis, Benisch used to dictate his leading articles to Myers – a useful induction into the craft of journalism.[1]

Like most Fleet Street editors of the time Myers was a professional journalist working for a proprietor. He was a fellow of the Institute of Journalists, the foundation of which signified that the era of the printer-publisher-proprietor-editor was coming to an end.[2] Indeed, there is a good deal of confusion about how much editorial control he actually exercised. The agreement under which he was appointed stated that 'All reasonable efforts will be made to carry out the instructions of Israel Davis as to insertions and omissions, general tone and policy of the paper and prominence of particular topics.' John Shaftesley, who edited the paper in the 1950s, identified at least one occasion on which Davis overrode the convictions of his editor – a symptom of the 'editor-owner syndrome'.[3] The author of Myers's obituary on 16 May 1902 (possibly the acting editor, Morris Duparc), declared that 'Of the editorial comments in the *Jewish Chronicle* he wrote but little, though he suggested much.' In an interview published on 27 March 1908, the historian and journalist Joseph Jacobs claimed that he had written most of the editorials during 1881. The most disparaging comment came twenty years later from the Revd Isidore Harris. Reflecting on the eightieth anniversary of the paper he recalled that Myers had been no more than the 'general and literary manager'.

Yet Myers was editor at a critical juncture for the newspaper industry. During the 1870s, costs continued to decline while revenues increased. The steady rise in the standard of living, the growth of consumerism and the accelerating pace of fashions in clothing and furnishings generated more advertising. Technical advances in pictorial printing led to greater use of, and demand for, illustrated display advertisements. Financial buoyancy enabled newspapers to enlarge their staff so that they could cover more events and print more news: newspapers got bigger and bigger. Better communications and distribution led to a larger amount of provincial news in the London papers. The emergence of trade unions and their political activity prompted the appearance of columns dealing with labour news. The last decade of the century also saw an extravagant interest in fashion and the conspicuous display of wealth: newspapers carried extensive gossip columns and 'society news'. Finally, the 1870 Education Act stimulated the growth of the children's and juvenile press. The trend was set by the *Boys' Own Paper*, established in 1879.[4]

There were changes in the tone and style of journalism, too. In 1868 the *Daily Telegraph* had revolutionised the industry by pioneering the one-penny daily newspaper, offering a wide coverage of news written in a more vigorous style. The tempo quickened in the mid 1880s under the influence of W. T. Stead of the *Pall Mall Gazette*, who wrote vividly about subjects that were previously taboo. As fresh titles entered the market the battle for circulation intensified. Exploring new techniques to attract readers, editors were drawn irresistibly to the lower end of the market by the promise of mass circulation. Even the religious press was affected. By the 1870s, established religious papers were being driven to the wall by a wave of attractive penny dailies and weeklies.[5]

The short-lived *Jewish Recorder* (1868–72) and the much more successful *Jewish World* (1873–1937) were expressions of these trends within the Jewish publishing milieu. Founded by George Lewis Lyon, a financial journalist on the *Daily Telegraph*, the *Jewish World* was edited by Myer

Davis until 1875, then by Lyon with the help of Lucien Wolf and Jacob de Haas, amongst others. In 1897 the paper was bought by S. L. Heymann, a merchant who had prospered in South Africa. The paper had three successive editors in as many years until, in 1900, it was acquired by a group of wealthy communal figures. Wolf was brought back as editor with the assistance of Jack Myers, son of Asher Myers. Under their direction, it was lively to read, well illustrated and unashamedly populist in its politics. With the ample resources of the proprietorial group behind it the *Jewish World* forged ahead of its rival.[6]

Guided by Myers the *Jewish Chronicle* responded to developments in the national, religious and Jewish press. Between 1878 and 1906, its provincial coverage was expanded, a column of labour news was started and an attempt was made at a sports section. There was more use of illustrations and, from the mid 1890s, photographs. Coverage of society weddings billowed, in imitation of the prevailing fashion and, possibly, as an incentive to marry within the faith. Descriptions of the marriage ceremony, the roster of guests and lists of wedding gifts could occupy an entire page. All accompanied, of course, by the ubiquitous photograph of the happy couple.[7]

There were more frequent reports in the style of 'society news' about Jewish dignitaries, particularly after the ennoblement of Sir Nathaniel Rothschild as the first Jewish peer in 1885. More than mere gossip, these reports displayed evidence that English Jews had become intrinsic to the country's social fabric. By celebrating the appointment of Jewish Lord Lieutenants and masters of the hounds they were intended to show that Jews were rooted in landed society. The ritualised references to public service by Jews in high office were both a demonstration of patriotism and a signal of gratitude. Although the attention lavished on Sir Moses Montefiore on his 100th birthday in October 1884 and on his death in July 1885 was *sui generis*, here, too, there was an exemplary lesson. The accent was on Montefiore the great Jew who was also a great Englishman. Indeed, he was characterised as virtually a national institution.

The expansion of space devoted to news and features was made possible by the healthy level of advertising revenue. On 24 September 1880, the paper carried its first full-page advertisement (for Cadbury's chocolate drink). The range of display advertising in the paper was typical of the general press, even including promotions for turtle soup. Nor was the paper immune to the circulation wars that were beginning to rage. In October 1881, the editor printed a notice asserting that, despite claims to the contrary, its circulation was 50 per cent higher than for any other Jewish title. The entries in *Mitchell's Newspaper Press Directory* testify to the ferocity of the battle now underway between the *Jewish World* and the *Jewish Chronicle*.[8]

For most of the period that Myers was editor the news and editorial columns were dominated by the mass immigration of Jews from eastern Europe. Between 1881 and 1906, 150,000 Russian, Polish, Galician and Romanian Jews arrived in Britain.[9] The *Jewish Chronicle* had always expressed middle-class concern about the concentration of poor, immigrant Jews in east London, and the linkage between the unhappy condition of the Jews in Russia and immigration was well established.[10] However, events in Russia radicalised the dimensions and implications of Jewish immigration.

In March 1881, Tsar Alexander II was assassinated by a group of revolutionaries. Although only one Jew was involved in the plot, the anti-Semitic press blamed the Jews as a whole. A wave of anti-Jewish riots swept through southern Russia and spread to Warsaw at the end of the year. These riots, and the punitive legislation which followed, provoked a panic flight of Jews from Russia. Jewish communities in the West raised money for the victims and sent emissaries to the Russian border to assist the refugees, but this inadvertently aggravated the stampede.[11]

The *Jewish Chronicle* naturally covered the riots in depth. It printed long dispatches by its own correspondents, one of whom was David Gordon, the owner-editor of the infuential Hebrew weekly, *Hamaggid*. These were supplemented with reports from the news agencies, the British and foreign press. Editorially it called for protests on the scale of the Bulgarian Agitation. The paper brought out two editions to cover the great public meeting held at the Mansion House on 1 February 1882 and the dozens of lesser rallies around the country. 'At no previous moment in the career of this journal', Myers wrote solemnly on 27 January 1882, 'have we felt so strongly as now the sense of responsibility under which we lie as an organ of Jewish opinion and Jewish necessities.'[12]

Refugees streamed into England, but the prospect of large numbers of poor Jews arriving in the country was not welcomed. The *Jewish Chronicle* considered that selection, at the very least, was essential. The paper never considered Britain a suitable haven for masses of refugees. It fully concurred with the policy of Anglo-Jewish relief agencies, like the Russo-Jewish Committee, of sending emigrants on to America, where it was assumed there were better prospects of their finding homes and work. A report on the refugees in London stated that those who were not 'real refugees' or were 'doubtful and hopeless cases, which should not have been assisted hither' should be sent back.[13]

Communal policy on immigration was not contested within Anglo-Jewish circles until late March 1885. Then Myers published a letter by

Oswald John Simon, giving an account of an informal shelter for poor immigrants set up by a Jewish baker in Church Lane, Whitechapel. The shelter filled a crucial gap since the immigrants did not qualify for help from the Board of Guardians until they had been in the country for six months. However, conditions in the shelter were primitive and it was abhorrent to adherents of 'scientific philanthropy' because access was free and residence was of unlimited duration. On 3 April 1885, the *Jewish Chronicle* declared that 'such places encourage "loafing" and idleness'. When officers of the Board intervened to close the shelter, Myers backed them to the hilt. 'More and more foreign Jews', he warned, 'would be enticed to this country only to live a life of degradation and beggary, with no prospect of bettering their condition ... Surely it is better that men such as these should be returned to their native places.'[14] Letters subsequently poured into the paper. The majority supported the editorial, including one from the president of the Master Tailors' Association deploring the prospect of competition from lowly paid foreign Jews.

In the spring of 1885 the expulsion of Jews from eastern Prussia provoked a renewed spate of immigration. It coincided with a trade depression and public anxiety about unemployment, poverty and poor housing in east London. Fearful of an anti-Jewish backlash, Nathan Joseph, chairman of the Russo-Jewish Committee which channelled aid to the Jewish victims and fugitives, suggested asking the Government to place restrictions on immigration. Myers was taken aback. In 'Notes of the Week' on 26 February 1886 he objected that 'Such a proposal is full of danger. The letters which spell exclusion are not very different from those which compose expulsion.' It would be better to deter would-be emigrants from leaving and exert pressure on Russia to treat its Jews better.

With little prospect of relief from that direction, the letters columns of the *Jewish Chronicle* filled with anguished debate between the leading figures in the London community. Myers was personally in two minds. He certainly saw the force of Joseph's argument. 'With all our sympathy for our brethren in Russia', he wrote at the beginning of December 1886, 'this state of affairs can no longer be permitted to continue. The refugees who come here do no good to themselves and by oversupply of the labour markets they do harm to others.' But two weeks later he asserted that, 'we must be no party to shutting the gates of the prison house in Russia'. In one editorial after another Myers applauded the Board of Guardians' policy of assisted onward migration and direct repatriation as the lesser evil to restriction by the state.

In March–April 1887, anti-alienism, the term for opposition to Jewish immigration, was taken up in Parliament and the national press. The

Jewish Chronicle responded by appealing to the traditions of English hospitality and the principle of asylum. It trenchantly put the case for an open-door policy based on liberal doctrine concerning the free movement of people and goods, and a series of practical points that were to be reiterated endlessly. The number of Jewish immigrants was small; they could not 'swamp' the labour market or threaten the jobs of English people; and, finally, if they were a burden because of their poverty, it was a weight which Anglo-Jewry was glad to bear on its own account. The paper accused anti-alienists, such as the publicist Arnold White, of fostering Continental-style anti-Semitism in England.[15]

During 1888–9 select committees of both Houses of Parliament examined the immigration question, but a slackening in the numbers of Jews reaching England eased the problem and the reports were not unfavourable. Yet, before Anglo-Jewry could draw its breath in relief, a new phase of persecution opened up in Russia. As part of the campaign to modify Tsarist policy, from 17 July 1891 the *Jewish Chronicle* printed and distributed a supplement *In Darkest Russia*, 'with the object of bringing to the knowledge of the civilized world authentic facts relating to Russia's persecution of her Jews and Nonconformist subjects'. Edited and mainly written by Isidore Spielman, the supplement was a valuable propaganda weapon, although some *Jewish Chronicle* readers thought it went too far in its attacks on the Tsarist regime. The paper also sought to discredit apologists for Russia, like the influential Madame Novikoff, who wrote for the British press.[16]

The latest wave of immigrants arrived at a time of escalating unemployment and social distress in east London. Local unrest now combined threateningly with political opportunism. In the course of the 1892 General Election candidates for east London constituencies vied to satisfy anti-alien feeling. Even Jewish candidates, who published their election addresses in the *Jewish Chronicle*, felt obliged to espouse exclusion or advertise their success in diverting immigrants from England.[17]

During the winter of 1891–2, the Jewish relief organisations in the East End found themselves close to breaking point as large numbers of unemployed and hungry Jews, mostly recent arrivals, queued at the Board of Guardians for small hand-outs of cash. As money drained away without any long-term result Nathan Joseph recommended a radical overhaul of relief work. His 'new departure' aimed at a more active intervention amongst the Jewish poor to encourage their dispersion from the East End and place them on a more secure economic footing. The corollary of this was the rigid denial of aid to 'helpless and hopeless' cases: they would be assisted to return to Russia, or left to fend for themselves.[18]

Myers congratulated Joseph on the boldness of his proposals, but regretted that the language in which he advanced them sounded as if it had been borrowed from the anti-aliens. He warned against 'a dictatorial insistence upon theoretical views' and was sceptical about the 'new departure'. 'Paper projects', he cautioned, 'however persistently advocated will not necessarily prove workable.'[19] But his tone was modulated at around the time that he became a member of the Board of Guardians in 1893. His editorials then hailed the institution of visiting and case work by the Russo-Jewish Committee as a 'new epoch' in Jewish philanthropy. The *Jewish Chronicle* rejoiced when the Board was persuaded, in the teeth of strong opposition, to accept Joseph's medicine. By the end of the year, the 'new departure' was declared a 'distinct success'.[20]

It is impossible to know whether Myers was a genuine convert to Joseph's point of view or whether, as a member of the Board, he succumbed to institutional pressure to toe the line. But he still stopped short of any suggestion for government interference in immigration matters. He was staggered that Benjamin Cohen, a Tory MP and president of the Board of Guardians, declined to intervene in the parliamentary debates on immigration legislation. The paper was equally astonished by Nathan Joseph's declared preference for government measures. An outraged correspondence, which went on for weeks, showed widespread concurrence with the stand Myers had taken.[21]

Between June 1892 and June 1895 the Liberal Party, which was ideologically opposed to interfering with the free migration of labour, was in government. It fended off demands for restrictive legislation emanating from MPs and the Trades Union Congress. The fall of the Liberals in June 1895 removed this shield, while anti-alienism overshadowed the campaign in east London constituencies during the ensuing General Election. Jewish candidates again bowed to popular pressure and endorsed restriction or claimed personal success for dissuading potential emigrants. The manipulation of anti-alienism in electioneering posed a dilemma for the *Jewish Chronicle*. Traditionally it disparaged the mobilisation of a 'Jewish vote' and condemned appeals by Jews to Jews, especially in the East End. But in this case it conceded that anti-alienism was a Jewish issue which affected Jews as a group and logically warranted a group response.[22]

Surprisingly, the new Conservative Government chose not to respond to persistent efforts by lobbyists to curb immigration. Meanwhile, agitation within the labour movement tailed off during 1897 as unemployment fell. Optimism was generated by more stable conditions in Russia. In October 1894, Tsar Alexander III had died and was succeeded by Nicholas II, who, Myers believed, was 'imbued with benevolent intentions'. Seeing a glimmer of hope for Russian Jewry, the *Jewish Chronicle* repeated its conviction that: 'it is to a relaxation of Russian policy and not to any restrictive legislation here that we must look for a decrease in so-called "pauper-alien" arrivals'.[23]

In fact, the next influx of Jewish immigrants came from Romania, where anti-Jewish discrimination and occasional violence was a fixture of national life. During the winter of 1899–1900 the country was plunged into a financial crisis. Famine struck Bessarabia, one of the centres of Jewish population, and Jews began to stream out of the country. The *Jewish Chronicle* again contributed powerfully to the protests of western Jewry by distributing the *Romanian Bulletin*, an exposé of the iniquities of the Romanian Government modelled on *Darkest Russia*.[24]

Yet protests did little to stop the flight of Romanian Jews. On 22 June 1900, the paper warned that, 'anybody with eyes to see must know that there are limits to the receptive capacity of this country. Already we have a large immigrant body camped down East, which is a rock of offence to many Gentiles, and taxes the resources of our community to exhaustion point ... Is there not a danger of raising an outcry... against Jewish refugees from whatever land they may hail?' As groups of bedraggled and desperate refugees congregated on street corners and besieged the Board of Guardians, the Jewish organisations adopted a ruthless policy of repatri-ating as many as possible. There were objections, but Myers, who saw the chaos at first hand when he went to the Board's headquarters for its business meetings, staunchly defended repatriation. He intervened in person at a meeting of the Board in July 1900, arguing that it was cruel to allow Romanian refugees to remain in the country and criticising opponents of the Board's repatriation policy.[25]

During 1898 and 1899, anti-alienism had continued to simmer in east London, monitored anxiously by the *Jewish Chronicle*'s reporters. Griev-ances against east European Jews for housing shortages and high rents were aggravated by the chauvinistic mood nurtured during the Boer War. In the General Election campaign of September–October 1900, candidates throughout the East End paraded their credentials as proponents of restriction on the hustings and in the advertising columns of the Jewish press. The election brought into the House of Commons a cadre of Tory MPs representing East End constituencies who were committed to restricting immigration.[26]

These MPs responded to, and harnessed, grass roots antagonism to Jewish immigration by forming a mass movement, the British Brothers' League (BBL), in May 1901. The *Jewish Chronicle* observed derisively that 'There appears to be very little British and nothing brotherly in the new League.' But in the House of Commons MPs formed a Parliamentary Pauper Alien Immigration Committee to press for legislation. Simon Gelberg, a young *Jewish Chronicle* reporter who as Simon Gilbert would become a senior member of the editorial staff, covered its first meeting and closely questioned Sir Howard Vincent MP, the veteran restrictionist and protectionist, who was its chairman. Gelberg's incisive analysis of anti-alienism was soon evident in the editorial columns. In August 1901, the paper observed shrewdly, 'a Government anxious to retain seats captured in East London may well pander to popular opinion by taking vigorous action in this matter'.[27]

Anglo-Jewry was confused and divided. Benjamin Cohen acceded to American pleas that no more Jews should be sent over to New York and tacitly endorsed a reduction of immigration. The *Jewish Chronicle* condemned his actions unreservedly, since, 'if the Jews themselves counsel restrictions the State cannot be blamed for accepting them'. After Harry Samuels, recently elected Jewish MP for Limehouse, joined a deputation of restrictionists to the Prime Minister in July 1901, a leading article fulminated that restriction was not the appropriate response. The question was 'one of diffusion, not restriction ... how to decentralise, not whom to exclude'. Myers remained unequivocal on this alone: over the preceding two decades, the *Jewish Chronicle* had veered between selection, voluntary restriction and repatriation of the immigrants. The reasons for this havering policy lay in Myers's and Anglo-Jewry's attitude towards east European Jews in London.[28]

Anglo-Jewry and the immigrants

The idea, which acquired a vice-like grip on Anglo-Jewry, that Jewish immigration was a 'problem' rested on a set of beliefs which were constructed, elaborated and disseminated in the course of public debate. First, there was the conviction that the majority society would not, even could not, tolerate that which made immigrant Jews different. Next was the fear that English-born Jews would be lumped together with the immigrants and that the rejection of the latter would extend to the former. For almost two decades these assumptions went virtually unchallenged. Asher Myers and the *Jewish Chronicle* were to a great measure responsible for making them orthodoxy within Anglo-Jewry and setting the agenda for the discussion of immigration and the immigrants.[29]

Myers's attitude towards the immigrants resembled the distaste which the Ostjuden (Jews from eastern Europe) aroused in the emancipated Jews of Paris, Berlin and Vienna. It combined a thorough identification with England and English culture with pride in an enlightened form of Judaism that excluded what were held to be superstitious beliefs and archaic practices. This did not preclude a genuine feeling of kinship with the immigrants, even if it was a case of holding your nose and doing your duty. But the fear of an anti-Jewish movement based on dislike of the immigrants, and the resurrection of claims that Jews were clannish and alien, vied with these sympathies.[30]

Consequently, the *Jewish Chronicle* did little to challenge the cultural assumptions of the majority society about the immigrants. This is not to say that it failed to defend them or portrayed them only in a negative light. On the contrary, it constantly argued that they were intelligent, thrifty, hard-working, sober and pious. It seized on every scrap of evidence from non-Jewish observers testifying to these virtues. But they were the values of English society. While the *Jewish Chronicle* did dwell occasionally on the Jewish traits of the immigrants – their religious practices, culture, social organisation and political views – on the whole it treated these attributes as a regrettable hang-over from the 'old country' to be eliminated as speedily as possible.

The *Jewish Chronicle* set the tone at an early stage. It is exemplified by this comment about the immigrants from an editorial on 12 August 1881:

They come mostly from Poland; they, as it were, bring Poland with them, and they retain Poland while they stop here. This is most undesirable; it is more than a misfortune, it is a calamity ... Our fair fame is bound up with theirs; the outside world is not capable of making minute discriminations between Jew and Jew, and forms its opinion of Jews in general as much, if not more, from them than from the Anglicized portion of the community ... It is tolerably clear what we wish to do with our foreign poor. We may not be able to make them rich; but we may hope to render them English in feeling and conduct.

The paper looked to the United Synagogue, the Board of Guardians and the Jews' Free School as the triad of institutions which could accomplish this task.

The *Jewish Chronicle* relentlessly campaigned against the *chedarim*, Hebrew and religious classes, and *chevrahs* established by the immigrants. It pronounced that their effect was 'to preserve a narrow parochial feeling which is, at the same time, not even an English feeling'. Like Michael Henry, Myers urged the United Synagogue to embrace them under its improving aegis. 'The great task before the London Jewish community is to Anglicise "the foreign contingent" that has arrived in such numbers during the past few years. And these can only be approached through the Hebras [*sic*].'[31] For this reason the *Jewish Chronicle* supported Samuel Montagu's initiative to unite the *chevrahs* in a Federation of Synagogues that would fund improvements to their facilities, help to anglicise the forms of worship and assist decentralisation.

Even though he later on became disillusioned with the Federation for allegedly poaching members from the United Synagogue, of which he was a council member, Myers continued to defend the idea it represented. When Benjamin Cohen suggested in a letter to the *Jewish Chronicle* that the best policy would be to demolish as many 'minor synagogues' as possible, Myers replied that: 'The advocacy of a policy of extinction is not calculated to promote that improvement in the chevras, physical and religious, which he ... so ardently desires.'[32]

Between 1890 and 1895, the United Synagogue produced ambitious plans for a large synagogue, with plentiful cheap seating, in the heart of the East End. This was intended as both an anglicising device and a death sentence on the *chevrahs*. But the *Jewish Chronicle* agreed with Samuel Montagu that the much-vaunted East End Scheme had major defects. After the plan was shelved, the paper commented on 8 May 1891 that an appeal for funds 'might have been misconstrued as an indication of provision being made for a large influx of foreign Jews to the East End'. Anything which contributed to Jews remaining in east London was a bad thing. When the scheme was revived in 1893–4, Myers objected tellingly that a major synagogue in the East End might fall under the control of east European Orthodox Jews. 'It is surely obvious that we are conjuring up no imaginary danger. So vast a congregation, with its far reaching social and educational adjuncts, cannot fail to wield enormous influence, and hence its powers must be very closely formulated and jealously watched unless the other constituents of the United Synagogue are to become mere appendages to the "People's Synagogue".'[33]

Myers also turned to philanthropy as a means to remould the immigrants. 'They must be taught to conform to English ideas about dress and cleanliness', he asserted in a leading article on 11 December 1885. Consequently he praised the doughty ladies of the United Synagogue and the Conjoint Committee (of the Russo-Jewish Committee and Board of Guardians) who visited foreign Jews in their homes. Another way to rework their domestic habits was to place them in an improving environment. Myers explained in an editorial on 20 February 1885 that: 'We want the foreign poor, for example, to live like Englishmen; but we shall not make much progress towards realizing our wish while we allow them to inhabit houses which, in respect of cleanliness, almost compel them to live like Russians ... The Russian immigrant must be taken by the hand. His civilization is not his affair, but the community's, which desires as much for its own sake as for him to improve his condition.' So the *Jewish Chronicle* was an enthusiastic proponent of the Four Percent Industrial Dwellings Company, which erected several tenement buildings, notably the Rothschild Buildings, specifically to house the immigrants.[34]

Above all, Myers put his faith in the educational system to instil English culture and middle-class values into the younger generation of immigrants and the children of foreign-born Jews. The Jews' Free School was lauded as the antidote to the 'pestilential atmosphere' and 'dens' of the *chedarim*. It played its part in combating anti-Jewish feeling by showing that 'we are doing our best to make Jews Englishmen'. The school provided immigrant children with a 'bridge by which, mentally and morally, they may pass from Russia to England'.[35]

Myers unremittingly opposed anything that promoted or preserved the alleged isolationism of the immigrants. Although Yiddish culture had taken root in the East End from the early 1880s, the *Jewish Chronicle* steadfastly ignored its manifestations until the end of the decade, and then treated it with contempt.[36] The editor's prejudices were confirmed when several people died during the panic which followed a fire alarm at one of the earliest Yiddish theatres in London on 18 January 1887. A month later the paper asserted that 'one of the direct causes' of the catastrophe was the 'persistent isolation' of foreign-born Jews. It concluded that, 'The recent event ought to be a lesson to avoid such performances of strolling minstrels acting in the jargon, and helping to keep up the alienation of the foreign contingent.'[37] The *Jewish Chronicle* condemned the use of Yiddish at school prize-givings and even called on the Board of Guardians to refuse to help anyone who could not speak adequate English.[38]

When reality could no longer be denied, and possibly also because of market pressures, articles on Yiddish culture began to appear. From 1898, the paper carried reports on the Yiddish theatre, including interviews with celebrities from the British and American stage. In 1901 the use of Yiddish to publicise the census gave official recognition to the existence of an immigrant culture, and the *Jewish Chronicle* was compelled to admit that it was fighting a losing battle. Debate about Yiddish, the desirability of its survival, its vivacity or decay, would persist for another two decades. But in his antipathy to 'the jargon' Myers was entirely at one with a very large part of native-born Anglo-Jewry.[39]

Under his direction the *Jewish Chronicle* promoted a host of other anglicising institutions. Many were first broached in the letter columns of the paper and subsequently relied on it to puff the appeals that funded them. Myers drew up the plan for what became the Jewish Working Men's Club, and was its honorary secretary and treasurer for many years. Another initiative funded by Samuel Montagu, the club was intended to help the immigrants 'to cast off the almost Oriental shackles which they have imported with them into this country'. Myers was also a warm supporter of the Jewish Lads' Brigade (JLB), founded by Colonel Albert Goldsmid under the initial supervision of The Maccabaeans.[40]

Jewish workers made their own efforts to improve their working and living conditions. The *Jewish Chronicle* was broadly sympathetic to these early movements, usually organised under the guidance of a Jewish or non-Jewish cleric, a social worker, or a personality from local or national government.[41] The subject of one of the first 'celebrity interviews', published in the paper on 29 January 1886, was the Government Factory Inspector, John Lakeman. He aroused the deepest admiration and gratitude from Myers for his assistance to the Jewish tailors' unions. The master tailors, however, resented the spotlight that was turned on them. Avid readers, who advertised regularly in the paper's columns, they protested that the agitation over wages and working conditions was got up unfairly. But stung by the negative publicity about the alleged role of foreign Jews in 'sweating', the *Jewish Chronicle* applauded Samuel Montagu's efforts to organise Jewish workers in a paternalistic union. The paper hoped that by organising Jewish workers in this way it would be possible to defuse the charges of exploitation, without, at the same time, encouraging what 'Notes of the Week' on 2 September 1887 described as 'the claptrap of socialist agitators'.

The *Jewish Chronicle* studiously ignored the growth of a socialist and anarchist culture amongst immigrant Jews in east London. This activity was based around several long-lasting publications and clubs. The first of these was the *Di poylishe yidel*, founded by Morris Winshevsky in July 1884. The 'Little Polish Jew' transmuted into *Tsukunft* in October 1884 and was taken over by anarchists. Winshevsky then started a new socialist weekly, *Der arbyter fraynd*, which ran from 1885 to 1932; it too adopted an anarchist line after 1891. The best-known and longest-lasting of the socialist and anarchist clubs was the International Workers' Educational Club (later the International Workingmen's Educational Association). The club was based in Berner Street from 1884 to 1892, and it was here that *Der arbyter fraynd* was printed. Despite these achievements, the Yiddish press was not mentioned by the *Jewish Chronicle* until 1887; the club never.[42]

This effective blackout may have accounted for the outrage and astonishment which greeted the first major public demonstration by Jewish socialists in London. In March 1889, Jewish radicals led a Sabbath march to the Great Synagogue, where the delegate Chief Rabbi was officiating, to demand that he condemn sweating. The *Jewish Chronicle* rushed to place as much distance as possible between Anglo-Jewry and the immigrant agitators. A strident leading article on 22 March declared: 'It is a fact that the demonstrators on Saturday were men of Jewish birth, who are not particularly nice as to their modus operandi or the opinions they express, provided they can further their own private ends. But it is clearly idle to talk of these persons as Jews and to pretend that socialism is a distinguishing feature of East End Judaism.'[43]

However, the unremitting public attention to 'sweating' made the absence of Jewish trade union activity a communal embarrassment. This accounts for the wry humour with which 'Notes of the Week', on 6 September 1889, greeted the news that thousands of Jewish tailors had struck for shorter working hours and more pay: 'The worm has turned at last. It is to be hoped that the agitation will really result in the amelioration of the lot of the poorer class of tailors. Seeing that the greatest of the communal problems springs to a large extent from the misery of the tailors the aspiration is not altogether unselfish ... On every ground, then, the movement is deserving of sympathy.' *Jewish Chronicle* coverage of this important strike was adequate, but nowhere near as thorough or engaged as that of *Der arbyter fraynd*, which brought out special strike issues. Although up to 10,000 Jewish tailors were involved, with many thousands more in their families affected by the strike, it was not deemed worthy of as much space as a Maccabaean dinner or elections to the council of the United Synagogue. The paper also did its utmost to play down the role of the socialist trade union leaders like Lewis Lyons and William Wess, concentrating instead on the mediation of communal leaders.[44]

After 1889, there were regular reports from the East End on labour matters. These served well-to-do Jews like Montagu who had an interest in the Jewish labour movement, but they were also read locally. Master tailors like Mark Moses, who lived in the East End, wrote to the *Jewish Chronicle* frequently on labour matters. Masters who needed skilled workers advertised in its employment columns, and Jewish workers placed notices under 'Situations Wanted'. Judging from these a significant portion of the Jewish workers and employers in the East End read enough English to utilise the *Jewish Chronicle* instead of, or along with, the burgeoning Yiddish press. This gave it some purchase over East End Jewish opinion and suggests that its increasingly frequent editorial comment on labour matters was not projected into a void. Equally, while coverage of the East End was still skewed, the *Jewish Chronicle* was at last inducting its West End readers into the realities of life there.

Publicity about, and support for, the Jewish labour movement was fraught because Jewish unions were unavoidably led by socialist and anarchist ideologues at a time when their ideas were treated with horror by most of middle-class society. The popular conception of anarchism associated its practitioners with crime and violence, while the linkage between Jews and criminality was already commonplace in anti-alien rhetoric. At the same time it urged Jews to unionise, the *Jewish Chronicle* had to fend off allegations in the anti-alien press that there were thousands of immigrant anarchists or criminals in the East End.[45]

Myers exercised the utmost delicacy in dealing with such matters, to the point of self-censorship. The *Jewish Chronicle* carried only occasional reports of crime in east London, usually of an anecdotal nature. The case of Israel Lipski, an immigrant Jew accused of a capital offence, was hardly mentioned until it culminated in the pronouncement of the death sentence in August 1887. This meagre coverage must be contrasted with the enormous attention paid to the affair by the *Pall Mall Gazette*, which took up Lipski's cause, and the rest of the press, which followed the trial avidly. The Yiddish papers, which loved nothing better than a juicy murder story, were riveted by the case. The rival *Jewish World* covered the trial blow by blow, and after Lipski's hanging even set up a testimonial fund for his lawyer. But the *Jewish Chronicle*, which did not wish to appear to be interested in a Jewish criminal just because he was a Jew, confined itself to a few judicious editorial asides.[46]

Such circumspection was exemplified by the paper's coverage of the so-called 'Jack the Ripper' murders, which began in August 1888. The killings occurred in and around the districts of east London with dense Jewish populations. However, the *Jewish Chronicle* avoided any mention of the crimes until the general press began to insinuate that the killer might be a Jewish butcher, and trouble threatened. At that point it intervened to combat the suggestion, made by the Vienna correspondent of *The Times*, that a ritual murder case in Austria might shed light on the Whitechapel events. Myers personally visited the City divisional surgeon to show him a set of knives used by a *shochet* (a man qualified to carry out animal slaughter according to Jewish Law) to demonstrate that they were unlike the murder weapon. For the rest of the year the murders obsessed the press, including the Yiddish papers, but the *Jewish Chronicle* dropped the topic, aside from three items in 'Notes of the Week'. It was left to several anguished letters printed in the paper to indicate the widespread anxiety triggered by the killings.[47]

Overall, the paper's treatment of Jewish crime, when it was reported, resembled its handling of socialism and anarchism – discreet and apologetic. With a hostile press and anti-alien politicians on the look-out for any evidence that immigration was having an adverse effect on the economy, morals and culture of English society, this discretion could be justified. It was, and still is, a matter of opinion whether it was the best tactic to adopt. Later editors would change the paper's policy, but none could avoid the dilemmas which face editors of a denominational or community paper, like the *Jewish Chronicle*, over reporting ugly incidents or behaviour concerning members of their group.

The treatment of immigration and foreign-born Jews in the *Jewish Chronicle* cannot be divorced from the paper's coverage and analysis of anti-Semitism at home and abroad. Just when Myers took the editorial chair, the 'Jewish Question' in Europe revived. Throughout the next two decades, editorials frequently discussed the phenomenon and how best to respond to it. In Britain itself the period between 1879 and 1902 saw a distinct heightening of anti-Jewish feeling, in addition to the tensions which were expressed in anti-alienism.[48] Myers was in no doubt that Russian and Polish Jews, with their 'hard shell', were at least partly to blame. On 25 October 1881 he wrote, 'They give rise to the Jewish Question everywhere; in their future amelioration lies the only hope of its permanent settlement.' Fifteen years later he bemoaned that 'the rehabilitating work of nigh upon a century of emancipation in the Occident is being clogged by the mediaevalised overflow of the Russian and Roumanian Ghettos'.[49]

Given this predisposition to attribute the origins of anti-Semitism to the behaviour of its victims, it was inevitable that the 'isolation' of the immigrants would assume nightmarish significance and become the object of drastic palliatives. Myers's analysis may have been flawed, but at the time this was not obvious and there were few alternative prescriptions for Anglo-Jewry to follow. With the connection between the two firmly established, each convulsion of anti-Semitism on the Continent that was reported in the *Jewish Chronicle* only confirmed the fears of Anglo-Jewry and guided its response to the immigrants.

The rise of modern anti-Semitism and Zionism

By the start of the 1880s the foreign coverage of the *Jewish Chronicle* was comprehensive and well honed. Its own network of (anonymous) correspondents reported in long dispatches and shorter cables on every development considered to be of interest to Jewish readers. The paper still drew on Reuters and the British or foreign press, but mainly to supplement its own reports. Its coverage of anti-Semitic movements and the Dreyfus Affair was outstanding. Alfred Harmsworth told the *Daily Mail*'s shareholders that 'The Dreyfus case ... did not materially affect the sale of English newspapers ... The public wearied of it before the end ... Circulation was on several days less than normal.'[50] The same could not be said for the *Jewish Chronicle*. Vast amounts of newsprint were devoted to the affair in order to satiate demand for the latest news and analysis of its implications for Jews in France and England.

Modern political anti-Semitism appeared first in Germany in the 1870s. In a series of three leading articles in November 1879, the *Jewish Chronicle* quickly exposed its pseudo-scientific basis and diagnosed the new *Judenhetze* as a product of the reactionary politics in Germany fomented by the slump of the 1870s. Initially the paper was not inclined to take the anti-Semites seriously, but the movement did not die away and English Jews watched it with concern. Extensive coverage was devoted to the national and local elections in Germany between 1881 and the late 1890s, when the anti-Semitic parties foundered. By the time of the Kaiser's visit to England in November 1899, the *Jewish Chronicle* felt confident enough to assure its readers that 'under his beneficent sway antisemitism in Germany is becoming a declining force'.[51]

The *Jewish Chronicle*'s explanation of anti-Semitism in Germany reflected a less than flattering view of German Jewry and, by implication, a certain conceit about the position of Anglo-Jewry. According to the paper, German anti-Semites were motivated by jealousy of the Jewish 'race'. This conclusion rested on partial credence of the claim, repeated by its correspondent, that the Jews dominated business, culture and politics in Germany. At times the paper appeared to blame German Jews for the prejudice which afflicted them. For example, it asserted haughtily in a leading article on 19 November 1880 that 'They have to a large extent, brought down all this envy on their heads by the ostentatious manner in which they have paraded their success.'

From its editorial columns the *Jewish Chronicle* proffered advice to German Jews about how best to cope with the upsurge of racial hatred. Its suggestions grew logically from its analysis of anti-Semitism. German Jews should cultivate unity, behave in an exemplary fashion, and avoid ostentatious or prideful behaviour. An editorial on 4 November 1881 disparaged active communal defence: 'We are inclined to believe that much of the resonance caused by the anti-semites' utterances of late years has been due to the ultra-sensitiveness of the Jews in Germany. For every pamphlet against the Jews there appeared seven in their favour magnifying the importance of the original attack seven-fold.' The *Jewish Chronicle* put its beliefs into practice three years later when Pastor Stoecker, the leader of the Berlin anti-Semitic party, visited London. Following a public outcry Stoecker was prevented from using the Mansion House for a rally, and his meeting was condemned in several quarters. But the *Jewish Chronicle* stressed that this was 'entirely spontaneous and uninfluenced by any prompting of leading Jews'. It reiterated its aversion to demonstrations and refutations.[52]

Political anti-Semitism took root in the Austro-Hungarian Empire, too, especially in Vienna. Here the paper tended to blame the Roman Catholic Church. Its commentary on the notorious ritual murder trials at Tisza-Eszlar in Hungary in 1882–3 and Polna in Bohemia in 1899–1900 dismissed them as temporary revivals of 'medieval' Jew-hatred and the the consequence of a 'Clerico-Reactionary Conspiracy'. One editorial, on 18 July 1902, explained that 'wherever antisemitism has raised its head, it has almost always been in the garb, so to speak, of the Roman Church'.[53]

Much the same diagnosis was eventually applied to the Dreyfus Affair. Captain Alfred Dreyfus was arrested and tried for espionage in 1894. During the hearing, Edouard Drumont's anti-Semitic paper *La Libre Parole* magnified the fact that Dreyfus was a Jew to support the specious claim that Jews were potentially disloyal aliens.[54] When Dreyfus was found guilty, the *Jewish Chronicle* was instantly suspicious of the verdict. To its eternal credit it declared in 'Notes of the Week' on 28 December 1894 that: 'For our part we decline emphatically to believe that any Jewish officer can have been guilty of the treasonable practices imputed to Captain Dreyfus, and we shall cling to this belief until it is made quite clear to us that the evidence against him was in itself conclusive and that its genuineness was properly tested.' However, the case temporarily rested there. For the next twelve months silence descended over the matter in France while French Jews kept their heads down.

In May 1896, Emile Zola published in *Le Figaro* an article denouncing the anti-Semitic politicians. It was immediately translated and republished in the *Jewish Chronicle* on 22 May even though Myers was not keen on such exchanges. Indeed, the following August he commented that it was foolish to argue with anti-Semites: 'To us the whole subject is a tiresome and disagreeable one.' However, Dreyfus had acquired a champion in Bernard Lazare, a French-Jewish journalist. In November 1896 Lazare issued a pamphlet refuting the charges and triggering a debate in the French Chamber of Deputies. The *Jewish Chronicle* now repeated its doubts about the case. A year later the affair exploded. Mathieu Dreyfus, brother of the convicted man, accused another officer, Major Esterhazy, of forging the documents on the basis of which Dreyfus had been found guilty. The case was taken up by the foreign press, notably the liberal *Daily Chronicle* and *Daily News* in London.[55]

On 28 January 1898, Myers published a four-page supplement devoted to Zola's 'J'Accuse', a devastating exposé of the calumny. The demands for a retrial and their painful progress then dominated the paper's foreign coverage from January 1898 to December 1899. Such militancy was not regarded without misgivings. When Max Nordau criticised French Jews for their passivity, the *Jewish Chronicle* reproached him, saying that it would be a folly to 'rush as a body to the defence of Dreyfus, to identify themselves as a people with him'. The paper fully supported the official French Jewish organisations: 'The only rational course for the Jews of France to take was to hold aloof as far as they could from the agitation, to leave an ordinary offence to be dealt with in an ordinary way, and to refuse to give a racial colouring to the matter ... Never was a policy more justified by events.'[56]

The *Jewish Chronicle*'s response mirrored the behaviour of French Jewry, which was reluctant to protest as Jews, for fear of confirming the accusation that Jews stuck together. But evidence exists that the paper's stance was not universally approved. 'There have been some', it commented on 9 June 1899, 'who have thought Jews and their press lax and halting in their resistance to the terrible injustice done to their coreligionists.' To these critics it repeated the argument that corporate agitation by Jews on behalf of Dreyfus would only have rebounded on their own heads. Myers was torn between accepting the fact that since Jews were indeed being singled out and lumped together it was necessary to respond in kind, and fear that such an admission would only make things worse.[57]

Like much of the British press the *Jewish Chronicle* held French Roman Catholicism and the Jesuits, in particular, culpable for the affair. On 6 January 1899, the editor wrote that 'Jews have now to confront everywhere in Europe the Jesuit enemy; a bitter and relentless force which has pursued its course from generation to generation with steady determination ...' Responsibility for this lay at the door of the Papacy itself: 'The Jesuits may be the irregular cavalry of the Catholic army, but that does not relieve the supreme commander from responsibility for their actions.'[58]

Modern European anti-Semitism was the background against which Myers studied the large-scale migration to Palestine that began in the wake of the anti-Jewish riots in Russia in 1881–2 and the rise of the Zionist Movement. He was sceptical about grandiose schemes for resettling the Jews in Palestine, and sympathised with Orthodox objections to such initiatives: 'We are exiled from our land by the decree of Heaven and even, from a sentimental point of view this decree is absolute until the proper time arrives.' But he allowed generous space for the more idealistic to expound their schemes. One of these was his friend Laurence Oliphant, the writer, journalist and English eccentric. Oliphant's book *Land of Gilead*, which contained his blueprint for the restoration of the Jews, was serialised in the paper in December 1880. Myers was not impressed: 'the Diaspora of the Jews has been by no means the curse as is usually assumed'.[59]

The flight of Jews from Russia opened an urgent debate as to whether it was better to go to America, the policy of the Am Olam Movement, or to Palestine.[60] The argument was echoed in the letter columns of the *Jewish Chronicle* in March–April 1882, which also carried detailed reports of the initial gatherings of pro-Palestine groups. Its editorials recognised the lure of Palestine and expressed admiration for the pioneers who set out to work the land, despite the obstacles in their way. Moreover, if they insisted on going, the paper thought that Anglo-Jewry had a duty to ensure the success of their efforts and should contribute funds to viable settlement projects.[61]

The paper's coverage of Palestine grew in quantity and quality. It boasted its 'own correspondent' in Jerusalem and received dispatches from Oliphant, who lived in Haifa until his death in December 1888. During the mid 1880s, the *Jewish Chronicle* also noted the formation of Chovevei Zion associations and kindred Zionist bodies in eastern Europe and England. Editorial comment on their activities was usually luke-warm. Myers commended the communal dignitaries who launched Chovevei Zion, though not because he saw their involvement as an endorsement of Zionism. He opined in a leading article on 20 March 1891 that 'The right policy to adopt is not to laugh at it or to ignore it, but to recognise it fully and generously, and to direct it into safe and practical channels.' Zionism was 'a preferable alternative to the wild dreams of the socialists'. The paper printed regular reports on Chovevei Zion 'tents', but at the same time opened its columns to Jewish anti-Zionists.[62]

In November 1895 Theodor Herzl, the famous Budapest-born Viennese journalist and playwright, came to London to canvass support for his scheme to establish a Jewish state. He had been introduced to Israel Zangwill by Max Nordau and through him was invited to meet a group of Anglo-Jewish intellectuals at the home of the Revd Simeon Singer. Myers attended and was instantly at odds with Herzl over religion. Nevertheless, he asked Herzl to put his thoughts on paper for the *Jewish Chronicle*, where they appeared on 17 January 1896 – the first version of *Der Judenstaat [The Jewish State]* (1897).[63]

The response was hardly encouraging. There were a couple of letters in the following issue, and none at all the week after that. The painter Holman Hunt, whose letter was published on 21 February, was one of the few correspondents to respond positively. Myers himself devoted a weighty editorial to Herzl's article on 17 January. He treated the idea as the product of unnecessary panic about anti-Semitism and concluded that although 'this proposal cannot be dismissed with a sneer ... We find it ourselves hard to accept these gloomy prognostications. We hardly anticipate a great future for a scheme which is the outcome of despair.'

While objectively reporting the work of the Zionist Movement in a weekly column that started in 1897, editorially the *Jewish Chronicle* emerged as one of Herzl's most bitter opponents. It echoed the arguments of Israel Abrahams, Claude Montefiore and Lucien Wolf, who were the chief ideological antagonists of Zionism. The paper feared that Zionism, an attempted solution to the 'Jewish Question', would only aggravate it. A leading article on 12 March 1897, dealing with the success of the anti-Semitic party in Vienna, explained that 'The battle against antisemitism must be fought in Europe, not in Asia; it is a campaign that will need centuries of patient endurance, and the fight cannot be won by a single *coup*.' When Herzl announced the convening of a congress to found the Zionist Organisation, the *Jewish Chronicle* was aghast: 'The very notion of an "International" Congress was an insult to the patriotism of Jews of various nationalities, and antisemites have not been slow to avail themselves of the groundless insinuations that Jews are now confessedly unpatriotic and half-hearted as citizens of the states in which they live.'[64]

For Myers and the so-called 'assimilationist' opponents of the movement, Zionism was purely spiritual and universalistic: 'The mission of Judaism ... is in the conception of the true Zionist bound up with Zion in the sense that Zion was, and must remain, the inspiration of Judaism. But the Zion of this hope is the greater Zion of the prophets, a Zion co-extensive with humanity.'[65] As he put it in a leading article on 1 October 1897, 'Our Zion is here or nowhere.'

The *Jewish Chronicle* fought Herzlian Zionism every step of the way. It endorsed the action of the 'Protestrabbiner', the German Reform rabbis in Munich who stopped Herzl from holding his first Zionist Congress there. Herzl's diplomatic odyssey during the early 1900s was conscientiously reported in the paper, but the editorials mostly damned with faint praise. They did not go unchallenged. The letter columns of the paper swelled after each outspoken attack as defenders of Zionism took up their pens.

Notwithstanding the paper's editorial line, a huge amount of space was assigned to the First Zionist Congress in Basle in July 1897, complete with verbatim reports from its own correspondent, Morris Duparc. When the Fourth Zionist Congress was held in London there were two heavily illustrated supplements totalling more than twenty pages on 17 and 24 August 1900. This was doubtless the result of sound commercial policy, since the Congress generated enormous public interest.

The paper took a dim view of Herzl's followers in England and their antics. As a result of its attacks on the English Zionist Federation (EZF), founded early in 1899, it was inexorably drawn into the arena of communal politics. At almost every gathering of the EZF the *Jewish Chronicle* was subjected to angry criticism, and Myers was repeatedly forced to defend its reputation for objectivity. Zangwill emerged as a particularly vitriolic, if witty, critic. Significantly, he attributed the slow progress of Zionism in England to the negative attitude of the Jewish press. This prompted Myers to write that 'if a *Jewish Chronicle* did not exist the Zionists would be driven to create one in the sacred interests of the cause'.[66]

Israel Cohen, journalist and Zionist activist, recalled that under Myers the paper 'had been a relentless opponent of the Jewish national cause'. Yet it won grudging respect for the continued objectivity of its news reports, if not its leading articles. Jacob de Haas, himself a journalist, told the delegates at the Fifth Zionist Congress: 'If in our English-Jewish press the *Jewish Chronicle* is unfavourably critical and the *Jewish World* is neutral and silent, we have obtained from those papers which express the opinion of the anglicised section of the community a respectful and continuous hearing; a fairly impartial record of our doings is heard through them on the continent and even in America and Australia.'[67] This was a just tribute to Myers and a testament to the influence now wielded by the *Jewish Chronicle* throughout the world.

The high noon of Anglo-Jewry

The crisis posed by mass immigration, the shadows cast by anti-Semitism on the Continent and the strife engendered by Zionism were only some of the preoccupations of the *Jewish Chronicle* and Anglo-Jewry in the high-Victorian period. It would be unbalanced to focus solely on these topics. For much of the first decade of Russian–Polish immigration, the paper was equally preoccupied with issues that had first arisen in the 1870s. The 1880s and 1890s were also a period of scholarly achievement and artistic creativity, when Jewish intellectuals and communal activists launched numerous initiatives to cope with the challenges of Jewish life in the post-emancipation era. Many of these undertakings survived well into the next century and supplied the communal and cultural framework in which the children of the immigrants orientated themselves.[68]

To begin with there was the continuing feud with Gladstone and the Liberal Party. In his survey for the Jewish year in 1878, Myers objected that, 'In this great country we have witnessed scurrilous and discreditable attacks on the Prime Minister, because his grandfather was a Venetian and a Jew' by men who claimed to be 'the champions of liberalism'. Gladstone was himself held to be guilty of 'strange extravagances... a want of discretion', an impression that was not allayed by conciliatory gestures towards Jewish Liberals.[69]

In December 1879 Morris Oppenheim, a barrister who had written travel pieces for Michael Henry, touched off a controversy concerning Jewish political allegiances when he reported from Sheffield that Jews were organising support for a Tory candidate. Gladstone later used this information as justification for a mealy-mouthed statement concerning the treatment of Jews in Romania and Russia. He wondered why he should extend a helping hand to Jews who apparently put Jewish loyalties before party or the national interest. The *Jewish Chronicle* frowned on the Sheffield Jews who paraded their support for the Tories, but still expressed annoyance with Gladstone.[70]

When the Liberals returned to power in 1880, Myers must have felt queasy. Indeed the outbreak of the anti-Jewish riots in Russia provoked a small-scale re-enactment of the Eastern Crisis. On 11 January 1882, Myers followed the example of Benisch and wrote to Gladstone appealing to him to act on behalf of the Russian Jews. In view of the anticipated public demonstration at the Mansion House, Gladstone's endorsement would have been most significant. Gladstone delayed his reply for several days and in the mean time read a pamphlet, 'Persecution of the Jews in Russia, 1881', which deeply shocked him. In his letter he wrote, 'The spirit of your appeal to me commands my respect and sympathy', but he never sent it. Instead, he wrote to Madame Novikoff pointing out the clamour in the press and calling on her to refute the allegations against the Tsarist authorities if this was possible.[71]

A few days later, Gladstone and Myers met. Gladstone recorded the encounter in his customarily terse but equivocal prose in his diary: 'I saw the Jew today to whom I wrote a letter afterwards and cancelled on Gr[anville's] insistence. I authorised him to quote me as having said that in my opinion the interference of foreign Govermts in such cases is more likely to do more harm than good.' Gladstone was conspicuous by his absence from the Mansion House meeting in February. Later, when questioned in the House of Commons by the Jewish Liberal MP Serjeant Simon, he repeated his argument that despite his conduct as a private citizen in 1876–9 it would not do for him or the Government to intervene now in the affairs of another state.[72]

The *Jewish Chronicle* noted Gladstone's abstention with concern, since Russian newspapers allegedly drew comfort from his silence. The lack of a major debate in the House of Commons was also attributed to his influence. Despite a subsequent thaw in relations between Gladstone and English Jews, the *Jewish Chronicle* was ambivalent towards the Grand Old Man for the remainder of his career.[73]

Myers was as concerned as his predecessors with secularising movements and gravely monitored the evidence of erosion and drift.[74] In 1886, Anglo-Jewry was stunned by the news that a daughter of Baron Henry de Worms had married out and, worse, that her father had attended the church ceremony. The first item in 'Notes of the Week' on 7 May 1886 expostulated that 'one would expect an expression of sorrow at the secession from the ancestral faith, some kind of protest against the defection, at least the absence of public countenance and visible approval. The total want of any open expression of regret is merely an encouragement to backsliding in others.'

Throughout the 1880s, articles and sermons dwelt painfully on Judaism's apparent loss of adhesive power. Several editorials in September 1886 dealt with the special problem of young Jews and social life. Even at home the revolution in leisure in late-Victorian society hid a new set of traps. For the middle classes in general the increasing time and wealth available for leisure activities caused introspection about how to combine social mingling with the preservation of social boundaries. How more acute this was for Jews: should they mix with non-Jews in clubs, sports activities and the pursuit of hobbies? If they did, this increased the chances of intermarriage or, at least, impatience with the constraints of traditional Jewish life; if they did not, they would be guilty of 'clannish' behaviour.[75]

Concern about 'unattached Jews' and the alleged aridity of Jewish life in England prompted a number of initiatives with which Myers and the *Jewish Chronicle* were closely involved. During the 1880s, Myers was part of a circle of friends who lived in the 'Jewish Bohemia of Kilburn'. The group, known as 'The Wanderers', included Moses Gaster, Israel Zangwill, Israel Abrahams, Lucien Wolf, Joseph Jacobs, Oswald John Simon, Arthur Davis, Herbert Bentwich and Solomon J. Solomon. All were frequent contributors to the Jewish press. Around 1885, Myers recruited Solomon Schechter to the circle, and he remained its intellectual mentor until he took up a post in Cambridge in 1890. These men shared a conviction that 'official Judaism' was moribund and that it was essential to revitalise Jewish life through intellectual and cultural initiatives. They met regularly at the homes of Schechter and Myers, where they discussed Jewish issues amidst a haze of cigar and cigarette smoke. Norman Bentwich, whose father was a regular attender, described Myers as 'the compère of the society'.[76]

In November 1891, this group formed The Maccabaeans, 'with the object of bringing together Jews who are interested in literature, science, artistic or professional pursuits'. The *Jewish Chronicle* explained that 'The organisation is essentially the outcome of circumstances which did not exist a generation ago. We take it that the scheme is the outward and visible sign of a deep-rooted attachment to the Jewish race among those whose pursuits have tended to withdraw them from close personal association with other Jews which was common enough thirty years ago.'[77] The paper devoted a huge amount of space to Maccabaean events, usually dinners followed by witty, erudite, but always earnest speeches. The debates, printed almost verbatim, had a valuable function since other communal institutions were closed to political debate or avoided the discussion of sensitive issues, especially those which might have sectarian implications.

The *Jewish Chronicle* also became a vehicle for studies in Jewish, particularly Anglo-Jewish, history and culture. These lengthy essays helped to clarify Jewish identity, explore Jewish thought and construct a past of which Jews could feel proud, without making them feel detached from

English culture and society. They were also intended to rebut allegations made by hostile commentators, such as Goldwin Smith, who asserted that Jews in medieval England had been an essentially parasitic community. Frustrated by the absence of any Jewish scholarship to disprove such allegations, during 1883–4, Myers published a series of impressive articles on Anglo-Jewry by Joseph Jacobs and Israel Abrahams.[78]

In a letter published in the *Jewish Chronicle* on 16 April 1886, Sir Isidore Spielman bruited the idea of an exhibition devoted to Anglo-Jewish 'archaeology'. Myers, who already saw the importance of preserving communal records and making use of them in history writing, was enthusiastic. When the Anglo-Jewish Historical Exhibition finally opened in the Royal Albert Hall in April 1887, it was given extravagant coverage. A series of richly informative supplements described the contents and printed the associated lectures. The exhibition led directly to the notion of a permanent society devoted to Anglo-Jewish history, although several years elapsed before the Jewish Historical Society of England was established. Myers played a key part in its creation and served on several of its committees. Sir Isidore later described him as 'one of its originators, one of its keenest supporters, one of its hardest workers'.[79]

The critical line of defence against drift or apostasy remained the teaching of Judaism. Myers served on the councils of the United Synagogue and Jews' College, and was a founder of the Jewish Religious Education Board. So his deliberations in the editorial columns were informed by first-hand knowledge. For this reason, he could also be reasonably sure that his editorials would carry authority. His institutional connections, however, did not prevent him from taking a progressive line on the revision of Jewish worship and related issues such as the rights of Jewish women.

Throughout the period of Myers's editorship, the *Jewish Chronicle* took the lead in advocating a systematic review of all aspects of Jewish belief and observance. A characteristic agenda-setting editorial on 28 October 1881 argued that 'Each age has its own way of looking at truth, and we have to adapt the cardinal principles of Judaism to the *weltanschauung* of the epoch and the country in which we live. Only by this means can we insure a sincere adherence to our faith by the most cultured of the community, those who, as it were form its brains.' The point was greatly elaborated in a leading article, 'Jewish Law and Modern Life', running over three weeks, commencing on 7 July 1882.

Myers observed how Christianity had adapted itself to current trends in order to retain its following, and he applied these lessons to the synagogue. The *Jewish Chronicle* repeatedly proposed the summoning of a Jewish 'synod', comparable to the central, deliberating bodies which almost every other denomination possessed. In a series of four major editorials on 'A

Jewish Synod' during October–November 1882, the paper set out radical proposals for the reform of Jewish law and practice which such an assembly might undertake. These editorials set off an avalanche of correspondence, including a querulous intervention by 'Lambda' (Lionel Cohen). But the *Jewish Chronicle* held that the alternative to a reforming synod was drift and then anarchy. It displayed little affection for the existing ecclesiastical authorities: 'The truth is, that what is wanted nowadays is a more liberal interpretation of Jewish law than the *Beth Din* in its existing form is inclined to give.'[80]

Letters to the *Jewish Chronicle* were amongst the most powerful weapons at the disposal of the Revd A. L. Green and Lionel Cohen in their campaigns to achieve modifications to the liturgy of the United Synagogue during 1879–80. The paper gave its backing to proposals which were submitted to Chief Rabbi Nathan Adler for his consideration, although the results were considered to be meagre.[81] His death in 1890 appeared to open the door to change. In its eulogy for Adler, the paper regretted the slow pace of reform under his stewardship because of the 'existence of a reactionary section which strenuously opposed even harmless modifications of established ritual practice'.[82] To its dismay, however, the new Chief Rabbi, Dr Hermann Adler, Nathan's son, proved to be a conservative influence. The paper strongly supported the reforms instigated by the Revd Morris Joseph at the Hampstead Synagogue in 1892, and was indignant at the 'inquisition into men's minds' when the Chief Rabbi vetoed his appointment as its minister.[83]

Myers's vision of what a Jewish cleric should be was inspired by the new Church of England clergymen who were carrying forth the social gospel and 'muscular Christianity'. The *Jewish Chronicle* encouraged a more sophisticated, professional training for the Jewish clergy and sought to reverse their lowly status. Through the publication of sermons and writings by ministers, the paper did its best to engender respect for their skills and abilities. Myers also argued that the Chief Rabbi should be willing to confer the rabbinical diploma, *semicha*, on graduates of Jews' College so as to give them greater authority and so balance the influence of rabbis from eastern Europe who were congregating in the East End.[84]

Jewish women were generally regarded as the Achilles' heel of the defences against assimilation. As before, the *Jewish Chronicle* promoted religious education for Jewish women of all classes and recommended involving them more in the synagogue service, but such efforts were hampered by the conservatism of male Jewish society.[85] Myers was something of a radical on the 'women question'. He published Amy Levy's scathing attack on the 'oriental' attitudes of Jewish men and frequently printed letters from Jewish women demanding recognition of their rights.

The anonymity of these contributions was probably vital in enabling women to speak out.[86] During the 1890s, the *Jewish Chronicle* called for more Jewish women to be employed in communal organisations like the Board of Guardians, and once women had achieved positions of responsibility, it supported their demands for a share in communal governance. In two editorials on 1 and 8 June 1900, for instance, the *Jewish Chronicle* endorsed the right of Jewish women to sit on the committees of the Anglo-Jewish Association and the Board of Guardians. Myers and his wife were on close terms with the founding figures of the National Union of Jewish Women, and the *Jewish Chronicle* proved an unstinting ally in women's progress towards autonomy in the public sphere.[87]

In the last two decades of the nineteenth century, Myers heralded a 'Jewish revival' in England. It was personified by young Jewish scholars such as Claude Montefiore (1858–1938), Solomon Schechter (1847–1915) and Israel Abrahams (1858–1924) who were equipped to take up the challenge posed by the Higher Criticism on its own terms.[88] Myers was also aware of the importance of popular culture and constantly regretted the paucity of Jewish novelists in England. Yet, when late-Victorian Anglo-Jewry at last produced a writer of originality and thoughtfulness, the reaction of the *Jewish Chronicle* was unfavourable.

In marked opposition to the apologetics of Aguilar and Farjoen, Amy Levy's novel *Reuben Sachs* (1888) was a spirited critique of the 'materialistic', complacent life of middle-class Jews living in Maida Vale. The *Jewish Chronicle* devoted a full leading article to excoriating this portrait: 'In non-Jewish authors this might be innocuous, especially as want of sympathy invariably results in faulty art not likely to win belief. But with the outside world the effect of such performances by Israelites is the more deleterious as it is impossible for the general public to know on what superficial knowledge of Jewish society such ill-natured sketches are founded.' *Reuben Sachs* opened the way to a series of similar novels, all of which were disliked by the *Jewish Chronicle*, which did its best to influence both the cultural tastes of Anglo-Jewry and the sensibility of Jewish authors.[89]

In May 1892, an editorial on 'Jews in Fiction' grumbled, 'why is it that the great writers of England avoid the Jew when seeking for a hero?' Desperate for a great work of fiction that would embody a favourable depiction of the Jews, it placed its hopes in the forthcoming novel by Israel Zangwill, *Children of the Ghetto*. Acclaimed upon its appearance, Zangwill's book was a sympathetic account of the immigrants (although when it turned to middle-class Jews the tone was harsher). An associate of Myers and a patron of The Maccabaeans, Zangwill (and his brother, Louis) often featured in the *Jewish Chronicle* as the subject of reviews, or as the writer of articles or letters. The *Glasgow Evening News* remarked somewhat cruelly that the 'literary horizon of the *Jewish Chronicle* is rather limited, being bounded, as it were, by the Zangwills'.[90] The paper's search for a wholly acceptable fictional representation of Jewish life was met finally by Samuel Gordon with *Sons of the Covenant* in 1900. The paper's reviewer thought that 'Mr Gordon has, besides writing an admirable novel, indirectly rendered the community a signal service.'[91]

This concern for the portrayal of Jews in fiction indicates how sensitive Anglo-Jewry was about its public image. It helps to explain the repeated demonstrations of patriotism and the proclaimed symbiosis of English and Jewish values. Like the rest of the press, the *Jewish Chronicle* devoted a large amount of space to the royal family. The Diamond Jubilee in 1897, Queen Victoria's birthday in 1899 and her death in 1901 were occasions for enormous outpourings of patriotic feeling; but they also served to crystallise the identity of Jewishness and Englishness.[92] On 26 May 1899, the *Jewish Chronicle* lauded the Queen because 'above all she has realised in her own existence the most exalted Jewish ideals of purity and domestic virtues'. Patriotism led the paper into controversy over revision of the prayerbook in 1897. Oswald John Simon, the Revds Simeon Singer and A. A. Green, Joseph Prag and others contributed copious letters on the question of whether or not to omit references to the Messiah redeeming the Jews and restoring Palestine. Myers argued forcefully that extruding Zion from Judaism was undesirable, but insisted on its purely abstract meaning: there was no dual loyalty.

The most direct expression of patriotism was military service. The *Jewish Chronicle* exhorted Jews to serve in the armed forces even if it necessitated infringing Jewish Law. As it explained on 9 September 1892, 'it is a question of ignoring the smaller considerations out of regard for the higher'. On balance, however, the paper stressed that it was possible to be a good Jew and a good soldier. During the Boer War, 1899–1900, it printed letters from men on active service which contained exciting accounts of military actions and photographs of Jews under arms. Editorial comment constantly stressed the patriotic Jewish response of both servicemen and civilians.

The paper gave prominence to the casualty roll of Jewish servicemen and highlighted the celebrations in the East End on the relief of Mafeking for more than just their public-service or news value. They were intended as proof that anti-alienism was ill founded and to rebut attacks by the pro-Boers who said that the war was being fought for the benefit of Jewish diamond- and gold-mine owners.[93] The relationship between patriotic rhetoric and anti-Semitism was exemplified by an editorial on 22 June 1900, devoted to answering the charge that the paper had gone over the top in its coverage of Jewish participation in the war. The *Jewish Chronicle* replied that: 'The patriotism and willingness of other creeds to make sacrifices were never in question, ours are being doubted and challenged at every turn.' It concluded frankly that 'Our references to Jews in the war must be regarded mainly as a defensive proceeding.'

Asher Myers died in May 1902, his last months as editor overshadowed by the controversies surrounding the Royal Commission on Alien Immigration. By temperament he disliked polemics, but he was a stout defender of Jewish interests and never shied away from a public retort if he felt it was necessary. Yet he preferred to believe that prejudice against Jews resulted from ignorance about their beliefs and errant behaviour on their own part, and so was open to correction. Through the *Jewish Chronicle* he strove to eliminate mutual misunderstanding and patronised the Anglo-Jewish scholarship which it was hoped would generate a more positive view of Judaism and Jewish history.

Myers saw Judaism and English values as akin to one another: a correct appreciation and practice of Judaism would lead naturally to harmony between the two. This influenced his policy towards native and foreign-born Jewry: improvements to the service in the United Synagogue and anglicisation of the immigrants were two sides of the same coin. By the turn of the century, this conviction was part of the consensus within Anglo-Jewry, and those who challenged it, such as the Zionists, were a small and marginal group. Myers and the *Jewish Chronicle* thus stood at the heart of Anglo-Jewry. During the years that he had guided it, the paper had increased its authority immeasurably. It was inconceivable for a communal cause or issue to attract attention if it was not publicised in or by the paper. A window on the world, it also guided the cultural tastes of its readers and educated them. The tributes paid to Myers on his untimely death expressed a deep grief that a valued communal activist and sensitive spokesman for Anglo-Jewry had been lost. Recalling him thirty years later, the Revd A. A. Green reflected that 'In his quiet strong way he managed the community without it knowing that it was being managed.'[94]

Israel Davis and the struggle over the Aliens Act, 1902–1906

On Myers's death, Morris Duparc (1852–1942), the assistant editor, took over as 'working editor'. Duparc, who was born in Holland, had been a staff reporter since 1873, concentrating on foreign news and Zionist affairs. He had a wealth of experience, a wide knowledge of languages and good foreign contacts. But the real power lay ever more firmly in the hands of Israel Davis: from his home outside London he exercised a minute control over the paper via the telephone and the page proofs.[95]

Israel Davis was born in March 1847 in Blackheath, and educated at the City of London School and Christ's College, Cambridge. He played football for the university and was the first Jewish vice-president of the union. After taking a first in classics, he was called to the Bar and practised from 1870. A man of enormous energy and varied interests, he was for a time secretary to Sir David Salomons and from 1873 to 1884 was a frequent, authoritative contributor to *The Times* on financial legislation. He served on the council of the Anglo-Jewish Association and on the executive committee of the Jewish Historical Society of England. In the evenings, he gave adult-education lectures. Davis was also something of a prude. The historian Cecil Roth noted that he had a 'fastidious' pen and displayed a 'hyper-delicacy of feeling'. He took offence at matters which could only have shocked someone of 'the most prurient imagination'. And while he had strong opinions, he seemed reluctant to upset anyone who expressed theirs.[96]

Despite being born with a love of newsprint (Davis edited a family newspaper while a child and sent juvenile poems to Benisch for publication), he had little feel for modern journalism. His writing was formal and stilted, like his attitudes. At a time when journalism was being revolutionised by Cecil Harmsworth and the *Daily Mail* (1896), Arthur Pearson and the *Daily Express* (1900), Northcliffe and the *Daily Mirror* (1903), Davis was an anachronism. In the battle for mass circulation the popular daily press was going steadily down market. There was less political coverage, fewer verbatim speeches, more sport and illustrations.[97] Within the realm of Jewish newspaper publishing, the *Jewish Chronicle* faced competition from the lively *Jewish World* and the burgeoning Yiddish press. By 1910, the *Newspaper Press Directory* listed a penny Yiddish daily, the *Yidisher Ekspress* (1895, Leeds; 1899, London), the penny weekly *Yidisher Telefon* (1897), and two half-penny weeklies, *Bril's Speshel* (1902–7) and the *Yidisher Zhurnal* (1907).[98]

Yet Davis clung to outmoded standards of journalism and displayed an almost suicidal attitude to the ratio between advertising space and editorial copy. He published long supplements with hardly any advertising that bit deeply into the paper's profitability. The shrinkage of advertising may be attributed to his 'prudish' tastes. Like Northcliffe, he seems to have had an aversion to 'vulgar' display advertisements for certain medicinal remedies, corsetry and other underwear. A long and acrimonious legal case between Solomon Davis (the paper's business manager) and its advertising agent did nothing to help.[99]

It is likely that the combined pressure of diminishing income and increasing expenditure on new features and supplements forced the management to hold down labour costs. The paper was hit by a bitter strike in 1902 which temporarily disrupted production and resulted in printing being transferred to a non-union plant. Nor was Davis on particularly good terms with his editorial team. The paper's star reporter and leader writer, Simon Gelberg, once threatened to resign over an editorial, while Duparc and Davis quarrelled incessantly. The expanding size of the *Jewish Chronicle* hid deep internal strains and an incipient financial crisis.[100]

In spite of these troubles, between May 1902 and December 1906, Davis led the paper in a heroic struggle against anti-alienism. Edition after edition devoted unprecedented amounts of coverage to the Royal Commission, with supplements that often ran to eight or ten pages giving verbatim reports of the proceedings. The *Jewish Chronicle* encouraged all forms of defence activity and made a direct contribution itself with the publication of pro-alien articles in the form of handbills for distribution.[101]

In August 1903 the Royal Commission issued its report. The majority of its members called for measures to diminish and control the inflow of immigrants by eliminating 'undesirable' aliens. Other recommendations included the demarcation of 'restricted areas' where the settlement of aliens would be prohibited. The *Jewish Chronicle* deplored the prospect of legislation along these lines: 'It would be pointed to by demagogues in future days as an admission by Parliament that the immigrant is an evil thing.'[102]

Frustration with the outcome of the Royal Commission was heightened by appalling news from Russia. On 1 May 1903, the *Jewish Chronicle* carried cabled dispatches and Russian press reports of anti-Jewish riots in the town of Kishinev. During the following weeks the *Jewish Chronicle* printed harrowing reports from its own correspondent, and from other papers, along with horrifying photographs of the carnage. The paper called for immediate protests and brought home to the restrictionist lobby the message that the immigrants were refugees from a wretched tyranny. The Tsarist authorities were so annoyed by this coverage that they censored issues of the *Jewish Chronicle* sent to Russia.[103]

At the close of 1903, the Government announced that immigration legislation would be brought before Parliament. In a pugnacious leading article on 11 December the *Jewish Chronicle* protested that the proposed bill really had nothing to do with the Jews, but was a protectionist measure intended to appease the working classes at a time of unemployment and so help to retain the seats of Conservative MPs in the East End. Duparc bolstered moral indignation with facts by sending Simon Gelberg to east London. During January and February 1904, Gelberg assiduously provided weekly reports showing that immigration was declining and pressure on the housing market was easing.

When the Government placed legislation to restrict alien immigration at the top if its business agenda for 1904, the *Jewish Chronicle*'s editorial on 5 February voiced the astonishment of Anglo-Jewry. 'The British Parliament is going to devote the best of its energies to discussing how a number of Jewish refugees can be prevented from earning a crust of bread in a free land.' It concentrated its fire on the most controversial aspects of the bill, such as the establishment of prohibited areas, and made free use of the suggestion that the agitation was really anti-Semitic. 'We cannot believe that the Home Secretary has seriously considered the danger of generating such dangerous distinctions in the popular mind, and of creating the beginnings of an anti-Jewish sentiment under Government patronage.'[104]

The threat of anti-Semitism in Britain was no longer as far-fetched as it might once have seemed. During 1902 and 1903, there were disturbances in South Wales at Dowlais and Pontypridd during which Jews were physically assaulted. At Limerick, in Southern Ireland, a local priest incited his congregation to mount a crippling boycott of Jewish traders.[105] However, the *Jewish Chronicle* practised the policy which it preached to German and French Jews: lying low and hoping that the agitation would 'blow over'. To a great extent this was also the stand taken by the Board of Deputies. Despite criticism of such quiescence, over a year after the Limerick Affair started, the *Jewish Chronicle* declared: 'We are reluctant to stir up the memories of a half-forgotten, if still continuing scandal.'[106]

Throughout April, May and June 1904, the *Jewish Chronicle* printed exhaustive accounts of the parliamentary debates. The paper carried the division lists so that Jewish voters could scrutinise the conduct of their MPs and pointedly lavished praise on the bill's Liberal opponents. No effort was spared to rebut the assertions of the restrictionists; above all, the paper stressed that the bill would end up creating animosity against the Jews, as Jews. Yet, when the bill was dropped after a savaging in Grand Committee, editorial comment was careful to ascribe its defeat to the efforts of the Liberal Party and denied that there had been any Jewish pressure.[107]

The 1905 revolution in Russia unexpectedly offered a way out of the agonies of the immigration debate. Jews in the West were filled with hope that, at last, conditions in Russia would be so improved that emigration would become unnecessary. Should the revolution succeed, 'It would relieve the Jewish race of that dominating problem of redistribution which goes under the name of the alien problem in various countries, and which threatens the peace of Jewry.'[108] By this time, the *Jewish Chronicle* was receiving dispatches from Russia within seven days, as well as almost instantaneous cables. From its correspondents' reports and thanks to the analysis by Lucien Wolf and other specialists, it was soon obvious that the revolution contained terrible dangers for the Jews. During the turmoil, thousands of Jews were massacred by pogromists and the reactionary Black Hundreds. Nothing like it had been seen in modern times, and the paper marked these new horrors with black-bordered pages.[109]

Anglo-Jewry rode a roller-coaster of hope and despair during 1905–6: it was a race between reform in Russia and immigration restriction in England. A second, much revised bill was introduced in April 1905, and made rapid progress through the Commons. The *Jewish Chronicle* expressed 'despair and bewilderment' at the repetition of 'old fallacies and delusions'.[110] But the bill passed its last stage in August 1905 and came into force on 1 January the following year. Under its provisions, aliens could enter the country unimpeded if they had sufficient means, while others were subject to examination by immigration officers and could be refused leave to land on grounds of undesirability, such as ill-health or criminal record.

By a twist of political fate, the Conservative Government resigned at almost the same time as the Aliens Act became operative. Although the paper delivered its usual eve-of-poll disavowal of a Jewish vote, it was quick to attribute certain Tory losses and Liberal gains to Jewish voters, and it could hardly conceal its delight at the Liberal landslide.[111] Anglo-Jewry anticipated a generous interpretation of the Act, not only because of the Liberal Party's espoused principles, but also as a result of the grim turn of events in Russia. During December 1905 and January 1906 Jack Myers, Asher Myers's son, toured the pogrom-struck centres of the Pale and sent back distressing accounts of murder, rape and brigandage.

Duparc also secured the services of Nahum Sokolow, the journalist and Zionist activist. Correspondence uncovered in the Central Zionist Archive gives a rare insight into the mode of hiring foreign reporters. Duparc wanted reports and analysis, but specifically requested pictures of pogrom victims. Sokolow was paid between £1 and £10 for a month's contributions, and Duparc tried to insist that he limit his services to the *Jewish Chronicle*. The job was not without dangers given the repressive conditions prevailing in Russia. The editor told Sokolow that his dispatches would appear without accreditation if he wished. Sokolow also advised the paper on whom it could engage as an additional Russian correspondent. Duparc only insisted that it be someone with journalistic experience and no political axe to grind.[112]

Despite the events in Russia the Liberal Government displayed no interest in repealing or even ameliorating the Act and left its enforcement to local officials whose conduct bore no relation to the sympathy for refugees evinced by the Liberals when they were in opposition. The *Jewish Chronicle* now emerged as the fiercest critic of the Act, although only after an internal struggle between Gelberg and Davis. When the aliens legislation came into effect, Davis wanted the paper to accept defeat and aver loyalty to the law of the land. Gelberg refused to write the necessary leading article and instead tendered his resignation. Davis relented and the paper announced defiantly that, 'On our part the Act should be fought as Church-rates were once contested in the days when they were still imposed, as the laws against free speech were eluded ... Let not anyone be afraid of the epithet "evading the law".'[113]

The talented parliamentary journalist and writer M. J. Landa was recruited to report on the operation of the Act. Throughout 1906, he provided damning accounts of the arbitrary nature of its enforcement. On the basis of these reports the *Jewish Chronicle* argued that the Act was ineffectual and cruel. In November 1906, its own correspondent, probably Landa, delivered a file of material to the Home Office exposing the abuses in the application of the Act.[114]

During the debates on the aliens legislation the public gaze remained fixed on the Jews of east London. *Jewish Chronicle* policy on East End Jewry initially remained consistent, but circumstances forced some curious deviations from earlier editorial positions. From early 1906 the *Jewish Chronicle* began to enthuse over Yiddish culture. In May it carried an interview with the Yiddish writer Sholom Aleichem. Articles acknowledged the growth and vibrancy of Yiddish in London. In a leading article on 17 August it suggested that 'It should be a serious consideration whether, even at some risk of appearing to accentuate our separation as a people, it would not be to our interest to submit to the prevalence of Yiddish with a view to its becoming a Jewish Esperanto, a *lingua franca*, making for our greater solidarity and linking more closely the sympathy between our brethren throughout the world.'

This startling turnabout climaxed with the publication, in June 1906, of a 4–6-page 'Language Supplement' with sections in Yiddish and Hebrew. The reversal of policy was doubtless the result of competition from the *Jewish World*, which had earlier started a Yiddish section, and the Yiddish press itself. It also showed that the sales potential of the East End could no longer be neglected. Market forces had breached the policy of complete anglicisation advocated by the *Jewish Chronicle* for three decades.

In another attempt to keep up with the *Jewish World*, the *Jewish Chronicle* produced lavish reports and supplements on communal events and cultural activities. Numbingly comprehensive coverage was afforded to the lectures and annual conference of the Union of Jewish Literary Societies and meetings of the Jewish Historical Society. The fiftieth anniversary of the founding of Jews' College was accorded a mammoth sixteen-page supplement.

The same prodigality was extended to the Zionist Movement, although the *Jewish Chronicle* remained at odds with its policy. On 17 July 1903, the paper printed a letter from Richard P. Yates suggesting that the Jews should settle in east Africa. This was a kite for Joseph Chamberlain's offer of territory in the British colony of Uganda. The proposal was presented to the Sixth Zionist Congress by Herzl, but his readiness to consider it alarmed the pro-Palestine faction. Israel Davis personally favoured Jewish settlement in Palestine and sympathised with the opposition to Herzl. While Duparc filed the copy for a twelve-page supplement on the Congress, on 28 August, a leading article warned that 'The future of Jewry does not lie in the tropics.' It would be the 'grimmest anti-climax' of Jewish history and 'the most savage piece of historical irony' should the Jews end up there.

The paper expressed 'a feeling of repulsion' at the faction fighting and polemics that divided the movement, especially in England.[115] Herzl's death on the eve of the critical Seventh Zionist Congress stunned the Jewish world and threw Zionism further into disarray. The *Jewish Chronicle* paid Herzl the tribute of a black-bordered issue, and a moving panegyric on 8 July 1904 characterised him as a tragic figure broken on the wheel of the Jewish problem. 'This journal did not always see eye to eye with the dead leader', it mourned. 'But it had learnt to recognise in Dr. Herzl a man hewn of noble clay.'

When the Congress finally rejected the 'Uganda' plan, the Zionist Organisation split. Those who believed that the Jewish situation compelled the acquisition of a territory anywhere in the world seceded and formed the Jewish Territorial Organisation (ITO). The 'pandemonium' at the congress so disillusioned the *Jewish Chronicle* that it declared Zionism to be 'on the rocks'. For a time it gave its qualified support to ITO, whose champion in England was Israel Zangwill. However, although the paper commended ITO as 'sober, practical and statesmanlike' and put coverage of its activity on a par with the Zionist Movement, it maintained a distance from both.[116]

Davis's unwillingness to take sides may have reflected a desire to avoid alienating readers. During 1905–6 the *Jewish Chronicle* desperately tried to increase its circulation, resorting to a variety of expedients. To boost sales outside London, it started devoting more and more space to regional Jewish centres and echoed the call from correspondents in Manchester and Leeds that these communities were neglected by the Jewish organisations based in London. In June 1906, the paper carried a six-page supplement on Manchester and a smaller one on Leeds and Bradford. East End readers were wooed with columns on friendly society and trade union news as well as 'East End Notes', a gossip column of daily life written by Gabriel Costa, a native East Ender. It courted religious readers with a feature on the weekly portion of the Law and communal activists with a series on Jewish communal bodies. It even began a children's column by 'Aunt Naomi' (pen-name of Annie Landa).

None of these experiments had the desired effect. Older readers of the paper were irritated by the profusion of supplements and their bulk, while the paper lost money on them. It had made an overall profit of nearly £3,000 in 1905, but since then circulation had increased only slightly, advertising revenue had diminished and profitability was falling. Solomon Davis, the business manager, pursued advertisers sluggishly and may even have been running the paper down in the hope that the owner would abandon it to him.[117] Exhausted after nearly five strenuous years at the helm of the *Jewish Chronicle*, in December 1906 Israel Davis went looking for a buyer.

4   The hegemony of Leopold Greenberg, 1907–1931

The new Jewish journalism, 1907–1914

On 12 December 1906, Leopold Greenberg, the owner of a successful advertising agency and publisher of the *Jewish Year Book*, wrote excitedly to his Dutch friend and fellow Zionist, the banker Jacobus Kann: 'I heard yesterday that the "*Jewish Chronicle*" is in the market for sale, and I today saw the proprietor and asked him if he would be willing to sell it to me. Of course I need not tell you what "me" in this regard means.' Greenberg was a leading English Zionist and a member of the Inner Actions Committee of the World Zionist Organisation, as was Kann. 'I have an idea', he continued, 'that it would be a most excellent thing if our Movement could have the paper, assuming the price asked is not exorbitant and will show a fair return on the outlay.' He was spurred on by knowledge that the syndicate which owned the *Jewish World* was also interested in acquiring the *Jewish Chronicle*. Its members were strongly pro-ITO and were their bid to succeed, 'This would be an absolute disaster.' Whereas, 'There is no necessity for me to point out to you the extreme value to Zionism in having such an organ, not only in so far as England is concerned, but because I believe that the future of our Movement is largely dependent upon this Country, and the J. C. has an influence outside the community.'[1]

Greenberg proposed to Kann an arrangement whereby he would pay the £10,000 for the paper demanded by Israel Davis and then sell it on to the Jewish Colonial Trust (JCT) for a nominal profit. Within five days Greenberg had obtained an option on the business at the desired price, but he had second thoughts about the transfer of ownership to the JCT, the bank of the Zionist Movement. He told Kann that 'if the journal became publicly recognised as the Organ of the JCT it would lose a good deal of its influence and circulation. I think so far as the public is concerned it must be a private holding, besides which some individual will have to control its working.' He therefore suggested that the JCT advance the money to a company formed to buy the paper. The money would be secured by the issue of debentures, but the ultimate control would be vested in the Trust.[2]

David Wolffsohn, president of the World Zionist Organisation, was informed of the project and gave his agreement after hesitating over the price. A week later, the JCT executive met and worked out the details. Wolffsohn, Dr Nissan Katzenelson of Libau, Joseph Cowen in London, Kann and Greenberg were to be the principal shareholders (although the JCT retained the right to purchase Greenberg's shares). On 21 December 1906, Greenberg telegraphed Kann to let him know that the transfer was completed.[3] But just at this moment the purchase of the *Jewish Chronicle* blew up into a political squall that briefly rocked the Zionist organisation and almost ruined Greenberg.

Nahum Sokolow, a member of the Inner Actions Committee and one of the most prominent Russian Zionists, complained that Wolffsohn had acted behind the Committee's back. Moreover, Sokolow thought the purchase was a bad deal. Having often written for the paper he knew something about the Anglo-Jewish press scene and warned that the *Jewish Chronicle* had been outstripped by the *Jewish World*. He also doubted whether its influence would be maintained once word spread that it had been purchased in the Zionist interest. All of which he proposed to say in an article for the Zionist paper *Die Welt*.[4] Kann explained to Sokolow that it had been essential to conclude the matter rapidly, while Greenberg and Joseph Cowen pleaded that secrecy was essential to the success of the venture. If it had to be announced, then it was most desirable for ownership to be attributed to Greenberg or his firm.[5] Indeed, once the purchase became widely known, indignation welled up on various counts.

Since Herzl's death the Zionist Movement had been split between the 'politicals', the followers of Herzl who maintained that the first priority of Zionism was political and diplomatic work to secure Palestine, and the 'practicals', who wanted the movement to do more to buy land in Palestine and support the existing Jewish settlements. The practicals complained that under Wolffsohn the WZO did too little for the settlements. They interpreted his role in the purchase of the *Jewish Chronicle* as further evidence of his willingness to plough precious resources into purely political schemes. Russian Zionists were particularly irate. The Warsaw *Tageblatt* denounced the deal as a 'Ein Jüdischer Volksskandal' and accused the Zionist leaders in the West of squandering the pitiful savings of Russian and Polish Jews on buying newspapers. Sokolow warned that 'Die Jew. Chronicle Geschichte macht mir viel Sorgen ... Dieser Casus wird zu einem Gaehrungserreger à la Uganda werden.' ['The *Jewish Chronicle* business has given me much concern. The venture will become a Uganda-type agitation.']⁶

The paper now became a political football, kicked around by the various factions within the Zionist Movement. The JCT disengaged from the enterprise, and Greenberg faced the prospect of financing the deal by himself. He salvaged the position by setting up a company to provide the necessary capital and enlisting Israel Davis as chairman with himself, Kann, Joseph Cowen and Leopold Kessler as the principal shareholders, along with David Wolffsohn and Katzenelson. The directors were Joseph Cowen (1868–1932), a well-to-do clothing manufacturer and member of the Actions Committee and the JCT, Leopold Kessler (1864–1944), a German-born mining engineer who led the El Arish expedition, and Jacobus Kann (1872–1944). Greenberg held the largest tranche of shares, was a director for life and became controlling editor of the paper.[7]

Had the *Jewish Chronicle* now fallen under the control of a political faction? After he acquired it Greenberg said that the paper had been receiving subventions from the Rothschilds. This impression was certainly widespread. In 1905 the young Chaim Weizmann wrote to Menahem Ussishkin that 'The *Jewish Chronicle* and the *Jewish World* are mean little papers belonging to Rothschild & Co.'[8] During 1901–2 Asher Myers was, indeed, receiving regular payments from Lord Rothschild through the family's charity accounts. In 1901, he received over £50 in this way, for no obvious reason.[9] After Davis became effective editor these transactions appeared to stop. It is not clear whether the payments to Myers constituted some form of covert remuneration or justified the claim that the Rothschilds exercised an influence over the paper's editorial policy. But Greenberg was fond of exaggeration and it suited him to spread the story, enhancing his image of the 'small man' pitted against the establishment of Anglo-Jewry. It was also a convenient smokescreen for what had, in fact, just occurred.

At the turn of the century it was still common for newspapers in Britain to be owned and manipulated by political parties or factions, and the new proprietors of the *Jewish Chronicle* appeared to fit that profile. Cowen, like Greenberg, was an early admirer of, and aide to, Herzl who had long served the Zionist Movement. Kessler had led the commission which investigated the possibilities for Jewish settlements in Sinai. Kann was on the Inner Actions Committee. Cowen, Kessler and Greenberg had served together on the East Africa Consultative Commission in 1903 which had handled Chamberlain's offer of territory to the WZO.[10]

Yet, although Greenberg certainly did put the *Jewish Chronicle* to the service of Zionism, it remained quite independent of the Zionist Organisation or any constituent faction. True, while Greenberg held office in the English Zionist Federation, it tended to reflect his own position during the in-fighting which racked the organization. In 1910, the anti-Greenberg Zionists in England were so annoyed by this that they set up their own paper, the short-lived *Zionist Banner*, published monthly in Manchester.

But by 1914 Greenberg no longer held office in the movement, or any other communal body, and could not be accused of institutional allegiances.[11]

More interesting than these early squabbles was the manner in which Greenberg used the *Jewish Chronicle* to project Zionism as an ideology. His devotion to Jewish nationalism was driven as much by the belief that it was vital to fight assimilation as by the need to create a Jewish state. This enthusiasm for the regeneration and strengthening of Jewish life in the diaspora was shared with a range of Jewish activists who were antagonistic to political Zionism. For example, Israel Abrahams, who was responsible for book reviews, was happy to work for the paper even though he was a dedicated anti-Zionist.[12]

To understand Greenberg's Zionism and the way he reshaped the *Jewish Chronicle* it is necessary to look at his origins and early activity in Anglo-Jewry. He was born in Birmingham in 1861, the son of Simeon Greenberg, a successful jewellery manufacturer. Although he was educated in London, at a private Jewish school in Maida Vale and at University College School, he contributed widely to the cultural and intellectual life of the Jews in his home town. In his youth he was a radical and graduated into Liberal Party politics. He idolised Gladstone, whose portrait hung on his office wall, and admired 'Radical' Joe Chamberlain. Greenberg and Chamberlain later became acquaintances, a contact that was to play a vital part in Zionist diplomacy in the 1900s.[13]

At the same time, Greenberg was deeply committed to Jewish causes. From the early 1880s, when he started work in London as a journalist, he lived on the northern fringes of the 'Jewish Bohemia' of Kilburn and was one of 'The Wanderers' who gathered around Solomon Schechter and Asher Myers. It is likely that Greenberg's forthright Jewishness and contempt for 'flunky Judaism' was formed during this period. In 1886, he was the secretary of the Anti-Demolition League, which succeeded in preserving Bevis Marks, the oldest surviving synagogue in London, from demolition. In the course of this campaign, he worked alongside the Haham Moses Gaster and Lucien Wolf. He was an active member of the Hampstead Synagogue Movement, which championed changes in the service, and represented the board of management on the United Synagogue council.[14]

In the early 1890s, Greenberg emerged as a vociferous champion of unrestricted immigration. He did not allow his admiration for Joseph Chamberlain to prevent him from addressing forceful letters to the politician when he announced his support for restriction.[15] In 1896, Greenberg founded the *Jewish Year Book*, which became his first platform for declaiming on Jewish affairs. At the height of the anti-alien campaign in the 1900s he published a trenchant and widely admired defence of immigration. As a result he was invited to give evidence to the Royal Commission on Alien Immigration. Greenberg was scathing towards Leonard Cohen, president of the Board of Guardians, and others who endorsed repatriation, loudly opposing this policy at the Board's meetings.[16]

This militancy set the tone of his initial foray into periodical publishing. In March 1897, Greenberg and his friend Joseph Jacobs launched *Young Israel*, a monthly magazine for Jewish youth. As the title suggests, with its echo of Young Ireland and Young Italy, *Young Israel* was intended to assert Jewish values and identity. But this was to be achieved without detriment to being English. The first editorial announced that: 'The English ideals apply to what a man is to do and feel towards his fellow men; the Jewish ideals apply to what he should feel towards God.'[17] *Young Israel* was boldly conceived and well executed, but it was never economically viable and ceased publication in 1901. It did, however, give Greenberg further valuable experience in newspaper publishing.

Greenberg had worked as a journalist on two Liberal papers, the *Pall Mall Gazette* and the *Daily News*, before setting up his advertising agency in 1883. Although he left the *Pall Mall Gazette* before W. T. Stead arrived, he was aware of the way Stead and other editors were revolutionising the style of newspapers. When he assumed control of the *Jewish Chronicle* he shook off the Victorian mustiness which had cloaked it in the last years of Asher Myers and under Israel Davis. Flaccid writing was eliminated and articles shrank in size. The typography was revamped, under the influence of art nouveau, and the page layout was tidied up, with a rule down the centre to separate the two columns. Sub-headings were employed to guide the reader. Cartoons, by Joseph M. Coplans and 'McLevy', were introduced. Greenberg regularised the coverage of Jewish labour affairs, friendly society and *chevrah* news. He increased the amount of regional news, reflecting the growing size and political influence of communities beyond the metropolis. There was more writing on sports and pastimes, largely imported from *Young Israel*, which was revived as a *Jewish Chronicle* supplement in January 1907. Every week the paper carried an interview with a leading personality, usually with a photograph, a typical feature of contemporary newspapers.[18]

These were halcyon days for the *Jewish Chronicle*. By 1911 circulation and advertising outside London were deemed sufficiently profitable to warrant the opening of branch offices in Leeds and Manchester. Greenberg boosted the quantity of advertising and cut down on overheads by funnelling it through his own agency.[19] Advertising revenue benefited from the diversification of consumption and the increasing disposable income of the working and middle classes. In August 1907, the paper carried its first advertisement for the motor car. The migration of the Jewish population from the East End to north-west and north London generated advertising for homes, and the furnishings that they required.

The *Jewish Chronicle* also profited from the religious reshaping of Anglo-Jewry. From the 1900s onwards the amount of advertising for kosher foodstuffs grew enormously, reflecting the increased purchasing power of the immigrants and the extent to which the social and dietary habits of English Jews were changing. Jewish boarding houses in south-coast resorts bid for the custom of Orthodox Jews, who emerged as a significant force in the market for holiday facilities. As kosher food manufacturers and suppliers proliferated, they fought for custom in the advertising columns of the Jewish press. When one advertised, the others had to respond on an equal or larger scale, an inflationary spiral that did nothing but good for the *Jewish Chronicle*'s balance sheet. Barnett's, the kosher butchers, outclassed all rivals with its large, humorous display advertisements.[20]

The waxing Jewish New Year supplements were further evidence of this evolution. Greenberg encouraged the publication of New Year greetings and astutely collected them in a supplement which also carried the paper's traditional review of the year. This more than paid for the copy and the annual cartoon by Joseph M. Coplans. The broadened interest in religious affairs was also serviced by the 'Sermon of the Week', a regular feature inaugurated in 1912. A weekly review of Yiddish books and theatre by Jacob Hodess on the 'Books and Bookmen' page catered for the secular cultural tastes of the immigrants. Israel Abrahams edited the literary section. Erudite commentaries on novels of Jewish interest and scholarly works were collected in a monthly supplement often as much as eight pages in length.

The redesigned *Jewish Chronicle* was a great success. By 1913 its circulation had doubled and it was earning a profit of £2,200–2,500 a year. Flush with money, Greenberg looked for expansion. For a while, he toyed with buying the French Jewish paper *Israélite*.[21] Finally, in 1913, he bought the ailing *Jewish World*. Running the two papers in tandem put him in a very strong commercial and political position. He informed Kann that 'The great advantage of having bought it will come in the course of a few months when we shall be able to raise the price of advertisements in the J. C. It will be justified by constantly increasing circulation and it will not in any way be thwarted by there being another paper in the slightest sense in competition.' The purchase of the *Jewish World* enabled Greenberg to cast the *Jewish Chronicle* as the authoritative voice of Anglo-Jewry, a 'communal publication – the organ of Anglo-Jewry', while the *Jewish World* became 'a medium of personal thought and individual aspiration'.[22]

Greenberg further invigorated the paper with his muscular writing style. Until October 1909 he confined his pen to the editorials. Then he replaced his friend, the Revd A. A. Green, who, as 'Tatler', had been writing a column entitled 'In the Communal Armchair'. Greenberg took the pen-name 'Mentor' for his page-long commentaries on Jewish affairs, often in the form of an open letter. In these he could be generous, particularly towards a person or a cause that aroused his affection; but he could also be vituperative, sarcastic and savagely critical.

The new approach to Jewish journalism made itself apparent in the way the paper dealt with Jews involved in crime. During the 1890s–1900s, the strains of migration and settlement, as well as the movement across the globe of thousands of young Jewish women, had contributed to a major escalation of individual and organised prostitution in which Jews were unfortunately prominent. Jewish agencies in several countries, but notably England, had been in the vanguard of efforts to fight the so-called 'White Slave Trade' since the 1880s. The *Jewish Chronicle* had intermittently commented on the work of the Jewish Ladies' Society for Preventative and Rescue Work, formed in 1885, which became the Jewish Association for the Protection of Girls and Women in 1896. But it would have been hard to learn from these coy snippets what the problem really was.[23]

While debate raged throughout the Jewish world as to the merits and dangers of openly reporting Jewish involvement in the 'White Slave Trade', the *Jewish Chronicle* was decisive. In the course of a full-page editorial on 30 October 1908, Greenberg declared that 'for years past it has been known that this vilest of all trades throughout a large portion of the world is carried on by Jews. It is idle to deny it; it is only making matters worse to ignore it; it is cowardly not to face it.' Although not excusing the Jewish role in white slavery, he attributed it to the corrupting effect of life under oppressive conditions in the Pale of Settlement and the forces which led to mass migration.[24]

These conditions were also blamed for Jewish involvement in a series of terrorist incidents committed in London: the 'Tottenham Outrages' in January 1909 and the 'Houndsditch Murders' and 'Siege of Sidney Street' in December 1910 and January 1911. These events were given a lurid treatment in the city's press. A barrage of hostile comment was directed at Jewish immigrants, and there were calls for the Aliens Act to be tightened up.[25] Uncowed, the *Jewish Chronicle* argued in the wake of the 'Houndsditch Murders' that the solution lay not in aliens legislation, but in ending the oppression of Jews in Russia which bred violent crime. Two other notorious cases, the trial of Oscar Slater in Glasgow in 1909 and 'Stinie' Morrison in London in 1911, were also covered openly and without apology that the perpetrators were Jews.[26]

Yet Greenberg was not wholly consistent. He oscillated between a blazing defiance of anti-Jewish prejudice and the belief that Jewish behaviour determined the extent of anti-Jewish feeling. Without compunction, he pinned the label of prejudice on politicians, campaigners against *shechita* or journalists who indulged in negative comments about Jews or Jewish practices. But he also railed against various classes of Jew for their alleged proclivity for gambling, 'ostentation', low standards of commercial behaviour and propensity to resort to law in the course of business disputes. His declamations on gambling and crime touched a raw nerve in his readers and were always followed by a heavy post-bag.[27]

During the years before the First World War, anti-Jewish feeling in Britain intensified appreciably. The most dramatic eruption occurred in August 1911, in the valleys of South Wales. For three days the small, isolated Jewish communities suffered intermittent rioting and vandalism. A special reporter dispatched by the paper arrived in time to witness some of the final disturbances and stayed to evaluate the extent of the destruction. Greenberg leapt on the riots to vindicate the Zionist argument that Jews, as a minority in the diaspora, were always vulnerable to anti-Jewish attack and that, in this respect, Britain was no different from Continental Europe. Again, Jews used the letter columns of the paper to reflect on these worrisome developments and debate the appropriate response.[28]

Journalists, writers and publicists in general seemed less inhibited from inserting anti-Jewish themes into social and political commentary and belles-lettres. Hilaire Belloc, MP and G. K. Chesterton were in the forefront of this tendency. Perhaps uncertain whether to engage with them or dismiss them utterly, the paper carried interviews with both. Belloc took the opportunity to declare his belief that the Jews were unassimilable and should be legally segregated from the rest of society. Publication of the interview, on 19 August 1910, was followed by pained letters from readers who thought that it was foolhardy to offer him a platform. In a leading article the next week, Greenberg replied that: 'Safety lies not in bottling up but in exposing the fallacies of the anti-semites ... We sympathise with our correspondent's sensitivities, but, alas!, in this world did we only heed that which is pleasing, should we ever be pleased – or instructed?'[29]

Belloc's pernicious role in the 'Marconi Scandal' later earned him Greenberg's undeviating enmity. The Marconi Scandal and the Indian Silver Affair in 1912–13 were further evidence that ideological anti-Semitism had migrated from the Continent to Britain. In both cases, allegations of parliamentary impropriety and corruption centring on Jewish MPs were whipped into scandal by Belloc's journal, *New Witness*. G. K. Chesterton, the editor, deployed the stereotypical images of Jews as clannish, conspiratorial and powerful to explain these admittedly murky transactions.[30] The *Jewish Chronicle* retorted that the stories appearing in the press were the equivalent of 'scavenging in the rubbish heap'. They were 'significant of the lengths to which certain enemies of the Jews even in this country are prepared to go'. Yet, when reflecting on the parliamentary investigations and their repercussions, the paper was more equivocal and rebuked those whose indiscretions were responsible for the bad odour.[31]

Greenberg's combative approach to the Aliens Act was displayed in the paper from the moment he took over. On 11 October 1907, a thundering article launched a major series exposing the fallacies and weaknesses of immigration control. The series concluded with a train of declamatory phrases such as 'We denounce this Act and its administration as a cruel concession to clamour and prejudice', and ended with a patriotic appeal to scrap the law on the grounds that it stained England's reputation. Not everyone agreed with this full-frontal assault, and Greenberg had to defend the paper from accusations that it had used too strong language.[32]

His insistence that the Board of Deputies press for the repeal of the Act, rather than its amelioration, led to his first blistering editorial attack on the communal leadership. On 17 January 1908 Greenberg wrote, 'The political emancipation of Jews in England is reduced to a sham when its representative body feels that, because an Act specially affects Jews, Jews must put up with it – with bated breath and whispering humbleness proclaim sufferance to be the badge of all our tribe – when Jews feel they may not do what every citizen in the land jealously cherishes the inalienable right to do – to protest against it and to appeal for its removal.' Such onslaughts were to become a regular feature of the *Jewish Chronicle*.

Greenberg's conflict with the Jewish establishment was aggravated by a clear difference of approach to political lobbying and the use of the Jewish vote. He was in favour of Jews employing whatever influence they had in electoral contests and encouraged Jewish voters to press candidates hard on relevant issues.[33] He intervened personally with Churchill, the Home Secretary, after it was revealed that transmigrants were kept locked in a ship's hold while their cases were being dealt with. However, in spite of his efforts to keep the matter before the Jewish public, in September 1912 he had to confess that the Act was 'almost forgotten'.[34]

Criticism of the communal leadership extended beyond its acquiescent attitude towards the Aliens Act. Greenberg thought that the Board of Deputies was out-dated, inefficient, secretive and unrepresentative. Until this changed, only a fraction of Anglo-Jewry would take any interest in its work, and its leaders would operate in a vacuum. Prior to the Deputies' triennial elections in 1910, the *Jewish Chronicle* dismissed its activity as 'make-believe'. On the occasion of the Board's 250th anniversary in November 1910, the paper suggested that it 'should so remould its constitution and its practice as to become really a representative body, in the true sense of the term, of Anglo-Jewry'.[35]

The paper's constant sniping at the Board and its president, David Lindo Alexander, drew many letters of reproach. In an editorial on 27 October 1911, Greenberg wrote that: 'We cannot hide from ourselves the fact that a good deal of resentment is felt among some members of the Board of Deputies at the criticisms which have been levelled at the Board in this journal.' However, it acted out of a sense of public duty and the conviction that the Board had to 'democratise itself and its methods'. In 1911–13, the paper associated itself with a reform movement spearheaded by Manchester deputies. At the Board's meeting in January 1912, Alexander and his allies took issue with the *Jewish Chronicle*'s stance and virtually demanded the paper's loyalty to the official leadership. Greenberg rejoined that the Jewish press was almost the only place where free discussion of constitutional reform was possible. Yet even the friends of change could be alarmed by the *ad hominem* attacks on the president. Following one broadside, Louis Kletz, a Manchester deputy whom Greenberg admired, reproached Mentor for the 'exceptionally violent attack'.[36]

This new assertiveness also found expression in the adoption of previously marginal and unpopular domestic causes. Greenberg put the weight of the newspaper behind the campaign to build a Jewish hospital, though the project was viewed with displeasure by Lord Rothschild and other powerful communal leaders.[37] There was far more coverage of the lives of east London and working-class Jews, including affectionate pieces on East End Jewish life by 'Halitvak' that were spattered liberally with Yiddishisms. The paper carried far more news about Yiddish cultural events and interviews with personalities from the world of Yiddish culture.

The *Jewish Chronicle* also reported on the explosion of artistic talent amongst young East End Jews, the children of the immigrants. It published interviews with Alfred Wolmark and Mark Gertler, and features on David Bomberg, Bernard Meninsky and other artists. The paper carried a major report on the Twentieth-Century Exhibition at the Whitechapel Art Gallery, at which Gertler organised a section of Jewish artists. However, its reporter at the opening declared that the painting by Modigliani was 'beyond our comprehension'.[38]

Jewish Orthodoxy was amongst the formerly unfashionable causes taken up by Greenberg. When, in April 1909, a financial crisis threatened the survival of the Machzike Hadath, an independent Orthodox synagogue and community, the *Jewish Chronicle* supported its appeal for funds. Yet,

Greenberg was no friend of 'ultra-Orthodoxy'. After a gathering of immigrant rabbis in Leeds in 1911 reiterated the traditional ban on mixed dancing and protested against theatre going, Greenberg was almost apoplectic: 'These narrow-minded, dark asceticisms are not, thank God, even remotely connected with the essentials of Judaism. They are parasitic growths which like dank mould, clustered round it in the noisome ghetto.'[39]

In effect, the paper projected the editor's own eclectic religious views. Initially he defended the progressive Jewish Religious Union, founded in 1902 by Claude Montefiore and Lily Montagu. However, when it mutated into Liberal Judaism he treated it as an unpleasant neologism.[40] In December 1908 the paper launched a ferocious attack on Sir George Faudel-Phillips for attending the marriage of his son in a church. (Faudel-Phillips, a vice-president of the Orphan Asylum, retaliated by withdrawing the advertising of a subscription list – an interesting example of the importance of such advertisements.) Although Greenberg's first wife, Marion Gates, was a non-Jew who converted to Judaism, he praised endogamy and seized on eugenic theory as a modern 'scientific' justification of the practice.[41]

The death of Chief Rabbi Hermann Adler in July 1911 rekindled hopes for a more dynamic religious leadership. As in 1844 and 1890, the *Jewish Chronicle* had pronounced views on the election of a successor. Such was its influence that Greenberg was lobbied (unsuccessfully) by Jacobus Kann on behalf of Rabbi Dr Lewenstein of Denmark. In the course of the long and messy election process editorial notes alternately disparaged Dayan Hyamson and puffed Rabbi Dr J. H. Hertz.[42] The paper had followed Hertz's career since his tenure of office in Johannesburg during the Boer War had brought him to public attention, and welcomed his eventual triumph. But Hertz assumed office over a ministry that was ill paid, poorly regarded and divided. Greenberg did what he could to enhance the position of the rabbinate. Enormous space was devoted to reports from the Anglo-Jewish conference of ministers in May 1909, June 1911 and June 1914 in the hope that they would assist the professionalisation and improve the status of the ministry.

Russia continued to dominate the foreign news, and the story was depressingly familiar. During 1911 and 1913, the ordeal of Mendel Beilis, victim of a blood libel accusation, filled the overseas news pages much as the Dreyfus trials had done. However, the scope for intervention by British Jews was limited since the conclusion of the Anglo-Russian Entente in 1907. Greenberg was perturbed both as a Jew and a Liberal that a Liberal Government was responsible for drawing Britain closer to autocratic Russia. The British press, too, debated the desirability of the alliance.[43] Several Liberal papers did not hide their unease, but *The Times*, the *Pall*

Mall Gazette and the *Daily Mail* clashed with the *Jewish Chronicle*. W. T. Stead even accused it of wishing to drive America and Britain into war with Russia. The Tsarist regime itself was stung by the paper's constant, well-informed and fully documented criticism. The Russian Ambassador in London issued counter-statements to stories in the *Jewish Chronicle*, while the Tsarist authorities censored columns of news and occasionally confiscated entire issues destined for readers in Russia.[44]

On the eve of the First World War, Anglo-Jewry was in many ways at a peak of security and wealth. England's Jewish élite had advanced to unprecedented heights of political influence and social eminence under King Edward VII.[45] Yet, the fifty years since emancipation had also posed a challenge to Jewish continuity which remained perplexing to observers. On 17 November 1911, the *Jewish Chronicle* celebrated its seventieth anniversary with an edition packed full of reminiscences, historical anecdotes and analysis. One of the paper's greatest achievements was its role in facing, if not surmounting, the problems of Anglo-Jewry. Greenberg, with his pride in Judaism and the Jewish people, extended that tradition into the twentieth century. By its attention to the mores of the immigrant communities, its adaptation to the new religiosity of Anglo-Jewry and its continued involvement in mainstream communal affairs, the paper was helping to forge a new community. It provided a meeting ground for immigrants and Anglo-Jews, an English education for the children of the foreign-born and instruction in the ways of inner-city Jews for those who lived in the suburbs. The comprehensive appeal of the paper was also the clue to its commercial success. Yet the war years and their divisive aftermath would test to the limits Greenberg's ability to preserve the inclusiveness of the *Jewish Chronicle*.

Doing its bit: the *Jewish Chronicle* in the First World War

The Great War of 1914–18 opened up unforeseen opportunities and dilemmas for the Jews in Britain. Despite the patriotic response of the overwhelming majority of British Jews, international conflict inexorably focused public attention on the loyalty and allegiance of immigrant minorities. The war would cruelly test the limits of emancipation and expose the frailties of Anglo-Jewish identity.[46]

The *Jewish Chronicle* got off to an uncertain start by backing the wrong side. On 31 July 1914, following the assassination of the Archduke Franz Ferdinand at Sarajevo and Austria-Hungary's ultimatum to Serbia, Greenberg declared 'we cannot forebear a feeling of sympathy with both parties'. The Habsburg and Serbian regimes had each shown benevolence towards the Jews; Jews served in the armies of each country and would end up fighting other Jews. Above all, it was desirable to avoid any British entanglement on the same side as Russia, Serbia's ally and protector: 'For England to fight alongside of Russia would be as wicked as for her as to fight against Germany, with whom she has no quarrel whatsoever.'

The next week, Greenberg performed a glaring U-turn, adducing Germany's violation of Belgian neutrality as an adequate justification for joining with Russia in a war on Germany. He coined the famous slogan that was to be displayed on a giant placard outside the *Jewish Chronicle* building throughout the war: 'England has been all she could be to the Jews; the Jews will be all they can to England.' His leader on 7 August 1914 repeated this formulation three times, and it was to be pronounced ritually on every anniversary of the outbreak of war and on other suitable occasions. He also announced that the supplement 'In Darkest Russia' was suspended, in spite of reports that anti-Jewish action in Russia was persisting. 'For the moment', he wrote, '"Darkest Russia" can serve no useful purpose, except perhaps by the contribution of its silence to the hushing of dissensions in the field in which the first duty of every Englishman now lies.'

Prior to 1914, the *Jewish Chronicle* had been unrestrained in its criticism of Tsarist Russia. But once Britain was at war on the same side as the Russian Empire, Greenberg had to negotiate a tricky path between criticising an ally in the Entente and abandoning Russian Jewry. When ill-treatment of the Jews by the Russian authorities continued, he devised an explanation that can only be termed apologetic. On 4 September 1914, Mentor argued that: 'From the Russian people Jews have never experienced anything but the deepest sympathy, and with the Russian people they have ever felt on mutually agreeable terms.' It was the threat of German aggression that had led to repression and the damaging policy of Russification. In addition – and in something of a contradiction to the foregoing – it was the 'Germanised' bureaucracy and ruling élite of Russia which were responsible for these dreadful impositions.[47]

This rather dubious rationalisation appeared with increasing frequency in the paper's editorial columns and in Mentor's regular screed throughout late 1914 and 1915. It was not without critics. On 7 May 1915, the paper published a letter from Albert Hyamson, the writer and communal activist, asking for evidence of German influence. Hyamson pointed out that the main perpetrators of Tsarist anti-Semitic practices were fanatically anti-German, while the most pro-Jewish ministers, like Count Witte, had been pro-German. Greenberg's equivocation was exploited ruthlessly by elements of the American Jewish press that remained committed to an anti-Russian (and in certain cases pro-German) line. In January 1915, for example, the New Orleans *Jewish Leader* accused the paper of a 'change of heart'. Greenberg retorted on 12 February that 'It is no part of Jewish interest, as such, to become the catspaw of German intriguers.'

When Mentor was chided by the *American Hebrew*, the authoritative voice of American Reform Jewry, for his 'perverse theory', Greenberg was goaded into a ratiocination so desperate that it is understandable only in the light of the intense pressure under which Anglo-Jewry was labouring. He retorted that no one could know exactly what was going on beneath the 'fog of war' on the Eastern Front and continued: 'The Russian persecution of the Jews – terrible and reprehensible as it has been – their position in Russia as citizens of that country – indefensible from every point of view as it is – form after all a smaller question, a localised question, when compared to the great issues that are at stake in the war.' A few days later, in a letter to Nahum Sokolow, Weizmann commented sarcastically that the *Jewish Chronicle* was 'taking up the defence of Russia and its persecution of Jews'.[48]

While the attacks by the American Jewish press were not without foundation, the *Jewish Chronicle* did continue to report on the suffering of east European Jews. In spite of all the pressure to desist from the pursuit of sectional Jewish interests Greenberg published reports detailing the cruel expulsion of Jews from the war zone on the Eastern Front. The paper was actually reprimanded under the Defence of the Realm Act in 1915 for publicising this information.[49] So it was with joy and relief that the *Jewish Chronicle* reported the Russian Revolution of February 1917 and the promise of a new deal for Russian Jews. The entire editorial comment on 23 March 1917 was given over to rapturous felicitations and optimistic prognoses. 'The vilest tyranny that the modern world has seen, and which withstood for so many years every effort of enlightenment and progress has at last been humbled to the dust … At last, the long, long night for the Russian Jew is ending.'

Greenberg was disappointed that the Jewish establishment did not share his enthusiasm and regretted that the Board of Deputies refused to extend a welcome to the new regime in Petrograd. Yet, before long, he too became more circumspect. Despairing at the new regime's lack of stability he declared on 4 May 1917 that what Russia – and the Allies – wanted was 'ordered progress'. Greenberg was also troubled by the tendency to ascribe continuing unrest and defeatism in Russia to the influence of Jewish agitators and the increasingly widespread conjoining of Jews and Bolshevism. The nexus of Jew and Bolshevik was being forged, frequently in combination with the myth of a Jewish world-conspiracy, and to counter it the paper publicised instances of Bolshevik hostility to Jewish interests. After the Bolsheviks took power, the paper returned to a more familiar mode of reporting Russia. It gave prominence to news of pogroms and anti-Jewish measures, by the Soviets or the counter-revolutionary forces. By 16 August 1918, the *Jewish Chronicle* was backing Allied intervention in the Russian Civil War to 'hasten the collapse of the whole discredited system and help Russia to regain its voice and direct its own destinies'.[50]

The *Jewish Chronicle*'s tortured course on Russian Jewry cannot be fathomed unless placed in the domestic context. The war stimulated an intense national chauvinism. Anglo-Jewry was under enormous pressure to conform to a popular outlook that made few allowances for the anomalous situation of minorities. In October 1914, enemy aliens of military age were interned, including Jews who had migrated to England many years before from the German- and Austrian-ruled areas of Poland. The *Jewish Chronicle* courageously challenged this policy, but to its astonishment the more timorous Board of Deputies refused succour to the internees.[51] Immigrant Jews of whatever background, even if they were naturalised British citizens, were regularly lumped together with Germans. Greenberg frequently and vainly resorted to the correspondence pages of other journals to stop the victimisation of Jews who just happened to be German or Austrian by birth. In his leader columns he forlornly contested the general confusion of Jews with Germans.[52]

Wartime anti-alienism reached its first crescendo after the sinking of the *Lusitania* in May 1915. Rioting occurred in London and Liverpool during which mobs made little distinction between Germans and anyone else with a non-British name. A week later, the Prime Minister announced the internment of enemy aliens of military age and the compulsory repatriation of those who were younger, older or female. Greenberg thought that the Board of Deputies ought to take up the cases of Jews threatened with internment or deportation who had lived in England for many years and who were performing useful war work. However, the president of the Board, David Alexander, ruled that it should not 'interfere'. This attitude disgusted Greenberg, who remarked that the Board's deliberations 'were marked by a nervous terror of the impugnment of Jewish patriotism, which played havoc with the logical faculties of the members'.[53]

War frenzy obliged Jews to demonstrate their fealty with redoubled vigour. Evidence of Jewish war service was the most obvious and essential proof of this. The *Jewish Chronicle* performed a vital function by giving prominent coverage to Jewish volunteering in the opening weeks of the war. On 11 September 1914, it announced an 'Honour Record' listing the names of all Jewish officers and men serving in the forces. However, before long the paper was fielding derogatory comments in the press about the Jewish contribution to the war effort. To ensure evidence of impressive figures for Jewish enlistment it appealed to Jewish servicemen to get in touch with the paper or tell Jewish army chaplains of their denomination.[54]

Foreign-born Jews who attempted to enlist were usually turned away, even if they were naturalised. Jews of Russian origin anyway felt little inclination to fight on the same side as the Tsar and used evidence of discrimination to justify their aloofness. A flamboyant English Jew, Captain Webber, hoped that an all-immigrant unit would overcome the reluctance of non-British-born Jews to enlist and bypass any discrimination. His scheme, publicised through meetings and the Jewish press, won Greenberg's measured support. However, the senior Jewish chaplain to the armed forces, the Revd Michael Adler, feared that it would lead to a Jewish 'ghetto' regiment. With the support of Edmund Sebag-Montefiore (the War Office liaison officer with the Jewish community) and Denzil Myers (London Jewry's chief recruiting agent) he intervened at the War Office to stymie the plan. Greenberg was outraged. He maintained that a Jewish regiment would be not different from the Pals' Brigades that were being formed at the time. He was convinced that a Jewish unit would increase the numbers of Jewish volunteers and help to counter the charges of 'shirking'.[55]

On 6 December 1914, the contending parties met at a London hotel to resolve this divisive issue. The opponents of the plan were drawn largely from the 'assimilationist' establishment of Anglo-Jewry. They feared it would detract from the principle of equality and, implicitly, challenge the 'emancipation contract' by placing Jewish ties above those of citizenship. Greenberg attended the meeting along with Dr David Eder and Joseph Cowen, all of them Jewish nationalists. They believed that a Jewish unit would strengthen recruitment and add weight to Jewish demands at the anticipated peace conference. In the face of this commotion the War Office vacillated, and when official policy turned against 'fancy' units the enterprise was doomed.[56]

The British press naturally covered all aspects of the war in huge detail and with a suitably patriotic emphasis. Anglo-Jewish newspapers paralleled this trend, although there were particular Jewish preoccupations underlying coverage and comment. Allegations of Jewish 'shirking' continued throughout 1915, and it was possibly to refute them that the *Jewish Chronicle* published a special War Issue in November 1915. Much space was devoted to examples of Jewish bravery, promotions and citations, of which there was no shortage. When a Jew, Acting Corporal Issy Smith, won the first Victoria Cross of the war in August 1915, the Jewish press lavished attention on him.

The *Jewish Chronicle* expressed relief when conscription was introduced in spring 1916, hoping that it would put an end to carping about the Jewish war record by removing any possibility of so-called 'shirking'. In fact, conscription provided new fuel for the debate. Some Jews appeared before the conscription tribunals pleading exemption on the grounds that Judaism enjoined pacifism. These instances were picked up by the general press and became the subject of disparaging observations. While Greenberg disliked militarism, he was no pacifist. Mentor remarked that 'The Jewish ideal of peace has no real connection with the doctrine of non-resistance.' The *Jewish Chronicle* asserted that 'In our belief no Jew ought or can claim exemption qua Jew.' But the paper showed its objectivity by publishing a letter from Lily Montagu attacking Mentor's 'derisive, contemptuous challenge to the Jewish "conscientious objectors"' and from others arguing the case for conscientious objection on Jewish grounds.[57]

Conscription also highlighted the anomalous status of the 25,000–30,000 foreign-born Jews of military age who were ineligible for conscription because they were subjects of another, albeit allied, power. The Government explored various schemes to end the anomaly, but discussions dragged on for over two years. Meanwhile, the shocking loss of life on the Western Front helped to stoke up popular hostility to this apparently immune residue. In May 1916, the War Office announced that it would allow foreign-born volunteers to enlist. By June, however, it was clear that the mass of Russian-born Jews were apathetic. The Government then declared that 'voluntary' enlistment would be backed by the threat of deportation for those declining to serve. Although Greenberg was dismayed by the lacklustre response and infuriated by the vociferous opposition of a few Left-wing Jews in the Foreign Jews' Protection Committee, he was indignant at the use of deportation. In July 1916 he put his cogent objections into a two-part 'open letter' to Herbert Samuel, the Home Secretary. The *Jewish Chronicle*'s opposition contributed to the final abandonment of the plan.[58]

Eventually, early in 1917, Britain reached an agreement with Russia under which Russian-born Jews could either serve in the British army or return to Russia to fight there. Since this development occurred almost simultaneously with the overthrow of Tsarism, the *Jewish Chronicle* anticipated that many Russians would now choose to return home of their own accord. Nor could those choosing to remain in England reasonably object to serving in the British army. Yet the saga was by no means over. The *Jewish Chronicle* found egregious faults in the 'Convention', and Russian-born Jews persisted in their manifest reluctance to serve.[59]

In an apparent effort to assist the integration of Russian-born Jews into the army, in July 1917 the War Office announced that it intended to create a Jewish regiment. This came as a complete surprise to Anglo-Jewry, which had not been consulted, and stirred up a hornets' nest. Greenberg had championed the idea of a Jewish unit in 1914 and again in 1916, when he put the paper behind Vladimir Jabotinsky's attempt to raise a Jewish battalion. But this latest idea aroused his deep misgivings. He was acutely sensitive to anything which savoured of discrimination or exceptionalism. In a leading article on 3 August 1917 he regretted the designation of the unit and the choice of a Star of David as its emblem, since, 'when the Jew dons the British or the French or the Russian uniform, he does so as a British, French, or a Russian soldier, and not as a Jewish soldier. There is, therefore, neither point nor relevancy – there will, we fear, be ground for actual offence – in imposing the symbol of the Jews or Judaism upon his accoutrements.'

On 31 August, Greenberg, writing as Mentor, published a long open letter to Lord Derby, Minister of State at the War Office, advising him that the plan was ill considered and 'threatened to divide Anglo-Jewry into segments'. In an unprecedented step, he joined a deputation to meet Derby at the War Office to plead with him to amend the proposal. Unhappy with the outcome, in an editorial the next week Greenberg declared that the project was 'a trifling with the Jewish idea' and one that 'does at least savour of discrimination and differentiation'. Following this strenuous protest, the Government dropped the name and insignia. The unit became a line battalion of the Royal Fusiliers, although it was soon known as the Judaeans and the soldiers bore a representation of the seven-branched candelabrum – symbol of the ancient Hebrew state – on their uniforms. A monument to the Royal Fusiliers stands in Holborn, not far from the present *Jewish Chronicle* building in Furnival Street.[60]

With the introduction of widespread food-substitution in late 1916, and rationing, from early 1918, the *Jewish Chronicle* acquired an important public-service function. It ensured that Jewish readers were aware of relevant new legislation and monitored Government regulations for their impact on Jews and Jewish interests. The paper fought for the adequate provision of acceptable substitutes for foods that were subjected to controls, such as meat, sugar and cooking oils. When selective rationing was introduced, it supported Jewish requests to be allowed to exchange coupons for bacon or animal fats for kosher foodstuffs and argued that Jewish food suppliers should be allowed extra deliveries of these items. To non-Jews this looked like preferential treatment, and the paper was at pains to show that the contrary was the case. In this way, it acted as a semi-official conduit for transmitting governmental decisions to the Jewish population. It also performed a policing role, for example, noting cases in which Jewish food retailers were prosecuted for contravening price regulations.[61]

The *Jewish Chronicle* was itself a casualty of wartime rationing, inflation and labour shortages. In November 1915, Greenberg told Kann that 'The work at the office is horribly harassing, for everything is against one.

Shortage of labour, by reason of a large number of men in the Army, rise of prices – both of material and labour and various other little amenities'. The cover price had to be increased from 2d. to 3d. in June 1916, and to 4d. in February 1918. In 1917, Greenberg was forced to take special measures to raise enough capital to buy paper in sufficient quantity to cover future production. Paper shortages led to straitened print runs. By May 1918 a smaller type was being used and the sale or return arrangement was suspended as a result of Government anti-waste regulations.[62]

It was clear to Greenberg that the strains of war were eroding the position of Jews in British society. In 1917–18, the paper anxiously monitored the growing volume of anti-Jewish comment in Parliament and the press. On 15 March 1918, Mentor warned Anglo-Jewry that 'these attacks are growing in virulence and that the anti-semitic feeling is being energetically fostered against us to an extent that has no precedence in modern times'. Disturbed by the xenophobia and intemperance that now characterised much of public life, Greenberg grasped at every peace proposal. With the end of hostilities in sight, he confided to Zangwill that 'Throughout the war, thank goodness, despite much trouble and considerable temptation, I think our papers have run on an even keel and have never in any circumstances been demeaned by brutal militarism. It has not been easy from me to accomplish this, as you can imagine. But I am proud of the fact that we have never had the word "Hun" appear in our columns.'[63]

On 15 November 1918, the *Jewish Chronicle* reprinted the telegram which it had sent to the King on the cessation of hostilities and repeated the pledge of loyalty to Great Britain 'redeemed in the blood and the lives of those Jews who have fallen or been maimed in battle and in the willing help of all classes of our community throughout more than four years of the struggle'. The *Jewish Chronicle*'s list of these casualties, its Roll of Honour, testified to the scale of sacrifice. In the first year of the war it had recorded modest losses, but as the volunteers were inducted into the ranks and the first major trench battles were waged in spring 1915, the lists extended. The vast expenditure of lives in the battles of the Somme and Passchendaele resulted in columns of names spilling down the page, one after another. In 1917, the layout was reorganised, possibly to minimise the sheer visual horror of these lists. The paper recorded the loss of those who had featured in its pages in happier days as the leaders of Jewish boys' clubs, Lads' Brigade officers and communal workers. For the small, tightly knit élite of Anglo-Jewry, even more intensely than for the élite of the country as a whole, the war was a demographic catastrophe. Seen in the longer term, it also produced a social revolution that transformed the Jews of Britain.

The *Jewish Chronicle* and the Zionist Movement, 1907–1931

When Greenberg took over the *Jewish Chronicle* the Zionist Movement had never been at a lower ebb. The World Zionist Organisation had barely recovered from the death of Herzl, the east Africa dispute and the secession of the Territorialists. Riven between the 'politicals' and the 'practicals', it failed either to make much impression in the diplomatic sphere or to expand settlement activity in Palestine beyond a pitifully small scale.[64] The English Zionist Federation was torn by personal and ideological disputes in which Greenberg and Gaster were the chief antagonists. In 1907, Gaster assumed the presidency of the EZF, with Greenberg on the executive. The two men disagreed vehemently on policy, the former supporting the 'practicals', the latter cleaving to the 'politicals'. Conflict, at the most petty level, between the two men and their respective factions paralysed the Federation between 1909 and 1910. Greenberg did not resist using the *Jewish Chronicle* to lambast his opponents, particularly Gaster.[65]

During 1913–14, the WZO became bogged down in a wasteful dispute over whether the official language of Zionist enterprises in Palestine should be Hebrew or German. When Sir Francis Montefiore, one of the few Anglo-Jewish notables who identified with the Zionist Movement, resigned from the EZF in protest against the pro-German attitude of the Zionist Central Bureau in Cologne, Greenberg begged him not to publicise his action. At a time when anti-German feeling in England was running high, such news could have seriously damaged Zionism in public opinion. Greenberg told Kann that more than once he had kept sensitive news out of the paper.[66]

The First World War reshaped the landscape in which Zionism operated. In October 1914, the Ottoman Empire entered the war as Germany's ally and two days later Britain began hostilities against Turkey. To Herbert Samuel, a member of Asquith's Cabinet, this foredoomed the break-up of the Ottoman Empire and opened the way to the revival of the Jewish nation in Palestine. He discussed the idea with senior Cabinet colleagues and had private consultations with Moses Gaster and, through Gaster, with Weizmann. Alongside these informal and secret contacts, the Conjoint Foreign Committee of the Board of Deputies (CFC), acting through Lucien Wolf and the Anglo-Jewish Association, presented its ideas for Jewish prospects in Palestine to the Foreign Office.[67]

Greenberg knew little of these developments, but he had an acute sense of both opportunity and peril. His editorials in November 1914 warned that Turkey's entry into the war endangered the Jewish settlements in Palestine, which depended on succour from Jews in the belligerent countries. During December 1914 and January 1915, he contacted the

Foreign Office to help to arrange for relief supplies to get through to Palestinian Jews. He also understood that British foreign policy might now work to the advantage of Zionism and welcomed Asquith's speech in November 1914 which declared that the days of the Ottoman Empire were numbered.[68]

Through its excellent network of correspondents, the *Jewish Chronicle* kept an eye on German diplomatic activity. It noted ominously that Germany was considering a pro-Jewish declaration and urged the Allies to offer as much. Ironically, Weizmann was annoyed by these promptings. In a letter to Moses Gaster in December 1914, he referred to Greenberg and Cowen as 'the enemies in our camp' and complained that Greenberg 'has neither any ideas nor any plans how to set about our work'. Soon after Greenberg speculated that the British might occupy Palestine, Weizmann moaned to Judah Magnes that 'The JC kept writing and keeps writing on this subject and does harm.' Weizmann personally cautioned Greenberg that such open proclamations of pro-British sympathy would place in jeopardy the settlements in Palestine which he was so eager to safeguard.[69]

This warning seems to have had the desired effect, since no further leading articles appeared on this theme for many months. Instead, Greenberg turned his attention to the Conjoint Foreign Committee. English Zionists expected that the Board of Deputies would play a crucial role in representing Jewish interests at any future peace conference. Yet the CFC comprised representatives of both the Board and the Anglo-Jewish Association, a non-elected body which was dominated by two trenchant critics of Zionism – its president, Claude Montefiore, and its secretary, Lucien Wolf. So as to dilute their influence, from November 1914 the *Jewish Chronicle* launched a campaign to broaden the CFC by including the representatives of other Anglo-Jewish organisations. The attack on the unelected CFC spilled over into criticism of the undemocratic basis and conduct of the Board itself. Throughout the spring of 1915 and spring 1916, the paper loudly and insistently supported calls for the Board's democratisation.

At the same time, it pressed for the CFC to adopt a position on Palestine and urged it to co-operate with the Zionist Federation and representatives of the WZO in formulating policy. Despite extensive negotiations, the two sides came no closer to co-operation and the Board remained without official policy on Palestine or Zionism. Nevertheless, Sokolow and Weizmann continued to develop their contacts with the Foreign Office. During 1916–17 they made significant advances towards securing recognition of their objectives.[70]

Greenberg played a small but not insignificant part in the intensive negotiations that led to the Balfour Declaration. In January 1917, he acted as an intermediary in arranging a meeting between Weizmann, Mark Sykes of the Foreign Office and James Malcolm, a member of the Armenian National Delegation who was pursuing Armenian interests. Malcolm was probably acting on behalf of Sykes, who wanted to meet leaders of the Zionist Movement other than Gaster. Unable to make a direct approach, he exploited Malcolm's acquaintance with Greenberg. Malcolm went to the *Jewish Chronicle* office and explained that Sykes wanted to meet the leading Zionist activists: Greenberg provided the necessary information. The meeting was crucial in introducing Sykes to Weizmann, who was thereafter to supersede Gaster as the chief representative of the Zionists.[71]

Greenberg naturally concealed what he knew, although it must have chafed against his instinct as a journalist. The *Jewish Chronicle* did not comment on the Palestine campaign until 6 April 1917, when a leading note remarked that it was an 'open secret' that the Allies were considering Jewish claims to nationhood. Greenberg preferred to concentrate on that element of the Zionist strategy that he could best assist with the resources at his disposal: the battle for public opinion. On 20 April 1917, a leading article entitled 'Say "Palestine"' explained the propaganda effect that advocates of a pro-Zionist declaration hoped it would have on Jewish opinion in war-weary Russia.[72]

The battle for opinion was also being fought closer to home. In November 1916, the *Fortnightly Review* published an anonymous attack on Zionism, probably by Lucien Wolf, accusing it of being a form of dual loyalty. The article was so potent that Greenberg, writing as Mentor, devoted four consecutive articles to a rebuttal. Sensing the trend of events at the start of 1917, Wolf redoubled his efforts on behalf of the CFC to torpedo any pro-Zionist Government statement. When it became evident that the tepid Palestine policy of the CFC would satisfy neither the Zionists nor the Government, Wolf, Montefiore and Alexander abandoned thoughts of a compromise and resolved on a powerful public statement against Zionism.[73]

On Thursday 24 May 1917, an anti-Zionist manifesto claiming to represent the views of Anglo-Jewry appeared in *The Times* over the names of David Alexander, the president of the Board of Deputies, and Claude Montefiore, the president of the Anglo-Jewish Association. Although no copy was forwarded to the *Jewish Chronicle*, Greenberg managed to hold the paper long enough to devote a massive leading article to a reply. Entitled 'A Grave Betrayal', it accused the CFC of being 'hopelessly estranged from the general body of Anglo-Jewry'. Avoiding the controversial issue of Zionism *per se*, he trained his fire on the manner in which the manifesto had been issued. There had been no mention of any such intention at the meeting of the Board just four days earlier, or at the last gathering of the CFC: 'It is the chicanery, the double-dealing, the hypocrisy, the trickery of those responsible for this action and their contempt for public amenities that concerns us infinitely more than the contents of the manifesto itself.' He concluded with a rousing summons to the Board's membership to assert itself.

Over the subsequent four weeks, the *Jewish Chronicle* was inundated with correspondence, most of it furious with the communal leadership. Incensed by their high-handed behaviour, scores of Jewish communities and organisations around the country held protest meetings. The paper printed news of each disgruntled gathering and used the reports to buttress the editorial demand for change in communal governance. When the Board met on 17 June 1917, a resolution censuring the action of Alexander and Montefiore was passed by a narrow majority. Alexander resigned his office, and the CFC was dissolved. Though the result was less about Zionism than it was due to the frustration of middle-class Jews, especially outside London, with the autocratic manner of the Board's leadership, it was unambiguously a victory for Jewish public opinion. In this regard, the *Jewish Chronicle* had played a profound role in voicing the ire of Jews excluded from the magic circle of communal leadership.[74]

The paper did not have it all its own way. The Revd Ephraim Levine, of the New West End Synagogue, objected that the *Jewish Chronicle* and *Jewish World* were aligned with the Zionist Movement and, therefore, biased. The former retorted that it had always printed contrary views, but the accusation may have hit home. In July, Greenberg introduced a new column, 'Leaves from a Jewish Log Book', which was intended to provide a platform for anti-Zionist views. It was directed by Diarist, who was actually Laurie Magnus, son of Sir Philip Magnus, MP, a director of the publishing company Routledge.[75] The experiment was not a happy one. By November–December 1917, editor and Diarist were metaphorically at each other's throats. The arrangement lasted only until March 1918, when Magnus gave up writing for the *Jewish Chronicle* and concentrated on the preparation of a publication connected with the anti-Zionist League of British Jews.

The Zionists were now in constant touch with the Government and preparing the way for the long-awaited Declaration. External and internal factors delayed this until 2 November 1917, when Arthur Balfour sent his famous letter to Lord Rothschild. The Government held up the publication of the Declaration so that it could be made known to the world first of all in the *Jewish Chronicle*. Thus on 9 November 1917, under the headline 'A Jewish Triumph', Greenberg wrote a blazing editorial that linked the emancipation of Russian Jews as a result of the revolution with the promise of a Jewish national home in Palestine. He used the fact that support for

Jewish nationalism was now Government policy to turn the argument of dual allegiance against his old foes and gleefully accused the anti-Zionists of disloyalty.[76]

Subsequently, the British Government made liberal use of the *Jewish Chronicle* in its propaganda around the world, and it was hoped that the Declaration would win over Jewish opinion in America to the Allied cause as well as persuade Jews in Russia to help keep their country in the war. The pro-Zionist and, just as important, pro-British statements in the paper, as well as its reports of speeches by communal leaders approving the Declaration, were widely circulated in Foreign Office material sent abroad in various languages.[77]

However, shortly after the announcement, leading figures in Anglo-Jewry combined to form a League of British Jews dedicated to the principle that the Jews were a denomination rather then a nation. Although it supported the right of Jews to settle in Palestine, it did so only on the basis that they should be equal with other citizens: a Jewish state was unnecessary and dangerous. The *Jewish Chronicle* inveighed against the League, deeming it unpatriotic and divisive. Such was the intensity and frequency of these attacks that Diarist asked: 'Has the *Jewish Chronicle* really done its best to present the League fairly and squarely to the public?' A month later, Magnus and Israel Abrahams left the paper.[78]

Not unsurprisingly, the Leaguers were aggrieved at this treatment. Convinced that they would never get a fair deal in the existing Anglo-Jewish press, on 18 March 1918 a literary sub-committee of the League met to discuss the establishment of a new Jewish newspaper. Lucien Wolf was the prime mover. He reported that he had seen the secretary of the wartime Paper Commission, who was responsible for granting licences to new journals, and had made a submission on the following grounds:

1. That the two existing Anglo-Jewish newspapers, which had been acquired by the Zionists before the war, represented only one party in the Jewish community.
2. That both papers support a theory of a separate international nationality for the Jews, which is opposed and repugnant to the great mass of British-born Jews.
3. That the Company owning these papers is only partially British. Of the 20 shareholders 9 are foreigners domiciled abroad and they hold nearly half the share capital. Two of the other shareholders resident in this country are probably not of British birth, but of this nothing certain is known.
4. That since the establishment of the Paper Commission and the issue of the prohibition against the publication of new periodicals, a licence has been issued for a third Jewish paper in this country which is also Zionist – namely 'The Zionist Review'.

The Paper Controller delayed a decision, despite personal approaches by Sir Charles Henry, MP. Meanwhile the committee agreed to raise the

£25,000 necessary for the venture should it be approved, of which £3,000 was quickly promised. One member of the League, S. G. Asher, regarded the *Jewish Chronicle* as 'a danger to the community' and told Wolf he wished it were possible to buy the paper and place it in 'responsible hands'. Since he recognised that this was impracticable, he pledged £1,000 for 'a new organ in which the views of British Jews may be fairly represented'.[79]

Eventually, the League brought out *Jewish Opinion* in December 1918, as a monthly bulletin. For a year this served as its mouthpiece until a more ambitious project was fulfilled with the publication in October 1919 of the *Jewish Guardian* as a full-blown rival to the *Jewish Chronicle*. The motives for this venture were clear. Sir Isidore Spielman, who served on the Board of the *Jewish Guardian*, told Zangwill that 'Master Greenberg has run the community long enough & it seems to me that he tries to "boss it" with his J. C. and J. W. as Northcliffe tries to "boss" the country with his Times and Mail.'[80]

Ironically, by this time the *Jewish Chronicle* was no more enamoured of the Zionist Organisation, if for quite different reasons. Weizmann led a Zionist Commission on an exploratory trip to Palestine in March 1918, but kept a discreet silence on his return. Greenberg, never a Weizmann devotee, began to express impatience with the delay in any practical steps to implement the Balfour Declaration. In October and November 1918, editorials in the *Jewish Chronicle* began to press the Zionist leadership for a clarification of policy. Greenberg was suspicious. He wrote to Israel Zangwill, 'Naturally, we all have to be very careful not to "queer the pitch". But on the other hand, we have to be equally vigilant in seeing that there is a pitch.' Regardless of old enmities, Greenberg, Zangwill and Moses Gaster found themselves sharing the same reservations about Weizmann, based on their adulation of Herzl and his 'political' Zionism.[81]

The *Jewish Chronicle* now became one of the most constant and severe critics of Weizmann's conduct of Zionist policy. Greenberg accused the movement's leaders of engaging in secret diplomacy at the peace conference in Versailles. He charged that Weizmann was too vague in defining Zionist goals and wanted him to state clearly that 'Palestine must be politically Jewish.' He worried that in the face of Arab opposition to Zionism, within Palestine and without, the wording of the Balfour Declaration would enable the British to slip out of their commitment. He told Zangwill in January 1919:

it seems to me that they have sucked the Jewish orange and are now throwing the pulp into our face. Having got the kudos they wanted out of their benevolent intentions to the Jewish people, they are now disposed to hold us at arm's length and to place an interpretation upon their Declaration strictly in accordance with the ideas of the League of British Jews. Of course, technically they are unimpeachable because the wording of the Declaration can mean so little, while it was intended to appear to be so much.[82]

The absence of hard information about the negotiations rendered Greenberg even more pessimistic. He wrote to Kann that 'I am afraid that Weizmann got less than nothing.'[83]

Greenberg was not merely carping. He had a shrewd appreciation of British policy and little faith in politicians. In 1917, soon after the Balfour Declaration, he had submitted to the Zionist Organisation a memorandum setting out the concrete steps necessary to establish a Jewish political entity in Palestine. He defined 'National Home' as the setting up in Palestine of a Jewish Commonwealth. The role of Britain was to do all that was needed to achieve this, as laid out in a constitution. The constitution included the appointment of a Jewish governor, the selection of a governing council dominated by Jews, the establishment of Hebrew as the official language of the country and the creation of a legal system based on Jewish law. It would limit the period of British protection and assistance to fifteen years. Greenberg could thus claim to have seen all the pitfalls that lay ahead of Weizmann and done at least something on his own part to help the Zionist Movement to negotiate a path through them.[84]

With great prescience, he told Kann that 'So far as I am able to judge, the proposals he [Weizmann] made to the Peace Conference and the general scheme are far too indefinite and are based far too excessively on Chovevi-Zionism. There is not sufficient political guarantee in the whole thing and without political guarantee, we cannot have what we really want – however much we may disguise it – a Jewish state (of course, I do not mean at once but ultimately).' Greenberg did not underestimate the difficulties which Weizmann faced both in Palestine and at Versailles. But he thought that if the Zionist leader had been more insistent in 1917, some of them could have been avoided.[85]

In October 1919, the *Jewish Chronicle* carried an important interview which Greenberg conducted with the Emir Feisal, leader of the Arab nationalist forces. Feisal told Greenberg that the Arabs would welcome Jewish immigration and settlement in Palestine; but they would never accept a Jewish state. Greenberg was taken aback when Feisal told him that he understood Weizmann's goals to fall far short of a such an outcome. This only fuelled Greenberg's suspicion that Weizmann was sacrificing too much in a bid to appease the Arabs and the Allied powers. All through the early months of 1920, the *Jewish Chronicle* questioned Weizmann's intentions. It went so far as to accuse him of deceiving the Jewish people.[86]

Weizmann resented these attacks. He complained to Sokolow in

November 1920 that they 'do a lot of harm, tear one's nerves to pieces'. Given the balance of population in Palestine and British intentions, he regarded the demand that he adhere to the maximalist position of immediate statehood as politically quite unrealistic. Moreover, statements such as those made by Greenberg in the *Jewish Chronicle* provided Arabs and British anti-Zionists with evidence that the Zionists were making unreasonable claims. Several times the pro-Weizmann *Zionist Review* chided the *Jewish Chronicle* for its florid pronouncements and its treatment of the Arab question.[87] Indeed, the Haycroft Commission, which investigated the causes of the disturbances in Palestine in April 1921, blamed them, in part, on the 'extreme' Zionist statements carried by the *Jewish Chronicle*.[88]

In the summer of 1921, a delegation of Palestinian Arabs spent several months in London attempting to persuade British politicians and public opinion that under the plan for the British Mandate an alien, Jewish presence would be imposed on Palestine. The *Jewish Chronicle* watched the delegation closely. The anti-Semitic vein running through the propaganda conducted by pro-Arab forces in England made it easy to discredit the Arab case. This also made it easier to avoid facing Arab fears that Zionism represented a threat to their self-determination in Palestine. The *Jewish Chronicle*'s skimpy coverage of the 'Arab Question' and its dismissive attitude towards Arab anxieties were fundamental in shaping the response of English Jews to Arab anti-Zionism. It bore a large measure of responsibility for their closed minds to any notion that the Palestinian Arabs had a case, even if it was an inferior one.[89]

Opposition to Zionism now centred on Parliament, which had yet to approve Britain's acceptance of the Mandate. Since the pro-Zionist policy was associated with Lloyd George, his enemies, who included the 'press barons', Northcliffe, Rothermere and Beaverbrook, set upon it. During the spring of 1922, Zionism was subjected to an 'absolute barrage of detraction'. *The Times*, the *Daily Mail*, the *Daily Express* and the *Morning Post* claimed that Palestine was being invaded and despoiled by Bolshevik Jews, while at the same time the international Zionist Movement exploited the country's people and resources. It was a vicious and unscrupulous campaign, drawing on ancient anti-Semitic images and the more recent 'Protocols of the Elders of Zion'.[90]

Greenberg responded energetically, addressing open letters to Northcliffe, whom he had once known quite well (they had both lived in Pandora Road, London NW6), and using the columns of the *Jewish Chronicle* to rebut falsifications. In June 1923 he arranged for Weizmann to lunch with Beaverbrook, proprietor of the Express newspapers, in the hope that a face-to-face meeting would help to modify some of the latter's prejudices concerning Palestine and Zionism. Northcliffe's death in August 1922 curtailed the worst excesses of *The Times*, but in the other papers the campaign continued without remission. Greenberg later confessed to Nahum Burstein that 'It has been some job for us here to keep "neck to neck" with all the lying mistatements that have been made under the direction of Lord Beaverbrook and Lord Rothermere.'[91]

In order to placate both the Arabs and his domestic critics, Winston Churchill, Secretary of State for the Colonies, presented the Mandate in the most anodyne way possible when it finally came before the House of Commons in the form of a White Paper in July 1922. Greenberg was mightily aggrieved. In an editorial on 7 July he wrote: 'Instead of a National Home for the Jewish people in Palestine, we have the prospect of only a mere Jewish "community" there. The Return about which we have heard so much, and in such lyrical terms, these last four or five years, boils down to the straggling in of a few Jews who are able to crawl through the narrow meshes of the drastic restrictions of Palestine immigration. The day of the Balfour Declaration has passed. That of the Churchill Renunciation has come.' Although Parliament confirmed the Mandate, the *Jewish Chronicle* editorials continued to be dominated by attacks on the White Paper, Churchill, Herbert Samuel, the High Commissioner, and Weizmann.[92]

Until Greenberg's death in 1931, the paper remained fixated on Weizmann and Zionist affairs. Greenberg attacked any policy that could conceivably be interpreted as a sign that Weizmann was compromising fundamental principles. He vigorously opposed the efforts to bring non-Zionists into the work of the Zionist Movement via the Jewish Agency, describing it variously as a 'ridiculous scheme', a 'blundering folly', a 'screaming farce and deep tragedy'. In private, he wrote to Weizmann that 'Nothing will give me greater pleasure than to record its [the Jewish Agency's] breakdown, because as you know I think its success must be fatal to our Movement and *you* are really made for better things.'[93] Followers of Weizmann in England, and Weizmann himself, were angered by the constant barracking. They responded in the *Zionist Review*, at Zionist meetings and, not least, in the paper's correspondence columns.[94]

Yet, at the same time as he denounced the terms of the Mandate and what he saw as the betrayal of the Zionist Movement, Greenberg made the *Jewish Chronicle* into a firm and influential champion of Zionism. Weizmann and the Zionist Organisation gave special thanks to Greenberg for his work in stemming the wave of anti-Zionism during 1922.[95] The paper fostered public interest in the *Yishuv*, the modern Palestinian Jewish community, by its increased coverage of Palestine affairs and illustrated features. This positive depiction of Zionist work was vital for sustaining fund-raising efforts, which Weizmann well understood. He briefed Greenberg before a major drive by the Keren Hayesod (Foundation Fund) in February 1923, telling him 'I feel sure that you can render inestimable service at this critical juncture by leading public opinion in the direction which I mentioned to you.' The *Jewish Chronicle* constantly urged British Jews to donate money to the Fund and berated the lacklustre response to its appeals.[96]

By contrast, Greenberg censored bad news from Palestine. At the nadir of the Zionist Movement's fortunes, in 1927, Jacobus Kann visited the country and returned with a very pessimistic impression. He sent Greenberg his observations of unemployment, hunger and Jewish emigration, adding that 'All this of course is only for you and not for the *Jewish Chronicle*.' Greenberg replied: 'I am not a bit surprised at what you tell me as to the condition of affairs in Palestine, because I have suppressed a great deal of what has been sent by correspondents with regard to it, in the hope that it was merely temporary and might improve.'[97]

In August 1929, a wave of rioting by Palestinian Arabs resulted in the horrifying destruction of Jewish lives and property. The *Jewish Chronicle* on 30 August reported the riots in an issue partially bordered in black, with the headline 'DISASTER!', and berated the Palestine administration for allowing the breakdown of law and order. The vehemence of Greenberg's editorial comment was such that even Kann was worried about its effect. He counselled him to let up on the relentless criticism: 'Don't you think it would be advisable to stop for the moment further comments and see what measures will be taken by the administration in the near future?' Greenberg replied in a characteristically defiant tone, 'All I can say is that I have not said half about the Palestine Administration and their responsibility for what has happened that I should like to.'[98]

Unlike Kann, Greenberg was sure that honest criticism would not alienate the British Government. He had an almost mystical belief in British honour and could not conceive of Britain abandoning its pledges to the Jews. This conviction was at the root of his conflict with Weizmann. Greenberg believed that if the Zionist Organisation had more faith in essential British goodwill, it would be more robust in its demands. Compromise, determined by a mistrust of British intentions, was only perceived as weakness and encouraged Whitehall not to take Zionism seriously.[99]

The report of a commission of inquiry appointed by Lord Passfield, the Colonial Secretary, attributed the disturbances to Arab fears that their political and economic interests were being neglected. It led in turn to a White Paper in October 1930 setting out a new policy on Palestine. This included stricter regulation of Jewish immigration and land purchases. The

Jewish Chronicle dubbed the Passfield White Paper 'A Great Betrayal'. It was 'not merely an anti-Zionist document', but 'anti-Jewish'. Greenberg raised the spectre of electoral retribution: 'We cannot believe that any Jews in this country will care now to be associated with the present [Labour] Government, and we shall not be surprised if the supporters among us of Mr Ramsay MacDonald will seriously reconsider their position.'[100]

By coincidence, the death of the Labour MP for Whitechapel precipitated a by-election in a constituency in which 30 per cent of the electors were Jewish. Greenberg had no doubt that the White Paper justified the employment of the Jewish vote: it was the duty of Jewish voters to do all they could to defeat the Government candidate. The selection of Barnett Janner, a Jew and a Zionist, as the Liberal candidate meant that 'no Jewish vote need be lost'. 'In ordinary circumstances', he wrote, 'the fact of a candidate being a Jew would not constitute any sort of obligation on Jewish voters to give him support, but the present are clearly not circumstances which, in the least, can be called ordinary.' Although Janner narrowly failed to win the seat, the by-election result was a tremendous moral victory for the Zionist cause.[101]

The *Jewish Chronicle*'s blanket coverage of the riots, the White Paper and the reaction of Jews around the world, including the Whitechapel by-election, had an impact on the decision-making process in Whitehall. Indeed, the Prime Minister, Ramsay MacDonald, was so alarmed by the 'Jewish hurricane' that buffeted his fragile administration that he ordered a revision of the White Paper. In February 1931 he addressed a letter to the Zionist leadership which amounted to a humiliating climb down. This was a considerable accomplishment for Zionist diplomacy, although the *Jewish Chronicle*'s negative editorial comment on the letter was an example of Greenberg's vendetta against Weizmann distorting objectivity.[102]

The *Jewish Chronicle* made many enemies during this controversial period. After the demise of the *Zionist Review* in 1926, the *Monthly Pioneer* (1928–33), edited by Phineas Horowitz, carried the banner for Zionism in England. It was intended to interest a broad readership in the work of the Jewish National Fund, the funding arm of the Jewish Agency. Understandably, the *Jewish Chronicle*'s 'vendetta' against the Agency elicited frequent expressions of regret and irritation. During the House of Commons debate on the Passfield White Paper, Sir Herbert Samuel retorted to another member who cited the paper as the 'real back of Zionism' that 'the *Jewish Chronicle* represents no one but the opinion of its editor'. Dr David Eder, one of Weizmann's supporters on the Zionist executive, complained that the *Jewish Chronicle* 'did not, in his opinion, give an entirely unbiased view of what was going on in Zionist circles'.[103] The *Jewish Chronicle* might have been the foremost advocate of Zionism in the Jewish world, but it reflected the independent, eclectic, proud Jewish nationalism of its controlling editor.

Anglo-Jewry between inner city and suburb, 1918–1931

During the inter-war years, the Jewish population of Britain mutated from one that was largely of recent immigrant origin, inner-city and working class into one that was mainly British-born, suburban and middle class. The *Jewish Chronicle* both reflected and influenced this fundamental change. In a leading article on 17 August 1928 entitled 'Jewish Migration', Greenberg remarked of London that 'The preference the Jew once showed for the North side of the town is as obsolete as is the East End as a more specifically Jewish quarter than any other.' Before 1914, Hampstead had been the northernmost point of Jewish settlement. Since then buses, trams and the underground railway had turned the further reaches of north-west London into accessible and desirable suburbs.[104] Advertising for domestic accommodation marked and then accentuated this shift. The typical location of houses for sale became north and north-west London, with the latter gaining the edge from the late 1920s onwards. Certain estate agents operating in these districts clearly used the *Jewish Chronicle* to target the Jewish market.

Advertising reflected the social trends within Anglo-Jewry that had their origins in the 'Khaki boom' of the war years. By the mid 1920s, display advertisements for consumer durables, leisure activities and homes outstripped those for traditional staples such as clothing or foodstuffs. At the start of 1927, Greenberg followed the rest of the press and launched a column on securities and investments. This suggests that a large enough section of readers possessed the disposable income necessary to join the rush to speculate on the Stock Exchange. Jacobus Kann, a *Jewish Chronicle* director and a banker, disapproved of the column, but Greenberg pointed out that it attracted advertisements from investment companies. He told Kann that the *Jewish Chronicle* had a reputation as a prime medium for notifying the public of company flotations and investment opportunities.[105]

Although the prosperity of 1915–18 had enabled many Jews to raise their standard of living, peace came amidst an orgy of jingoism and xenophobia. The post-war years saw a heightening of anti-Jewish feeling expressed in anti-alienism, anti-Bolshevism and anti-Zionism. Running through, and linking, each theme was the myth of the Jewish world-conspiracy. Greenberg deplored the 'rampant prejudice and the political weakness that truckles to it'. But, in 1919, Parliament extended the wartime Aliens Act into peacetime and made it even more stringent. He regularly inveighed against the Draconian power of the Home Secretary to deport, without appeal, aliens convicted of even minor offences. Editorials belaboured the Board of Deputies for not doing more to ameliorate the Act and reprimanded the majority of Jewish MPs who stood by as the legislation was passed and then enforced.[106]

The appointment of the anti-alien and anti-Zionist William Joynson-Hicks, MP as Home Secretary in the new Conservative Government in 1924 sent a shiver of apprehension through Anglo-Jewry. It was accurately captured in the *Jewish Chronicle* headline 'A Threat to Aliens?'. Joynson-Hicks met their worst fears and ordered immigration officials, police and magistrates to tighten up the application of the Aliens Act, with particularly harsh effect on immigrant Jews. Greenberg denounced these measures as 'an anti-semitic attack aimed at the community as a whole' and amplified the ultimately ineffective pleas from the Board for some amelioration of the legislation.[107]

Anti-Bolshevism facilitated the most virulent expression of anti-Jewish feeling. During the Russian Civil War, reports from the Russian correspondents of *The Times* and the *Morning Post* and Foreign Office dispatches, influenced by British army officers assisting the anti-Bolshevik forces, stressed the role of Jews in the revolutionary movements. With incredible speed, the separate terms 'Russian', 'Bolshevik' and 'Jew' became virtually synonymous. The high-Tory *Morning Post* was the chief bug-bear of Anglo-Jewry and repeatedly challenged British Jews to denounce the Bolsheviks. Greenberg saw the trap. If British Jews refused to denounce Bolshevism, they could be accused of covert sympathy with the revolutionaries. If, on the other hand, they did condemn it as Jews, it would appear that Jews had a special reason to distance themselves from Bolshevism, which would only confirm the original fabrication.[108]

He had further reasons for not playing this game. Greenberg welcomed the death of Tsarism and saw much that was worthy in the Bolshevik programme. On 28 March and 4 April 1919, writing as Mentor, he tried to express his views in two typically challenging, if verbose and theoretically naive articles. Although the atheism and dictatorial methods of the Bolsheviks were abhorrent, so was Tsarist autocracy and militarism. 'Bolshevism', he declared, 'is at once the most serious menace to, and the best hope of, Civilization.' It was 'in essence... the revolt of peoples against the social state, against the evil; against the iniquities – and the inequities – that were crowned by the cataclysm of the war'. In what may have been the most controversial statement of his career as a journalist, he delivered his opinion that 'There is much in the fact of Bolshevism itself, in the fact that so many Jews are Bolshevists, in the fact that the ideals of Bolshevism at many points are consonant with the finest ideals of Judaism.' This phrase was a hostage to fortune. The *Morning Post* pounced upon it to justify its assertions that there was an inherent link between Jews and Bolshevism. A few days later the paper issued a further summons to British Jews to dissociate themselves from the Bolsheviks.

On 23 April, a letter signed by ten prominent Jews appeared in the *Morning Post* in direct response to this invitation. It stated: 'We have read with the deepest concern and with sincere regret certain articles which have recently appeared in two closely associated Jewish newspapers [the *Jewish Chronicle* and *Jewish World*] in this country on the topic of Bolshevism and its "ideals". In our opinion, the publication of these articles can have no other effect than to encourage the adoption of the theoretic principles of Russian Bolsheviks among foreign Jews who have sought and found a refuge in England. We welcome your suggestion that British Jews should "disassociate themselves from a cause which is doing the Jewish people harm in all parts of the world"'. They also concurred with the *Morning Post* that British Jews were 'being served very badly by their newspapers'.[109]

The 'Letter of the Ten' triggered an outburst comparable to that which followed the anti-Zionist manifesto of May 1917. Greenberg raged against what he termed 'Treachery – or Folly'. In writing to the *Morning Post* the 'Ten' had 'grovelled abasingly before this anti-Semitic organ' and forfeited all right to communal authority. Correspondence and reports of protest resolutions from Jewish bodies flooded into the *Jewish Chronicle*. Greenberg himself entered into a long and futile correspondence with the *Morning Post* to counter the implications of the letter. However, the imputation of Jewish sympathy for Bolshevism spread ever more widely. The *Jewish Chronicle* and Mentor were soon battling against *The Times* and even Winston Churchill, who also embraced the fiction of Jewish Bolshevism.[110]

The unifying element in post-war anti-Semitism was the myth of an international Jewish conspiracy to undermine Christianity and the stability of the existing governmental systems. This fantasy found its most malevolent expression in the notorious forgery 'The Protocols of the Elders of Zion'. The 'Protocols' were first published in England as *The Jewish Peril* in January 1920. By April, they had attracted the attention of the press, including the watchful *Jewish Chronicle*. However, a leading article in *The Times* on 8 May 1920, speculating on the origins, significance and reliability of *The Jewish Peril*, catapulted the 'Protocols' into the limelight.[111]

In a leading article on 14 May 1921, Greenberg jeered that 'The whole thing is a nightmare, the figment of a disordered brain, the emanation of a man fit either for a gaol or a criminal lunatic asylum.' But soon 'respectable' journals such as the *Spectator* were seriously proposing an inquiry into the activities of the Jews. In July 1920, the *Morning Post* serialised a version of the 'Protocols' which later appeared in book form as *The Cause of World Unrest* with an introduction by H. A. Gwynne, the paper's editor.[112] Despite Lucien Wolf's exposé of the forgery, reprinted as a leaflet by the *Jewish Chronicle* for wider distribution, the alleged Jewish conspiracy continued to fascinate the Right-wing Conservative press. Greenberg was at his wits' end to cope with the tide of vilification, which he dubbed 'Hebrabies'.[113]

Greenberg's analysis of anti-Semitism forms the background to his controversial decision to expose Jewish criminality to public scrutiny in the Jewish press. He stated more than once that Jews themselves contributed to anti-Semitism by their own bad conduct. If Anglo-Jewry could purge itself of malefactors, then anti-Semites would be denied at least one pretext for attacking them. Publicity was necessary to make law-abiding Jews aware of the problem and shame the guilty ones. It might be used by anti-Semites, but they would never lack mud to throw at the Jews anyway. For these reasons, in April 1924 the *Jewish Chronicle* started a separate column, albeit tucked away at the back of the paper, which collated law cases and crime news in which Jews were concerned as either victims or perpetrators.

The Board of Deputies did not share Greenberg's analysis. In January 1926, Dr Israel Feldman steered through the Board a motion advising its press committee to request that the *Jewish Chronicle* discontinue its law and crime reports. The motion was passed by 58 votes to 46, with Philip Guedalla, the committee's chairman, in the minority. Subsequently, the committee rejected the advice on grounds similar to those used by Greenberg to justify the column.[114] The decision to continue it illustrated the autonomy of the *Jewish Chronicle*. While it co-operated with the Board on defence matters, for example in rebutting another campaign against *schechita*, it remained quite independent.[115]

The willingness to espouse risky causes was shown by the paper's sponsorship of the campaign to retry Oscar Slater, convicted of murder in Glasgow in 1909. Greenberg was persuaded by advocates of Slater's cause, notably Sir Arthur Conan Doyle, that there had been a mistrial. The paper called on the Board to take up the case and started a defence fund to pay Slater's lawyer. Greenberg admitted the danger of seeming to favour a criminal just because he was a Jew, so he argued the case mainly on legal grounds. But he was aggrieved that the Board and other communal organisations steered clear of Slater's appeal precisely because they feared that their involvement would justify claims of Jewish 'clannishness'. In the end, Slater's conviction was set aside and the *Jewish Chronicle* was vindicated.[116]

The apparent increase in delinquency amongst young Jews during the

1920s was commonly attributed to the strains on the children of immigrants, the break-down of parental control and the erosion of Jewish values because of assimilation. The *Jewish Chronicle* was the leading arena for exploring the 'problem of youth', a popular euphemism for this complex of phenomena. Discussion in the paper reflected the concern of middle-class Jews when they confronted the conditions in areas of dense Jewish settlement such as the East End of London, or similar regional centres. Correspondents and editor clashed over the merits of Jewish boys' and girls' clubs which assisted the assimilation of the children of immigrant families, but possibly neglected the Jewish values that would give moral ballast to their lives.[117]

Awareness of the threat posed by ignorance and irreligion prompted initiatives to revivify the religious institutions of Anglo-Jewry. On 25 April 1919, the *Jewish Chronicle* suggested that the most appropriate memorial for the Jewish dead of the Great War would be a fund to support Jewish religious education and the improvement of the ministry. Greenberg saw in the Jewish Memorial Council the finest opportunity for the regeneration of Anglo-Jewry. Sadly, the £1 million scheme was too ambitious and was wrecked by internal disputes. The paper continued to give extensive coverage to the Anglo-Jewish Preachers' Conferences which now tackled questions of assimilation among Jewish youth and the dilemma of modernising the ritual and liturgy. Greenberg wanted more positive action from the United Synagogue's spiritual leadership to counter what he regarded as the alarming growth of Liberal Judaism.[118]

The paper's coverage of cultural affairs reflected Greenberg's varied interests. In the monthly supplement in November 1923, David Eder, Freud's friend and colleague, introduced *Jewish Chronicle* readers to psycho-analysis. The paper's art criticism by 'K' was outstanding. Between 1919 and 1931, the art column reviewed exhibitions of work by Jewish artists including Jacob Kramer, Pilichowski, Amshewitz, Modigliani, Lipschitz, Katz and Chagall. Greenberg himself ventured into the world of art criticism at the time of the public controversy over Epstein's *Christ* in February–April 1920. At the other end of the cultural spectrum, the paper wrote up new plays and 'movies'. Silent films were especially popular with the immigrants, whose grasp of English was uncertain, and the advertisements were often in English and Yiddish. In 1928 the *Jewish Chronicle* sponsored a festival of Jewish music.

With the departure of Israel Abrahams in 1919, literary and scholarly publications were covered by a group of talented reviewers that included Cecil Roth, Hugh Harris, Maurice Myers and Charles Landstone. Zangwill's death in 1926 was a personal blow to Greenberg. Although the two men had quarrelled often and furiously, they still corresponded with one another and on many topics, notably Weizmann, were in complete agreement. Greenberg honoured his old friend and sparring partner by running black borders around the pages of the edition that carried the sad news. Zangwill's place in the Jewish literary firmament was gradually, if only partially, filled by Louis Golding. He was discovered by the *Jewish Chronicle* in April 1921. Eight years later, the literary supplement printed a section from what was to be his first, major Jewish novel, *Magnolia Street.*

Women writers, like Hannah Trager, were prominently featured, too. This was indicative of a generally more supportive, or pragmatic, attitude towards women's issues. Greenberg followed the rest of the press in experimenting with women's sections before the war. They dealt mainly with fashion, furniture and family, and had proved immensely successful as well as lucrative. During the 1920s, women's features became a permanent part of the *Jewish Chronicle* for the first time. In 1926 Greenberg brought out two women's supplements and introduced regular columns on clothing and cooking. The latter was written by his second wife, née Florence Oppenheimer, a multi-talented woman who had been decorated for service as a nurse at Gallipoli during the war. Her recipes ruled Jewish cuisine in Britain from the 1920s to the post-1945 era.

Foreign coverage during the 1920s was dominated by events in Germany, Poland and Russia. In each country, Jews were caught between parties contending for power and suffered from the chronic instability that persisted into the mid 1920s. The struggle of the Weimar Republic to establish itself was of enormous concern. Correspondents in Germany reported the poisonous Jew-hatred which flared up in the bitter aftermath of defeat. The paper's Berlin correspondent noted Adolf Hitler early on, and *Jewish Chronicle* readers first encountered him in the editorial columns in May 1923. But the proclamation of his downfall on 11 May was premature: a few months later, Hitler staged an abortive putsch in Bavaria. The paper was one of the few English publications to pay close attention to his subsequent trial in April 1924.[119]

The rise of the Nazis on the back of Germany's economic crisis led Greenberg to send a special correspondent there in April 1930. His first, disturbing, report appeared in the paper's supplement on 2 May and came to the notice of the German Foreign Office, which assiduously monitored its coverage of German affairs. The paper's excellent reporting of the German political scene left no doubt about the threat which Hitler posed to German Jewry. When the Nazis became the second largest party in the Reichstag in October 1930, Greenberg sounded the tocsin. He berated Lord Rothermere for the *Daily Mail*'s presentation of Hitler as a patriotic, energetic reformer and pointed to the violence against Jews that accompanied the Brownshirts wherever they went. The *Jewish Chronicle* begged the world to take Hitler seriously and quoted extensively from papers like the *Volkischer Beobachter* to show the British people what the Nazis were saying about the Jews. Editorials in 1930–1 stressed that, on their own track record, the Nazi leadership meant exactly what they said.[120]

The chaotic and bloody establishment of the Weimar Republic was innocence itself compared to events in Poland in 1919–20. Greenberg pleaded with the Allies, and especially the Americans, to prevent the slaughter of Jews as the Red Army and Polish forces campaigned over the areas of densest Jewish settlement. Jews in England, many of whom were from Poland and the Ukraine, could do little more than march in protest, hold days of mourning and raise money to aid the victims of the pogroms. The *Jewish Chronicle* gave much publicity to these events, and tried vainly to arouse public opinion to the depredations visited on the Jews in eastern Europe.[121]

The optimism which Greenberg harboured for Russia after the revolution was quickly dissipated. War and famine in the 'Ukraine Gehenna' (hell) claimed an estimated 200,000 Jewish lives by 1922. The tragedy was highlighted in the *Jewish Chronicle* by the appeals for relief funds and the pathetic lists of names submitted by relatives seeking information about lost members of their families. During the 1920s, the paper reported the effects of the anti-religious campaigns waged by the Jewish Section of the Communist Party and the destruction of the traditional economy on which Jews had depended. Disillusioned, it spoke out against the Labour Government's resumption of diplomatic ties between Britain and the Soviet Union in 1930.[122]

In the eightieth anniversary issue of the *Jewish Chronicle* on 2 December 1921, Greenberg told readers that the decade 1911–21 was the 'most strenuous experience' in the life of the paper. During the 1920s, the pressure eased off, but there were still unpleasant shocks and difficulties. The early 1920s were marked by industrial disputes, culminating in the General Strike in 1926, which interrupted production.[123] Inflation pushed up the cost of labour and raw materials, which had to be passed on by raising the price of the paper in June 1920 and May 1925. However, it remained profitable. In 1924, a bad year because of the uncertainty caused by the Labour Party's election victory in December 1923, net profits were £1,698. Net profits rose to £1,770 for 1928, after a run of good years.[124]

It was not all plain sailing. The loans to finance the purchase of the *Jewish World* were not paid off until 1928, and the acquisition failed to show much profit. In addition, during the 1920s, the *Jewish Chronicle* faced serious competition from the *Jewish Guardian* (1919–31) and a number of more short-lived publications such as the *Jewish Graphic* (edited by Barnett Friedberg, 1926–8) and the *Jewish Weekly* (edited by Abraham Abrahams, 1932). The *Jewish Guardian* posed the greatest challenge. Its statement of intent declared that it was founded 'in order to provide the Jews of Great Britain and the Empire with an organ of their own, their own in the sense that they own it, and that it will represent their views ... We believe that there is a need for a paper which will supply the Jewish community with trustworthy information on all matters pertaining to their interests as members of a single religious brotherhood.' This was a direct reproach to the *Jewish Chronicle*. Yet, although the *Jewish Guardian* claimed to be independent, it was financed by Claude Montefiore and several wealthy members of the League of British Jews. Laurie Magnus and Israel Abrahams, who had left the *Jewish Chronicle* in 1919 on account of its Zionist posture, were, respectively, editor and chairman of the Board of Directors.[125]

Laurie Magnus, son of Sir Philip Magnus, was a talented, if unlucky, writer. He had lost £40,000 on a newspaper in 1904, since when he had worked in publishing, notably as a director of Routledge. Under his guidance, and with the ample financial support of its owners, the *Jewish Guardian* challenged the *Chronicle*'s claim to comprehensive coverage and literary excellence. It also systematically undercut the latter's advertising revenue by reducing its rates.[126] Partly in order to fend off this newcomer, the *Jewish Chronicle* initiated a literary supplement in January 1921. The paper's design was revamped in 1928: the dated art nouveau cover and column headings were removed and it was given a crisper, modern appearance.

As previously in the history of the Jewish press in Britain, the market was too small for two Anglo-Jewish weeklies. The *Jewish Guardian* tended to attract high-quality advertising, reflecting its well-to-do readership, but its circulation was too small for it to be economical. Although its ideology changed gradually from anti-Zionism to non-Zionism and tepid support for the Jewish Agency, it barely moved beyond its initial constituency as defined by the League of British Jews. The League's membership never exceeded 1,200.[127]

In 1922 Greenberg turned sixty and it is evident from the tone of his editorials that he was growing weary. His letters to Kann around this time are a litany of medical complaints and observations on the diminishing circle of his ageing friends. A rheumatic complaint virtually removed him from the affairs of the paper for a year and finally led to his death on 15 November 1931. Jewish papers in every country paid tribute to him. The *Yorkshire Post* commented judiciously on his hegemony at 2 Finsbury Square that: 'His volcanic energy – and temper – made the *Jewish Chron-*

icle of which he was so long the Editor, the foremost Jewish paper in the world.'[128]

Greenberg had expressed the wish that he should be cremated and his remains buried, without any religious ceremony, near Mount Scopus in Palestine. This was a testimony to his Zionist ardour, but the fate of his ashes once they arrived in Palestine is a curious footnote to his stormy career as a Zionist. The casket containing them arrived in Haifa in November 1931, but the Orthodox rabbinate in Jerusalem insisted that since Jewish Law prohibits cremation, it could not be buried in consecrated round. Letters flew back and forth between London and Palestine as his son Ivan tried to resolve the impasse. In January 1932, Joe Linton, one of Weizmann's aides, suggested burying the casket in Herbert Bentwich's private garden near Mount Scopus. This would have been a nice irony since the two men had loathed one another. In any event, this solution was overruled by the rabbinate. By May 1932 the casket was still in the customs office in Haifa, and officials threatened to throw it out if something was not done about it. Eventually, through the combined efforts of Moshe Sharett (later Foreign Minister and Prime Minister of Israel) and Chaim Arlosoroff, both high-ranking officials in the Jewish Agency, a resting place for Greenberg's remains was found at Kibbutz Degania by the shore of Lake Galilee.[129]

5   Discordant interlude: J. M. Rich and Mortimer Epstein, 1932–1936

Leopold Greenberg's death precipitated a long period of strife within the management of the *Jewish Chronicle*. As long as he had been controlling editor the other directors had, perforce, to leave the direction of policy in his hands. In any case, there was a large measure of harmony between the original members of the group which purchased the paper in 1907. Leopold Kessler, Jacobus Kann and Joseph Cowen sat on the Board of Directors throughout this period. Israel Davis was chairman of the Board until his death in 1927, when he was succeeded by Cowen. However, Greenberg's death, followed by that of Cowen in May 1932, upset the equilibrium. Internal discord coincided with years of turmoil in Anglo-Jewry as it faced the challenge of Nazism in Germany, the influx of refugees from central Europe, Fascism at home and a renewed crisis in Palestine.

During the months before he died Greenberg was too ill to edit the paper. His son Ivan, who had been appointed assistant editor in 1925, deputised for him. Ivan anticipated that the editorial chair would be his by succession and was certain that his father intended this to happen. However, Dr Mortimer Epstein, the paper's managing director, told Ivan on the day after his father's death that he was not going to become editor. Instead, Epstein arranged for the position to go to Jack M. Rich, the secretary of the Board of Deputies. Ivan was furious: he protested to Jacobus Kann and even offered to buy his shareholding in order to strengthen his bargaining position. But neither Kann nor Cowen would intervene.[1]

Mortimer Epstein (1880–1946) had been appointed managing director in December 1931. Born in Kovno, Lithuania, he had been educated in Manchester and at German universities. For a time he had attended a Liberal Jewish seminary with the intention of becoming a minister. Instead, he turned to the study of economics at the London School of Economics. In 1910 he married Olga Oppenheimer and took on the management of her father's telephone manufacturing company. Epstein was highly gifted. By the time he was thirty-four he had written a number of books on economic history and had translated Werner Sombart's *The*

Jews and Modern Capitalism. In 1919 he became editor of the *Statesman's Year Book* and in 1921 added to this the editorship of the *Annual Register*. At Leopold Greenberg's suggestion in 1919 he began writing a weekly column for the *Jewish Chronicle*, 'The Letters of Benammi'. This popular feature ran for sixteen years. While he was managing director between 1932 and 1936 Epstein supervised both the editorial and business aspects of the paper.[2]

Jack M. Rich (1897–1987), whom Epstein appointed editor, was born in Hanley, in the Potteries. The son of a synagogue secretary, he attended Hanley High School and went through university on scholarships. During the First World War he served as an officer in one of the Jewish battalions of the Royal Fusiliers in Palestine. On his discharge, he studied law at Cambridge University, where he was active in student Zionist circles. After graduating he joined the staff of the Board of Deputies as an assistant secretary and worked alongside Lucien Wolf. After three years he was promoted to the secretaryship of the Board and succeeded Wolf at the Joint Foreign Committee.[3]

Through his years at the Board, Rich gained a thorough-going knowledge of communal issues and institutions as well as a wide range of contacts. He maintained close ties with the Board's leadership after he left, which affected his direction of the *Jewish Chronicle*. Neville Laski, who became president of the Board in 1933, more than once asked Rich to tailor news in order to assist him professionally or in communal affairs. In November 1935, for example, he asked Rich not to print news that he was going on a trip to the United States, since he was a barrister and was leaving before the end of the legal term. When Laski was criticised for failing to do enough on behalf of German Jewry, he sent Rich a personal account of his behind-the-scenes work and invited him to visit the Board to view a file of material backing this up.[4]

Since Rich was no journalist, the leading articles and the important weekly column of opinion, 'In the Communal Armchair', were entrusted to Simon Gilbert (1869–1946). He was an East Ender who had been educated at Stepney Jewish Schools, Jews' College and University College London, where he had obtained a BA in Semitics. Israel Zangwill had spotted his talents and propelled him into journalism. For several years Gilbert was a leader writer on the *Morning Leader*, the *Daily News* and the *Star*. He was also active in politics and stood as a Liberal candidate for the London County Council. While he worked at the *Jewish Chronicle* between 1897 and 1921, Gilbert played a major part in the paper's campaign against the Aliens Act. He then left journalism for the film and entertainment industry, but returned to the paper in 1931. Gilbert had a forthright style and characterised himself as a man of the people. In an early piece as

'Watchman' for 'In the Communal Armchair', he declared 'I am a proletarian of the proletarians.'[5]

Between 1932 and 1936, this team made a number of changes to the *Jewish Chronicle*. The weekly crime and law reports, which had never been popular, were discontinued. Several new features were introduced which mirrored the division in the Anglo-Jewish population between well-to-do suburbanites and inner-city proletarians, artisans and small traders.

The galloping suburbanisation of Anglo-Jewry was manifested in 'Property Notes'. During 1932–3, the column surveyed the London districts of Golders Green, Edgware, Hendon, Cricklewood, Willesden, Stamford Hill, Dollis Hill, Harrow, Wembley Park, Hampstead, Northwick Park and Stanmore. It also focused on Margate, Bournemouth, Brighton and Westcliff-on-Sea. Articles described new suburban residential developments, stressing the existence of synagogues, Sunday schools, shops, leisure facilities and means of transport into the city necessary for Jewish home-buyers. It frequently appended information about local estate agents too. While they testified to the efficacy of advertising in the *Jewish Chronicle*, the writer of 'Property Notes' encouraged Jews to utilise their services. In this way the paper strikingly influenced the formation of the Jewish neighbourhoods which were to become the foundation for modern London Jewry.[6]

By contrast, about 100,000 Jews remained in East London, and there were similar, smaller, concentrations in the Leylands in Leeds, Red Bank in Manchester and the Gorbals in Glasgow. The Great Depression superimposed a social and economic division on the geographical rift which separated these communities from suburban Jewry. Working Jews living in the suburbs drew their incomes from white-collar professional or managerial occupations which were relatively lightly affected by the slump. But Jews in inner-city areas, particularly in Manchester and East London, were clustered in districts and occupations that were badly hit.[7]

The social chasm which split Anglo-Jewry ran through the sports and leisure coverage of the *Jewish Chronicle*. It finally recognised the major involvement of working-class and lower-middle-class Jews in all aspects of boxing, as fighters, trainers, managers, promoters, referees and fans.[8] By contrast, in July 1935 a travel column was started, reflecting the disposable income and leisure time available to an increasing section of the readership. This expanded into an annual travel supplement which, like the regular column, attracted valuable advertising for cruises and holidays abroad. A women's page was launched as a weekly feature with the title 'Home Page'. It concentrated on fashion, make-up, child-care and domestic management, and drew advertisements from the producers of cosmetics, consumer durables and household appliances. Indeed, advertising became more and more concentrated on the middle-class female readership.[9]

The *Jewish Chronicle* once again expressed the anxieties of the Jewish middle class concerning social problems. In leading articles on 17 February and 3 March 1933, the paper drew renewed attention to the position of Jewish youth. Casual labour in dead-end jobs, long-term unemployment, the attraction of boxing and gambling all contributed to the emergence of a disaffected, sometimes disorderly, population of young Jews in the inner cities. Phrases such as the 'problem of youth' and 'assimilation' were a code for discussing this estranged generation and the erosion of control by the traditional communal agencies.[10] On 27 April 1934, Gilbert warned that the Board of Deputies was losing any influence over 'the new Jewry that has arisen in what is loosely called the East End...the children of the immigrants of the latter part of the last century'. 'It is', he wrote, 'a great mass at a stage of social and religious transition. Its relations with the deputies are nebulous. Many of its members, I make so bold to say, have rarely heard of the Board of Deputies.'

Anglo-Jewry in the 1930s was thus fissured along lines of generation, place of birth and class as well as an assortment of political and religious ideologies. But its institutions failed to embrace this pluralism. The shocks of the 1930s fell on a divided population, sections of which had no established representation. Despite efforts to widen the franchise of the Board, all of which were supported by the *Jewish Chronicle*, nothing much was achieved. The paper remained almost the only communal forum open to all portions of Anglo-Jewry. It became a crucial platform for every Jewish movement and reflected virtually the entire spectrum of opinion.[11]

The first issue to polarise Anglo-Jewry was the appropriate response to Hitler's assumption of power on 30 January 1933. Unlike the rest of the British press, the *Jewish Chronicle* had never underestimated Hitler and castigated British newspapers for swallowing pro-Nazi propaganda. In November 1932, it tried to highlight the Nazis' anti-Semitic campaign by running a feature 'In Darkest Germany'. It contained weekly reports attesting to the brutality of the Brownshirts, extracts from *Mein Kampf* and speeches of the Nazi leadership. Yet the paper responded cautiously once Hitler was made Chancellor. Editorial policy closely followed the line taken by Neville Laski and Leonard Montefiore, presidents of the Board of Deputies and Anglo-Jewish Association respectively. They counselled that British Jews should do nothing without consulting German Jews or endanger them through independent action.[12]

During March–April 1933, the Nazis enacted laws to drive the Jews out of the civil service and announced a boycott of Jewish businesses. British

Jews reacted by spontaneously organising a boycott of German goods and services. The *Jewish Chronicle* applauded this idea in a leader on 24 March: 'If, as seems evident from the flood of letters that has passed into this office, there is a strong longing to institute a boycott of German goods and services, by all means let it be done. Let Jews, here and in every land, borrow from the Germans their weapon of the boycott and turn it against them.' In addition, the paper suggested that every synagogue should pass resolutions of protest to be addressed to the Government and Members of Parliament. This issue sold out completely, giving some idea of the mood of Jews in Britain at the time.[13]

However, Laski and Montefiore were reluctant to give official sanction to a boycott. Despite intense pressure from within and without the Board, they even held back from arranging a protest in the name of Anglo-Jewry. The *Jewish Chronicle* quickly came into line with Laski. But in the absence of any official leadership numerous unofficial bodies sprang up to answer the call for action. This put Rich in an awkward position. There was no doubt that Laski was far behind Jewish public opinion, but the proliferation of committees and councils threatened to get out of hand. So, throughout March and April, the paper chided the communal leadership for its lethargy, while stridently denouncing the duplication of effort and advising Jews to rally behind the Board and the Joint Foreign Committee (JFC), however half-heartedly they were acting.

Rich helped Laski to buy time, but May arrived and still no official protest had been arranged. In a leading article on 19 May 1933 entitled 'What are our Leaders Doing?', the paper adverted to the 'undercurrent of dissatisfaction' at Board of Deputies' meetings. It suggested, however, that the problem was one of presentation and urged the leadership to be more open. Editorials meanwhile commended unofficial actions such as the protest march of 50,000 East End Jews to Hyde Park. At the same time as it published a stream of letters attacking the apparent inactivity of the Board's leaders the paper expressed sympathy with Laski's pleas for patience and unity.

The communal leadership could rely on the *Jewish Chronicle* to broadcast their views. Laski fed material to Gilbert in defence of his position and encouraged Rich to visit the Board for informal briefings. The paper frequently published unattributed reports 'explaining' the policy of the JFC.[14] A leading article on 22 September strongly reproved the formation of the Jewish Representative Council, which was intended to co-ordinate the boycott nationally. As a former secretary of the Board, Rich was sensitive to its prerogatives: 'the only body that can claim to speak in the name of British Jewry is, and must be, the Board of Deputies'. The *Jewish Chronicle* reiterated the leadership's argument that it would be

Plates 1–12, personnel of the *Jewish Chronicle* – owners, editors, directors

3 Dr Mortimer Epstein 1880–1946

2 Joseph Cowen 1868–1932

1 Leopold Greenberg 1862–1931

6 Leopold Kessler 1864–1944

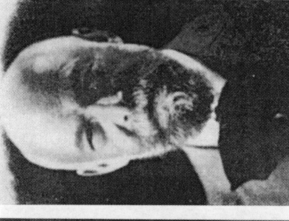

5 Jacobus Kann 1872–1944

4 Michel Oppenheimer 1884–1980

9 John M. Shaftesley 1901–1981

8 Edwin, Viscount Samuel 1898–1978

7 J. M. Rich 1897–1987

12 Philip Zec 1910–1983

11 Leonard J. Stein 1887–1973

10 Ivan M. Greenberg 1896–1966

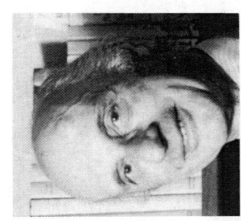

14 David Kessler

13 William Frankel, CBE

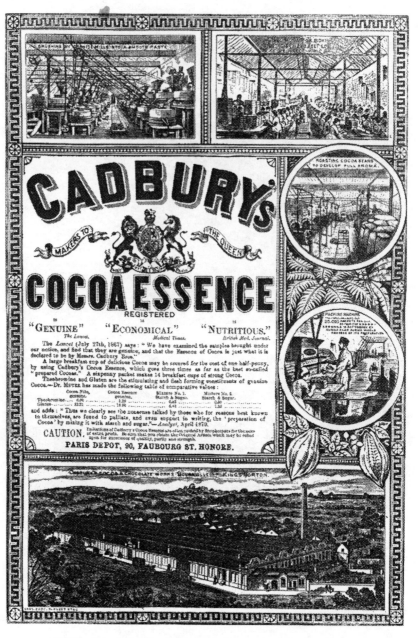

15 The first full-page advertisement to appear in the paper

"PERVERTING JEWS."

16 Cartoon by Joseph M. Coplans in protest at the work of Christian missionaries, from the *Jewish Chronicle* of 23 December 1910

out and discussed in preliminary investigations and experiments. There was no *Jewish Chronicle* in the old English Jewry; the only means of public announcements were by proclamation in the synagogues which could not be of any length. But half the battle of toleration is fought now-a-days by the press. In contrasting the two Jubilees of Anglo-Judaism, we might almost sum up the difference between the two periods by saying that the one had a *Jewish Chronicle*, and the other had no means of appeal to public opinion.

A LETTER FROM MR. GLADSTONE IN 1848.

The following is a *fac simile* of a characteristic Letter written by Mr. Gladstone in February, 1848, on the Jewish Disabilities Bill.

For the purpose of comparison we also give a *fac simile* of a post card written by Mr. Gladstone in 1891. It will be observed that the style and character of the writing have altered but little in the interval of nearly half-a-century :—

THE SYNAGOGUE FIFTY YEARS AGO.

BY THE REV. MORRIS JOSEPH.

When the *Jewish Chronicle* first saw the light half-a-century ago there were only six established synagogues (קהלות) in London : the "German" triad and the Sephardic synagogue in the East, and the St. Alban's Place and the Maiden Lane synagogues in the West. There was about the same number of minor synagogues. There were the Polish *Shools* in Gun Square, Cock and Hoop Yard, and Cutler Street, and the English *Chevras* in Rosemary Lane and Garden Court, Petticoat Lane. All these were in the Jewish quarter. The synagogue in Prospect Place, Southwark, and a small synagogue built by my maternal great grandfather, Nathan Henry, in his house in Market Street, Borough, provided for the requirements of the South London Jews. Fourteen years were still to elapse before the foundation of the little "Branch" synagogue in Great Portland Street, which was to serve as a chapel of ease to the three *Ashkenazi* places of worship in the city. The "chapel" of the congregation of British Jews in Burton Street was not yet in existence—it was opened in 1842 ; but the religious movement of which it was to be the outward and visible sign was already very much *en évidence*. The birth of the *Jewish Chronicle* was coincident, indeed, with the dawn of a new era in the religious history of the community. It was a time when the Anglo-Jewish body was beginning to feel the stir of a more vigorous spiritual life. The Reform agitation had begun—an agitation whose immediate result was the establishment of a synagogue independent of the existing Rabbinical authorities, but which was destined, through the succeeding half-century, to leave its impress upon the synagogue service generally, and to play an important part in the evolution of Anglo-Jewish religious thought. As for the latter, every succeeding phase in its development has been faithfully reflected in the pages of this journal. The child of the new age, the *Jewish Chronicle* has been its consistent representative and exponent. "The period for the moral regeneration of our people is advancing"—so write the editors, with keen insight, in their very first number ; and this power to feel and respond to every beat of the communal pulse has been the *Chronicle's* abiding characteristic.

Fifty years ago the Rev. Dr. Hirschel still occupied the Rabbinical chair. Systematic preaching, to which the appointment of Dr. Nathan M. Adler in 1845 was destined to give a considerable impulse, had yet to be acclimatised in the English synagogues. In London the *Rav*, before age and infirmity had sapped his physical powers, would deliver a semi-annual *derasha* in the Great *Shool* on the Sabbaths immediately preceding Passover and the Day of Atonement respectively ; but, except on these and a few special occasions, the pulpit at the Cathedral Synagogue was mute. The sermon was relegated like an אותה to the "Hall." Here the Rev. Dayan Levy—Reb. Aaron—would deliver a Sabbath discourse pretty regularly. In 1841 he had for a colleague in this task a Mr. Solomon Jacobs, whose preaching seems to have made a great stir. "Though a boy in years," we are told, "he was old in learning," and "he spoke the word of God in true and devoted earnestness." At the Hambro' Synagogue the Rev. I. M. Myers was delivering sermons once a month. Here the preacher was allowed to speak in the synagogue itself. Both in Duke's Place and Church Passage the sermon was delivered during the *Mincha* Prayer, so that the importance attached to a Sabbath Afternoon Service by the Hampstead people is not without respectable precedent. Other London preachers were the

17 Facsimile of a letter and postcard from William Gladstone, reproduced in the issue of 13 November 1891

100TH BIRTHDAY NUMBER

The Jewish Chronicle

THE ORGAN OF BRITISH JEWRY   INCORPORATING THE "JEWISH WORLD"

One Hundred and First Year   Established November 1841

No. 3,788.
REGD. AS A NEWSPAPER   **Friday, November 14, 1941 — Marcheshvan 24, 5702**   Price : 4d.

CENTENARY OF THE JEWISH CHRONICLE

Messages from State and Religious Leaders

From THE PRIME MINISTER

(The Right Hon. Winston S. Churchill)

On the occasion of the centenary of THE JEWISH CHRONICLE, a landmark in the history of British Jewry, I send a message of good cheer to Jewish people in this and other lands. None has suffered more cruelly than the Jew the unspeakable evils wrought on the bodies and spirits of men by Hitler and his vile regime. The Jew bore the brunt of the Nazis' first onslaught upon the citadels of freedom and human dignity. He has borne and continued to bear a burden that might have seemed to be beyond endurance. He has not allowed it to break his spirit; he has never lost the will to resist. Assuredly in the day of victory the Jew's sufferings and his part in the struggle will not be forgotten. Once again, at the appointed time, he will see vindicated those principles of righteousness which it was the glory of his fathers to proclaim to the world. Once again it will be shown that, though the mills of God grind slowly, yet they grind exceeding small.

Winston S. Churchill

From THE CHIEF RABBI :

This is the first time that a Jewish religious journal anywhere has lived to celebrate its centenary. Jewry would, in gladness, have taken note of such a landmark in our latter-day history, but for the appalling contrast between Israel's position and outlook in 1841 and the heart-breaking situation that confronts us a hundred years after.

THE JEWISH CHRONICLE was founded one year after the Jews of the Old and the New World had united, under the leadership of Sir Moses Montefiore, for their successful protest against the Damascus Blood Libel. This moral triumph was followed within a generation by the removal of every Jewish disability in England, and Jewish enfranchisement in the Central Empires and Italy. It is true that the word "pogrom" was soon to be added to the vocabulary of modern politics by the Tsarist regime; but the millions of Jews fleeing from its oppression strengthened immeasurably our older Communities in all English-speaking countries, and furnished the pioneers for the resurrection of the Holy Land. In the 20th century, despite all setbacks due to Reaction, Israel proceeded from strength to strength—till 1933, when Nazism, in outrageous defiance of all civilisation and humanity, outlawed the Jew, and announced the policy of his disappearance from Europe. Ten millions of our brethren have accordingly been hurled into the abyss of defamation and misery, and are facing annihilation.

All the changes in the fortunes of the Jew, his hopes and fears, during these eventful decades are faithfully mirrored in the columns of THE JEWISH CHRONICLE. It has from the very first been a wise defender of Jewry against dangers from without, and a fearless mentor of failings within. Pan-Jewish in its cultural consciousness, it has opposed every form of spiritual self-obliteration or revolution in religion; but given its utmost support to all movements that stood for Jewish life and the deepening of Jewish self-respect. It has aimed to be the voice both of our Unknown Warriors and of the architects of Israel's future; and that noble aim has been crowned with a gratifying measure of success.

"Each age is a dream that is dying, or one that is coming to birth," sings the poet. The nightmare which now holds Europe in its grip shows the correctness of the first half of the saying. Equally so is the second half. For it would be blasphemy to doubt that, in the cosmic struggle of the nations now raging, the hosts of freedom will prevail. Amid infinite woe, and at the cost of endless sacrifice, a new dream of humanity and justice is coming to birth; and, with the help of the God of Righteousness, we shall yet witness its triumphant realisation among all peoples. In that new day, may it be given THE JEWISH CHRONICLE to perform its

(Continued at foot of next column)

From THE ARCHBISHOP OF CANTERBURY :

I congratulate THE JEWISH CHRONICLE on having reached its centenary year. That it should have been issued regularly for these 100 years is a striking proof of the security which British Jewry have had in this country, in contrast with the cruel treatment to which their brethren in other lands have been subjected, especially in recent years. In this country we regard them as in every sense our fellow-citizens. In the present struggle the Jewish people have given abundant proof of their wholehearted association with the British Commonwealth and its Allies. I have always admired the remarkable generosity with which British Jewry have done their utmost to alleviate the lot of their brethren who, in other lands, have been so cruelly oppressed and driven from their homes. I join in their prayers that the tyranny of our common enemy may be overthrown and that their brethren everywhere may be able to live in security and peace.

same mission that it set before its eyes throughout the cycle of years just closing.

I know that I echo the good wishes of the whole House of Israel when I greet THE JEWISH CHRONICLE on its centenary with the words צלח ורכב על דבר אמת "Ride on prosperously in behalf of truth, in behalf of Israel, and continue to deserve God's blessing."

Messages from Allied Prime Ministers and other Lay and Religious Leaders on page eight

The Jewish Chronicle

THE ORGAN OF BRITISH JEWRY · INCORPORATING THE "JEWISH WORLD"

One Hundred and Seventh Year

Established November 1841

No. 4,102

Friday, December 5, 1947—Kislev 22, 5708

Price : 4d.

U.N. DECIDES FOR PARTITION

Separate Jewish and Arab States

On Saturday last, November 29, at 5.30 p.m., in a packed hall, and in an atmosphere tense with excitement, the General Assembly of the United Nations decided, by 33 votes to 13, with ten abstentions and one absentee, to approve the plan to partition Palestine into a Jewish State, an Arab State, and the City of Jerusalem, the last to be placed under a U.N. trusteeship.

A United Nations Commission, consisting of the representatives of five small Powers—Bolivia, Czechoslovakia, Denmark, Panama, and the Philippines—was appointed by the General Assembly to supervise in Palestine the carrying out of the decision.

British troops are to be withdrawn from Palestine and the Mandate laid down by August 1, 1948, and the new States are to come into existence within two months after the termination of the Mandate.

AN HISTORIC DECISION

From our United Nations Correspondent—FLUSHING MEADOWS

The General Assembly of the United Nations reached its historic decision to adopt the plan for the partition of Palestine on the night of Saturday, November 29, after a dramatic 24-hour postponement of the voting in a last-minute effort to see whether a reconciliation between Jews and Arabs could be effected. The effort failed as the suggestion submitted by the Arab delegations was merely a variant of their proposal for a unitary State which had previously been decisively defeated on the *ad hoc* committee.

The partition plan as finally adopted by the General Assembly sets up independent Jewish and Arab States, linked in an economic union, Jerusalem is to be placed under a United Nations trusteeship.

Voting on the plan was as follows:—

FOR

Australia	France	Paraguay
Belgium	Guatemala	Peru
Bolivia	Haiti	The Philippines
Brazil	Iceland	Poland
Byelo Russia	Liberia	Sweden
Canada	Luxemburg	Ukraine
Costa Rica	The Netherlands	South Africa
Czechoslovakia	New Zealand	The Soviet Union
Denmark	Norway	The United States
Dominica	Norway	Uruguay
Ecuador	Panama	Venezuela

AGAINST

Afghanistan	Iran	Saudi Arabia
Cuba	Iraq	Syria
Egypt	The Lebanon	Turkey
Greece	Pakistan	The Yemen
India		

ABSTENTIONS

Argentina	El Salvador	Mexico
Chile	Ethiopia	Great Britain
China	Honduras	Yugoslavia
Colombia		

ABSENT

Siam

British troops are to be withdrawn and the Mandate terminated by August 1. The new States are to come into existence by October 1.

The Arab State will occupy an area of 4,500 square miles with a population of 804,000 Arabs and 10,000 Jews. The Jewish State will have an area of 5,500 square miles, with 538,000 Jews and 397,000 Arabs.

Continued on page 9

STEPS TOWARDS A STATE

The following are the principal stages in the progress from the Balfour Declaration to a Jewish State in a partitioned Palestine

PALESTINE RIOTS

Many Casualties

(From our Own Correspondent)

JERUSALEM

The Yishuv's first enthusiastic reaction to the news of the U.N. decision on the partition plan was dampened this week by the outbreaks of Arab rioting. The troubles began on Sunday, when seven Jews were killed near Lydda in attacks on buses, and further incidents developed when a three-day Arab protest strike began on Tuesday.

The keynote of all the speeches and statements made by Jewish leaders on the announcement of partition was the desire and need to co-operate with the Arabs, but this brought no answering echo from responsible Arab circles. Individual Arabs pleaded for peaceful relations, but this did not stop the rioters.

Heavy Death Roll

Violent fighting, resulting in heavy casualties and serious damage to property, took place on Wednesday when, according to reports as yet unconfirmed, seven Jews and five Arabs were killed, and a large number on both sides were wounded in a "battle" lasting several hours on the Tel-Aviv-Jaffa border.

Continued on page 24

YISHUV CELEBRATES

Troops Join In

Cries of "Mazel Tov" resounded throughout Palestine on Saturday night, when the news of the United Nations decision was received. A wave of joy swept over the whole Yishuv, and jubilant crowds celebrated until the hours of daylight, when they streamed into the synagogues to recite Hallel.

The Jews of Jerusalem, who are normally rather reserved, at once poured into the streets, many not even waiting to change their night attire. Old and young joined in dancing the Hora.

British soldiers patrolling the streets in heavy armoured cars mixed with the crowds and wholeheartedly joined in the general merriment. They willingly gave the Jews joy rides in military vehicles, and, at 3.30 a.m., one mechanical monster carrying a human load of 50 tumbled into the forecourt of the Jewish Agency building. It was difficult to recognise the strange vehicle as a police armoured car. The sweating driver peered out of the narrow slit in the armour over which a pair of legs were dangling.

Well-earned Reward

Members of the Jewish Agency mingled with the crowds. Mrs. Golda Meyerson was recognised and she had to make a speech.

"We have laboured for this moment. We have hoped and made sacrifices for it. Above all, we have always believed that it would come," she said. "Therefore, every one of us has earned the reward."

"To the Jews in the camps of Europe," she said, "The end to your sufferings is in sight. Together with us, you will live in a free Jewish State, and together

THANKSGIVING PRAYERS

Instruction For Sabbath

The following letter is being sent by Dayan H. M. Lazarus, Deputy for the Chief Rabbi, to all ministers:

"In view of the decision of the United Nations on Palestine, I would suggest that the following Psalms be recited at the synagogues on Sabbath next, December 6, immediately after the Prayer for the King and Royal Family in the following order:

Psalm 97 (Authorised Prayer Book, p.110), v.10-12; Psalm 98 (Authorised Prayer Book, p.110); Psalm 87 (Authorised Prayer Book, p.211); Psalm 125 (Authorised Prayer Book, p.180); Psalm 126 (Authorised Prayer Book, p.180).

"Psalm 87 may be sung by the congregation so the traditional tune used at the termination of the Sabbath, and Psalm 126 to the tune of Hatikvah. At the conclusion of the service, after the Adon Olam, Hatikvah and the National Anthem should be sung.

"We pray that this great act of justice to the House of Israel may in our time begin the Divinely-promised era of universal peace.

...we will soon elect the first Jewish parliament.

Chief Rabbi Dr. Isaac Herzog toured the city in a car crowded with singing children. At dawn he arrived at the entrance of the suburb of Rehavia, and there he, his octogenarian father-in-law, Rabbi Samuel Hillman, and Rabbi Moshe Silver, father of Dr. Abba Hillel Silver, joined the worshippers.

In Tel-Aviv, loudspeakers had described hour by hour the proceedings at the United Nations, and when the final vote became known, the whole city went wild with joy. Singing and dancing went on in the streets throughout the night. Crowds swarmed into the streets shouting "Long live the Jewish State". Long live the United Nations.

[Accounts of the celebrations in London and elsewhere will be found on page 8.]

COMMISSION ON HUMAN RIGHTS

Joint Action by Jewish Bodies

(From a Correspondent—GENEVA)

Co-operation in the presentation to the United Nations Commission on Human Rights of problems of specifically Jewish interest has been agreed upon here by Mr. A. G. Brotman, representing the Board of Deputies, of the World Jewish Congress, and Rabbi Munk and Mr. H. A. Goodman, of the Agudat Israel (the latter also representing the Anglo-Jewish Association).

The British and other delegations are understood to be ready to support their attitude, and Moslem delegates are sympathetic in regard to the claim for the protection of Shechita.

The British delegation is urging the declaration and implementation of an International Bill of Rights.

Principal Contents

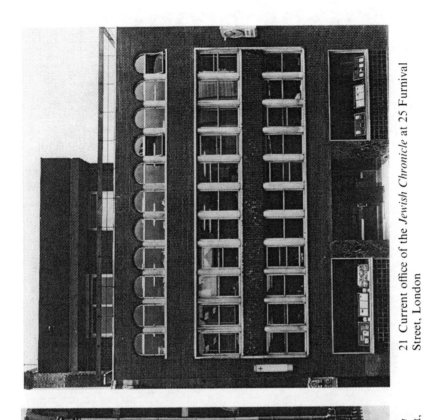

21 Current office of the *Jewish Chronicle* at 25 Furnival Street, London

20 Former office of the *Jewish Chronicle* at 32 Furnival Street, London

22 The front page of the 150th anniversary issue

23 A meeting at 32 Furnival Street. From left to right: Joel Cang, J. M. Shaftesley, David Kessler, L. J. Stein, Michel Oppenheimer

24 Graffiti on the wall of the *Jewish Chronicle* and Vallentine, Mitchell
Building, Cursitor Street

25 Moshe Dayan visiting the *Jewish Chronicle*, around 1976. Including, from left to right: Moshe Dayan, Ellis Birk, David Kessler, Geoffrey Paul

26 William Frankel greets the Lord Mayor of London, Sir Brian Jenkins, on the occasion of the *Jewish Chronicle*'s 150th Anniversary celebration in the Guildhall, London

dangerous for Anglo-Jewry to appear to be officially, as a community, at odds with Germany.[15]

At the same time, the Jewish press did its best to rouse British public opinion to the oppressive measures against German Jews. Stung by its criticism, the Nazi authorities banned the *Jewish Chronicle* from Germany in November 1933. Undeterred, the evidence of Nazi brutality was collected and held up as proof that the world was being duped into accepting the Nazi regime. On 13 September 1935, following the Nuremberg Race Laws, the paper coined the slogan 'No truck with the Nazi Reich'. While not endorsing the boycott, it campaigned against any form of contact with Nazi Germany, be it the Berlin Philharmonic's London tour in 1934, a visit by the British Legion to Germany or British participation in the 1936 Olympic Games. It bitterly reproached politicians and others who visited Germany and flirted with Nazism.[16]

The Nazi takeover triggered a flight of Jews from Germany in 1933, followed by a smaller, but steady emigration as discriminatory measures squeezed Jews out of society and the economy. Entry into Britain was governed by the highly restrictive Aliens Act, though there was little effort to challenge the Government's immigration policy. The *Jewish Chronicle* assumed that Britain would not be a primary place of refuge for large numbers of German Jews and raised the issue of asylum only once. Rather, Anglo-Jewry responded to the needs of the refugees by raising large sums of money for relief inside Germany and the resettlement of Jews who left. The Jewish press was essential to the fundraising drives of the Central British Fund for German Jewry between 1933 and 1936.[17]

As a Zionist, Rich preferred to see Jewish refugees settled permanently in Palestine. 'Land of Israel News' now formed a substantial part of the *Jewish Chronicle*'s overseas coverage. It published regular supplements on Palestine which were intended to raise public interest and stimulate donations to Zionist funds.[18] However, the content and tone of editorials on Zionist politics differed markedly from those by Leopold Greenberg. Rich and Gilbert were moderates. When Jabotinsky challenged the Zionist leadership's policy and demanded a tougher line with Britain, they dismissed him as 'one of those harmless fireworks intended for indoor use: they amuse the children, but do no damage'. The paper welcomed Weizmann's return to power at the head of the WZO in 1935 and was unequivocally against Jabotinsky's break-away new Zionist Organisation.[19]

Although the paper concurred with Weizmann's admonitions that nothing was to be gained from attacking the British Government, in the wake of the German crisis in 1933 it grew increasingly frustrated with the Palestine Administration's niggardly immigration policy. During 1934–5, it played an important part in the successful campaign to block a Government proposal to establish a legislative council in Palestine that would have been dominated by Palestinian Arabs. The *Jewish Chronicle*'s support was indispensable to the Zionist Federation's lobbying efforts in Whitehall.[20]

In April 1936, Palestinian Arabs, alarmed at increasing rates of Jewish immigration and disillusioned with British rule, turned to armed revolt. The *Jewish Chronicle* called on the Government to restore order, and as it became clear that this was more than just a spasm of violence, increased the scale of its coverage until each issue contained several pages of reports. They were collected beneath a general heading that indicated how many weeks of the disturbances had been allowed to pass. The paper accused the Palestine Administration of irresolution and a pernicious tendency to appease Arab opinion. There was little sympathy with Arab fears that increased Jewish immigration might lead to a Jewish majority. Rather, the paper conformed to the dominant Zionist interpretation which attributed the disturbances to the work of Muslim religious fanatics and anti-British propaganda emanating from Fascist Italy.[21]

The uncertainty that hung over Palestine was all the more distressing because of the spread of anti-Jewish movements throughout central Europe. From 1933 onwards, it appeared that Austrian Jewry was living on a knife edge as an armed pro-Nazi movement squared up to an equally determined and well-armed socialist movement. Maurice Myers, second son of Asher Myers, who was for many years the chief reporter of the *Jewish Chronicle*, travelled to Vienna in 1934 to cover the ensuing brief but bloody civil war. His vivid account of the assassination of the Austrian leader Dolfuss and the attempted Nazi coup on Wednesday 25 July was dictated over the telephone to the London office and appeared in the paper the following Friday.[22]

The fate of the Jews in Germany created a greater sensitivity to anti-Jewish activity in Britain. The *Jewish Chronicle* routinely reported evidence of discrimination against Jews in business and the professions, as well as highly charged campaigns against *shechita*. It carefully watched the activity of small, racist and Fascist groups which had been disseminating anti-Semitic propaganda since the 1920s. These anti-Jewish currents provoked widely differing prognoses and remedies.

The confused Jewish response to anti-Semitism was exemplified within the *Jewish Chronicle*. Simon Gilbert believed that religion and tradition inevitably set Jews apart from their fellow citizens and that it was, therefore, futile to strive for total acceptance as the Victorian Jews had thought was possible under emancipation. He had a keen eye for the stereotyping of Jews and understood the double-bind in which they were placed by a society with deeply rooted preconceptions about Jewish behaviour. Yet the editorials took a different line and repeatedly urged Jews to conform to the expectations of a society that was ambivalent to Jewish differences.[23]

Jewish defence came to the fore when Sir Oswald Mosley formed the British Union of Fascists (BUF) in 1932. Individual members were soon identified with anti-Jewish agitation, and the *Jewish Chronicle* challenged Mosley to disown them. His response was equivocal. He declared that the BUF was not anti-Semitic and would 'never attack Jews because they are Jews'. However, if Jews were 'international capitalists' or subversives and attacked the BUF, then it would respond in kind. The paper found this reply 'a little perplexing' and deplored the references to 'international finance' and Communists.[24]

For the next two years, the *Jewish Chronicle* and Mosley played a cat-and-mouse game. The paper cited speeches and publications by the Fascist leader, or his aides, hoping to flush him out or push him into openly denouncing anti-Semitism. When the anti-Semitism of the BUF became more explicit, after January 1934, the *Jewish Chronicle* strenuously pointed this out to Mosley's English admirers like Lord Rothermere. Meanwhile, Mosley haughtily ignored further challenges from the Jewish press. The paper felt vindicated when a BUF rally at Olympia, Earls Court, in June 1934 degenerated into savage brawling as Jewish and Left-wing hecklers were violently ejected. In the aftermath, Rothermere publicly broke with Mosley and accused him of harbouring anti-Jewish elements.[25] For the next year the BUF went into eclipse nationally, although the *Jewish Chronicle* continued to report and comment on the anti-Jewish incidents that frequently accompanied its activities.

In 1935–6, the BUF focused its campaign on the Jewish districts of east London. The eruption of open anti-Semitism on a wide scale in the East End triggered a debate on Jewish defence that sundered Anglo-Jewry. The Board of Deputies, under Laski's guidance, preferred to temporise in public and seek the assistance of the forces of law and order in private. Laski deplored anti-Fascism as an ideology and a course of action. In his eyes it was tied to the Left and apparently confirmed the claim that Jews were pro-Communist. To young, local Jews the Board was a distant and irrelevant organisation that did nothing to protect them. Many joined the Communist Party and other Left-wing parties that were militantly anti-Fascist. In the absence of leadership from Laski, a host of self-defence groups were formed by Jewish trade unions, friendly societies or individual militants.[26]

Opinion at the *Jewish Chronicle* was no less divided. As early as 16 February 1934, Gilbert had argued that Jews were under an imperative to fight Fascism politically since, as an ideology, it was intolerant of minorities. By contrast, the paper's editorial line was resolutely against Jews forming themselves into, or aligning with, anti-Fascist organisations. It warned on 11 May: 'That is our old friend the Jewish vote. It is perilous.' In August, Gilbert favoured the deployment of Jewish anti-Fascist speakers at Speakers Corner, Hyde Park, and urged the Board of Deputies to adopt an activist policy of self-defence. But the leading article on 7 September urged Jews to stay away from a Fascist meeting in Hyde Park.

For all its support of Laski, on 17 January 1936, the *Jewish Chronicle* had to admit that 'a great deal of dissatisfaction and anxiety exists in connection with this matter. There is a feeling that the question has been badly bungled.' Four months later, when the Board had little more to show, the paper warned that 'while we have slept, young men among us have grown fretful, so that there is a danger of them throwing themselves into the arms of anti-Fascist groups ready to help in defence against attack'. In June 1936, Gilbert galvanised the defence debate with an article on 'The Question of Self-Defence'. He called for measures to organise and train speakers, open-air meetings, and the printing and distribution of information sheets to counteract Fascist propaganda.[27]

From the end of June, the *Jewish Chronicle* collated news of anti-Semitic and Fascist activity, counter-measures and all aspects of the debate in a prominent news section under the heading 'Jewish Defence'. This feature often ran to four pages and in itself focused attention on the magnitude of the crisis. Notwithstanding Rich's association with Laski, the paper was now unsparing in its criticism of the Board's leadership. The headline over a leading article on 19 June that commented on the 'reign of terror' in east London was 'Still Fiddling'. While it lamented the prevarication by the public authorities, 'Gravest and most staggering of all, what are the Jews themselves doing for their own protection? Letters pour into the *Jewish Chronicle* from bewildered readers asking this question.'

A private letter which Jack Rich wrote to Joseph Leftwich in September 1936 reveals some of the motives which animated him at this juncture. Leftwich had argued that the counter-campaign only amplified the effect of Fascist propaganda. He pointed to the example of German Jewry as a sign of how useless and even counter-productive such measures could be. Rich replied:

The line which you take with regard to the present campaign that the Community is conducting against anti-Semitism is quite familiar to me. I know what was done in Germany, but I believe that even if we knew that we were going to be unsuccessful in this country, we should have no right to sit with folded arms. Not only do we not know this, but I am convinced that an anti-Jewish [*sic*] defensive campaign has a much better chance of being successful here because this country is not Germany and because the Fascist Movement has very little chance of success here. The fascists have adopted the offensive by making anti-Semitism a main plank in their campaign and we are bound, consequently, to be on the defensive. We cannot help it. If we do not answer the numerous calumnies that are spread about, we shall present our adversaries with an extra argument. I have had many letters from non-Jewish well-wishers, expressing wonder that the Jews did not long-ago take steps to answer anti-semitic allegations.

Rich was convinced that the British public could be won over against Fascism if only they were presented with the facts, and he made the *Jewish Chronicle* into a platform for enacting that belief.[28]

During July, the leaders of the Board saw the Home Secretary to call for tougher policing in the East End and finally announced a series of defence measures of their own. The *Jewish Chronicle* regarded this as a successful culmination of its campaign, and in a leading article on 24 July 1936 headlined 'Forward for Defence!' called for solidarity behind the Board's defence operation. It was too late. While the new defence co-ordinating committee struggled to establish itself and raise funds, Jewish trade unions and Left-wing Jewish political groups in the East End acted. A major conference of Jewish organisations resulted in the formation of the Jewish People's Council Against Fascism and Anti-Semitism (JPC). As the full title of the JPC indicated, it was founded on the principle that resistance to anti-Semitism was inseparable from the political struggle against Fascism. Its leading members also proclaimed that the Board of Deputies did not represent the Jewish population adequately and was insensitive to the needs of working-class Jews.[29]

The *Jewish Chronicle* was intensely hostile to the JPC from its inception: it was not even mentioned in the paper until October 1936. This was to be expected from an editor who had served the Board for over a decade. Yet although the Board's view was by and large supported in the editorial columns, Rich did not refrain from questioning its defence campaign. He gave full latitude to Maurice Goldsmith, the paper's 'special correspondent' in the East End, who had links with the JPC. Goldsmith, a freelance journalist who also wrote for the *East London Gazette*, regularly sent in copy that contradicted the 'official' line of the Board. For example, he commented on 21 August that: 'I disagree with those who give advice urging Jews to keep away from Blackshirt meetings. It is necessary to counter the foul lies and slanders of the Fascists immediately.' In further reports, Goldsmith praised the effectiveness of heckling and raised the highly sensitive issue of police bias. Rich printed these articles even though they contradicted the paper's editorial stance.[30]

The contrast was nowhere more evident than in the reports of the 'battle of Cable Street' on 4 October 1936. Mosley's earlier announcement that the BUF would march through the Jewish districts of the East End caused dismay and fear. The JPC, having failed to get the procession banned, joined the Communist Party, the Independent Labour Party and other groups to block the route it was to take. But on the Friday before the march, the *Jewish Chronicle* printed appeals from the communal leadership urging Jews to remain at home and avoid violent confrontations. These notices, which were not paid advertisements, were located prominently in the paper. Clearly, the communal leadership was using the co-operation of the editor to send a message to the Jewish population. The appeal went unheeded.

In its next issue, there was a glaring contradiction between the paper's editorial comment and the testimony of its reporters. The leading articles self-righteously denied that many Jews were amongst the crowd, estimated at 100,000, that resisted police charges to clear a path for Mosley's Blackshirts. The paper frowned on the violence and argued that it cast Mosley as a martyr to law and order. But the reports were couched in a triumphant and excited tone. They offered plenty of vignettes of the solidarity between Jews and non-Jews in the streets and at the barricades, and did nothing to disguise the extent of Jewish participation.[31]

Although Mosley had been forced to abandon his march on 4 October, it did not mark the end of Fascism or anti-Semitism in east London. Divergent views on the best response to political anti-Semitism continued to tear Anglo-Jewry apart. Rich remained a Board of Deputies loyalist, although even he could not conceal the deep structural faults in the communal governance over which Laski presided. Both he and Gilbert acknowledged that it was in need of an extensive overhaul and urged that something should be done to encompass Jewish youth and the working-class elements that displayed a 'tendency to revolt'.[32]

The divisions within the *Jewish Chronicle* were not confined to editorial policy. At the end of November 1936 Rich ceased to be editor. His departure was followed a month later by the resignation of his patron, Mortimer Epstein. This was the culmination of a power struggle that had been underway since the summer of 1932, when Kann and Kessler looked for a successor to Joseph Cowen on the Board of Directors.

Israel Cohen, the Zionist journalist and writer, and Sir Robert Waley Cohen, the managing director of Shell, put themselves forward to fill the vacancy. However, Kessler was not impressed by Israel Cohen, who had actually approached him to take over as editor after Leopold Greenberg's death. Nor was Kann enamoured of Waley Cohen, who visited him in The Hague. In communal life Waley Cohen was a vice-president of the United Synagogue and was well known for his luke-warm attitude towards Zionism. Kann later reported that Waley Cohen objected to articles by

Watchman (Gilbert) on the ministry and did not conceal his ambition to influence the *Jewish Chronicle*'s policy. 'We must see to it that the *Jewish Chronicle* remains pro-Zionist', he wrote to Kessler. 'Would you not see Dr Weizmann and talk the matter over with him? Maybe that [*sic*] some of the people who are interested in the Jewish Agency would like to take up a certain amount of shares. And that one of them could be put on the Board.' Waley Cohen would only be acceptable if he took up an adequate number of shares and was balanced by another appointment.[33]

Kann favoured Harry Cowen, Joseph Cowen's brother, but Kessler ruled him out as he had not taken any role in the paper's affairs. Instead, he suggested Leonard Stein, Laurie Magnus or Isidore Spielman. Failing these possibilities, Kessler put forward his son's candidacy. He was particularly keen to have a member of his family at his side, since he had growing doubts about Epstein. He was 'able and pushing, but perhaps not quite as trustworthy as our late colleagues'. Yet Epstein was evidently intent on amassing a considerable shareholding. His ambitions acquired substance because of the sudden availability of equity in the paper. Greenberg's widow, the beneficiaries of the Katzenelson legacy and the Cowen family were all willing to dispose of their holdings. Nearly 5,000 of the total of 13,000 shares were for sale.[34]

Kessler was adamant that 'it would not be desirable that he [Epstein] acquires a predominating influence' and asked Kann to help him purchase the bulk of the shares coming on to the market. But Kann was deeply unhappy at the idea of David Kessler joining his father on the Board and blocked the proposal. In March 1933, Leopold Kessler and Epstein split the 2,194 shares being disposed of by Harry Cowen. This increased the Kessler family holding substantially. To begin with, Kessler and his wife had held 800 shares, but this had been increased by 1,675 shares after the death of Israel Davis. In May 1933, Leopold Kessler was also able to secure the former holding of Nathan Katzenelson, totalling 1,872 shares, and the family now commanded over 5,300 shares.[35]

However, Epstein was now also a large shareholder and wanted a greater role in the paper. He had been reappointed for a second twelve-month period as managing director in October 1932, but pressed for a five-year contract. He also wanted a similar contract for Rich. In October 1933, Epstein travelled to The Hague to see Kann and lobby for the extensions. He adroitly played on Kann's growing sense of isolation and his frustration that Kessler was not consulting him enough about the management of the paper.[36] Kessler would not budge. He told Kann that 'Neither of the two men have really fulfilled our expectations when they were chosen to replace Greenberg. But acceptance of Dr Epstein's proposal would mean loss of control by us and I have quite definitely told him that I am absolutely opposed to it on principle. If he should continue to strive after sole control then the necessity might arise to ask him to resign.' He implied that Epstein was not personally trustworthy or reliable on Zionist matters: 'I feel that Dr Epstein requires watching.' Kessler reiterated his wish for his son, David, to join the Board. To support his case he pointed to the terms of trust under which his sons and daughter held shares in the *Jewish Chronicle*, obliging them to support the Zionist cause. Acceding to Kann's desire to increase the number of shareholders, he suggested that Kann's son, Maurits, join the Board at the same time and on a similar basis. In November 1933, Maurits Kann and David Kessler were elected to the Board of Directors.[37]

Epstein had been checked temporarily, but over the course of 1934, the disagreements between Kessler and Kann widened. In January 1934, Kann was annoyed by editorial attacks on the Jewish Colonial Trust, with which he was associated. He protested in May that he was not consulted about fixing the fee for the paper's directors. He also felt that he was not being kept sufficiently informed about Kessler's plans for the paper. The lease on the building in Finsbury Square was running out and the type-setting equipment was outdated. Kessler wanted to secure better quarters and purchase new Linotype machinery, which would prove very costly. Yet, Kann complained, neither he nor his son, who was a newspaper publisher in Amsterdam and knew about printing, was asked for his views.[38]

At this juncture, Epstein renewed the drive to strengthen his position on the Board. Again he exploited the divergence between Kann in The Hague and Kessler in London, also winning over Maurits to his cause. As a result of this pressure, Leopold Kessler reluctantly conceded a two-year extension to Epstein's contract. The irritation between Kann and Kessler now had a momentum of its own, and at the end of 1934 it exploded into an ugly row between the two men. Kessler was worried by the competition from a new twopenny weekly publication, *World Jewry* (1934–6, editor: J. H. Castel) and the *Jewish Daily Post*, a short-lived Jewish daily, edited by J. Puniansky. He felt it was imperative for the *Jewish Chronicle* to improve its premises and up-date its type-setting facilities. Overall, the cost would be £7,000 to modernise the building and £10,000 for the machinery. To pay for this, he proposed raising money through a combination of loans and debentures. Kann wanted more details of this planned expenditure, which to him seemed high, and asked Kessler to hold the next Board meeting in Holland, since he was too weak to travel. Kessler declined to do so and insisted on a quick decision whether or not Kann wanted to take up any of the debentures. Meanwhile he had arranged for them to be issued on his own authority. This was too much for Kann, who protested against

Kessler's behaviour and flatly refused to have anything to do with financing the loan.[39]

Maurits Kann attended the meeting of the Board on 31 January 1935 on behalf of his father, who was partially mollified by the report he received from his son. The scale of the loan to finance the move was set at £7,000, guaranteed by Epstein and Kessler. Maurits was also consulted on the choice of Linotype machines. However, the appearance of harmony was illusory. On 1 June, Jacobus Kann arrived unannounced for a Board meeting in London, accompanied by Maurits. One of the motions on the agenda in Kann's name was to limit the issue of debentures to £5,000. Kessler appears to have regarded the appearance of both Kanns as an ambush and lost his temper, accusing Jacobus of organising a conspiracy against him. He vacated the chair in favour of Epstein and a heated, wounding exchange with his old friend ensued.[40]

Over subsequent days, Michel Oppenheimer (1884–1980), Leopold Greenberg's brother-in-law and the trustee of the Greenberg interest, was called in to mediate between Kann and Kessler. But the tide was running against Kessler. He was obliged to accept the issue of debentures as proposed by Kann. When he attempted to restore the status quo ante and resume the chairmanship of the Board, he was rebuffed by Epstein, who told him that only the Board could make that decision. Moreover, Jacobus Kann backed Epstein. He told Kessler that it was not the matter of the debentures which had led to this denouement. Rather he was irked by what he understood to be Kessler's plans for the management of the paper. 'It has been clear to me for some time', he wrote to Kessler, 'that you wanted the control because you had the intention to provide a good position for your son.' The Jewish Chronicle did not exist to serve any 'private interests'. He was prepared to forgive the events at the Board meeting, 'But it should be clearly understood that the Board has appointed Dr Epstein as its chairman and this cannot be changed unless the Board decides to do so.'[41]

Kessler's son David was, indeed, returning from Palestine, where he had been working for Moshe Novomeysky, the Palestinian entrepreneur who had owned the concession to exploit the Dead Sea mineral deposits. David's father had earlier suggested that he return to London and assist him in his work, but the storm at the Jewish Chronicle now made his presence essential to prevent the Kessler–Greenberg interest losing control. Ruth Kessler wrote to her brother on 2 June that 'Dad is very worried about J. C. affairs at the moment. Epstein heard indirectly about your coming home "to take up an important position on the paper" and is apparently making a last attempt to gain control of affairs.' It later transpired that it was, in fact, misleading information stemming from

Jerusalem, to the effect that he had been given a job at the *Jewish Chronicle*, which had provoked the show-down at the Board in the first place. After an extended exchange of letters between London, The Hague and Jerusalem, Kessler had managed to persuade Kann that this was not true and his son's return was not part of a strategy to enhance his family's interests.[42]

In July 1935 the *Jewish Chronicle* moved from Finsbury Square to 49 Moor Lane, in the City. Thanks to Leopold Kessler's planning, the paper acquired new premises with a well-lit composing room that was large enough to accommodate up-to-date composing machinery. The new equipment enabled more rapid type-setting, better typography and greater economy. As the British economy recovered from the Depression, the quantity of advertising increased and the paper's financial position benefited. Relations between Leopold Kessler and Jacobus Kann also improved, and it was not long before the tables were turned on Epstein.[43]

At the end of the year, Michel Oppenheimer announced that he would stand against Jacobus Kann in the annual election of a director, despite protests from Kann's friends amongst the shareholders. On 23 January 1936, on the eve of the crucial Board meeting, David Kessler secured proxies from his brother and sister. With Oppenheimer he took legal advice on Epstein's right to remain a director. The Kessler family and Oppenheimer combined their strength: Jacobus Kann was replaced by Oppenheimer, and Leonard Stein (1887–1973) was appointed a director instead of Epstein. A barrister by training, Stein had been involved in Zionist affairs since before the First World War. From 1918 to 1920 as an officer in the army he had served in the Palestine administration. He was political secretary of the Zionist Organisation from 1920 to 1929 and became a confidant of Weizmann. Stein played a major part in the creation of the enlarged Jewish Agency and the negotiations with the Government following the 1930 White Paper.[44]

On 8 May 1936, Leopold Kessler had warned Rich that it was unlikely his contract as editor would be renewed after it expired in November. When the Board appointed Ivan Greenberg editor in December, Epstein's power was broken. After vainly seeking Oppenheimer's support he resigned from the *Jewish Chronicle* on 10 December. In a bitter letter to the directors Epstein protested that the paper was being run as a two-family concern. He cited the removal of Jacobus Kann and the employment of Ruth and David Kessler as evidence that the aim of appointments was not one of serving the interests of the business, 'but one of providing employment for members of the Kessler family'. The prospect of appointing Ivan Greenberg to the editorial chair 'has the appearance of a reward to the Greenberg family for their complacency in the Kessler appointments'. Rich was dismissed only because 'he stood up to Mr Kessler's interference in the Editorial Department'.[45]

The crisis at the *Jewish Chronicle* had many strands. Mortimer Epstein and Leopold Kessler were at odds over the running of the paper. Epstein was chiefly a businessman. He saw it as a profit-making enterprise and wanted to increase the value of his shareholding. Kessler placed the accent more on the public-service function of the *Jewish Chronicle* to provide Anglo-Jewry with objective news and comment even at the cost of making less money. As an old friend of the Greenberg family he felt uncomfortable with the way that Ivan had been passed over for the editorship and was uneasy about the close ties between Rich and the communal leadership. Epstein and Rich were both keen Weizmann supporters: but Kessler, as a Herzlian, was strongly critical of the way Weizmann was directing the Zionist Movement.[46]

Leopold Kessler was convinced that the Kessler–Greenberg alliance would best guard the interests of the *Jewish Chronicle*, Anglo-Jewry and the Zionist Movement. For two years he had fought off a sustained challenge, but by 1937 he was able to relax and withdraw from day-to-day management of the paper. By his efforts he had ensured that the second generation of the group which purchased the paper thirty years ago would now be able to take over and run it on the lines intended by their forebears.

6   Ivan Greenberg and the crisis years, 1937–1946

The deluge begins, 1937–1939

Following his father's death Ivan Greenberg (1896–1966) had always felt that the editorship of the *Jewish Chronicle* was rightfully his. The boardroom upheaval during 1935 ultimately cleared the way for his appointment. The youngest son of Leopold Greenberg and his first wife, Marion Gates, Ivan was born and educated in London. During the First World War he served in the Royal Field Artillery and was wounded in action on the Western Front. After demobilisation he travelled widely as a journalist, working on newspapers in South Africa and Australasia. He joined the *Jewish Chronicle* staff as assistant editor in 1925. When he became editor, he was succeeded in his former post by John M. Shaftesley (1901–81), a Lancashire-born journalist who had worked for the *Manchester Guardian* and served as Manchester correspondent for the *Jewish Chronicle* before moving to the London office. Simon Gilbert continued as associate editor, writing the leading articles and 'In the Communal Armchair'.[1]

The business side of the paper was now in the hands of Alfred Brown Guthrie (1874–1959), a Scot, and David Kessler. Guthrie had transferred to the *Jewish Chronicle* from Greenberg's advertising agency and became successively advertising manager and general manager. Good humoured, hard working and wholly devoted to the welfare of the paper, he held this post until 1955.[2] David Kessler was born in Pretoria in 1906, while his father was in South Africa working as a consulting mining engineer. He was brought up and educated in England, and graduated from Cambridge with a degree in economics and law. After working for a shipping company in London and Paris he was recruited by Antonin Besse, an unconventional French businessman, to manage the shipping and oil departments of his Aden-based trading empire. After three years, Kessler returned to England via Palestine, where his elder brother was a farmer. Delighted by what he saw there, he accepted an offer to work for the Palestine Potash Company and lived in Jerusalem until he was summoned home in 1935.

The *Jewish Chronicle*'s editorial policy now shifted in several respects. Like his father, Ivan Greenberg believed passionately in political Zionism and admired Vladimir Jabotinsky. Under Ivan's influence the *Jewish Chronicle* returned to criticism of Weizmann, accusing the Zionist leadership of failing to adopt a resolute stance towards the British Government. Paradoxically, although he was never as involved in communal institutions as Rich had been, Greenberg took a generally favourable view of the Anglo-Jewish establishment. Throughout his years as editor he stoutly defended Neville Laski, the Board of Deputies and the Anglo-Jewish Association against their detractors. His sympathy for Laski was particularly surprising, since one cause of Laski's unpopularity was his barely veiled hostility to the Zionist Movement.

The other change of emphasis concerned Jewish defence, which continued to dominate home coverage. An editorial on New Year's Day 1937 announced that Anglo-Jewry had to reform itself if it was to defeat anti-Semitism. It was necessary to stamp out 'the materialism which is rampant among some of our people' and the 'vice of vulgar display'. Close on the heels of this editorial, the paper launched a campaign to expose 'sweating' in the London trades most closely associated with the Jews. Over the next six weeks, its special investigator, Maurice Goldsmith, made the round of Jewish workshops, exposing poor conditions of work and low rates of pay. The series caused an uproar at the Board of Deputies, where the *Jewish Chronicle* was accused of giving ammunition to anti-Semites.[3]

In fact, this approach was shared by many prominent Jewish figures, including Neville Laski. The series helped to establish as orthodoxy the argument that a good deal of anti-Semitism was related to the allegedly low ethical standards of Jewish businessmen. It also contributed to the formation of the Trades Advisory Council of the Board of Deputies (TAC) in 1938. As well as monitoring discrimination against Jews, the TAC investigated claims that Jewish entrepreneurs were engaged in unfair business practices and arbitrated between Jewish employers and their workers to avoid damaging publicity arising from disputes between non-Jewish workers and Jewish 'bosses'.[4]

Defence work remained important. As diplomatic tension between Britain and Germany increased, Mosley accused the Jews of wanting to push the country into a war to serve their interests. By exploiting the widespread anti-war feeling between the Munich crisis, in the summer of 1938, and the outbreak of war, in September 1939, he reinvigorated the BUF. There was also increasing opposition to the influx of Jewish refugees from Germany and Austria. Newspapers, spearheaded by the Beaverbrook press, suggested that Britain was being invaded by hordes of aliens who were snatching the jobs of British people. The *Jewish Chronicle* counter-attacked, with some effect. One chastened editor, Hugh Cudlipp of the *Sunday Pictorial*, felt obliged to account for his paper's claim that a 'Jewish Question' existed in England. Other newpapers took advertising space in the *Jewish Chronicle* to state that they had no intention of fostering 'anti-alien' sentiment.[5]

The revival of British Fascism and the hostility to Jewish refugees rekindled the divisive argument over Jewish defence work. On 29 April 1938, Gilbert approvingly quoted Josiah Wedgwood, MP, who had said: 'It must no longer be thought that anti-Semitism can be stopped by improving the Jews.' Yet, when it was suggested that Jews were disproportionately numbered among doctors, lawyers and accountants, the paper seriously considered whether 'It might be a good or a bad thing if Jews were to ration, if they could, their representation in the professions.' The proposition was treated with such gravity that in June 1939, the *Jewish Chronicle* joined with B'nai B'rith in the establishment of a career guidance service.[6]

The *Jewish Chronicle*'s warmth towards the communal hierarchy was almost without precedent since 1907. It grew out of the convergence of views between Greenberg and Laski, who both, for quite different reasons, disliked the Zionist Movement in Britain. Zionist activists were amongst Laski's chief antagonists inside the Board of Deputies. Since the Zionist Federation was pro-Weizmann, whereas Greenberg was anti-Weizmann, the *Jewish Chronicle* tended to support Laski in his clashes with the Zionist bloc. Laski and Greenberg also shared an antipathy to plans for the partition of Mandatory Palestine into a Jewish and an Arab state. Partition was recommended by the Royal Commission, under Earl Peel, which had been sent to Palestine in 1936 to inquire into the causes of the Arab revolt and propose remedies. Weizmann and his supporters in the ZF leaned towards accepting it, even though the Jews would only have been given a mini-state in a part of Palestine. Along with other maximalist Zionists, Greenberg saw this as a betrayal of the movement's goal of a Jewish state in all of Palestine. Laski disliked the idea of a Jewish state, whatever its size. However, to defeat the Peel Commission's proposal, in the short term he was prepared to co-operate with any of the forces arrayed against it.[7]

On 9 July 1937, the *Jewish Chronicle* dubbed the Royal Commision's partition plan a 'Nightmare Scheme'. This was a view shared by a substantial number of MPs, peers, a majority of the World Zionist Congress and a large part of the Zionist Movement in Britain. A leading article on 24 September was scathing towards Weizmann for favouring partition as the best of a bad job: 'Dr Weizmann, it would appear, is devotedly, almost fanatically, in love with the Partition policy. But Dr

Weizmann, despite his eminent labours in the Jewish cause, is not the Jewish people. Jews have not yet embraced the idolatrous principle of a sacrosanct leadership. If the Zionist leader is unalterably intent on Partition, then let him, in a patriotic spirit, stand aside and allow others to present the case for the Mandate.'[8]

Greenberg, egged on by David Kessler, printed a series of assaults on the plan. These included a specially written article by Winston Churchill, the author of the 1922 White Paper, for the Jewish New Year Issue. Space was provided for canvassing numerous alternatives, such as Jewish and Arab cantons within a unitary state or a Crown Colony. The paper carried few pro-partition statements other than reported speeches by Weizmann and his followers in England. It published only one article in favour of the Peel Report, by the Marchioness of Reading. Even this was prefaced by an editorial statement making clear that it appeared purely out of the obligation to be fair.[9]

Jewish public opinion was a not inconsiderable factor in the Cabinet's thinking on Palestine. One of Weizmann's supporters in the Jewish Agency, Henry Mond, second Lord Melchett, told him on the eve of the Cabinet's final debate on the plan, in December 1937, that the *Jewish Chronicle* was being used by opponents of partition inside the Government to show that it would be unpopular with Jewish voters.[10] In this way the paper contributed significantly to the defeat of partition.

In desperation, Weizmann summoned his loyalists to whip up support for Jewish statehood. The Zionist Federation accordingly passed a resolution in favour of a Jewish Dominion within the British Empire. The Zionist bloc then forced a parallel declaration through the Board of Deputies in the teeth of resistance from Laski and his friends. Proponents of partition warned that if they failed, the Government was likely to enforce minority status on the Jews of Palestine. But Greenberg contemptuously rejected this argument and mocked the Dominion Resolution. He was also highly indignant at the rude treatment meted out to the leaders of the Board by the Zionist deputies.[11]

In the wake of the vote, Lionel Cohen, a non-Zionist who was Laski's closest ally, resigned as a vice-president. In the election to replace him, the Zionist bloc put up Dr Israel Feldman, the chairman of the Board's Palestine Committee. Greenberg threw the paper behind the rival candidacy of Otto Schiff, a non-Zionist who opposed partition and was favoured by Laski. Statements that were openly pro-Schiff were printed in the editorial columns of the paper in a brazen display of partisanship. Despite this, Schiff lost. The result demonstrated graphically how far the influence of the *Jewish Chronicle* was limited on issues which sharply divided Anglo-Jewish opinion.[12]

The Zionist Federation could rely on the *Zionist Review*, which worked equally assiduously on behalf of Israel Feldman. In the course of the election and the entire debate over partition, the two journals clashed frequently. The *Zionist Review* accused the editorials in the *Jewish Chronicle* of flagrantly ignoring the facts in Palestine and especially resented the imputation that Weizmann had not tried to seek an accommodation with the Arabs. Notwithstanding this criticism, the *Jewish Chronicle* continued to publish a stream of anti-partition articles and produced a 'poll' of American rabbis intended to show that American Jewish opinion was opposed to partition.[13]

Leonard Stein was not at all happy with the way in which the paper was covering the partition story. He took his directorial responsibilities very seriously. Every Friday copies of the paper were sent to him at his rooms in the Temple, or wherever he was on holiday, and he made copious notes on the content which were then delivered to the editor. In February 1938 he told Leopold Kessler, who was in Cyprus on business, 'I cannot conceal from myself that I am not fully in sympathy with the present Editorial policy in relation to Palestine. This applies not only to the views expressed as matters of opinion, but also to the selection and presentation of news.' As a director of the paper and a legal adviser to the Jewish Agency, Stein felt that he was in a 'false position' and proposed to resign from the Board. Kessler persuaded him not to act precipitately and, after further discussion, Stein narrowed down his objections to the contributions by the diplomatic editor. These, he thought, should be couched 'in a more amiable and less aggressive tone'. Kessler told his son that Greenberg had 'entirely misjudged Jewish feeling about dealings with the B.[ritish] Government'. He agreed to intervene and spoke to Greenberg, in the name of the Board. He also asked his son to get in touch with the author of the offending items.[14]

This was only the first of several occasions when Greenberg's guidance of the paper in relation to Palestine affairs would be called into question, and it signified a new, dynamic relationship between the Board of Directors, the chairman and the editor. Stein expressed his displeasure again, in June 1938, after the diplomatic editor made a sharp attack on Sir John Shuckburgh, Deputy Under-Secretary at the Colonial Office. As a civil servant Shuckburgh could not reply to the comments in the report, and Stein protested that this was not only unfair, but potentially damaging to relations between the Zionists and Whitehall. Kessler, who agreed, arranged to meet the writer and 'impress upon him the desirability of adopting a more conciliatory style'.[15]

Nevertheless, editorial policy remained uncompromising. When the Government finally announced in November 1938 that it had abandoned partition, this was hailed as 'A Wise Decision'. The paper welcomed the subsequent proposal to bring Palestinian Jews and Arabs into direct negotiations, along with representatives of the Arab states. Judging from the optimistic editorial comments at this time, Greenberg appears to have misjudged seriously the Government's thinking behind the St James's Palace Conference, which convened in February 1939. In fact, faced by intransigence on both sides, the Cabinet had resolved to impose a solution on the warring parties in Palestine: limited Jewish immigration for five years followed by independence, which meant, in effect, an Arab state with a permanent Jewish minority.[16]

This démarche caused outrage amongst Zionists. In an editorial on 3 March 1939 entitled 'A Fantastic Compromise', the *Jewish Chronicle* berated the Government for 'tearing up the Balfour Declaration'. It asked: 'Is it conceivable that any British Government would take such a crassly stupid, let alone grossly immoral, step?' The paper could not believe that it would. The lobby correspondent cited a British MP who allegedly said 'If only Dr Weizmann had the courage to say "I will not accept this solution. I will fight first", the whole bubble would burst.' Yet the Jewish Agency leaders had done all that was in their power, given that they had little with which to bargain; it was Greenberg's stance that was unrealistic.

Leading articles persisted in reassuring readers that the British would never break their word and impose an unjust settlement on Palestine. By contrast, the reports of the paper's diplomatic correspondent brimmed with fury. As the international situation deteriorated and British resolve with respect to Germany stiffened, editorials continued to anticipate that the Government would bend less to Arab demands. The paper argued that now war was in the offing Britain needed a strong Jewish Palestine as an ally. Once again, editorial policy was based on a flawed evaluation of British intentions. Given the prospect of war, the Foreign Office reckoned that it was infinitely more important to maintain the friendship of the Arab states. The Jews of Palestine were a negligible factor by comparison and, anyway, were bound to support Britain in any conflict with Nazi Germany.[17]

The appearance of the White Paper on Palestine in May 1939 should have disillusioned anyone who still saw British policy towards the Jews as benign. Yet the *Jewish Chronicle*'s editorial on 19 May counselled 'there is no need to despair'. It confidently predicted that the Government's action in limiting Jewish immigration to 75,000 over the following five years, with the promise of self-determination for a state with an Arab majority, would underscore the 'unanswerable case' of the Jews. But with war clearly on the horizon, the White Paper was bulldozed through every obstacle in order to secure stability in Britain's Middle Eastern backyard.[18]

Frustration with the drift of British policy and anger at Arab attacks on Jewish settlements drove some Palestinian Jews to desperation. The *Yishuv* held to its official policy of self-restraint in the face of violent harassment, but from 1937 the Irgun, the military arm of the Revisionist Zionists, began to organise reprisal raids. *Havlagah*, or self-restraint, had won the praise and admiration of the *Jewish Chronicle*, which at first refused to believe that Jews could adopt other methods. However, by 1938 it took the operations of the Jewish military underground for granted and began to explain, if not to justify, them. A harshness entered the tone of editorial comment: if no one else would defend the Jews of Palestine, why shouldn't they be allowed to do it for themselves?[19]

This mood of defiance fed off the indignation which the British Government's Palestine policy, especially the restrictions on immigration, aroused in the Jewish world. Germany's annexation of Austria in March 1938 placed a further 200,000 Jews under Nazi control, and a wave of brutal persecution ensued. Bruno Heilig, the paper's Vienna correspondent, was one of hundreds of Jews imprisoned in Dachau. He was only released after the intervention of David Kessler. Tens of thousands of Jews struggled to get out of the country, joining the mass of German Jews already seeking a haven, but where could these refugees go?[20]

With unemployment and anti-alienism in the background, the *Jewish Chronicle* never suggested that Britain should serve as a destination for any mass migration: the obvious refuge was Palestine. Throughout 1938 and 1939, the paper reiterated the arguments for large-scale refugee immigration into the Jewish National Home, but the Foreign Office proved inflexible. Initiatives to secure other havens produced few results. The paper accurately caught the Jewish public's despondency when the international conference on the refugee crisis held at Evian in 1938 begat little more than words of sympathy.[21]

The *Jewish Chronicle* hoped that the flurry of diplomacy at the time of the Sudeten crisis in the summer of 1938 would benefit the Jews. It anticipated that the French and the British would resist Hitler's claims on Czechoslovakia and force him to back down. This would put them in a position to demand concessions from Germany, including better treatment of the Jews. The Munich agreement showed the paper's sanguine analysis and understandably belligerent prescriptions to have been sadly wide of the mark. While most of the British press greeted Chamberlain's promise of 'peace in our time' with relief and cared little for the fate of Czechoslovakia, the *Jewish Chronicle* despaired. But since the Mosleyites were quick to denounce as 'war-mongers' those who called for continued resistance to Hitler, the *Jewish Chronicle* toned down its dismay at the outcome of the Munich talks and bent over backwards to avoid sounding hawkish.[22]

In the wake of the Munich agreement, more Jewish refugees sought sanctuary in fewer and fewer countries. Worse was to come. The *Jewish Chronicle* issue of 11 November 1938 carried a leading note on the assassination of Ernst vom Rath, a German diplomat in Paris. He had been shot by Herschel Grynszpan, a Polish Jew whose parents had recently been expelled from Germany and were languishing, unwanted by Poland, in the no man's land between the German and Polish borders. On the front page, in a box headed 'Stop Press', was a terse communication announcing: 'Terror campaign against German Jews broke out yesterday.' This was *Kristallnacht*, a pogrom which more than anything else alerted world opinion to the fate of the Jews in Germany. The *Jewish Chronicle* gave a massive amount of space to reports and press commentary over the succeeding weeks. It was a source of information, a platform for lobbying politicians to allow freer Jewish immigration to Palestine and a vital adjunct to fundraising for aid agencies. At such a time of crisis, each issue was pounced upon by readers. The columns of anguished letters epitomised the paper's function as a safety-valve for their feelings as well as a channel for the energies of those who felt compelled to act in some way.[23]

The scale of the human tragedy precipitated by the Nazis was registered in the personal columns of the *Jewish Chronicle*. Each week dozens of short notices conveyed plaintive messages from Jews in central Europe desperately seeking someone in Britain who would offer them employment, usually as domestic servants, so that they could obtain visas to enter the country.[24] The paper recorded the plight of Jewish refugees leaving south-eastern Europe on small ships in a bid to reach Palestine. The fate of the 900 refugees on the SS *St Louis*, turned away from port after port, captured the imagination as a paradigm for Jewish suffering and the apparent indifference of the world. For those who wished to take an interest – members of the public, journalists, civil servants and Government ministers alike – the ghastly predicament of the Jews was set out comprehensively in its pages. Certain refugee campaigners such as the MPs Eleanor Rathbone and Josiah Wedgwood utilised these data, but otherwise few people outside the Jewish communities took much notice.[25]

The Second World War and the Holocaust

When the war started in September 1939, it was anticipated that London would be bombed, and carefully planned civil defence measures swung into operation. Hundreds of thousands of children and pregnant women were evacuated from the capital to 'safe zones' in the countryside. The *Jewish Chronicle* had also prepared. Under the guidance of David Kessler and Alfred Guthrie, the editorial, composing and circulation departments were moved to High Wycombe, Buckinghamshire, where they were crammed into the offices of the *Bucks Free Press* along with the *Catholic Herald*, the Church of England *Guardian* and the *Mutual Magazine*, published by the Christadelphians. Initially the staff were located in a hostel, but they gradually dispersed to private houses in which they could accommodate their families. Some continued to live in London and commuted to and from the city through the black out. The arrival of the *Jewish Chronicle* had a considerable impact on High Wycombe. The staff furnished a *minyan*, the quorum needed for a prayer service, and hired a Methodist church hall for services on the High Holy Days. It attracted other Jews evacuated to the town and Jewish servicemen stationed in the area. Before long the *Jewish Chronicle* office became the kernel of a flourishing, if displaced and mildly disorientated, Jewish community.[26]

With the Jewish New Year issue on 8 September 1939, the *Jewish Chronicle* underwent the first of many mutations necessitated by wartime conditions. The glossy front and back pages disappeared, and news was printed on the front page for the first time in many decades. Because of the need to conserve paper a number of features were eliminated, notably 'In the Communal Armchair'. Regular columns which continued throughout the war adapted to wartime needs. The 'Home Page' now dispensed information on recipes with rationing in mind, on how to make clothes last longer and on ways to keep up morale. One contributor advised women readers to dress simply, but to avoid appearing 'frumpish': it was important to remain elegant in order to keep the men's spirits high. 'Perfect poise is so important', she advised, 'to offset war strain.' In the course of the conflict, this page also covered the difficult issues of child-rearing in divided families and the problems of education in wartime.[27]

Wartime exigencies affected the content of the paper in other ways. From the start of hostilities, it reported the names and, where possible, gave photographs of Jewish servicemen and women. There was a particular stress on brothers and sisters in uniform. This was not just out of 'human interest'. Greenberg told his assistant editor, John Shaftesley, that he was concerned to counteract claims that not enough Jews were serving in the British Expeditionary Force.[28] Nor did censorship leave the *Jewish Chronicle* untouched. Reports sent from Palestine were frequently intercepted by the censor, while copies of the paper were prevented from reaching readers there. In keeping with Ministry of Information regulations to deny intelligence to the enemy, details of some of the worst disasters during the blitz and, later, the V-1 and V-2 rocket attacks were also suppressed.[29]

Advertising quickly reflected the new situation. During the 'Phoney War' in 1939–40, schools and boarding houses boasted of their location in 'safe zones' or highlighted their air-raid precautions. Some even featured photographs of their shelter accommodation. Kosher butchers anticipated rationing by urging their customers to register with them and avoid the difficulties remembered from the First World War. However, from late 1940, the number and size of advertisements shrank dramatically. Unlike the rest of the press, the *Jewish Chronicle* did not benefit greatly from the Government's public information drives. The personal notices and classified advertisements bulked larger and larger by comparison with the amount of display advertising. This signified the decline of economic activity and wartime shortages on the one hand, and the function of the *Jewish Chronicle* as a means of communication between isolated individuals and families on the other.[30]

The war had serious financial consequences for the paper. From September 1939 to July 1940, the amount of newsprint consumed weekly by the press was reduced by 60 per cent. The Paper Control Office then introduced limits on the number of pages permitted to newspapers. To make matters worse, evacuation greatly disrupted the distribution of the paper and hit circulation. Efforts to improve sales in evacuation areas during the autumn and winter of 1940 were unavailing. David Kessler also attributed the fall in circulation to the blitz, which left people tired and unable to concentrate on reading newspapers.[31]

Newspaper circulation was officially pegged for the first time in March 1941, and, thereafter, papers were allotted a ration of newsprint sufficient for this alone. In November 1941 the restrictions being applied to the *Jewish Chronicle* necessitated the suspension of casual sales; copies were only supplied to existing subscribers. In 1942 the print run was further limited on account of tighter paper rationing: it was now even difficult to meet established subscriptions. The *Jewish Chronicle* advised regular readers who had finished with their copy to 'pass it on' and send used copies to servicemen at home and abroad. Those who could get hold of the paper had to contend with minuscule type that was reduced in size with each successive cut in the paper ration. To cram more on to each page and to make reading easier, in July 1943 the format was changed from three to four columns per page. The thin, discoloured paper on which it was printed testified eloquently to the drabness of life on the Home Front.[32]

Hostilities greatly affected the staffing situation, too. David Kessler, the managing director, volunteered in the summer of 1940, joining several other members of staff who had been in the Territorial Army before 1939 and were already in uniform. Isidore 'Izzy' Bernstein, a staff member who remained with the paper, brought out a special 'JC Newsletter' for those who were in the forces.[33]

As the Germans overran Europe, *Jewish Chronicle* correspondents decamped hastily. The lucky ones escaped unscathed. Maurice Franks, the British Pro-Consul in Amsterdam and the paper's Dutch correspondent, fled with his wife and two children just ahead of the German army.[34] Others were less fortunate. William Blumberg, the Paris correspondent, originally from Russia, was amongst the foreign-born Jews rounded up in Paris in the summer of 1943 and sent to Drancy. From there he was deported to Auschwitz on 18 July 1943, and murdered along with thousands of other Jews transported from France. The family of Jacobus Kann in Holland was virtually wiped out. Jacobus and his wife were deported to Westerbok, thence to Barneveld and ended up in Theresienstadt. He died there in October 1944, followed by his wife in April the following year. Maurits Kann was involved in the Dutch underground, but was captured and died in a concentration camp, as did his two brothers.[35]

A similar fate would have overtaken those involved in the production of the *Jewish Chronicle* had the Nazis conquered Britain. After the war it was revealed that Ivan Greenberg and Simon Gilbert were amongst those on a blacklist, compiled in 1940 by the *Sicherheitsdienst*, the Nazi Security Police, to be arrested at the first opportunity. The paper was to be suppressed, the directors arrested and all records seized.[36]

As it was, the Germans did immense damage to the paper. On 13 December 1940, David Kessler wrote to Greenberg expressing concern for the safety of the rare back volumes of the *Jewish Chronicle* which on his orders had been placed in the strong-room in the basement of the offices at 49 Moor Lane, in the City. However, as the nightly bombing of London continued, he became worried that this was insufficient protection and suggested moving them to a country house. Greenberg replied on 19 December that probably only a specially built shelter would suffice, although he promised to make inquiries about a haven in the country. It was too late. The offices were destroyed by bombing during a heavy air raid on the night of 29 December 1940. Irreplaceable files containing correspondence, accounts, press cuttings, obituaries, photographs and all the other material that forms the cumulative memory of a newspaper, along with back issues from 1841, were burned. By the time David Kessler reached the scene the devastation was complete. He told Greenberg: 'there is nothing inflammable left. The volumes are nothing but ashes and the contents of the safes were cooked to ashes too.'[37]

The temporary base set up in Queen Victoria Street after this calamity was also hit in a raid on 11 May 1941. The fact that the *Jewish Chronicle* appeared without missing a single issue throughout the war years despite the bombing, paper shortages, loss of staff and other privations was a tribute to the ingenuity, determination and unflagging devotion of the entire staff. Indeed, in 1941, the employees actually took a pay cut in order to help the paper survive. More than once Michel Oppenheimer used his own capital to keep it going.[38]

The apotheosis of this period came with the centenary issue on 14 November 1941. The anniversary history of the *Jewish Chronicle* which had been commissioned before the war and entrusted to Cecil Roth had to be delayed, but the occasion was marked in as great a style as possible. On the front page were tributes from Winston Churchill, the Chief Rabbi and the Archbishop of Canterbury. There were also messages from Chaim Weizmann, General Charles de Gaulle, leader of the Free French, General Sikorski, head of the Polish Government-in-exile, and Ivan Maisky, the Russian Ambassador. Roth contributed a concise article on the paper's history and the changes in Anglo-Jewry over the century 1841–1941.[39]

During the war, the overall direction of the paper was in the hands of Michel Oppenheimer, the chairman of the Board of Directors, Leonard Stein, Alex Gumb and Neville Laski. At the outbreak of hostilities Leopold Kessler had travelled to New York, where he died in 1944. His son-in-law, Alex Gumb, sat on the Board in his stead, pro tem from July 1941 and then permanently after Leopold's death. Laski acted as the alternate for David Kessler from the start of 1940. The dynamic between the Board and the editor was significant. On home affairs, there was a substantial degree of harmony. Indeed, in its sympathetic commentary on controversies involving Laski and Stein between 1940 and 1945, it is hard not to suspect a degree of bias. But on matters concerning Palestine, a serious gap opened between the directors and the editor.[40]

In September 1939, Neville Laski faced another drive for constitutional reform of the Board of Deputies led by the Zionist group. Under the banner of democratisation, it demanded the creation of a broad, elected executive that would curtail the wide-ranging powers of the honorary officers. The war offered Laski and his allies a way of blunting these demands and simultaneously muzzling their critics among the deputies. On 12 September, at a meeting of prominent Anglo-Jews at New Court, headquarters of the Rothschild bank, Anthony de Rothschild proposed suspending the Board and replacing it with a wartime directorate. Laski presented this plan to the next Board meeting, but it was vigorously opposed and he was forced to drop it. Instead, the proposal for an enlarged and democratic executive remained in place.[41]

Laski turned to Greenberg for help. He wrote to him on 7 November explaining how the Zionist activists from London, orchestrated by Lavy

Bakstansky, the general secretary of the Zionist Federation, dominated the Board's proceedings and left him virtually their prisoner. In his letter he gave statistics which detailed the attendances of deputies, but added: 'I should be glad if you will treat this matter as confidential for the moment, and not even print as yet the analyses of the meetings of the Board as I may need to use them at the next meeting, and if they are printed beforehand there may be thought to be some sort of collusion.'[42] In fact, the material from Laski's letter appeared, almost verbatim, in the *Jewish Chronicle*'s leading article on 17 November, on the eve of the Board's monthly meeting. Repeating Laski's desperate plea the editorial warned that, because of apathy, 'the Board at its depleted meetings takes on, more and more, the appearance of a Zionist Committee rather than an organisation whose primary *raison d'être* is the Anglo-Jewish interests as such'. And it echoed the President's warning that the Zionists comprised 'a group out to capture the Board and make it first and foremost another subsidiary instrument of Zionist purpose ... a servant of the Zionist Organisation'.[43]

However, at the Board's next meeting Laski announced out of the blue that he was resigning as President. The news would have come as less of a surprise to Greenberg; Laski had informed him in the letter of 7 November that his professional, and financial, situation was in jeopardy through his concentration on communal business. The way was now open for a presidential contest, and it was soon clear that Professor Selig Brodetsky, a leading figure in the Zionist Movement, was going to stand in the name of democratisation and, implicitly, the Zionist cause.[44]

As in the vice-presidential contest in 1938, the paper's editorial comment was singularly partisan. Brodetsky, who was Laski's *bête noire*, was peremptorily ruled out as being too busy with other matters. When it was evident that no other leading figure in Anglo-Jewry had the stomach for a fight, the paper actually suggested postponing the election until a more suitable candidate could be found. But, despite the opposition of the *Jewish Chronicle* and the antagonism of powerful interests in Anglo-Jewry, Brodetsky won the contest.[45]

The broader coverage of Jewish life on the Home Front in 1939–40 was heavily preoccupied with the persistence of anti-Semitism. Irrespective of the declaration of hostilities, Mosley and the BUF continued to campaign on an anti-war platform and fought three by-elections during 1940. The *Jewish Chronicle* reported that his followers made free use of anti-Semitism in their propaganda and disclosed cases in which Fascists in the armed forces and civil defence made life difficult for Jews.[46] The role attributed to the Fifth Columnists in the Nazi conquest of Norway, Belgium, Holland and France provided the paper with a powerful weapon against anti-Semitic agitators whom it tarred (not always correctly) with Fascist and pro-German sympathies. 'Scratch an antisemite', it declared on 12 April 1940, 'and you will find a conscious or unconscious Hitler agent.' Having implored the Government to suppress the British Fascists, it was gratified by the Emergency Powers Act, passed in May 1940, which enabled the Government to gaol Mosley, his wife and other BUF figures along with suspected pro-Nazis.[47]

However, the fall of France in May 1940, the evacuation from Dunkirk and the threat of imminent invasion were also responsible for the imposition of drastic measures against 'enemy aliens' in Britain. Although the Government was determined to avoid the mistakes of 1914–18 and a rush into mass internment, press agitation and scare stories in May–June made it harder to stick with this policy. By stages, the Government was stampeded into interning 27,000 'enemy aliens' of all categories, the bulk of them German and Austrian Jewish refugees.[48]

The *Jewish Chronicle* expressed 'little surprise' at the first wave of detentions and considered it a sound measure. When the net widened, it thought this should be 'cheerfully accepted'. By the end of May, 'Category C' aliens, who included the bulk of Jewish refugees, were suffering from unofficial discrimination and official uncertainty. The paper then recommended internment or, preferably, transferring them overseas to end the tension. In fact, on 11 June 1940 the mass internment of all enemy aliens had already been ordered.[49]

Internment and deportation proceeded virtually without opposition until the SS *Arandora Star*, carrying internees to Canada, was torpedoed and sunk with heavy loss of life on the morning of 2 July 1940. The *Manchester Guardian*, the *Daily Herald* and Eleanor Rathbone, MP now bitterly criticised the policy. By the end of July a chastened Government had already set changes in motion that would lead to the release of nearly 10,000 internees before the end of 1940. The *Jewish Chronicle* was curiously reticent. A new Jewish paper, *The Jewish Standard* (1940–9), published in London by the Zionist Revisionists and edited by Abraham Abrahams, launched editorial attacks on internment in its issues of 5 July and 12 July; but the *Jewish Chronicle* refrained from comment in its leader columns until 19 July.[50]

Greenberg and Gilbert waited until the counter-campaign had already gathered force and they could express support for leading non-Jewish figures, rather than engaging in what might appear to be special pleading as Jews. Only then, on 19 July 1940, did the *Jewish Chronicle* make a powerful statement: 'At the beginning of the war, British sanity and humanity took a wise and kindly course. Later this policy began to be whittled away. There came cruel, indiscriminate and wasteful round-ups of men whose *bona-fides* had been scrutinised again and again and who had always been vindicated.' From this date, the paper added its authoritative voice to the parliamentarians and journalists who denounced the 'internment scandal'.[51]

Anti-Semitism in Britain was not curbed by the internment of key Fascist personalities. In the midst of the blitz, newspapers printed stories hinting that alleged Jewish cowardice lay behind the clamour to open underground tube stations for use as shelters. Following claims that Fascists were disseminating anti-Jewish propaganda in air-raid shelters and tube stations, the *Jewish Chronicle* detailed a special correspondent to report on the situation. His findings revealed that, while some shelters had committees that worked to eliminate discrimination and discouraged prejudice, in others racism was openly displayed. The paper adverted to the many examples of courageous behaviour by Jews serving as air-raid wardens or on shelter committees as the soundest reply to anti-Semitism. But it also demanded that better facilities should be provided in the shelters.[52]

The durability of anti-Jewish feeling made itself apparent in the widespread identification of Jews with the black market. By the middle of 1942, the intensity of anti-Semitism had grown so worrying that the paper demanded action by the Government. It campaigned for legislation against community libel, arguing in its support that anti-Semitism facilitated pro-Nazi propaganda and was defeatist.[53]

Editorial comment in 1942–3 was often dominated by events on the Home Front or Zionism and Palestine, rather than news from occupied Europe. Domestic anti-Semitism was perceived as a real danger by Jews in Britain, haunted as they were by the speed of the disaster which overtook the Jewish populations in Europe. At the same time, it was tempting to inveigh against anti-Semitism at home. This was an enemy which Anglo-Jewry could battle with directly, while the truly evil exponents of anti-Semitic policy were beyond its reach. In similar vein, if British Jews could do little to aid Jews under Nazi control, they could help those who succeeded in escaping by demanding that they be granted refuge in Palestine. The deep anxiety aroused by the critical position of Jews across the English Channel was refracted through the extensive discussion of the Palestine Question.

Forthright statements on the treatment of European Jewry appeared gradually and were sparing in proportion to the unfolding disaster. This pattern may be accounted for in several ways. The confusing and ambiguous nature of the information from the occupied countries all contributed to demoting the place assigned to it in the paper. To print unverified reports would have exposed it to accusations of irresponsibility, scare-mongering and spreading 'atrocity stories'. In addition to their own professional scepticism, the editorial staff were compelled to look over their shoulders at the watchful eye of Government. At the outbreak of war, the Ministry of Information instructed that reports of Jewish suffering should be played down in propaganda, since anything that fostered sympathy for Jewish refugees attempting to reach Palestine was frowned upon. 'Atrocity stories' were deemed counter-productive in view of the disillusionment following their use during the First World War.[54]

Even when the evidence was clear, the response of British Jews to the persecution of the Jews in Europe was muted and oblique. At a time of national crisis and generalised suffering, accompanied by a high level of anti-Semitism, it was considered impolitic to focus on the plight of their co-religionists. In consequence, the Jewish communal organisations avoided public protests and noisy demands for rescue measures. When aid for European Jewry was raised, it was overwhelmingly in the context of immigration to Palestine, and was soon caught up in the complexities of the Government's Middle Eastern policy and the conflicts surrounding Zionism. The *Jewish Chronicle* was part of this consensus.[55]

Initially, the quantity and quality of data that reached Britain concerning the Jews in Nazi Europe were remarkably good. Throughout the first year of the occupation of Poland, the *Jewish Chronicle* managed to obtain precise information on the situation of Jews in Warsaw and other Polish ghettos. Much of this news came via Lithuania, until it was occupied by the Red Army in July 1940. The *Jewish Chronicle* also made use of Swedish newspapers, a source that gained in value after the Baltic states were annexed by Russia. The Polish Government-in-exile in London, which included Jewish representatives, supplied the British press with material from its underground network in Poland.

By these means, the *Jewish Chronicle* followed the consolidation of Germany's grip on Poland and the Nazi plan to establish a new Pale of Settlement around Lublin. Reports of massacres and killings were accepted as routine occurrences and were carried deep inside the paper, rarely meriting editorial comment. One front-page article on 1 December 1939 spoke of a 'campaign of extermination of the Jews'. It was followed by another, two weeks later, headlined 'Mass Murder in Poland', which appeared on page 15. The first such front-page story in 1940, which claimed that there were 200 executions in Poland every day, passed without editorial embellishment. A few weeks later on 26 January a report that 1,900 Jews were massacred at Chelm merited an editorial note. There was apparently an ambivalence towards constantly leading with stories about Jewish suffering. Yet these early reports of large-scale killings may actually have desensitised the editorial staff, and readers, to later accounts of events that were actually more far-reaching and awful.

The paper was able to construct a highly textured picture of the overcrowding, malnourishment and disease that began to afflict the Polish ghettos from the winter of 1940–1 onwards. Much of the response centred on speculation about the future of the Jews in post-war Poland. It was also tied to fundraising appeals for immediate relief work. Yet editorial concern was at a considerably lower level than at the time of comparable crises in 1919–20, 1933 or 1938–9. At the height of the blitz, the *Jewish Chronicle* faced emergencies closer to home that required an editorial opinion. It was a moment when the whole of the British population was under bombardment and civilian casualties were very heavy. The reticence concerning Polish Jewish affairs can be understood as a tactical silence to avoid giving the impression that the paper was only concerned with the fate of the Jews.[56]

As the war spread, the paper chronicled the misfortunes of the Jews in France, Holland, and the Balkans and those in the Baltic states who fell under Soviet rule. Again, information was relatively abundant.[57] However, the opportunities for reportage and analysis were drastically curtailed with the start of 'Operation Barbarossa', the German invasion of Russia in June 1941. Swedish newspapers continued to provide some information on the ghettos of Poland and the Baltic states; Turkish reports gave an inkling of developments along the Black Sea coast of Bessarabia and Moldavia; but like the rest of the press the *Jewish Chronicle* obtained little solid intelligence about the activity of the *Einsatzgruppen*, the mobile killing units. It was consequently unable to appreciate the scale of the disaster that overtook the Jews of the Baltic states, White Russia and the Ukraine.[58]

At just the moment when the application of the Nazis' genocidal policy towards the Jews was being crystallised and implemented, the supply of news dried up. The Soviet authorities, previously silent on Jewish matters, adjusted to the new geo-political constellation and issued press statements about the oppression of Jews in Nazi-controlled Poland and western Russia. But until the recapture of areas in which the killing units had operated, it could only obtain fragmented data from partisans and escaped prisoners. *Jewish Chronicle* readers were furnished with particles of information that had no self-evident connection. There were, for instance, detailed reports on the role of quislings and collaborators in the former Baltic states and the Ukraine. The paper obtained lucid accounts of new ghettos being set up. Side by side with this, but with no obvious relationship, there was news of massive human destruction.[59]

The natural tendency was to make sense of the atrocities by placing them in a framework derived from the Jewish historical experience. In its retrospective for the Jewish year on 19 September 1941, the paper spoke of a 'policy of crude persecution' against Jews in Germany and Austria and commented that: 'The alternatives seem to have been extermination or expulsion to the hopeless, starving, disease-infected Lublin Ghetto.' In the occupied territories, it detected only a poor response to Nazi anti-Semitic incitement. There could, as yet, be no inkling of a systematic plan of extermination.

For the first months of the German onslaught against Russia, the *Jewish Chronicle* supplied evidence of carnage on a huge scale, but in common with other news agencies could not conceptualise the scope or organised methods of the *Einsatzgruppen*. The paper's difficulties in getting hold of, and evaluating, news are exemplified by a story, culled from *Pravda*, on 17 October 1941. This reported that Jews in Kiev were being forced to wear distinctive armbands; yet, unbeknownst to the editorial staff, two weeks earlier 30,000 of Kiev's Jews had actually been massacred at Babi Yar.

The level of editorial comment during late 1941 remained modest in proportion to the reports carried by the paper. The problem of sifting rumour and contradictory fragments of information explains some of this editorial hesitation. In addition the *Jewish Chronicle* was under intense pressure not to appear solely concerned with the plight of Jews. Despite the entry of the USA into the war in December 1941, the Allies continued to suffer military reversals. The most intensive phase of the German extermination programme coincided with the nadir of the Allies' military fortunes. Confusion and caution both played a part in restraining its comment on stories trickling out of occupied Europe.

For example, on 24 October 1941, a front-page item headed 'Ghastly Pogroms in the Ukraine' described thousands of corpses in the Dniester River. It also cited reports by Hungarian officers on leave from the Russian Front to the effect that 15,000 Galician and 8,000 Baltic Jews had been murdered. This report was not the subject of editorial comment, possibly because it was unsubstantiated. However, the following week, a leading article was devoted to the killing of hundreds of non-Jews in retaliation for the assassination of two German military personnel. The same pattern was repeated in November and December. At the start of November, the *Jewish Chronicle* simply reported that one-third of Bessarabian Jewry had been 'exterminated'. A few weeks later, on 19 December, there was an editorial about a hundred Frenchmen being held hostage after the killing of a German soldier.[60]

There was no leading article explicitly about the news of the massacres until 28 November 1941, when a letter from a distraught reader triggered an editorial. Adverting to the previous week's report that 25,000 Romanian Jews had been killed, Jacob Sarna, an inveterate correspondent, wrote: 'One is staggered by the utter apathy with which this ghastly and unprecedented destruction of Jewish life has been received by the public, both Jewish and non-Jewish.' The editorial response gives some indication of the reasons behind the oscillating character of the *Jewish Chronicle*'s commentary. 'It is not that Britons, who have fed daily on horrors in these last two terrible years, have grown inured to them, and become less humane than their fathers, but that they have come to the conviction that torture and murder must continue so long as the foul Nazi system endures and have determined to devote every ounce of energy and treasure they possess to extirpate it.' The horror aroused by the catastrophe engulfing the Jews was subordinated to the larger cause of winning the war. This was not an atypical reaction: on the contrary, it was Sarna's letter that was an isolated expression of outrage and grief. The *Jewish Chronicle*'s tempered language and intermittent, explicit attention were characteristic of a general tendency in Anglo-Jewry at the time.[61]

From the autumn of 1941, Jews were being deported from central Europe to the Lublin area in the first stages of the pan-European scheme of annihilation. The first mass murder of Jews by gas occurred at Chelmno in December 1941. Purpose-built killing centres with fixed gas chambers were established at Belzec in March 1942, followed by others at Sobibor, Treblinka, Birkenau (part of the Auschwitz complex) and Majdanek. The transportation of Jews from Poland to the death camps began in March and was extended to western and central Europe in the summer.[62]

Yet the full dimensions of the 'Final Solution' emerged only slowly and unevenly. On 7 November 1941, the *Jewish Chronicle* documented the deportation of German Jews to Poland and the following week announced that the Germans had banned further Jewish emigration from Europe. On 16 January 1942, it noted that the Polish Government-in-exile had published a report that 80,000 Poles had died since the war started. In the same issue it disclosed that, Molotov, the Soviet Foreign Minister, had demanded retribution for Nazi war crimes, including the murder of 52,000 Jews in Kiev. At the start of February 1942, the *Jewish Chronicle* publicised rumours that 18,000 Jews had died in Poltava and a month later carried a report, emanating from Russian partisans, that 15,000 Jews had been killed at Borisov. On 10 April 1942, a small article on the front page gave the news that 1,200 Jews had been deported to Mauthausen concentration camp and some killed by 'poison gas' in an experiment. This was the first hint of mass murder by gassing. A Soviet statement printed on 1 May reported that 13,000 Jews had been killed in Lvov.[63]

Although the paper aired the question of punishment for war crimes in a leaderette on 16 January 1942, editorials from then until July focused on domestic issues such as religious education and defence against anti-Semitism at home. The true enormity of what was happening was known only to the murderers, and any connection between the disparate, terrible stories which leaked out eluded commentators in the free world. Indeed, the *Jewish Chronicle* was the only newspaper to deem the story about the use of deadly gas at Mauthausen worth printing.[64]

Of course, the reports were no less horrifying for appearing random, and it is striking that the level of editorial animation was lower than at the time of *Kristallnacht*, for example. However, the pressure on the paper to avoid special pleading had not diminished. In the summer of 1942, German armies were pushing into Egypt towards the Suez Canal, and thrusting towards the oilfields in the Caucasus. Nor were there grounds for suspecting an overarching structure of annihilation. News was interpreted according to the pattern familiar from Jewish history, namely ghettoisation and pogrom violence, which, ultimately, the mass of Jews would survive.

On 19 June 1942, the *Jewish Chronicle* announced in bold type on the front page: 'News is filtering through of recent ghastly massacres of Jews in Nazi Europe. Some 85,000 men, women, and children are mentioned in the reports to hand.' The story, which came via Stockholm, concerned only massacres in Lithuania. Then, on 3 July 1942, in a page 1 article headlined 'Mass Murder in Poland ... Nazis' Bestial Extermination Plan', the number of Jews exterminated leapt to 700,000. This information was provided by Shmuel Zygielbojm, a member of the Polish National Council in London, to whom it had been transmitted by the Polish underground. Zygielbojm, who was concerned that the report should not appear initially in a Jewish paper, had actually fed the material to the *Daily Telegraph*, which broke the story on 25 and 30 June. For the first time a British newspaper referred to the use of gas in a daily process of mass killing and named Chelmno as one of the sites.[65]

Zygielbojm knew his report would face a credibility problem, which accounted for his determination that it should first appear in the non-Jewish press. Even the *Jewish Chronicle* stressed that the substance of the story had been checked against other sources. Its editorial on the communiqué, on 3 July 1942, exemplified the dilemmas of dealing with news that beggared belief: 'The hideous details now coming to hand of the wholesale butchery by the Germans of Jewish men, women, and children in Poland and Lithuania read like tales from the imagination of some drug-maddened creature seeking to portray a nightmare of hell. The average mind simply cannot believe the reality of such sickening revelations, or that men, even the vilest and most bestial, could be found to perpetrate such disgusting orgies of sadistic mania.' The writer admonished readers against the temptation to discard the story as fantastic or exaggerated, if only as a defence mechanism: 'unhappily there is only too much ground for the belief that even now the whole story has not been told'.

Groping for a response, the editorial fastened on domestic themes and

Palestine. It drew the moral that extermination was the terminus of Fascism and anti-Semitism if they were not stoutly resisted. It also demanded the creation of a Jewish army as 'one immediate consolation' and suggested that Jews beseech the churches to take some action. The *Jewish Chronicle* reflected the agony and bewilderment of Anglo-Jewry when confronted by the horror of events in Europe, but without the power to make a meaningful intervention. Hamstrung by anti-Semitism on the Home Front and afraid of drawing attention to Jewish suffering at a time of war when the entire country was in danger, the Jewish leadership lacked the freedom of manoeuvre or the confidence to risk a sustained, public agitation.[66]

In May and June 1942, the *Jewish Chronicle* had carried reports that Jews in Holland, France and Belgium were being forced to wear the yellow badge, the precursor to deportation. During July, August and September a picture emerged of Europe-wide transportations 'to the East'. There were front-page accounts of round-ups in Warsaw, Vienna, Holland, Paris, Slovakia and Belgium. On 21 August the paper printed a comprehensive report of operations involving gas vans at Chelmno, derived from Jews who had escaped. It also carried news of the suicide of Adam Czerniakow, the leader of the Warsaw Ghetto Jewish Council, which had occurred four weeks earlier.

Despite the volume of intelligence concerning Nazi action against the Jews across the Continent, the leading articles were mainly preoccupied with local matters, notably disputes about the Trades Advisory Council and its role in fighting anti-Semitism at home. It was not until 28 August 1942 that an editorial, occasioned by the day of prayer which the Chief Rabbi, Dr Hertz, had ordained a month earlier, focused on the awful trend of events. Accounts of the seizure of Jews in Vichy elicited only a general editorial note on 16 October; the main leader concerned the 450th anniversary of the discovery of America. A protest meeting at the Royal Albert Hall was relegated to the inside pages in the issue of 6 November, while the main leader dealt with the twenty-fifth anniversary of the Balfour Declaration. Three weeks later the paper reported that, according to the Polish Government-in-exile, 250,000 Polish Jews had died in the last six months at Sobibor, Treblinka and Belzec, and that a plan existed to kill half of Polish Jewry by the end of the year. It was discussed in the third leaderette, in the context of dealing with war crimes.

The editorial staff at the *Jewish Chronicle* faced a problem: there was simply a limit to what the readership would tolerate. This was both because the news was so ghastly and also because Jews had internalised the ethos of sacrificing self-interest and allegedly narrow concerns to the greater cause of the nation's survival.[67]

Jewish protests and pleas for Allied intervention gained momentum from the summer of 1942, after reliable and comprehensive information delineating the 'Final Solution' reached Jewish organisations in the free world. The *Jewish Chronicle* assisted this clamour with a black-bordered issue on 11 December headlined: 'Two Million Jews Slaughtered. Most Terrible Massacre of All Time'. The content of the leading article suggests that the paper's earlier coverage of Nazi atrocities had been constrained as much by what readers would tolerate, or believe, as anything else. It asserted that 'Week after week ... this paper has striven to awaken the public mind to the facts of the Jew-extermination being carried on by the Nazi monsters in Europe. Again and again it has cried aloud that the oft-repeated Nazi threat of Jewish annihilation was seriously intended.' But this 'was regarded in some quarters as sickening iteration'. Many Jews could not believe it, and several 'complained that they could no longer read the *Jewish Chronicle* because the facts it recorded so harrowed the feelings'. Now it was vindicated and it was time to impress the truth on the British public, to demand retribution against the guilty and to seek the rescue of as many Jews as possible.[68]

In December lobbying by Jewish representatives and a public outcry at the published reports led the Allied Governments to issue a joint declaration deploring German conduct. In Britain the storm of indignation culminated in a statement by Anthony Eden, the Foreign Secretary, in the House of Commons on 17 December 1942, followed by a minute of silence during which MPs stood with bowed heads. Over subsequent weeks, the paper reported the expressions of outrage that swept the Allied powers and Jewish communities in the free world. It welcomed the declaration of the United Nations that war crimes would be punished.[69]

Yet, in the course of 1943, the sense of urgency tailed off. This was not due to any interruption to the flow of information. On the contrary, Anglo-Jewry was able to follow the Warsaw Ghetto uprising blow by blow. The paper obtained accurate data on the decimation of the Jewish populations in Belgium, Holland, Vilna and Salonika. Readers learned the approximate meaning of Treblinka, Sobibor, Belzec and Auschwitz, although the latter was never clearly perceived as the nodal point of the extermination programme. There were reports describing the gas chambers, the crematoria and the 'medical' experiments in the death camps.[70]

At home, communal life went on. Throughout the first part of 1943, and even at the height of the Warsaw Ghetto uprising, the *Jewish Chronicle*'s leading articles dealt predominantly with controversies at the Board of Deputies and the development of Jews' College. In despair at the general apathy, Zygielbojm committed suicide. He left a note explaining that by his death he hoped to draw notice to the destruction of the Jews. The *Jewish*

Chronicle carried an obituary, but like the rest of the press did not mention that he took his own life as a deliberate gesture of protest.[71]

Comment on the murder of Europe's Jews became entangled with discussion of rescue projects, the role of Palestine and the creation of a Jewish army. The protest movements and lobbying efforts by Jewish agencies in Britain and the USA found themselves up against a wall of governmental indifference or tergiversation. *Jewish Chronicle* editorials mirrored the fragmented Jewish response, the in-fighting between various groups and the absence of an overall strategy. Above all, they faithfully expressed the conviction of Zionists that the most relevant steps would be increased immigration to Palestine and the formation of a Jewish fighting force.[72]

Anguish over the destruction of European Jewry undergirded the paper's frequent, angry commentaries on the niggardly response by governments in the free world when asked to provide sanctuary for refugees. In January–February it voiced astonishment at Britain's refusal to allow 5,000 children to enter Palestine. The Bermuda Conference on refugees, called into being by Britain and America in response to the public outcry in December 1942, was essentially a public relations exercise. The leading powers had no desire, or intention, to save large numbers of Jews from Europe by allowing them into Britain, America or Palestine. The *Jewish Chronicle* observed wearily on 23 April 1943 that 'Even the most irrepressible optimists can scarcely fail to experience a rapid chilling of their hopes for the future of refugees of all kinds as they read the reports of the Bermuda Conference.' When it was over, on 7 May, the paper lamented: 'And so the greatest tragedy in modern history must go on.'[73] The editorial on 3 September 1943 marking the fourth anniversary of the war reflected that sympathy for the 'Jewish martyrdom' was rarely translated into positive action. 'Some have detected even a note of impatience with the pleas pressed by the Jews', a phrase which alluded without much attempt at concealment to bureaucratic sclerosis and prejudice.[74]

Ivan Greenberg channelled his rage into demands for a Jewish army and the opening of Palestine to Jewish immigrants. During this period he was becoming ever more deeply involved in Revisionist Zionist politics and was actually writing leaders for the *Jewish Standard*, which took a far more shrill approach to these issues. He imported a Revisionist perspective into the *Jewish Chronicle*, too. Editorials on the need for a Jewish fighting unit appeared with increasing frequency, as did articles with an aggressive Zionist edge to them. The slogan 'Palestine or Extinction' summed up their tone and content.[75]

As the Russians liberated the Ukraine and White Russia and then swept on into the Balkans and eastern Poland, hard facts about the 'Final Solution' began to accumulate. The murder of Jews, however, went on. In March 1944, the Germans occupied Hungary and began to deport its Jewish population. This was known in Britain virtually as it was taking place, and Jewish leaders engaged in another flurry of deputations, demanding emergency measures such as the bombing of the rail link between Budapest and Auschwitz. Shocked by the lackadaisical reaction of the Allied Governments and public, the *Jewish Chronicle* proclaimed starkly on 30 June 1944: 'Slaughter Passes Unnoticed.' It struggled to comprehend how the spectacle of Hungarian Jewry being transported to the gas chambers before the eyes of the world could be allowed to pass without any intervention: 'Few cries of indignation are heard in this country, perhaps because the chords of human sympathy have been dulled or atrophied by sheer over-use – one of the sinister by-products of the orgy of German official murders. Perhaps, too, the imaginations of really kindly and civilised men boggle at these accounts of wholesale and systematic human slaughter. One can understand this reaction, but not justify it.' The paper's suggestions that reprisals be threatened, or that German citizens should be seized as hostages to protect Jews, were in vain.[76]

On 24 July 1944 the Red Army captured Majdanek death camp virtually intact. For the first time, newsreels and photographs of crematoria and the skeletons of dead Jews appeared in British cinemas and newspapers. The *Jewish Chronicle* took advantage of this incontrovertible evidence to reiterate that it was no longer feasible to hide from, or deny, the truth. But not everyone shared these feelings. *The Times* asked if was really necessary to show newsreels of Majdanek in its full horror. Although the *Illustrated London News* printed photographs of the crematoria, it added an apologetic commentary on the perils of 'atrocity propaganda' and barely mentioned the fact that most of the victims were Jews. This 'squeamishness' earned the *Jewish Chronicle*'s scorn: unless the world faced up to the horrors of the death camps, it would learn nothing. To underline this point, the paper regularly demanded action by the War Crimes Commission to exact condign punishment and ensure that Nazism could never revive.[77]

The press was shocked and sickened by what was finally revealed with the liberation of the concentration camps in western Germany. But the response was fleeting, even ambivalent. Much of the coverage was tinged by 'squeamishness'. For example, the *Illustrated London News* placed photographs of Bergen-Belsen in a special detachable supplement 'intended for our adult readers only'. The specific intent behind the 'Final Solution' was blurred by the fact that the British, French and Americans liberated camps in which the Jews formed only a proportion of the inmates.

The extermination centres in the East, whose victims had been solely Jews, remained shrouded in mystery.[78]

Certain journalists and politicians grappled with the gigantic scale of the disaster and paused for introspection. For a short while, the *Jewish Chronicle* was no longer isolated when it insisted that the persecution of the Jews was a central feature of Nazi rule. The parliamentarians who visited Buchenwald in April 1945 gave a harrowing account of what they had seen. Hannan Swaffer, who wrote for the *People*, asked how it had been possible to ignore the weekly reports in the Jewish press. The *Spectator* declared that the worst of fears were now confirmed. But an editorial in the *Jewish Chronicle* on 27 April asked bitterly 'Why have we had to wait till now for this widespread revulsion?' Even then, the end of the war against Japan induced a degree of relativism which it found obnoxious. In August it inquired why there was there such an emotional debate over the use of the atomic bombs at Hiroshima and Nagasaki, against an enemy population, when the slaughter of the Jews, who were innocent of any crime, had been allowed to proceed in virtual silence.[79]

All through the war the paper had commented on the evolution of strategy, the major battles and the political developments at home and in other Allied countries. In the darkest hours of the winter of 1940–1, it hailed President Roosevelt's 'Four Freedoms' and at the end of 1942 welcomed the Beveridge Report which laid the foundations for the welfare state. On the occasion of the meeting between Roosevelt and Churchill at Casablanca, in January 1943, it praised the policy of unconditional surrender and declared that the war was now being prosecuted with a view to scourging Nazism and anti-Semitism from the world. The liberation of Rome and D-Day received full, front-page coverage; the tone of excitement was at one with the sense of wonder and pride that infused the whole press. The paper also cultivated support for Soviet Russia and published reports on the activities of the Jewish anti-Fascist Committee. Yet pride in the achievement of Allied arms and joy at the coming of final victory were tinged with melancholy at the Jewish tragedy and alarm at the eruption of conflict in Palestine. The ending of the war enjoined relief, but also nervousness: what was to become of Anglo-Jewry after the destruction of the great reservoirs of Jewish population, learning and culture in eastern Europe?[80]

Furthermore, to the consternation of the *Jewish Chronicle*, anti-Semitism was not discredited. In May 1945, several Conservative MPs began questioning the Home Secretary when refugees in England would be repatriated. They were echoed in the press, while in the London borough of Hampstead a petition was circulated blaming refugees for the housing shortage. Nor was Britain's restrictive immigration policy substantially altered in favour of Jewish Displaced Persons (DPs) and concentration camp survivors. On 8 March 1946, the paper observed that 'One of the most astonishing phenomena of the times is that the martyrdom of the Jewish people, instead of being followed by universal sympathy and reparation, has begotten only a new spate of anti-Jewish feeling.'[81]

The immediate impact of the attempted genocide of the Jews was undeniable, but it paled quickly. The *Jewish Chronicle*, embattled in the struggle for Palestine, barely had time to dwell on the catastrophe. The volume of stories related to the Holocaust diminished during the latter part of 1945, and almost disappeared in the following year. Instead, the torment of the Jews formed a mute backdrop to the events unfolding in Palestine.

The *Jewish Chronicle* and the struggle for Palestine, 1937–1948

Ivan Greenberg had always admired Jabotinsky's fiery brand of Jewish nationalism, but the fate of the Jews during the war radicalised his outlook still further and pushed him beyond mere sympathy with Revisionism. His close ties with activists in the Revisionist Movement in Great Britain eventually compromised his editorial independence. They gave him suggestions about the editorial content of the *Jewish Chronicle*, and Greenberg himself started writing leaders for the rival Revisionist *Jewish Standard*.[82] He also became involved with a group of young Palestinians associated with the Irgun, the military wing of the Revisionists, who were agitating for the creation of a Jewish army. The *Jewish Chronicle* became one of their strongest allies. Greenberg's maximalist Zionism had a tangible effect on the paper's editorial policy and, finally, provoked his dismissal.[83]

When war was declared, Zionists in Britain felt sure that the Jewish population of Palestine would be seen as a valuable ally. They anticipated that the Government would soften its stand on the White Paper, but in vain. The *Jewish Chronicle* then followed the model of 1914–17 in urging the Government to modify its Palestine policy so as to influence public opinion in neutral America. This contention had some force, since American Jews were dismayed by the interception of refugee ships attempting to reach Palestine in defiance of the White Paper. The *Jewish Chronicle* stoked the fires of indignation by routinely denouncing the policy of the Palestine Administration and the Colonial Office.[84]

Drawing again on the experience of the First World War, Zionists were convinced that if Jews made a substantial military contribution to the Allied war effort they would be rewarded at the eventual peace conference. Britain's military weakness in the Middle East soon forced it to utilise the resources of the *Yishuv*, and the *Jewish Chronicle* seized on this intitial contribution to campaign for Palestinian Jews to bear arms.[85] With the emergence of news about the massacre of the Jews in Europe, the notion of a Jewish army was further seized upon as a way of hitting back. Even though it was a misplaced effort, it served as a release for anger and gave the impression of doing something. However, complex political and diplomatic obstacles stood in the way of a Jewish fighting force. The issue, and its backers, including Greenberg, became entangled in Jewish domestic politics, too.

During 1942, Greenberg was drawn into the affairs of the Committee for a Jewish Army. This body was formed in America under the inspiration of Palestinian Jews who had been dispatched to America in 1939–40 to agitate on behalf of Revisionist Zionism. Their agent in England was Captain Joshua Halpern, a former merchant seaman. Halpern enlisted the support of politicians and writers including Lord Strabolgi (formerly Commander Kenworthy, MP), Colonel Josiah Wedgwood, Joseph Left-wich, and Greenberg. From April 1942, the *Jewish Chronicle* enthusiastic-ally reported on the committee's work and endorsed its objectives. The amount of editorial comment it received between April 1942 and December 1942 actually exceeded that devoted to the news of the slaughter in Europe which was emerging over the same period.[86]

The official Zionist leadership was antagonised by the connection between the Committee for a Jewish Army and the New Zionist Organisation. In addition it duplicated the work they had been doing along the same lines since 1939 and complicated their lobbying in Whitehall. Much of the ensuing conflict took place behind the scenes, but hints of it can be found in the frequent editorials in the *Jewish Chronicle* which argued, disingenuously, that the Jewish Army campaign was not a Zionist party-political objective.[87] The suspicion that Greenberg was imple-menting a hidden agenda was furthered by several frankly pro-Revisionist leading articles.[88] Writing to his friend Meyer Weisgal after a spate of articles on the Zionist position in America, Weizmann accused the paper of deliberately trying to undermine confidence in the Zionist Organisation. He spoke to Greenberg personally and tried to explain to him the damage that these editorials could do.[89]

Greenberg's relations with the Zionist Movement in Britain deteriorated still further as a result of his position in the bitter power struggle being waged within Anglo-Jewry. Haunted by the attempts of the anti-Zionists to derail the negotiations for a Jewish National Home in May 1917, the Zionist Federation was anxious to counteract any interference in the formulation of Jewish claims at the anticipated peace conference. Conse-quently, it planned to sever the tie between the Board of Deputies and the Anglo-Jewish Association, which was regarded as a bastion of non- and anti-Zionists. Lavy Bakstansky, the ZF general secretary, came up with the expedient of offering to fund the representation of small, almost defunct synagogues on the Board providing the ZF could choose the deputy. Once there was a large enough block of Zionist deputies, they would simply vote the old Joint Foreign Committee out of existence. This practice, clothed as a drive to democratise the Board, was intended to climax with the election of its president, executive and committees in July 1943.[90]

The *Jewish Chronicle* never denied the need to reform the Board, but it strongly opposed the programme of the Zionist bloc. Greenberg distrusted Bakstansky, who was staunchly pro-Weizmann. Neville Laski, who was temporarily a director of the paper, had already been a victim of Zionist machinations. Leonard Stein, another director, was president of the AJA. To those in the Zionist Federation, it was therefore little surprise that the *Jewish Chronicle* was implacably hostile to the ZF and its allies, the World Jewish Congress and the Trades Advisory Council. Writing in the *Zionist Review* in March 1943, Rebecca Sieff accused the *Jewish Chronicle* of using its monopoly to 'present private views of Jewish affairs, as if they were those of the community'.[91]

The *Jewish Chronicle* retorted that the Zionists were guilty of factionalism. It warned that if they succeeded in dominating the Board of Deputies, they would drive non-Zionists into open resistance to Zionist policy and reveal divisions in the Jewish population. Knowledge that the Zionists had 'captured' the Board would devalue its pronouncements in the eyes of the Government. Inspired by these considerations, a leading article on 14 May 1943 made a direct intervention in the power struggle: 'We urge every member of a synagogue or other constituent to stamp on the plots and faction, to exercise courageously and independently his voting right, and to employ it only in support of a candidate not chained to a party machine but determined to work in accord with his conscience and the charge of his constituents, for the general communal good.'

This rallying call to the independent members of the Board of Deputies infuriated the Zionists. During May and June, the *Jewish Chronicle* and the *Zionist Review* traded invective and editorial blows. The correspondence columns of the *Jewish Chronicle* were packed with negative comments on Bakstansky's tactics. However, when the new and greatly inflated Board finally convened on 4 July 1943, it proceeded to re-elect Brodetsky as president and, by a narrow margin, ended the connection with the Anglo-Jewish Association.[92]

The following week, on 9 July 1943, the *Jewish Chronicle* ran a front-page story headlined 'The Deputies Captured' and printed pages of indignant correspondence. The leading article protested: 'Even the caucus, flushed though it may be with success, can be asked to pause for a moment.

Under the impact of its assault, the Board is no longer a free representative body of British Jewry but a partisan committee meddling in Anglo-Jewish communal affairs.' The controversy dragged on into the autumn, frequently taking editorial precedence over the news from Europe. Each week Greenberg published letters attacking the latest developments, but few endorsing them. After the Zionist bloc had obtained control over all of the Board's vital committees, the paper dramatically declared on 17 September that 'as far as its function of representing the Community is concerned, it has as good as committed suicide'. For the rest of the war, the *Jewish Chronicle* reported the affairs of the Board in almost funereal tones.[93]

Paradoxically, while Greenberg had placed himself in stark opposition to the Zionist Movement in London and aligned himself with non- and even anti-Zionists in relation to the Board of Deputies, his brand of Zionism and his opinions about events in Palestine grew increasingly radical. The fear that Jewish interests might be totally overlooked in any peace settlement led Greenberg to look more sympathetically on the extremists in the *Yishuv*. The *Jewish Chronicle* defended Palestinian Jews who were arrested for gun-running and condemned the arms raids conducted against Jewish settlements. It even accused the Mandatory authorities of 'a deliberate and systematic effort to goad the Palestinian Jews into a state of revolt'. This was considered so inflammatory that copies of the paper were intercepted by the British authorities before they could reach readers in Palestine. Meanwhile, dispatches from Julian Meltzer, the paper's Palestine correspondent, were censored and prevented from reaching London.[94]

In February 1944 the Irgun, now under the direction of Menachem Begin, issued a 'declaration of war' against the British. A wave of terrorism broke over Palestine to which the authorities responded with curfews and other forms of collective punishment. The *Jewish Chronicle* commented on 31 March 1944 that 'Nobody in his senses can have feelings of anything but utter abhorrence for the recent outrages in Palestine.' Yet its suggestion that the perpetrators might not have been Jews made its strictures rather less than convincing. One front-page story on 7 April was headlined '"Pinning it" on the Yishuv?'. This was nonsensical, since in Palestine the Irgun was doing everything it could to publicise and take the credit for acts of violence against the British.[95]

During August 1944, the Irgun killed six British policemen, and Lechi, an underground terrorist faction allied with it, narrowly missed assassinating the High Commissioner, Sir Harold MacMichael. A few weeks later, Lechi shot dead a key British police officer. The *Jewish Chronicle* considered these 'outrages' 'un-Jewish' and counter-productive; they were 'morally indefensible'. However, a leading article on 6 October went on to qualify the words of reprobation by adding that 'These acts of violent gang-war reflect a deep-seated weakness, or worse, in the local administration.' In what was close to an exoneration of the terrorists, it laid the causes of the unrest at the door of the Palestine Administration which tolerated 'grave corruption among certain elements of the local police force'. Two weeks later it scorned complaints by the British authorities that the Jewish population hid members of the Irgun and Lechi: 'is it to be wondered at if Palestinian Jewry is found to be fretful, gloomily indifferent, and non-collaborationist with the powers-that-be?'.

The drift of editorial policy, and the use of language such as 'collaborationist' to describe co-operation with the Mandatory power, was worrying the directors. In January 1942, Leonard Stein repeated the action he had taken in 1938 and submitted his resignation from the Board. Although he was persuaded to stand for re-election, his uneasiness was not allayed. When the Board met in October 1943, it adjourned 'for a private discussion of editorial policy'. In April 1944 and at the start of 1945, Stein wrote personally to Greenberg to protest at the way the paper treated certain Zionist leaders. His tone was amiable, but concerned.[96]

In October 1944, two weeks before a Board meeting, Michel Oppenheimer, the chairman, made a concerted attempt to influence editorial policy. He spoke to Greenberg about the paper's coverage of the disturbances in Palestine and followed this up with a friendly, but explicit letter:

It may be that some measure of responsibility lies on the shoulders of the [Palestine] police and the administration; it can also be true that numbers of willing informers are too terrified of the consequences to themselves to aid the authorities; nevertheless in my view it would be a major disaster if we were in our paper even to hint that the government were in some means to blame. In that case our enemies (and Lord knows we have enough) would seize on the opportunity to say that we condoned the excesses, no matter how false the accusation.

Oppenheimer assured Greenberg that he understood 'how deeply you are stirred by the many tragic reports you received', but feared they might unbalance his judgment. 'At this juncture when the slightest false move may do irreparable harm, it requires almost superhuman care on your part to see that we do not damage the cause in the slightest degree.' He concluded, 'I hope you will feel it sufficient in addition to condemning the crimes, to urge our people to assist the authorities in every way possible to restore law and order.'[97]

In fact, the Jewish Agency had already decided to mount operations against the Irgun and Lechi. This developed into open co-operation with the British after members of Lechi assassinated Lord Moyne in Cairo in

November 1944. The *Jewish Chronicle* echoed the Jewish Agency's statement denouncing the murder and called it 'a blunder and a crime'. Yet it cast doubt on the identity of those responsible and gave only lukewarm endorsement to the eulogies for Moyne. When the Prime Minister threatened that terrorist acts placed the Jewish National Home in jeopardy, the paper defiantly replied that the future of the *Yishuv* was no longer in the gift of the British.[98]

With the end of the war in Europe in May 1945, the Jewish people waited expectantly for a decision on Palestine. The *Jewish Chronicle* reflected on 11 May that the Jews 'are the greatest martyrs of all the peoples of the world. And to-day they stand the only undelivered ally among the United Nations.' But Churchill could not forget the assassination of his friend, Lord Moyne, and remained icily disposed towards the Zionist Movement. The Foreign Office, with the support of the military, dropped renewed moves towards partition and reverted to a policy of enforcing the Mandate. This trend was ironically confirmed by the results of the General Election, in August, which put the Labour Party in power. Although the party was formally committed to overturning the White Paper, Ernest Bevin, the new Foreign Secretary, was soon convinced that Britain could not risk giving up Palestine.[99]

By November 1945, the hope generated by Labour's victory had evaporated, and it was apparent that demands for immediate mass immigration would not be met. In Palestine, frustration at the plight of Jewish survivors in the DP camps prompted another surge of anti-British violence. The Haganah, the pre-state Jewish defence organisation, combined with the Irgun and Lechi and mounted a series of attacks on British targets. The paper condemned the raids, but in calling them 'spectacular' made it clear that admiration was barely held in check by the need to express regret.[100]

An Anglo-American Commission of Inquiry was now sent to Europe and Palestine to investigate the question of immigration and the future of Palestine. When the Commission held hearings in London in January 1946, Greenberg gave testimony. His forceful statement of Zionist aims was a sure sign that he was the guiding hand behind the *Jewish Chronicle*'s editorial policy.[101] The paper no longer spoke of potential harmony between British and Jewish interests. In a convoluted leader on 4 January 1946, it explained that Anglo-Jewry, the *Yishuv* and the British Government were locked into an irreconcilable conflict: 'Any divergence of interests between Anglo-Jewry and the *Yishuv* could not but be viewed here with the profoundest regret. Nevertheless ... it would be foolish in the extreme either to attempt to smother it and "pretend" it away or, on the other hand, to fall into panic and resort to the usual alternatives of that emotional state in such circumstances: violent bad temper against, or patriotic heroics for, one or the other of the parties concerned.'

The *Jewish Chronicle* accused the British forces in Palestine of a 'terrorism of their own' and called Jewish terrorist acts 'Jewish Resistance Operations'. From the start of March 1946, reports of sabotage and attacks on the British forces were gathered together on the front page under the headline 'Jewish Resistance Movement'. Coming so soon after the war, the term 'resistance' had connotations that could not have been missed by contemporaries. Set against the events in Palestine and the darkening mood of public opinion in Britain this was deeply provocative. One Conservative MP, Earl Winterton, demanded that the paper should be prosecuted for seditious libel. It made little difference that editorials formally repudiated such acts as the killing in cold blood of six British paratroopers in April and the kidnapping of five army officers in Tel Aviv two months later. When the paper argued, somewhat illogically, that the 'resistance movement' was 'not anti-British' but simply seeking justice for the Jews, it gave the appearance of condoning the violence.[102]

This ambivalence was stretching the directors' patience to breaking point. Laski and Stein wrote several times to David Kessler, now a major and attached to the British Economic Mission to Greece, expressing their misgivings at the tone of the leading articles. In January 1946, Laski told Kessler that although he had a 'great admiration for the character, independence of mind and ability' of Ivan Greenberg, both he and Stein felt that Ivan's editorials and 'news settings' had justified 'grave criticism as detrimental both to the community and to the relations of the community with H. M. G.'. Laski complained that it was 'quite impossible to argue with IG. He has so supreme a self-confidence that he is impervious to argument.' And he revealed that the two directors had debated appointing a new editor. But Laski, who had not written to Kessler since his appointment as his deputy, did not feel able to take such a decision without prior consultation. In the mean time, he was so agitated at being held responsible for an editorial policy which he could not influence that he wanted to resign. When David Kessler returned to London in April 1946, he found the *Jewish Chronicle* in a state of disarray, operating in a climate such that it was feared one false move could trigger an outbreak of anti-Semitism.[103]

At noon on 24 May, a special meeting of the Board convened at the company's offices at 88 Chancery Lane. Michel Oppenheimer took the chair, with Stein, Kessler and Gumb present as directors. Laski was also in attendance, by invitation. Together they confronted Greenberg, who had come down from High Wycombe that day. Each of the directors, and Laski, 'expressed strong dissatisfaction' at the conduct of editorial policy.

They stressed that Greenberg had been 'entirely unreceptive' to 'suggestions put forward by either Mr Laski or Mr Stein'. The paper 'was not maintaining the high standard of journalistic good taste which the Board expected'. In particular, the policy on Palestine 'tended too far in the direction of Revisionism'. The Board condemned the language used in the attacks on 'Civil Servants and leading citizens'. In short, the 'presentation of news was frequently lacking in objectivity' and the paper 'had ceased to be an independent forum for the expression of all shades of opinion'. Greenberg 'replied fully to the charges which were levelled against him, and affirmed that it was his intention to edit the paper in conformity with the wishes of the Board, provided, of course, that the policy laid down by the Board did not offend against his conscience'.

The directors and the editor then discussed ways of establishing closer liaison between themselves. This proved impossible in view of Greenberg's reluctance to leave High Wycombe except to deal with necessary business in London each Friday. Instead, the 'main lines' of the paper's policy were set out so as to guide Greenberg in future. These were that the *Jewish Chronicle* should be: 'Moderate Zionist in respect to Palestine/Orthodox as regards the Jewish religion/Strictly loyal in relation to HMG.'. The Board concluded by telling Greenberg that 'henceforth they were resolved that the paper should pursue a policy which was acceptable to them. They were not prepared to tolerate any further breaches of these instructions and warned the Editor that if, in their opinion, serious infringements occurred again they would not hesitate to take the necessary steps to terminate his appointment.'[104]

Greenberg ignored the guidelines: the front-page stories and leading articles remained as inflammatory as before. Oppenheimer met with him again in June to demand a modification of the editorial accent, but Stein took a tougher approach. He wrote to Oppenheimer threatening to resign unless the Board sacked Greenberg. On 26 June, when the Board met again, Kessler backed Stein and noted how Greenberg had shown, 'in spite of every warning by the Board, that he was incapable of editing the paper, as the Directors desired'. Oppenheimer and Gumb were not convinced that the 'infractions' were so grave, and suggested another meeting with the editor. There was, for the moment, a stalemate and the Board agreed to meet again on 2 July.[105]

This time Kessler and Stein finally prevailed. Gumb, who had backed Greenberg, resigned. Oppenheimer refused to support the dismissal of the editor to whom he was related by marriage and for whom he felt a sense of responsibility, but when the Board reconvened on 2 July 1946, Stein and Kessler outvoted him. Greenberg's appointment was ended as from 5 July and he was awarded £2,000 for loss of office. The minutes recorded that this action was taken with 'the greatest regret and the fullest regards for the great services which Mr Greenberg had rendered to the paper over a period of 10 years as Editor preceeded by 11 years as Asst. Editor'. Despite these sentiments, Michel Oppenheimer tendered his resignation. He put his decision into abeyance only after Stein and Kessler 'pleaded with him to reconsider'.[106]

The *Jewish Chronicle* issue of 5 July 1946 was the last to bear the imprint of Ivan Greenberg. On the editorial page it carried a defiant message to Palestinian Jewry in response to the punitive arrest of the Jewish Agency's leadership: 'To our gallant fellow Jews in the Yishuv we would offer a word of brotherly love and deepest sympathy in the ordeal through which they are passing.' The article characteristically maintained that a peaceful community had been turned into fanatical resisters by a policy that was stupid and unjust. There was also 'A Personal Note' signed by Greenberg. In it he summed up his version of the crisis which had led to his departure:

With the developing tension of the Jewish position a growing divergence has manifested itself between the views my conscience compels me to hold and those held, equally conscientiously, by the Board of Directors of the paper. In these stern and searching times, honour can tolerate no compromise of principles in any of us. And so, with natural regret on my part, which the Directors graciously informed me they share, I relinquish this week the editorship of THE JEWISH CHRONICLE.

A statement by the directors was published in the same issue. 'The Government have argued the justification of their actions [in Palestine] on the purely logical grounds that their authority was being assailed, and that to permit such a development to go unchecked would be, in fact, to abdicate.' The Board agreed with that view; the editor did not. In consequence of the disagreement the editor had relinquished his position.[107]

Greenberg elaborated his side of the story in typically strident language to the *Evening Standard* diary on 11 July. He said that 'I will not condemn the resistance movement in Palestine any more than I would the French resistance, or the British resistance to Hitler. Force is not wrong or right in itself. If a government or any other body use force to do wrong, then the only alternative is to use force back. I demanded that the *Jewish Chronicle* criticise in the strongest terms the Government policy and the failure to redress the wrong done to our people. The directors felt that my view was not wise.'

Otherwise, Fleet Street took little notice of Greenberg's departure. The Revisionist press in South Africa, with which he had longstanding links, was indignant but ineffectual from such a distance. Julian Meltzer, the Jerusalem correspondent, resigned in solidarity; but he was the only journalist connected with the paper to make such a gesture. According to

Doris Greenberg, Ivan's wife, five hundred people wrote to console him, and she claimed that the *Jewish Chronicle* refused to publish an advertisement acknowledging this mail.[108]

Greenberg did not react passively to his dismissal. During September and October, he negotiated with Eliezer Hoofien, a director of the Anglo-Palestine Bank in Tel Aviv, in a bid to purchase the shares held by Mortimer Epstein. He also investigated the shareholdings of the Kann family and the Wolffsohn Trust. Greenberg told Hoofien that if he could get hold of the Wolffsohn shares, 'we shall be in a position to rescue the paper from its present undesirable direction and bring it back again to the support of Zionism'.[109]

A memorandum of the Anglo-Palestine Bank summed up the strategy: 'Mr Greenberg, who says that he left the *Jewish Chronicle* in protest against the policy of Mr Kessler who is in control of the Company, is trying to acquire a majority ... Mr Greenberg believes that he can get the Epstein shares. If he were to acquire the Kann and Wolffsohn equity too, he would hold a round £7,000 against Kessler's £6,000, acquire control and re-install himself.' But the author of the memorandum, probably Hoofien, was uncertain whether this was a good idea and wondered whether it might not be more desirable for the Jewish Agency to get hold of the Kann and Wolffsohn shares (which he thought it could do without too much trouble) and hold the balance between Kessler and Greenberg.[110]

At the same time as Greenberg thought that the Bank was about to help him, Berl Locker, a member of the Jewish Agency executive, gave Hoofien the green light to purchase the shares solely in its interest. The Agency, acting in concert with the Zionist Federation in London, considered the voice of *Jewish Chronicle* to be so influential that they were willing to buy a major holding in the company in order to effect its policy. Efforts to bring this plan to fruition persisted into 1947, but ran out of steam when difficulties appeared in the way of the share purchases. By then the *Jewish Chronicle* was securely under David Kessler's control.[111]

7 The post-war era: J. M. Shaftesley and David Kessler, 1946–1958

The establishment of Israel, 1946–1948

Taking on the editorship of a paper is a challenge at the best of times, but John Shaftesley became acting editor of the *Jewish Chronicle* in the middle of a crisis that tested his mettle to the limit. Born in 1901 in Salford and educated at Salford Grammar School and Manchester School of Art, Shaftesley was intensely proud of his Lancashire roots and self-made status. He had studied printing at London University and possessed a thorough grounding in all of the technical aspects of newspaper publishing. Indeed, while he worked on the staff of the *Manchester Guardian* he taught printing at the Manchester College of Technology. Shaftesley was appointed the Manchester correspondent of the *Jewish Chronicle* in the 1930s and moved to the London office as assistant editor in 1937. Loyal to his profession and the paper, he could, however, be opinionated and abrasive with colleagues.[1]

With the help of David Kessler and the Board he set about pouring oil on troubled waters. The distressing stories of terrorism and repression in Palestine were removed from the front page and placed inside the paper under 'Land of Israel News'. The tone and the content of editorials on Palestine were transformed. Written by several hands, including Simon Gilbert, until his death in October 1946, Aubrey (Abba) Eban, who was in London working for the Jewish Agency Information Department, Norman Bentwich and Jacob Hodess, they stressed the history of the Jewish–British partnership during the Mandate and the potential for a peaceful settlement. The paper's stance on the Jewish underground was completely revamped. Ambivalence was replaced by the assertion that terrorism was inimical to the ideals of Zionism. The bombing of the King David Hotel was dubbed, without qualification, an 'abominable and universally condemned crime'. While the paper chided the British authorities for the harshness of police measures in Palestine and unbending opposition to Jewish immigration, it reminded Anglo-Jewry that Jews had never had a better friend than the British people.[2]

British efforts to bring Arabs and Jews into negotiations failed dismally. At the end of 1946, the hard-liners of the Zionist Movement, led by Abba Hillel Silver, the leader of American Zionism, and Ben-Gurion, the leader of the *Yishuv*, succeeded in ousting Weizmann at the Twenty-second Zionist Congress. To the dismay of the *Jewish Chronicle*, Weizmann's carefully modulated, essentially pro-British approach was terminated along with his leadership. Britain and the Zionist Movement were now on a collision course. The conflict had a singularly threatening dimension for Jews in the United Kingdom who found themselves sandwiched between the contending forces. Anti-Semitism, which had persisted during the war, was inflamed by reports of Jewish attacks on British targets in Palestine. This resentment was easily manipulated by the veterans of the British Union of Fascists who gathered in east London in November 1946 to revive the movement.[3]

The general press inflamed the situation by printing scare stories about Jewish terrorists infiltrating Britain and planting bombs in Whitehall. Following the reprisal flogging of a British officer and three sergeants in Palestine, two synagogues in London were vandalised. The *Jewish Chronicle*'s editorial obloquy of those who committed the flogging had little impact on public opinion. In January 1947 a *Sunday Times* editorial challenged British Jews to denounce terrorism in Palestine. Leonard Stein wrote to the *Sunday Times* pointing out that the terrorists were repudiated throughout Anglo-Jewry, but his letter was not even printed in full.[4]

On 18 February 1947, Bevin told the House of Commons that Britain was going to hand the Palestine question over to the United Nations. In May the UN accepted its new charge and set up a UN Special Committee on Palestine (UNSCOP) to seek a solution. While the committee deliberated, the cycle of terrorism and counter-terrorism continued. In July the *President Warfield* – which became world famous as the *Exodus-1947*, chartered by the Haganah to take 'illegal' immigrants into Palestine – was intercepted by the British navy, boarded and taken into Haifa harbour. Maurice Pearlman, who had served with the British army in Greece with David Kessler before becoming a Haganah spokesman, provided the *Jewish Chronicle* with graphic accounts of the *Exodus* Affair. The drama gripped public attention for months and helped to swing world opinion decisively against Britain's immigration policy.[5]

For Jews in Britain the Palestine emergency reached a critical point in mid 1947 following the killing of two British sergeants in retaliation for the hanging of three Irgun men. Every British newspaper reported the story in detail. The *Daily Express* on 1 August carried a large photograph of the atrocity on the front page that fuelled popular wrath. Jewish communal organisations were quick to denounce the hangings and dissociate themselves from the perpetrators. The *Jewish Chronicle* headlined its editorial on the same day 'Murder', and offered its deepest sympathies to the families of the victims. However, over the bank-holiday weekend there was anti-Jewish rioting in Liverpool, Manchester, Salford, Glasgow, east London and other centres. Although no one was injured, crowds of youths destroyed and looted Jewish-owned property, synagogues were attacked, and cemeteries were desecrated. In Palestine, British soldiers went on the rampage and killed five Jews.[6]

At this nadir in British–Jewish relations the voice of the *Jewish Chronicle* was crucial. Its editorials explained to the British public the causes of the Palestine impasse and calmly put the Jewish case. Yet the anxiety to reach an understanding with the British Government and avoid a catastrophe was so great that one editorial suggested voluntarily suspending 'illegal' immigration while the UN committee's work was in progress.[7]

At the start of September UNSCOP issued its report, recommending the partition of Palestine into Jewish and Arab states. David Kessler had always disliked the idea of partition. He longed for a solution in which Jews and Arabs would live together in amity, but it appeared that a unitary state was no longer viable. On 5 September 1947 the *Jewish Chronicle*, presciently, asked who was going to oversee the transition period to ensure that chaos did not ensue between the departure of the British and the creation of the new states. In the absence of British goodwill, the hand-over turned into a bloody civil war between Jews and Arabs. When the UN General Assembly voted the state of Israel into existence on 19 November 1947 (in principle, if not yet in practice) the paper in a cool, judicious editorial surveyed the obstacles in the way of independence. It pointed out that no fewer than 42 per cent of the population of the Jewish state were destined to be Arabs.[8]

Israel's birth pangs riveted the attention of the Jewish world. The story dominated the *Jewish Chronicle*'s front page for the next twelve months, with reports furnished by its new Israel correspondent, Jon Kimche. Certain themes recurred in the editorial comment. Because of the singular position of British Jews, the paper was particularly concerned by the behaviour of the British Government and relations between Israel and Britain. It expressed frustration that Britain refused to recognise the new state and alarm when Israeli fighter planes skirmished with RAF fighters over the Negev, shooting one down. For British Jews the threat of a war between the two countries was appalling, so enormous relief greeted *de facto* and, later, *de jure* recognition of Israel. Bevin's influence was blamed for the tardiness of the reconciliation process, and the *Jewish Chronicle* did not conceal its delight when he left the Government in March 1951.[9]

Reconstruction and the emergence from austerity, 1946–1958

The news from Palestine created enormous demand for the *Jewish Chronicle*, so it was intensely frustrating to the publishers that continuing paper rationing made it impossible to print enough copies. The Jewish New Year issue for 1946 was completely sold out within a short time of appearing. Pressure from Fleet Street led to an easing of the restrictions on the print run allowed to newspapers, but hopes of full recovery were dashed by the fuel crisis in the winter of 1946–7. To save electricity, the Government ordered newspapers to reduce their size and imposed a two-week suspension of the periodical press, including the religious weeklies. For two successive Fridays, the printed *Jewish Chronicle* failed to appear, although postal subscribers received a skeleton edition on duplicated sheets.[10]

The enforced stoppage, described by the *Newspaper Press Directory* as a 'unique penalty in publishing history', was received with fury. During the war the financial position of the paper had become so precarious that it was only saved by guarantees of support from Michel Oppenheimer. A further loss of revenue would have extremely serious consequences. Shaftesley asked Selig Brodetsky, president of the Board of Deputies, to intervene with the Government, but his appeals to the Prime Minister and Emanuel Shinwell, the Minister of Fuel, were unavailing.[11]

The editors and managers of the religious and periodical press jointly complained to the Government, but without any effect. Their determination to prevent such treatment in the future led to the formation of a Periodical and Religious Weekly Press Group, in which the *Jewish Chronicle* played a leading part.[12] The group protested against a further Government order to restrict the number of pages during the dollar crisis in the summer of 1947. Although its composition shrank to the religious weekly press, the group continued to meet regularly into the 1970s and was an important forum for the exchange of views between members of various denominations.

From the start of 1949, the newsprint ration was increased, so that the *Jewish Chronicle* was able to take advantage of the pent-up demand for the paper. By 1948, circulation had almost doubled from the 1946 level of around 22,000 and reached a peak of 55,000 in 1951, before falling back slightly.[13] This was a boom-time for the press in general. As a result of the demand for news during the war readership of daily papers jumped from 10 million in 1937 to 15.5 million in 1947 and peaked in 1950, when the number of readers reached 17 million. The leaders of the popular press – the *Daily Express*, the *Daily Mirror* and the *Daily Herald* – achieved high circulations and healthy profits. However, the escalating cost of newsprint and labour began to erode this profitability. Competition from television and radio bit into readership figures from the mid 1950s and cut advertising revenue. This was the prelude to the 'shake out' in Fleet Street which led to the disappearance of three national Sunday papers and three long-established dailies, and the increasing concentration of ownership.[14]

As conditions permitted, the *Jewish Chronicle* was brought into line with developments in Fleet Street. Shaftesley quickly made a number of improvements in the paper's layout. In July 1947, he followed the daily press and added a fifth column in conjunction with larger type to make reading easier. The masthead was redesigned to be more in keeping with the format which the front page had taken since 1939. Ten years after moving to High Wycombe, the paper returned to a London address at 32 Furnival Street, between Chancery Lane and Fetter Lane. Old features that had been victims of wartime exigencies reappeared: cartoons by Sallon, travel notes by 'Green Flag' (F. H. Samuel) and pictures. New features included an opinion column, 'In My View ... ', which attracted the pens of Maurice Edelman, MP, Dr James Parkes and Tosco Fyvel, later the paper's literary editor, amongst other fresh voices. Shaftesley also used some of the techniques that were being employed in the circulation wars between the Fleet Street dailies. He obtained the exclusive English rights to serialise extracts from Chaim Weizmann's memoirs, in 1949, and Louis Golding's 1951 novel *Dangerous Places*.

With Britain's emergence from the worst of the post-war economic crisis and the easing of restrictions on paper, the amount of advertising expanded and it became possible to increase the number of pages. By the early 1950s, full-page advertisements reappeared, showing the rapid growth of consumption once controls were lifted. A motoring column, introduced in 1953, reflected the changes in leisure activity and spending power as the age of austerity passed.[15] There was hardly a pastime that was not covered: there were stamp notes, gramophone notes, art notes and an easy Hebrew column. The paper sponsored a football competition from November 1957. In August 1956, there was a further change in layout, bringing the paper into harmony with modern newspaper practice.

The *Jewish Chronicle* supplements were reinstated in November 1951. They focused attention on Jewish centres abroad, particularly Israel, communal institutions and regional communities. From April 1954, a northern edition, based in Manchester, afforded extra pages for local news. However, it was hard to compete with local papers in this market. The *Jewish Gazette* had been published in Manchester since 1946, and it was joined by the *Jewish Telegraph*, also printed in Manchester, four years later. In the early 1950s, the older paper ran into difficulties and sought a buyer. The *Jewish Chronicle* purchased the *Jewish Gazette* in April 1954, to strengthen its northern representation, although it has since been run independently.

Prior to 1931, changes in the editorial chair and policy of the *Jewish Chronicle* had resulted from death or a change of ownership. It was only after Leopold Greenberg's reign as controlling editor ended that the directors of the paper had scope to assert their will in the choice of his successors and the determination of policy. The dismissals of J. M. Rich and Ivan Greenberg had been a negative, reactive expression of this authority, but in the post-war era the Board of Directors took a more pro-active role in the paper's conduct.

Following Alex Gumb's resignation only Michel Oppenheimer, chairman of the Board, David Kessler, managing director, and Leonard Stein remained. To fill the vacancies, Kessler recruited Edwin Samuel in 1951 and, five years later, Ellis Birk. Edwin Samuel, the 2nd Viscount Samuel, had served in a Jewish battalion of the Royal Fusiliers in Palestine in the First World War and returned to work for the Mandatory Administration. He settled there after marrying into a distinguished Palestinian Jewish family. After the creation of the state of Israel he pursued an academic career, specialising in public administration. Kessler had known Ellis Birk since before the war. A prominent city solicitor, Birk had joined the Board of Directors of the *Daily Mirror*, which gave him valuable experience of newspaper publishing.[16]

The Board oversaw several important developments in the activity of the Jewish Chronicle Company. At the inspiration of David Kessler it established a subsidiary company, Vallentine, Mitchell, to provide the Jews of Britain with their own publishing house and further the sociological, historical and cultural awareness of Anglo-Jewry. Over a relatively short time, Vallentine, Mitchell was responsible for the publication of several major works on Jews and Judaism including Gerald Reitlinger's *The Final Solution*; the English translation of *Anne Frank's Diary*; *A Minority in Britain*, a collection of social studies by James Parkes, Hannah Neustatter, Howard Brotz and Maurice Freedman; and Leonard Stein's *The Balfour Declaration*. The Company also ventured into printing via the acquisition of George Barber Ltd and G. Barclay Ltd, and set up a news and features service. Finally, Jewish Chronicle Publications took over the *Jewish Chronicle Year Book*, inaugurated the *Jewish Chronicle Travel Guide* and published several editions of Florence Greenberg's cookery book.

The paper's steady growth and the diversification of activities were reflected in physical expansion. In 1956 the paper moved into bright new premises erected further along Furnival Street. However, the soaring cost of newsprint and other expenses flowing from expansion made it necessary to increase the cover price from 4d. to 6d. in May 1955, and to 9d. at the end of the year. Largely because of the power of the print unions, labour costs were also being pushed relentlessly upwards. Staff relations at the *Jewish Chronicle* were good, and there were many combined staff activities such as the annual outing. But it was unable to escape the problems of wage levels and industrial conflict which dogged the industry at large. The paper was caught up in a long and damaging dispute in the first six months of 1956, as a result of which it was obliged to change its printers. This had an unfortunate temporary effect on page size and format.[17]

Anglo-Jewry emerged from the war transformed. Evacuation and the bombing had disrupted almost every communal institution and inflicted extensive damage on buildings, especially synagogues in east London. The establishment of the welfare state by the 1945–51 Labour Government significantly affected the functioning of Jewish charitable and educational organisations. The *Jewish Chronicle* helped Anglo-Jewry to adjust to these changes and played a part in reconstruction. The leading articles on domestic affairs were written usually by Hugh Harris – the son of the Revd John Harris, a regular contributor to the 'Sermon of the Week' before the First World War – who had been in charge of the book page in the 1930s. His editorials threw light on the economic and social conditions of the Jewish population, reviewed the work of the central communal bodies, and offered suggestions and constructive criticisms.

One of the most obvious changes was the decline of the Jewish East End. The wartime evacuations and the blitz had more than halved the population of Stepney by 1943, and the number of Jewish inhabitants never returned to inter-war levels. In 1948 Shaftesley commissioned A. B. Levy, a member of the editorial staff, to write a series of articles on what had befallen Jewish life in the East End. He recorded that the Jews of Whitechapel and Stepney were now dispersed over the whole of London. Only a small percentage of London Jewry still inhabited what was once the heartland of the community.[18]

In October–November 1949, Levy made a study of occupations in which Jews were engaged. It revealed extensive changes in Jewish economic activity, mainly the growth of self-employment in various trades and increased penetration of the professions. The new pattern was reflected in the paucity of comment in the paper on the crisis in the clothing trades during 1952. The veteran trade unionist J. L. Fine contributed an article on the textile industry's plight, but only after criticism in the correspondence columns that the *Jewish Chronicle* had ignored the garment trades.[19]

To help repair the lack of solid information about the demography and social structure of Anglo-Jewry the *Jewish Chronicle* instigated a major research project, the results of which were later published by Vallentine,

Mitchell in *A Minority in Britain*, edited by Maurice Freedman. The results came as something of a shock. According to Hannah Neustatter, Anglo-Jewry was facing a demographic disaster through the cessation of immigration, a low birth rate, the small size of families and out-marriage. Neustatter, Brotz and Freedman all agreed that religious observance was declining. Zionism was the most widespread and cohesive ideology amongst Jews, but they believed it was not proving an adequate check to secularisation and assimilation. These disclosures stimulated a good deal of heart-searching in the editorial columns and a vigorous analysis of communal institutions.[20]

One of the most pressing communal matters in the immediate post-war years was the absence of a Chief Rabbi since the death of Dr J. H. Hertz in January 1946. The *Jewish Chronicle* pressed for an appointment to be made and was then involved in the long, unhappy debate over the terms on which the Federation of Synagogues would be invited to participate in the choice of his successor. The United Synagogue insisted that representation on the electoral college should be determined by the financial contribution which synagogues made to the upkeep of the Chief Rabbinate. This resulted in the allotment of a small number of delegates to the Federation, which the *Jewish Chronicle* called 'strange and high-handed treatment'. Eventually, the Federation withdrew from the process and an important opportunity for co-operation was lost. The successful candidate, in a field that included Alexander Altmann and Kopul Rosen, was Rabbi Israel Brodie, a former chaplain to the forces. Brodie was strongly promoted by Sir Robert Waley Cohen, the president of the United Synagogue, although the *Jewish Chronicle* sympathised with the claims of Altmann and Rosen. However, the former was ruled out because he was of German origin, the latter because he was considered too young and inexperienced.[21]

The new Chief Rabbi and the *Jewish Chronicle* were soon to clash over the paper's attitude to the Liberal Synagogue and its insistence on the right to criticise the Chief Rabbinate. In December 1949, in a deliberate display of openness and tolerance, the paper carried an article by the Liberal Rabbi Israel Mattuck discussing questions relating to Jewish marriage. It was attacked at the Beth Din by Dayan Isidor Grunfeld and Chief Rabbi Brodie, who labelled it 'the higher anti-semitism'. While disclaiming any intention to interfere with the freedom of the editor, Brodie said 'it was right to point out that this particular article with its contents, its unfair generalisations and its non-Jewish approach had deeply offended many conscientious Jews who read the paper'. He also took offence to a biographical reflection by Charles Solomons, the assistant editor, on the way that in Anglo-Jewish life the 'Anglo-' part commonly eliminated the

'Jewish'. Paradoxically, the paper was defended by the *Jewish Review*, the journal of the Mizrachi Federation, the religious Zionists, which characterised Solomon's article as 'a live piece of unpleasant contemporary reality'.[22]

Dr Bernard Homa, a leading figure in the Federation of Synagogues, echoed the Chief Rabbi's criticism. He claimed that 'for some time there has been a growing feeling in the orthodox community that the *Jewish Chronicle*, under its present ownership, has become a propaganda organ for the Liberal and Reform Jews', a reference to the fact that Kessler and some of his colleagues belonged to these synagogues. Homa suggested that 'the leaders of the community should consider what steps should be taken against the pernicious policy of the *Jewish Chronicle*'. The same line was taken by Harry Goodman, a leader of the Union of Orthodox Hebrew Congregations, in a broadside against the paper in 1952.[23]

Brodie did not take kindly to criticism of his person or his office. After an editorial note mildly disparaging his views on the correct pronunciation of Hebrew (between the usage in Israel, *Ivrit*, and that traditional to Ashkenazi Jews in the diaspora) he accused the *Jewish Chronicle* of deliberately publishing comments that detracted from his authority. Brodie asserted that 'for our survival's sake and for the cohesion of the community, central authority must be exerted'. In reply, Shaftesley, a member of the United Synagogue, defended the paper's independence and criticised the assumption of infallibility amongst certain communal figures. The retort, though pointed, was couched in respectful language to avoid causing offence.[24]

Intermittent conflict with the Orthodox community continued. In 1955, after an article in the paper called the *mikvah*, ritual bath, 'a barbaric hangover from ancient days', Rabbi Dr Schonfeld declared that it might be necessary to pronounce an *issur* against the *Jewish Chronicle*, forbidding observant Jews to read it. One dayan in Manchester publicly compared the paper to *Der Stürmer*. These attacks were signs of a growing assertiveness in the Orthodox community that would lead to bitter controversy surrounding the paper.[25]

The Board of Deputies was still overshadowed by the dissension of the war years, and its prestige had never been lower. The *Jewish Chronicle* agreed with Neville Laski that lack of interest in the Board's work stemmed from its domination by the Zionist bloc. It sympathised with the group of independent deputies, led by Laski, who tried to organise an opposition and retrieve the initiative. Their efforts were nullified after they received a drubbing at the hands of the well-drilled Zionist faction. Nevertheless, Zionists and supporters of the British Branch of the WJC, notably Lady Reading and Israel Sieff, were so irritated with the paper's insistent criticism that during 1946 they explored the possibilities of a takeover or the creation of a rival paper. In the event, paper rationing thwarted their intention to found an alternative Jewish weekly and the *Jewish Chronicle* remained completely independent. To its despair, factionalism increased as the World Jewish Congress sought to involve the Board in its work, while the Sephardi and Liberal congregations threatened to secede over other issues. On 9 April 1948 after the failure of another reform movement, the paper lamented that 'An ever-increasing sense of unreality seems to pervade the Board's proceedings.'[26]

The heightening of anti-Jewish feeling in 1946–7, due partly to the events in Palestine, aggravated conflict within Anglo-Jewry and became one of the *Jewish Chronicle*'s chief preoccupations. Comparable to 1936–7, the agitation was all the more disturbing as it came so soon after an anti-Fascist war which had exposed the horrors resulting from racism. The Jewish public was equally perplexed by the apparent lack of Government concern. On 12 September 1947, the *Jewish Chronicle* argued that 'too much complacency appears to be shown by the responsible authorities towards the growing Fascist menace'. It demanded official action, particularly the passing of a community libel law.

Six months later the degree of anti-Jewish agitation and violence in east and north London had become so serious that on 19 March 1948 the paper warned: 'This is a time for plain speaking... because the Jews of this country are aware that they are living in a social climate which is becoming increasingly stormy. Some are thinking in terms of emigration; and some of desperate fight [*sic*], believing that even in Britain, with its great democratic and tolerant traditions, anti-Semitism is making such headway as to threaten seriously their well-being as Jews.' Ridley Road, in Hackney, was the scene of regular Fascist meetings, and, as in the 1930s, young Jews acted to protect themselves, believing that the communal organisations were doing too little. The *Jewish Chronicle* condemned their behaviour while expressing sympathy with their motives. History repeated itself as the paper urged the Board of Deputies to do more to combat anti-Semitism.[27]

During 1947–8, Sidney Salomons, secretary of the Board's defence committee, pleaded with Shaftesley to curb the publicity the paper was giving to independent defence organisations such as the 43 Group. He even asked him to ban the advertisements which they placed in the paper. Shaftesley refused the request. While the *Jewish Chronicle* always assisted defence work, it never allowed itself to become an instrument of the Board's committee or any faction in the community. Kessler tried to promote communal defence in other ways. He suggested to the journalist and former police officer C. H. Rolph that efforts should be made to infiltrate the British Union of Fascists, but the idea was not taken further.[28]

Fascist activity tailed off during the late 1940s, but social anti-Semitism remained widespread in certain circles. The *Jewish Chronicle* associated this with the general pattern of racism that was becoming apparent in British society and began to take note of the colour bar operating in many pubs and places of entertainment, particularly after the Notting Hill riots in August 1958.[29] In its coverage of the Seretse Khama Affair, the introduction of apartheid in South Africa, and the battle for desegregation in the southern states of the USA, the *Jewish Chronicle* repeatedly warned Jews that anti-Black racism was *their* problem, too.[30]

As well as examining and suggesting ways to improve communal institutions, Shaftesley, Charles Solomon and Hugh Harris tried to enlarge the cultural awareness of their readers. The expanded book page gave due prominence to pre-war writers, among them Louis Golding, William Goldman and Arthur Koestler, but also embraced the work of a new generation that included Alexander Baron, Wolf Mankowitz, Danny Abse, Bernard Kops, Barnett Litvinoff and Brian Glanville. Baron and Mankowitz, who were the first to establish themselves in the public eye, were recruited as reviewers. The *Jewish Chronicle* played an influential part in the establishment of Jewish Book Week in 1954 and the Jewish Book Council. Its art correspondent, Peter Stone, trumpeted the arrival of a new wave of Jewish artists in Britain, led by Josef Herman and Lucien Freud, whose early exhibitions created a stir similar to the excitement that greeted Gertler and Bomberg in the 1920s.

The paper continued to maintain a benevolent interest in Yiddish culture. It featured profiles of A. N. Stencl, I. A. Lisky, Itzig Manger and other survivors of that once flourishing literary milieu. Discussion of Yiddish revolved increasingly around the prospects for its continuity. The closure of the daily *Di Tsait* in November 1950 signalled the erosion of the demographic base for Yiddish in Britain. Only *Loshn Un Lebn*, heroically edited by Stencl, survived.[31]

To mark the tercentenary of the resettlement of the Jews in England a special supplement was produced, on 27 January 1956, that included no fewer than forty articles by a wide range of scholars, authors and artists. Over 64,000 copies of this issue were printed, and it was completely sold out. This was the zenith of Shaftesley's editorship, combining his devotion to the *Jewish Chronicle* with his interest in Anglo-Jewish history and culture. At the height of the year-long celebrations, he was awarded the OBE in the Queen's Birthday Honours List, the first editor of the *Jewish Chronicle* to be so honoured.[32]

Covering the Jewish world, 1946–1958

The birth of Israel tended to overshadow other foreign news between 1946 and 1948, but during these years the *Jewish Chronicle* re-established its network of foreign correspondents and resumed a full coverage of Jewish affairs across the globe. Polish-born Joel Cang, who had been the east European correspondent of the *Manchester Guardian* before the war, became the foreign editor and was subsequently appointed assistant editor. Kessler, who travelled widely, helped with the recruitment of correspondents and wrote leading articles on Israel and the Middle East.

Beyond the Middle East, the focus was initially on Germany and Austria, where tens of thousands of Jewish DPs lingered in camps, several of them former concentration camps, waiting for a decision that would allow them to enter either the USA or Palestine. The paper published grim articles on the plight of the survivors, adding impetus to Jewish relief operations and the lobbying by Zionist groups. Naturally, the *Jewish Chronicle* paid close attention to the fate of Nazi war criminals. Peter Calvocoressi sent back vivid copy on the Nuremberg Tribunal in 1945–6, but as the interest of the general public waned, it was almost alone in reporting subsequent war crimes trials.[33]

Jews regarded the establishment of the Federal Republic of Germany (FRG) in 1949 with deep suspicion, a feeling that was keenly reflected in the *Jewish Chronicle*. After the war, the paper consistently refused to accept advertisements for German goods or services. Editorials noted with concern that the Basic Laws governing the new state did little to ensure that the crimes of Nazism would be remembered or atoned for. As distinct from the rest of the British press, the *Jewish Chronicle* closely monitored the elections to the Bundestag (the lower house of the Federal German Parliament) and constantly drew attention to the existence of far-Right splinter parties. Their marginal success did not allay nagging doubts as to the wisdom of allowing Germany to rebuild itself.[34]

Articles on the Federal Republic always provoked a large letter bag. Not surprisingly, the issue of German rearmament was especially controversial. In the climate of the Cold War, the paper welcomed the creation of NATO and the Council of Europe in 1949 as guarantees against both a recurrence of German totalitarianism and Soviet aggression. However, the logic of the paper's stance on the Cold War obliged it to accept the need for rearming Germany so that the FRG could play its part in the defence of western Europe. A long and torturous leading article in November 1949 consequently justified the policy of reconciliation (on the lines advocated by Victor Gollancz and others) and German rearmament. This editorial was the subject of heated debate and was condemned by AJEX, the Association of Jewish Ex-Servicemen.[35]

Relations between the *Jewish Chronicle* and the Soviet authorities deteriorated from mid 1947, when the Russian press accused it of anti-Soviet bias. Since 1945 the paper had reported Soviet Jewish affairs with deep interest and pleaded with the Soviet Government for a more open policy towards the Jews. It praised Soviet policy on the Palestine Question and hoped that Russian support for Jewish statehood would lead to increased toleration for the two and a half million Soviet Jewish citizens. When the Soviet authorities began to suppress Jewish political and cultural organisations in 1949, the editorial attitude changed. It noted with anxiety that anti-Israel and anti-Jewish themes were becoming a staple element of Soviet propaganda, with similar trends visible in the Soviet satellite states in eastern Europe. From 1949, it became increasingly difficult to obtain information about events concerning the Jews inside the USSR.[36]

Pogroms initiated by anti-Semitic and nationalist mobs in post-war Poland were followed by the Communist-inspired elimination of Jewish institutions and the curtailment of emigration to Israel. In 1949 Polish Jewish Communists broke the connection between Polish Jewry and the World Jewish Congress. This clamp-down impinged on the *Jewish Chronicle*. A year later the Central Committee of Polish Jews engineered the expulsion of B. Zilberberg, the paper's Warsaw correspondent, who had provided sensational eye-witness reports on the Kielce pogrom. In reprisal for a leading article that criticised Polish policy towards the restitution of property to former Polish Jews now living in Israel, Zilberberg's Polish passport was confiscated and his citizenship was revoked.[37]

With substantial Jewish populations still in eastern Europe, the *Jewish Chronicle* maintained as high a level of coverage as was feasible, taking news from whatever source was available and sifting fact from propaganda. During the first years of the post-Stalin era, the lack of firm information left the paper largely in the realms of speculation. With the liberalisation under Khrushchev in 1956 contacts with Soviet Jews improved, as did both the quantity and quality of its reports. In August 1956, an editorial actually discussed how Jewish vistors to Russia could assist Soviet Jews by questioning the authorities about their treatment.[38]

Interest in the Jews of the USSR and the Eastern Bloc quickened after 1956. This was a result partly of the glimpse of Jewish life afforded during the 'thaw', the period of liberalisation following Stalin's death, and partly of the threatening utterances by Khrushchev on the alleged excessiveness of Jewish influence in the Soviet Union. Thanks to Cang's extensive contacts, Soviet and east European Jewish affairs assumed a regular and larger place in the paper's foreign coverage. In June 1957 the paper sent a special correspondent to Moscow, but his findings were not cheering. An editorial on 8 November protested about the 'brutal isolation' of the Jews.

Israel remained the leading overseas news story. Fighting along the country's borders with Syria, Jordan and Egypt occurred with depressing regularity all through the early years of the state's existence. In October 1953, Israeli forces responded to one cross-border raid by attacking the Arab village of Qibya, in Jordan, with heavy loss of civilian life. The Israeli Prime Minister, Ben-Gurion, denied that the Israeli army was responsible (it was in fact a special unit commanded by Ariel Sharon known as Unit 101), but the attack was condemned by the British Government and the UN.[39]

The *Jewish Chronicle* was ill at ease with the policy of reprisal attacks. After Qibya, Kessler protested in an editorial entitled 'Right Is Might' that: 'a well-armed body of Israelis carried out reprisals ... and, in a violent attack, indiscriminately killed some fifty or more Arab villagers of both sexes and of all ages'. He insisted that Jews in the diaspora had a right to comment on such matters and judge them according to the ethical precepts of Judaism: 'This was not self-defence against armed attack. It was reprisal of the same kind that was perpetrated by our enemies in the last war.' Not only was it morally unjustifiable, but it was not even politically expedient since it alienated Israel's friends. In conclusion he demanded that the Israeli Government dissociate itself from the attack and discipline those responsible for it. Finally, he scolded the Anglo-Jewish leaders who 'tagged along' with the Israeli Government and insisted that they condemn it, too.[40]

This hard-hitting editorial did not please the Israeli Embassy. The Israeli Ambassador, Eliahu Elath, rapped the paper across the knuckles, although six months later he admitted to Kessler that the criticism had been justified. It stimulated a good deal of correspondence, too, much of it supporting the paper's stand. Ernst Simon, a prominent academic at the Hebrew University, commended the 'admirable and courageous' editorial. The article was praised by Selig Brodetsky, who called the raid 'a terrible and unjustified revenge'. Leo Baeck, the philosopher and spiritual leader, congratulated Kessler personally.[41]

Palestinian Arabs who had voluntarily left, or been driven out of, Palestine during the War of Independence formed a deep reservoir of hatred for Israel that supplied the impetus for many of the border incidents. The *Jewish Chronicle* had commented ruefully on the flight of Palestinian Arabs in 1948 and urged the Israeli Government to offer them some form of reparation, if not to permit their actual return. It praised the abortive offer to accept back 100,000 refugees as a 'courageous', if risky, gesture. Beyond this early attempt to solve the Palestinian Question, the paper commented only intermittently on the refugee problem. The fate of the Palestine Arabs and the complex issues underlying the problem were rarely discussed editorially.[42]

By contrast, Israel's complicated and often obscure internal affairs were the subject of constant, sometimes admiring and sometimes bemused commentary. The paper's attitude to these political events was summed up by the title of a leading article on 3 November 1950: 'Much Ado ... '. Ben-Gurion was hugely admired, but the *Jewish Chronicle* was pleased when he left office and was succeeded by Moshe Sharett, whose moderate foreign policy was more to the paper's liking. It regretted that Ben-Gurion continued to interfere in politics and was unhappy when he returned to oust Sharett.[43]

The integration of the immigrants, especially those oriental Jews who had been forced to leave north African countries, was watched with fascination. Less affection was displayed for the political behaviour of the religious population. The *Jewish Chronicle* sympathised with the construction of an intense religious life, but not the interpolation of religion into affairs of state – even a Jewish state. For example, when Orthodox Jews demonstrated against the conscription of women into the Israeli Defence Force, the paper commented on 24 July 1953 that 'much of the present opposition comes from elements which, in Israel, still have as their background habits and conditions of medieval or ghetto life, in which women are kept very much in the home'.

The *Jewish Chronicle* always hoped that the Western Powers, including Britain, would guarantee Israel's precarious borders. The frontier warfare between 1950 and 1955 reinforced this wish, but it was constantly frustrated by the Foreign Office policy of supporting the Arab states, even at the cost of sacrificing Israel's security. This policy reached its apogee under the Prime Minister, Anthony Eden, in November 1955. In a speech at the Guildhall Eden declared that it might be necessary to impose a settlement on the region and adjust Israel's borders to pacify Arab opinion. The *Jewish Chronicle* was appalled by such a notion and apprehensive of the clash of loyalties which the proposal threatened to revive.[44]

Editorials repeatedly contended that Arab nationalism, as represented chiefly by Abdul Nasser in Egypt, could not be appeased and represented the real threat to western interests in the region. The British Government was urged to see Israel as a loyal ally in the Middle East and a potential bulwark against both Soviet influence and Arab ambitions. When Nasser, bolstered by Russian arms supplies, nationalised the Suez Canal, the *Jewish Chronicle* argued that this proved how vital Israel was to the West. 'The choice before the Western powers', it declared on 3 August 1956, 'seems to be reduced to this: either they support Israel and maintain their foothold in the Middle East, or they abandon Israel and make it infinitely more difficult to defend their position.'[45] The Suez War of 1956 and Israel's campaign in the Sinai appeared to vindicate the line which the paper had been taking, and it basked in the era of harmonious relations between Britain and Israel which followed.[46]

In the short term, however, the Suez War provoked enormous controversy and Anglo-Jewry did not go untouched. The paper had prophesied on 19 December 1947 that with the creation of the state the spectre of 'dual loyalty', which had hung over the Zionist Movement since the days of Herzl, would vanish. It prodded the Zionist Organisation to disband and turn itself into an essentially pro-Israel philanthropic institution. In reality, the nexus between diaspora Jews and Israel proved harder to define, let alone institutionalise. A decade later, the paper acknowledged mournfully that 'the establishment of the State of Israel has presented us with a new set of ideologies which sometimes drive us into sharp conflict with our previously held notions'. In November 1956, Jewish MPs had to decide how they would vote when Parliament debated the Sinai campaign. Of the nineteen Jews in Parliament, seventeen were in the opposition Labour Party and two were in the Conservative Party. Labour was hostile to the Suez expedition and charged the Government with 'colluding' in Israel's attack on Egypt; the Conservatives staunchly supported Britain's new ally in the Middle East. In the subsequent vote the Jewish MPs followed their respective party's line, to the disgust of large swathes of Anglo-Jewry. Letters poured in to the *Jewish Chronicle* belabouring the Labour MPs and accusing them of 'betraying' Israel. There was especial ire against Barnett Janner, MP, who was president of both the Board of Deputies and the Zionist Federation. But the paper asserted firmly that 'Jewish MPs in their capacity as Members of Parliament, do not represent Jewish interests.' In any case, the issue was the conduct of the British Government and not the behaviour of Israel.[47]

The question of Israel–diaspora relations remained a conundrum to which editors of the *Jewish Chronicle* turned their thoughts over and over again. The paper strenuously disagreed with Nahum Goldmann, the influential leader of the World Jewish Congress, when he demanded that Israel should give priority in its foreign policy to Jews in the diaspora and create a real partnership in which the two sides consulted and determined policy. An editorial on 28 March 1958 objected that: 'Acceptance of such a plan would have meant for Jews in many countries the explicit surrender of all that they had fought for in the past century or longer in the way of emancipation and equal rights as citizens.'

Despite these domestic complications and its equivocal diplomatic outcome, the war stabilised Israel's border situation for a decade. The *Jewish Chronicle* celebrated Israel's tenth anniversary in 1958 with a forty-eight-page supplement bearing a striking cover designed by George Him. Covering every possible aspect of Israel's political, economic, social, cultural and religious life, it exuded a mood of confidence and joy.[48]

8 The *Jewish Chronicle* under William Frankel, 1958–1977

Angry young men and Anglo-Jewry, 1958–1967

John Shaftesley had originally been appointed acting editor as a stop gap while Kessler and the Board found someone of higher calibre to fill the post. He remained in the editorial chair for twelve years, because it proved difficult to find anyone suitable who could take over at once. As a solution to the Board's dilemma, it was decided to recruit a non-journalist and groom him for the job. In April 1955, William Frankel, a barrister, was appointed general manager to replace A. B. Guthrie on his retirement. Three years later, Shaftesley was made an executive director and assigned responsibility for the *Jewish Gazette* in Manchester. Frankel took his place as editor of the *Jewish Chronicle*.[1]

William Frankel was born in 1917 in Whitechapel, east London. His parents had come to Britain from Przemysl, in Galicia, about six years earlier. After a spell in business his father settled down to a modest career as a synagogue official. William, the second of three sons, was born in a one-up, one-down terraced house in Eastman's Court, off Petticoat Lane. He grew up in a closed environment of *shtiebels* and *chedarim*, and was educated at the Jews' Free Infants' School, Berner Street School and St George's-in-the-East Central School. This qualified him for a humdrum clerical position, but two of William's teachers encouraged him to sit the exams for secondary school. He passed and went to the Regent Street Polytechnic School, far from the East End. This experience, and his early teachers, opened up the wider world and instilled in him an appetite for ideas. Yet he remained grounded in traditional Judaism, the sphere in which he began his communal activities.[2]

Frankel studied medicine at the Polytechnic for one and half years, but left to find paid employment. During 1939, he got married and at the outbreak of war was working as the secretary of the Mizrachi Federation, the religious Zionist Movement. Having been rejected for military service on health grounds, he and his wife, Gertrude, left London because of the blitz. They ended up in Cambridge, where William enrolled with the evacuated London School of Economics to read law. In 1944 he started practising at the Bar and over the next ten years built up a substantial practice.

In February 1945, Frankel was appointed as the European, later London, correspondent for the American Jewish Committee. David Kessler, who was active in the Anglo-Jewish Association at this time, first encountered him in connection with this work, and they continued to meet regularly during the late 1940s and early 1950s. In 1954 Kessler asked Frankel to take over as general manager of the *Jewish Chronicle*, and Frankel accepted.

The paper he joined in July 1955 was, in his words, 'not a happy house'. Shaftesley did not take kindly to Kessler's practice of taking the galley proofs of the editorials home on a Wednesday night, where he read and commented on them before delivering them to the composing room the following day. There was a feeling amongst the directors and the younger journalists that Shaftesley had allowed the paper to fall into a dull routine. According to Chaim Bermant, who was later recruited to the paper by Frankel, 'Year after year during the feast days and fasts much the same articles by the same pens appeared under different titles, and the editorial columns seemed barely alive to the metamorphoses which had taken place in Jewish affairs.'[3]

In his three years as general manager, Frankel learned the newspaper business as well as the specific aspects of running the *Jewish Chronicle*. However, the Board was aware that he lacked journalistic experience. So, at the same time Frankel was made editor, Phillip Zec (1909–83) was appointed a director with a brief to act as his mentor. Zec had been the editor of the *Sunday Pictorial*, but was probably best known as a political cartoonist. During the war, he had incurred Churchill's wrath for a famous cartoon attacking the selfish attitudes of people on the Home Front. He later became a director of the *Daily Mirror* and was brought into the *Jewish Chronicle* by his colleague Ellis Birk. At the same time, Michel Oppenheimer retired from the chairmanship and was replaced by Kessler, who purchased his shareholding. Sidney Moss, who was the company secretary and accountant, was appointed general manager. A new era in the history of the *Jewish Chronicle* opened.[4]

Frankel was determined to introduce into the paper the issues that were agitating the wider society and the young voices which were challenging received wisdom. It was his ambition to make the *Jewish Chronicle* more than the 'organ of Anglo-Jewry': he wanted it to become an international Jewish newspaper, covering world stories with a corps of reporters of which any other paper would have been proud. The quality of the leader and feature writing was improved by bringing in a team that included

Alfred Sherman, Chaim Bermant, Terence Prittie and Geoffrey Paul. Frankel was not a journalist by training and accepted this limitation, but he was adept at getting his leader writers to produce a good first draft of what he wanted the paper to say, which he would then work on until it met with his satisfaction.

Other changes in personnel reflected the new priorities. Frankel recruited fresh Israel correspondents and a panel of feature writers from the United States to ensure that coverage of the largest and most vibrant Jewish centres was of the highest standard. Every week he made certain there was a foreign news story on the front page and a feature on either a foreign affairs subject or an item of current debate on the opinion page. Between 1958 and 1968, the *Jewish Chronicle* covered, or commented on, the Cuban Revolution, the emergency in the Congo, the end of French rule in Algeria, the Nuclear Test Ban Treaty, Kennedy's assassination, Vietnam and Rhodesia's unilateral declaration of independence. Naturally, it gave massive coverage to the Eichmann trial in 1961–2 and the controversies which it stimulated.

Gradually the old guard, several of whom had been with the paper since the days of Asher Myers, Israel Davis and 'L. J. G.', retired, and Frankel was able to advance younger talent. He introduced several new, regular columns and made greater use of photo-journalism. The innovations included 'Personal Opinion', a sparky commentary on the week's events by 'Ben Azai'; and 'Teenage Topics' for the teen-market, featuring David Jacobs, the celebrated broadcaster. The reviews and features bristled with names from the front ranks of journalism, criticism and scholarship such as Clare Rayner, John Gross and Jonathan Miller. The arts coverage by Charles Landstone and Pamela Melnikoff fastened on to the crop of youthful talent that included David Kossoff, Miriam Karlin, Warren Mitchell, Bernard Bresslaw, Helen Shapiro, Lionel Blair, Manfred Mann and Brian Epstein amongst many others. With this profusion of Jewish cultural creativity, there was never any shortage of personalities from the film, theatre, television or music world to feature in the paper.

Frankel also embraced the revolution in design that was sweeping through the publishing world, an area in which Zec took a strong interest. The format of the paper was overhauled again in 1961, and a more adventurous use was made of graphics. Allen Hutt and Terence Conran were brought in to advise on the paper's fresh look. It acquired a new typeface in 1960 (the first change since 1937), which was modified in 1963 and 1966. That year the masthead was redesigned under Conran's direction. The *Jewish Chronicle* looked snappier and more exciting than ever before.[5]

The Anglo-Jewish population which it now served was much changed. It had become predominantly middle class and suburban. Jews had deserted the old 'Jewish trades' of clothing, furs, footwear and furniture manufacture as workers, although they remained heavily involved as employers. Around one-fifth of employed Jews were in the distributive trades, with similar proportions in service industries, including the financial sector, and in the professions. Some 50 per cent were self-employed, one of the most distinctive features of the occupational pattern of British Jews. It was an 'affluent' population. *Jewish Chronicle* readership surveys indicated that over 50 per cent of the paper's readers – a skewed, but still significant sample – owned cars, and nearly 90 per cent had televisions, fridges and vacuum cleaners. Sixty per cent went away for holidays, half of them abroad, which was six times the national average.[6]

Affluence was reflected in the activities of Jewish youth: like other teenagers they were enjoying the booming 'youth culture'. This environment was not friendly to the continuity of traditional authority or tradition itself. According to the author Norman Cohen, addressing a symposium in 1962, 'the great bulk' of Anglo-Jewry had 'only the slightest concern with Judaism'. While there were a number of flourishing day-schools in London, Liverpool and Manchester, these catered for no more than 8,000 Jewish children in the country (out of an estimated 50,000), and only about half had a regular exposure to Jewish religious teaching.[7] While talented young Jews were making an impression on every area of cultural life, few applied their energy to Jewish learning. Frankel was disturbed by this discrepancy, and one of his first priorities as editor was to explore the reasons for it.

In 1958, Brian Glanville published *The Bankrupts*, a novel that depicted suburban Anglo-Jewry as materialistic and spiritually desiccated. Frankel asked him to do a series of interviews with other young Jewish writers 'to present to our readers the attitudes taken up by the younger generation of Jewish writers in England to Judaism and the Jewish community'. Over the succeeding weeks, Glanville interviewed Wolf Mankowitz, Peter Schaffer, Alexander Baron, Bernard Kops, Arnold Wesker and Dannie Abse. Almost every one of the interviewees was indifferent or hostile towards Judaism, could not define what it meant to be Jewish except in a negative sense, and complained that Anglo-Jewry was a cultural wasteland. Schaffer, for example, said that 'when people talk about Judaism they're simply talking about Yiddishkeit really, and I'm sick and tired of Yiddishkeit: it's the most boring thing in the world'. Baron declared: 'I don't think there's any real cultural life in the Jewish community.'[8]

Such views were displeasing to Frankel, but he regarded them as a challenge. The leading article in the *Jewish Chronicle* on 19 December

1958, accompaying the first of the series, retorted that 'To deplore the attitude of this generation is not enough: we must endeavour to change it. If we feel that young men would not be alienated from Judaism if they knew more about it, then we must endeavour to teach them ... The sickness from which Judaism in England is suffering shows itself, among other ways, in an attitude of aloofness to the perplexed.' The difference between his approach and that of John Shaftesley could not have been starker. Shaftesley wrote privately to a friend in 1963 that 'Some years ago, when I was still the Editor of the *Jewish Chronicle*, Glanville, who was already showing signs of becoming the blue-eyed boy of some of my colleagues, came to see me and we had a long talk. I gained the impression that he had a chip on both shoulders (and no doubt he thought me a fuddy-duddy). The trouble is that he and his contemporaries write without knowledge, and they tend to blame others for what is their own fault.'[9]

The series stirred up a hornets' nest and led to weeks of subsequent discussion on the letters pages, much of it angry. But the *Jewish Chronicle* insisted on 6 February 1959 that all was not lost: 'It is ignorance of, and indifference to Judaism, rather than hostility, which is the problem.' This conviction was to govern the future course of the paper, with significant repercussions for Anglo-Jewry as a whole. Frankel set out to show that Judaism had something to say on every major issue that cropped up; and he offered a platform for those exponents of Judaism who rejected reliance on authorities in favour of persuasion and the exercise of reason.

No major news story in the general press was allowed to pass without being tested for a Jewish angle. The *Lady Chatterley* obscenity trial and 'permissiveness', the drugs problem and the rise of the Campaign for Nuclear Disarmament (CND) were all the subject of rumination and investigation within the context of Jewish society. To show the relevance of Judaism, the *Jewish Chronicle* published the views of rabbis on contemporary issues. It ran a series of five articles on 'Living Judaism' in November 1959 intended to show that Judaism could be made to work in twentieth-century society. Reports and features on these subjects never failed to trigger a response from readers who were clearly divided on generational and religious lines. Older and more Orthodox readers found it hard to stomach the aspects of modern Jewish life which were being exposed to them.

Frankel gave the *Jewish Chronicle* a distinctly liberal inflection, particularly in its comments on race and immigration issues. He was impressed by the courage of American friends, rabbis, who participated in the Freedom Marches in the southern states of the USA. The paper commended the activities of the civil rights movement in America, consistently criticised apartheid in South Africa and lent its support to liberal voices in the Jewish community there.[10] Editorials frequently pointed to the links between anti-Semitism and anti-black racism, condemned racial violence in British cities and the colour bar, and praised legislation on race relations. Reminding readers of the 1905 Aliens Act and the Jewish immigrant experience, the paper declared the 1962 Immigration Act to be a 'retrograde step'. Frankel delighted in controversy and, on this issue, there was plenty. Ian Mikardo, MP, Alfred Sherman and Julius Gould wrote articles offering widely divergent points of view, while readers responded with large numbers of letters, often in furious language.[11]

Communal debate in Anglo-Jewry had tended to concentrate on minor issues which quickly degenerated into personal attacks. Frankel wanted controversy, but about principles, not personalities. He wanted the *Jewish Chronicle* to be critical of institutions and their established leadership, taking the role of a 'loyal opposition' over and above petty conflicts concerning place and individual authority. One of the paper's first targets was the Board of Deputies, which was about to celebrate its 200th anniversary. The *Jewish Chronicle* assailed the unreality of the Board's proceedings as it solemnly discussed foreign policy which it could not influence and took decisions on domestic issues which it lacked the machinery to enforce. 'Thus far', it concluded on 25 September 1959, 'the Board has failed to make a satisfactory adjustment to the changed conditions of the mid-twentieth century.' As hopes for reform were thwarted, impatience replaced the gentle prodding. By the mid 1960s, the paper considered that the Board had become ineffectual through 'obsolete machinery' and an equally obsolete mentality.[12]

A succession of anti-Jewish incidents throughout the 1960s exposed the Board's cumbersome workings. At the start of 1960, neo-Nazi activity in West Germany found an echo in Britain in the form of vandalism, including swastika daubings on communal buildings, synagogues and tombstones in Jewish cemeteries. Further waves occurred in the summer of 1962, the first part of 1963, and 1965. The *Jewish Chronicle* itself became the target for attack. The building suffered a broken window in January 1960 and was slightly damaged by a bomb in March 1963. It was the policy of the paper to counsel vigilance, although equally firmly to dispel panic and discourage Jewish vigilante groups. On the other hand, editorials accused the Board's Defence Committee of being 'rusty and antiquated' and observed that if the Board were seen to be acting decisively, public anxiety would be allayed.[13]

Although it maintained an impressive coverage of organised racism, editorially the *Jewish Chronicle* dismissed attacks on buildings and individuals as isolated incidents, the work of crackpots. The paper stopped short of the conclusion reached by black activists that racial attacks were symptoms of structural racism in British society. Yet four in-depth articles on the exclusion of Jews from certain golf clubs in April 1960 produced disturbing results. 'The careful investigations conducted by our correspondents', the paper commented on 8 April 1960, 'show beyond any doubt that this discrimination is widespread.' It was a 'grave reproach to the British reputation for fairness' and revealed 'a distressing symptom of the persistence of anti-Jewish prejudice in a particular economic and social section of the population'. In February 1961 an inquiry into the application of quotas against Jews seeking admission to public schools had a similarly unpleasant outcome.

While the paper's critique of the Board of Deputies provoked a reaction amongst readers and the debate over Jewish defence proved as resilient as ever, none of these subjects stimulated as much correspondence as the discussion of Judaism. As Kessler and Shaftesley had discovered, Orthodox Jews would not meekly accept criticism of their beliefs and practices in the paper. Yet Frankel believed passionately that Orthodoxy had to adapt and modernise if it was to survive, and, from the outset of his editorship, the paper's editorial comment projected this conviction.

The *Jewish Chronicle* did not find any signs of salvation in the United Synagogue, to which Frankel belonged. It scorned ambitious plans to build a large, prestigious 'cathedral synagogue' at Marble Arch. An editorial on 21 November 1958 remarked caustically that 'Neither a "cathedral" nor opulent banqueting halls will help to perpetuate our faith.' In general, the paper was worried by the trend towards a stricter interpretation of Jewish law and practice, which it dubbed 'militant orthodoxy on the offensive'. Such observations were not welcomed by the Orthodox rabbinate or congregations, and letters poured in contesting the paper's point of view. The Orthodox community in London went still further and attempted to exert its authority in an unprecedented fashion.[14]

At the end of 1960, Frankel was summoned before the Beth Din on account of an article, which it considered derogatory, concerning the views of Orthodox rabbis on mixed dancing. Before he responded, he consulted Rabbi Kopul Rosen, the head of Carmel College. Rosen advised him against appearing, since the Beth Din could hardly be neutral in the case of an alleged attack on a group of rabbis. Moreover, it would create a dangerous precedent: the Beth Din would effectively acquire the right to control the *Jewish Chronicle*'s religious reporting. In any case, Rosen advised that its jursidiction was limited to desecration of Jewish Law, and this matter was *ultra vires*: it was 'too absurd' for a religious court to claim authority over standards of journalism. Rosen proposed that the directors should send a polite note of refusal to its demand.[15]

However, Frankel thought it would be wrong for him to give the impression of sheltering behind the Board. He agreed to appear as an 'act of courtesy' to the Chief Rabbi, while rejecting the Beth Din's authority in the matter.[16] Frankel was defiant, but he felt let down by sympathetic rabbis who understood what was at stake in the Beth Din's challenge. He told Rosen that 'these are people who are trying to impose fanatical standards which debase Judaism. I will certainly carry on the good fight, but it would be nice if the responsible rabbinate were to join in.'[17] The conflict between the *Jewish Chronicle* and the Orthodox communities would shortly reach its climax in the course of the 'Jacobs Affair'.

The pressing need for scholars and religious leaders capable of facing the challenges of modernity imposed great expectations on Jews' College. When Rabbi Dr Isidore Epstein retired from the principalship, the *Jewish Chronicle* yearned for an appointment that would supply the wants of Anglo-Jewry. It proclaimed in a leading article on 24 July 1959 that 'The College needs to be strengthened in self-confidence, so that it can champion the combination of traditional studies with a contemporary approach. The need is to train ministers who can reason with the laity and thereby strengthen the hold of Judaism on the uncommitted.' The key word was 'reason', and it resonated with the title of a book on Judaism published in 1957 by Rabbi Dr Louis Jacobs, *We Have Reason to Believe*.

Louis Jacobs had become the minister at the New West End Synagogue in London in 1953, where he first met William Frankel. The two men developed a close friendship, and Frankel had played a large part in the appointment of Jacobs as moral tutor and lecturer in pastoral theology at Jews' College. In *We Have Reason to Believe* Jacobs restated Judaism attractively in a modern idiom, and to Frankel he embodied many of his own ideals for Judaism and Jewish learning. However, in the book Louis Jacobs had also reiterated his long-held convictions about biblical scholarship and human agency in the evolution of the Torah. Indeed, when Frankel and Jacobs discussed the book before its publication by Vallentine, Mitchell, of which Frankel was a director, he warned him that it might endanger his chances of advancement.[18]

On his appointment to the staff of Jews' College, Jacobs understood that he would become principal in due course. But the job was in the gift of the Chief Rabbi, and he was lobbied by Epstein and others who considered Jacobs unsound on theological grounds. After two years' delay, Brodie appointed himself principal, pro tem. The *Jewish Chronicle* had been suspicious about the reasons for the delay and had been affronted by Epstein's indirect attacks on Jacobs.[19] So it viewed the appointment of Brodie with dismay. In the Yom Kippur issue on 15 September 1961, the paper published a fulsome profile of Jacobs which concluded: 'If Anglo-Jewry can show the wisdom to provide opportunities for making the fullest use of his rare combination of qualities, it will not have to regret, when it is too late, the loss of yet another of its spiritual leaders.' The editorial commented pointedly that: 'A religious revival will never be brought about by prohibitions and denunciations, by exclusive claims to authenticity, or by mutual recriminations between different sections of the community.' This and subsequent broadsides did nothing to shift the opposition to the appointment of Jacobs. He resigned from Jews' College on 14 December 1961.

Frankel led with this news on 22 December, giving the inside story in great detail. An editorial the following week made it clear what he felt was at stake: 'It is whether the Orthodox Establishment in this country will successfully negotiate the transition to twentieth century Western life while maintaining Judaism's special vigour, relevance, and communal unity. The alternative is to lapse into narrow, dogmatic rigidity which must inevitably bring about disunity and decline.' The editorial accused the Chief Rabbi of submitting to Right-wing Orthodoxy which did not represent the mainstream of Anglo-Jewry.[20]

By nailing Louis Jacobs's flag to the masthead of the *Jewish Chronicle*, Frankel had inextricably linked the fortunes of both. Over the following months, letters poured into the paper – supporting Jacobs or Brodie. Rabbis, scholars, students, writers all expressed their opinions. The daily press picked up the story and turned it into a national issue, comparing it to the row in the Church of England over the controversial appointment of John Robinson as Bishop of Woolwich. The *Jewish Chronicle* was openly partisan. On 5 January 1962, it printed Chief Rabbi Hertz's 1932 definition of 'progressive conservatism' and a 'poll' of rabbis intended to show that the ministry was split. At the start of February, an article explaining the views of the Beth Din on Jacobs's suitability as a candidate noted that four of the five *dayanim* – rabbinical judges – were foreign-born and of ripe years. It clearly implied that they were not suitable to determine who could best serve Anglo-Jewry in the 1960s. A second leader in the same issue attacked an Orthodox rabbi in Cardiff who refused to allow a couple to use certain catering facilities because one of them had parents who were members of a Reform Synagogue.[21]

Rabbis and laymen in the Orthodox community struck back. In March 1962, the Union of Orthodox Hebrew Congregations issued an official warning 'to the Jewish public to beware of the anti-Torah influences which the *Jewish Chronicle* is bound to have especially upon youth'. Sidney, later Sir Sidney, Hamburger, a leading figure in Manchester Jewry, told Frankel that the *Jewish Chronicle* had 'veered from its central point of Orthodoxy'. Even those who had reservations about strict Orthodoxy looked askance at the paper's conduct. Norman Cohen pronounced that 'the attitude of the Organ of Anglo-Jewry merely makes inevitable the ascendency of the right-wing which it so frequently deplores. By adding to the bewilderment of the middle of the road [Jews], it is made more difficult than ever for them to assert leadership.'[22]

The *Jewish Chronicle* counter-attacked by alleging that there was an orchestrated campaign of pressure on Brodie from within the Orthodox communities reinforced by a concerted effort to swamp the correspondence columns of the Jewish press. Frankel sought allies at home and abroad. In a letter to Wolfe Kelman, professional head of the Rabbinical Assembly in New York, Frankel summed up the issues as: '(a) Reactionary versus Progressive orthodoxy. (b) The acceptance of the critical position in Bible Studies and (c) The infallibility of the Chief Rabbi. If the boys would express an opinion of these matters, it would be interesting.' However, as he told Kelman, the response was disappointing.[23] He suggested to the Jewish scholar Raphael Loewe that a collective letter by Jewish academics on the Jews' College fracas would be helpful. Frankel drafted a letter which was then circulated, with some success.[24]

In April 1962 the Chief Rabbi returned from an overseas pastoral tour and soon confirmed the veto on Jacobs. He justified his action by imputing that Jacobs lacked both scholarly merit and leadership qualities and was insufficiently Orthodox. These charges outraged Frankel. He wrote to Rabbi Louis Rabinowitz, the former Chief Rabbi of South Africa who now lived in Jerusalem, mocking the accusation that Jacobs was a 'crypto-Conservative', an adherent of the American Jewish movement which was anathema to the Beth Din. 'That seems to be a fashionable smear now for anybody in the orthodox camp who shows any signs of intellectual activity.'[25] The *Jewish Chronicle* launched a stinging attack on Brodie. Notwithstanding earlier assurances that it had no intention of impugning the authority of the Chief Rabbinate, it now clashed directly with the spiritual head of Anglo-Jewry. The crisis turned into one in which Brodie's authority was at issue, and, in reply, the Chief Rabbi roundly condemned the paper's stance.[26]

Relations between the *Jewish Chronicle* and the Orthodox communities worsened. Within the United Synagogue a memorandum was drawn up for the president of the US and the chairman of the Chief Rabbinate Council listing 'the planned and persistent attacks which appear in the columns of the Jewish Chronicle against orthodoxy in general and the central religious authorities of the Community in particular'. The paper was accused of abusing the reluctance of Orthodox Jews to issue writs on such matters and undermining the authority of Jewish religious leaders around the country. 'The interpretation by the Jewish Chronicle of communal trends and events is tendentious and its sympathies are clearly with the Reform and the American Conservative movements.' This bias was also allegedly made manifest by the selection of letters for publication.[27]

In an effort at conciliation, Frankel and Kessler met Brodie in October 1963. Writing later to the Chief Rabbi, Kessler summed up his thoughts on their discussion: 'I think we are agreed that it is time our relationship was put on a more constructive footing, and I shall indeed be pleased if we can find ways of narrowing the differences which have shown themselves recently. It must be in the interests of Anglo-Jewry that the Jewish Chronicle and your office should co-operate wherever possible. No doubt we shall continue to find ourselves at variance from time to time, but I think we should be able to respect one another's points of view even if we do not agree. Perhaps the essence of the matter is that there should be closer liaison between Hamilton Terrace [the Chief Rabbi's residence] and Furnival Street.' Kessler insisted that the paper 'never set itself out to be the mouthpiece of Liberal or Reform Judaism'. It stood for the 'Progressive Orthodoxy' typified by J. H. Hertz, a product of the Jewish Theological Seminary in New York with which 'editorially speaking' the paper was 'basically in harmony'. However, as a newspaper it sought to represent the opinions of every section of Jewry with the utmost objectivity.[28]

Brodie responded positively to this exchange: 'I think it helped to clear the air somewhat and create the desirability of further meetings with you and the Editor in the near future.'[29] However, the concerted attempt on the part of the *Jewish Chronicle* to heal the breach with the Orthodox community and its leadership was frustrated by the eruption of the second 'Jacobs Affair'. In December 1963 Rabbi Dr Chaim Pearl, who had succeeded Louis Jacobs at the New West End Synagogue, accepted a post in the United States, leaving the way clear for Jacobs to resume his former position. He was duly invited to do so by the synagogue board of management. But the zealous secretary of the United Synagogue pointed out to the Chief Rabbi that under its by-laws Brodie had to provide a certificate for the incumbent – even if he was resuming a position for which he had already been certified as fit and proper. Brodie declined to issue one. Despite appeals from the board and congregation, Sir Isaac Wolfson, the new president of the United Synagogue, upheld the Chief Rabbi's stand. With Jacobs banned from officiating at, or on behalf of, the New West End Synagogue, at the start of May 1964 his supporters formally seceded from it. They set up the independent New London Congregation in St John's Wood, with Jacobs as their minister.[30]

Following the Chief Rabbi's refusal to certify Jacobs as fit and proper to be a minister, the *Jewish Chronicle* took up his case again, with renewed vigour. It faulted the logic of the veto by pointing out that Jacobs had been allowed to hold the pulpit at the New West End after he had published *We Have Reason to Believe*. But the crux of the matter was political: would the Chief Rabbi allow the 'Right wing' to determine the standards for the formerly latitudinarian, 'Broad Church' United Synagogue? Again, the paper denied any intention of questioning the Chief Rabbi's authority, but it warned Brodie that by staking his authority on barring Jacobs he would be to blame if his office lost respect.[31]

Brodie responded to this challenge with a public statement rebuking the *Jewish Chronicle* for its position with regard to the 'Jacobs Affair' and indicting its attitude towards Orthodoxy in general:

The travesty of our traditional Judaism has been featured in our monopolistic Jewish press for some time. There has been a consistent denigration of authentic Judaism and religious authority which has tended to create religious confusion and a spirit of divisiveness within our community and which in no small measure has contributed to the present situation. While we believe in freedom of the press, we should not allow this freedom to be abused and even turned into a tyranny as is attempted by the *Jewish Chronicle* which, in recent years, no doubt for reasons of its own, has not presented an objective picture of the Anglo-Jewish scene, nor has it reflected the tradition and sentiment of Anglo-Jewry.

Of course, the statement was carried in the *Jewish Chronicle*, and Frankel derided the notion of a conspiracy. The paper had been scrupulous in reporting every strand of opinion as long as comment was vouchsafed to the paper's representatives, which was not always the case with some sections of Anglo-Jewry. It asserted that 'Our news columns report events: our editorial opinion is our own. While acknowledging the need for a free press the Chief Rabbi appears at the same time in surprisingly intemperate terms to deny our right to express reasoned opinions if he disagrees with them.'[32]

During the first phase of the 'affair', the general press followed the drama avidly. There was comment in the *Evening Standard*, *The Times*, the *Daily Telegraph*, the *Guardian*, the *Yorkshire Post*, the *Sunday Times* and the religious weeklies. Anglo-Jewry was ill at ease with this sort of exposure and did not share Frankel's belief in the merit of controversy. Letters arrived by the sackful, many of them bitterly hostile to the stand the *Jewish Chronicle* was taking. The 'affair' had international resonances, too. In June 1964, Richard Yaffe, the paper's correspondent in New York, reported a comment by Dr Yaacov Herzog, who was a candidate for the Chief Rabbinate, that the paper had been partisan and selected letters unfairly. Frankel replied that, of course, he was partisan, but 'apart from general tut-tuttings that I should have been so presumptuous as to have criticised a Chief Rabbi, there isn't any reasoned argument to suggest that my arguments were faulty'. As for the alleged selection of correspondence for publication, he had received 'up to 100 letters a week. They were equally divided pro and con. The letters I published, about 10 % of those received, were almost equally divided.' If there was any preponderance on the Jacobs side, it was because 'whereas all the pro-Jacobs letters were reasonably written and could all have been published, a very large proportion of the letters on the other side were either illiterate, abusive, or defamatory'.[33]

If the paper had been unable to affect the outcome of the struggle at Jews' College or the New West End Synagogue, its support was crucial to Jacobs's followers and to a large extent made it possible for them to establish and maintain a new congregation. In August 1964, Frankel wrote to Richard Yaffe that 'Of course this was a fight we couldn't win because the issue was decided by one individual with dictatorial powers. But it was impossible not to have made a fight of it, and, if nothing else, it brought some life into a lethargic community.' It was not by chance that in the spring of 1965, the paper ran a series on 'Jewish heresies', concluding with an editorial note that 'Where there is no heresy there is stagnation.' Frankel subsequently conceded that some of the attacks on the Chief Rabbi and the religious establishment had been 'unnecessarily offensive', but remained convinced that the controversy had been worth while.[34] If Louis Jacobs had not existed, the *Jewish Chronicle* would probably have had to invent him.

The appointment of a new Chief Rabbi in 1964 occasioned fresh acrimony between the *Jewish Chronicle* and the assertive, vocal elements of Orthodoxy. Frankel regarded the concept, and trappings, of a 'Chief Rabbi' as un-Jewish and faintly ridiculous. An editorial in July 1964 suggested that it was time to admit that the Chief Rabbinate of the United Hebrew Congregations of the British Commonwealth of Nations now only represented a part of Anglo-Jewry. The office was rooted in an age of 'Victorian paternalism', and its title should be amended to 'something less unreal'.[35]

As on earlier occasions, the paper discussed the prospect of the election, the qualities needed in a candidate and the scope of the office. At first it appeared that the favoured candidate was Rabbi Immanuel Jakobovits. Sir Isaac Wolfson, president of the United Synagogue, had met and been impressed by him on his visits to New York, where Jakobovits ministered to the Fifth Avenue Synagogue. Frankel, however, preferred Louis Rabinowitz, Chief Rabbi of South Africa. In November 1962 he told Rabinowitz that the *Jewish Chronicle* would support his candidacy. 'The militant ultras here are, I believe, fully committed to Jakobovits and the fact that there are Mizrahi people among them will probably make it even more difficult. But we have some years to work on it and, without flattering you, it would seem to me that it would not be difficult for any unprejudiced and impartial observer who is thinking of the good of the community, to make a choice between the two.' Initially, such assistance would be limited to keeping Rabinowitz before the Anglo-Jewish public, since anything more forthright would probably do harm rather than good to his cause. 'I think our function would be to keep the facts before the Community without advocating, at any rate until the very last stages, any particular candidate. I think the facts and the records will speak more strongly than editorial opinion.'[36]

However, the election machinery was cloaked in secrecy, and it was soon apparent that Sir Isaac Wolfson had virtually made the choice himself, reducing the selection committee of the Chief Rabbinate Conference to a 'rubber stamp'. Unexpectedly, Jakobovits was supplanted by Dr Yaacov Herzog, an Israeli Foreign Ministry official who was the son of a former Chief Rabbi of Israel and a qualified rabbi himself. The *Jewish Chronicle* expressed bemusement at these gyrations, but it approved the choice of Herzog. Frankel wrote personally to congratulate him, although he admitted that 'you know I had some doubts about it, but that's history'.[37]

Several months later, Herzog withdrew because of ill-health, and when he died soon afterwards the selection machinery resumed its operations. In September 1966, it was finally announced that Jakobovits would be appointed Chief Rabbi. The paper cautiously welcomed this outcome, but not long afterwards there were troubling signs that the appointment would do nothing to smooth relations between the *Jewish Chronicle* and the Chief Rabbinate. It became known to Frankel that Jakobovits had published in *Tradition*, a journal of American Orthodoxy, an article which referred to the *Jewish Chronicle* as 'a leader of the anti-Orthodox crusade'. The author implied that it was party to 'a modern blood libel' and had an effect comparable to the 'Protocols of the Elders of Zion'. Frankel wrote to Jakobovits 'to express my disappointment that you should make these unwarranted imputations against the JEWISH CHRONICLE'. Yet, in a gesture of conciliation, he chose not to write a letter to the journal for publication, 'because I am sure that it would be most unfortunate if, at this stage, you and the JEWISH CHRONICLE would appear to be in open conflict even though in replying to an attack and not initiating one'.[38]

When Immanuel Jakobovits was inducted into his office in April 1967, the *Jewish Chronicle* damned with faint praise and reiterated its distaste for the entire institution.[39] Notwithstanding the inauspicious exchange in the November of the previous year, it was not a question of personality: underlying the paper's unease was a differing conception of how best to preserve traditional Judaism. On 6 January 1967, the *Jewish Chronicle* declared that 'Unless strenuous efforts are made to give real leadership and guidance, especially to the younger generation, assimilation on an ever-wider scale is inevitable, and eventual disintegration is a real threat.' This anxious vision of the future and sense of urgency led to a harsh critique of communal institutions and leaders which was widely resented. Although it was the customary position of the *Jewish Chronicle*, the Orthodox population read Frankel's pleas for reform and progress, coupled with his resistance to extremism and intolerance, as an assault on their beliefs.

Clearly, a section of the Jewish population was alienated from the *Jewish Chronicle* by the 'Jacobs Affair' and its after-shocks, although the paper's circulation was not particularly affected. More serious were the challenges to its independence from powerful figures in Anglo-Jewry. Sir Isaac Wolfson, the chairman of Great Universal Stores and the president of the United Synagogue, expressed a serious interest in acquiring the paper, but was discouraged after taking the advice of Lord Thomson, the press magnate. At around the same time, John Shaftesley, who had been unhappy at his transfer from the editorship to the Board of Directors in 1958, was involved in some covert, and ultimately ineffectual, machinations to set up a rival to his former paper.[40]

These threatening moves gave more urgency to David Kessler's longstanding concern that steps should be taken to safeguard the paper's independence. The 'Jacobs Affair' and its aftermath thus accelerated the creation of the Jewish Chronicle Trust in 1969. The idea had been mooted long before. In November 1936, at the height of the struggle between Leopold Kessler and Mortimer Epstein, Harry L. Nathan, former Liberal MP for North-East Bethnal Green and later a Labour MP, minister and peer, approached Kessler, in his capacity as a solicitor, on behalf of a client (probably Sir Robert Waley Cohen) who wanted to buy 2,000–3,000 shares in the paper. Kessler told him that the shares under his control were not for sale. Indeed, he had arranged matters so that shares were transferred to his own children only on an undertaking that they would not allow them to pass out of the circle of Jewish people committed to the Jewish national cause.[41]

A few weeks later, Sir Robert Waley Cohen discussed with Kessler the idea of a *Jewish Chronicle* trust modelled on that of *The Times*. Kessler disparaged the notion: 'Unfortunately British Jewry has neither the enduring traditions, the unique institutions nor the brilliant and in-dependent journalists forming the rock on which to erect a structure intended to last.' He preferred to stick by the arrangements which he had made within his own family. Waley Cohen, who evidently fancied himself as a trustee, tried once more to persuade Kessler, but he was again rebuffed. Yet the proposal did not die altogether. In 1939, David Kessler made inquiries about the nature of *The Times'* Trust and was to return to the concept twenty-two years later.[42]

At the *Jewish Chronicle*'s 120th anniversary celebration dinner, held in the Stationers' Hall, David Kessler announced that the Board was contemplating the formation of a trust. The basis for this development lay in the fact that between 1939 and the 1960s, the Kessler family had gradually increased their shareholding in The Jewish Chronicle Ltd from just over 40 per cent to 80 per cent of the capital. The independence and integrity of the paper weighed heavily upon the shoulders of David Kessler, his brother and sister, who felt a duty to assure its future security after their passing. The creation of the trust proved to be an immensely complex undertaking that required extensive legal advice from the most esteemed authorities in the field, and it was not completed until October 1969.

In order to safeguard the legitimate interests of the shareholders and at the same time preserve the independence of the paper, the Board formed two new companies, both subsidiaries of Jewish Chronicle Ltd. The first, Jewish Chronicle Newspaper Ltd, assumed ownership of the goodwill, copyright and title of the newspaper itself. Everything else belonging to the parent company – the building, the composing department, and subsidiaries such as Vallentine, Mitchell and the *Jewish Gazette* – was retained in its hands. The directors of Jewish Chronicle Newspaper Ltd would be the same as those of the Jewish Chronicle Ltd, but the share capital was divided into two categories, 'A' and 'B' shares. The 'A' ordinary shares of a nominal value of £1 each were to be held by Jewish Chronicle Ltd and the 'B' ordinary shares of a nominal value of 1d. each were to be owned by the Jewish Chronicle Trust Ltd. The 'A' shares conferred the right to participate in the running of Jewish Chronicle Ltd, while the 'B' shares carried vital powers designed to safeguard the independence of the paper and control its policy.

The second company was the Jewish Chronicle Trust Ltd. The Kessler family agreed to hand over to it, gratis, all their 'B' shares. Subsequently, the Trust company acquired, from the shareholders, also free of charge, another 19 per cent of the 'B' shares, giving it 99 per cent control over the paper. This was the crucial element in determining the independence of the paper. The decision-making power was vested in the 'B' shares. Without the agreement of the Trust, the Board of Directors could not remove or appoint the editor or managing director, form any relationship with a third party permitting it to interfere in the paper's policy, or cease publication unless the paper was irredeemably uneconomic as certified by the company's auditors.

A majority of the trustees were always to be independent of the paper, and only a minority could be nominated by the Board of the *Jewish Chronicle*. The first chairman of the Board of Trustees was Lord Goodman. The independent members were the Hon. L. H. L. Cohen, the eldest son of Lord Cohen of Walmer and a former president of the Jewish Welfare Board, Mr Chaim Raphael, CBE, a research fellow at Sussex University and formerly a senior Treasury civil servant, and Dr J. B. Segal, professor of Semitic languages at the School of Oriental and African Studies, London University. The *Jewish Chronicle* Board nominated David Kessler, Viscount Samuel and Ellis Birk. The Trust was to be a self-perpetuating body which would be regulated by its Articles of Association designed to protect the autonomy and character of the paper.[43]

Israel, the Six-Day War and after, 1967–1977

Between 1958 and 1966, the *Jewish Chronicle* covered Israel's internal affairs and external relations in great detail. Editorial comment was always well informed and frequently critical. The paper disliked the endless political intrigues around Ben-Gurion, the routine irruption of religion into politics and what it saw as the mishandling of the state's economy. Yet the underlying treatment of Israel was marked by fascination, admiration and unflinching solidarity. It assailed the British Foreign Office for its complicity in the Arab boycott of Israeli produce and strongly objected to arms sales to Arab countries. There was also a noticeable change of attitude towards Israel's defence policy. The paper now dubbed cross-border actions 'retaliation' rather than 'reprisals' and consistently rejected international condemnation of Israel as the expression of a double standard. The raids were 'a regrettable necessity'.[44]

The tension between Israel and her neighbours in the months preceding the Six-Day War in 1967 gave Frankel time to prepare the paper for the looming conflict. He lined up several correspondents in Israel to cover the southern, northern and central fronts as well as army, navy and air force experts in Britain. Chaim Herzog, later to become President of Israel, was invited to become military correspondent. A close friend of Frankel since their days together at Cambridge, he was then a high-ranking officer in the reserves. Herzog accepted the commission provided that the front with Jordan remained quiet, which he expected would be the case. Otherwise, he explained to Frankel, he would be called up. His expectations were confounded, and his only reports were filed before war broke out. On the morning of Monday 5 June, Israeli aircraft destroyed the Egyptian air force on the ground and land forces rolled over the border into the Gaza Strip and Sinai. On the same day, the Jordanians shelled Jerusalem, and the war engulfed the area known as the West Bank.[45]

When the *Jewish Chronicle* went to press at the last possible moment on Thursday 8 June, it was obvious which way the tide of battle was flowing, but it was by no means clear when the fighting would end. Frankel settled for a front-page headline on 9 June 1967: 'Israel Sweeps to Victory', which, he reckoned, should cover most eventualities. The editorial rejected calls for Israel to withdraw from the conquered territories: 'It would be morally unjust, dangerous and futile. The impetus of Israel's military victory must be allowed to play its full and ultimately beneficent part in moving the region forward towards peace.' The essential task now was to establish 'viable strategic frontiers which will enable Israel to develop in peace and security'.

The mood amongst the *Jewish Chronicle* staff was jubilant. Like most British Jews, they had developed an enormous pride in Israel and identified closely with the state. In 1955, the staff had purchased an ambulance for the Magen Dovid Adom, the Israeli Red Cross, which was ceremonially handed over at Kfar Menachem by David Kessler in the presence of the British Ambassador. During the tense weeks before the war the atmosphere in the building had been apprehensive, and the relief at the scale of the military victory was consequently all the greater. When the news came through that Israeli paratroopers had driven the Jordanian forces out of the old city of Jerusalem, Kessler called the staff to the library to celebrate.

Yet the debate on the future of the occupied territories and Israel's frontiers began almost before the smoke of battle had cleared. Initially, the *Jewish Chronicle* insisted that Israel had to retain all conquered territory until a peace conference accorded her due recognition by her neighbours and viable, internationally guaranteed borders. The paper fully endorsed the extension of Israeli law, jurisdiction and administration over east Jerusalem. When Chief Rabbi Jakobovits intimated that it might be wise to announce a willingness to trade land for peace, the *Jewish Chronicle* cautioned him. A leading article on 30 June 1967 considered that 'There is no reason why Jews in the diaspora should not discuss and comment freely on Israeli affairs. But it must be remembered that on matters affecting its security the Government of Israel and its electorate alone bear the responsibility of decision-making.'[46]

In May 1968, Frankel toured the West Bank and reported on the 'invisible occupation'. It remained the view of the *Jewish Chronicle* that this was one of the most humane occupations in history, an ideal that was reinforced over the years by photographs of fraternisation and trading between Jews and Arabs. However, the paper brought to the attention of Jews in Britain the debate which developed in Israel on the fate of the occupied territories and the Palestinian Arab refugees. In August 1969, it ran a series of articles in which Shimon Peres, a leader of the Israeli Labour

Party, Paul Johnson, editor of the *New Statesman*, Moshe Sneh, head of the Israel Communist Party, and several other political figures and commentators from Israel gave their varied opinions on what should be done with the West Bank. In May 1970, an article appeared by Eliahu Sasson, a former Israeli Cabinet minister, explaining why it was essential, on demographic grounds, for Israel to leave the West Bank. A few months earlier, an editorial had advocated allowing refugees back into the West Bank and 'home rule'.[47]

The editorial policy of the paper towards the territories became starker and less restrained. A leading note on 27 July 1973 strongly criticised a statement by Moshe Dayan, the Minister of Defence, that Israel should set about 'creating facts', meaning Jewish settlements, on the West Bank: 'It is for Israel to decide on her own security requirements, and she is the only competent judge of them. But the "creation of facts" can very easily make the attainment of peace more difficult. Any Jewish community in the world, therefore, has the right to its own views on this matter and the right to point them out.' Unquestioning enthusiasm and a vicarious patriotism conditioned the way most British Jews regarded Israel, but the *Jewish Chronicle* gave its readers the opportunity to follow the internal debate on the fate of the West Bank and took an early stand on the settlements issue. In this it was not reflective of Anglo-Jewish public opinion, which, as later controversies would reveal, had hardly been influenced by the paper's outspokenness.

In the aftermath of the Six-Day War, successive peace initiatives on all sides came to naught. Kessler was troubled by the 'apparent lack of a long term policy for the occupied areas, and for dealing with Arab–Israel relations'. In March 1968, he wrote to several prominent Jewish figures, including Professor Norman Bentwich, Max Beloff, Bernard Lewis, Walter Laqueur, Ben Segal, Lord Segal, Marcus Sieff and Eli Lauterpacht with a view to forming a small group dedicated to 'formulating constructive suggestions which could perhaps form the basis for a debate in the columns of the Jewish Chronicle or elsewhere'. When, a year after the war, there was still no peace, the *Jewish Chronicle* commented ruefully that 'The brilliance which Israel displayed in the Six Day War has not been reproduced in her civil policy-making and political strategy.'[48]

A parallel disillusionment ran through the coverage of Israel's internal affairs. Between 1969 and 1972, Geoffrey Paul, in Jerusalem, covered the explosion of discontent amongst Israel's oriental population and the restiveness of the Orthodox community. His disturbing reports provided the raw material for some toughly worded editorials.[49]

The attack on Israel on 6 October 1973, on the fast of Yom Kippur, the Day of Atonement, came as a complete shock to world Jewry. By the time

the *Jewish Chronicle* went to press on 9 October, Israel's northern and southern fronts had been stabilised after being partially overrun, but it was clear that the assault across the Suez Canal and on the Golan Heights had been contained only at a dreadful cost to the tiny forces of Israel's standing army. The title of the editorial on 12 October 1973, 'Question of Survival', spelled out bluntly what was at stake. At first, the paper broadcast the commonly held view that Israel had been warned, but had declined to launch a pre-emptive strike in order to avoid being placed in the wrong by the international community. It later transpired that Israeli defence doctrine was seriously flawed. By 19 October, Yoram Kessel and Chaim Herzog, now respectively the *Jewish Chronicle*'s Israel and military correspondents, were providing alarming background material to the initial calamity. The paper's editorial line was to call for an immediate cease-fire. In the second week of the war, Israel received crucial supplies from the United States and its fully mobilized forces went on to the offensive. As the tide of battle on the northern and southern fronts was reversed, Egypt and Syria sought an armistice through the intervention of the USSR. At the end of the third week of fighting a cease-fire was brought into effect.[50]

The *Jewish Chronicle* calculated that Israel had been cheated of total victory by the super powers, but triumphalism was eschewed. A leading article on 26 October 1973 spelled out its sober and pacific attitude: 'it is understandable that many Israelis will take a simple hard-line view: having initiated this war, the Arabs should be taught a lasting lesson by the complete destruction of their military forces and that there should be no budging from the dogma that only buffer territories can ensure security. But this concept, like others which were held in Israel before the outbreak of this war, calls for calm and profound reappraisal ... This moment of post-war shock presents the appropriate occasion for Israel to explore Arab willingness to co-exist and to display a spirit of generosity.' It reminded readers that the great military victory of 1967 had not ensured peace and that the moment when the Arab countries felt they were in a position to be magnanimous was the best in which to negotiate.

After the Yom Kippur War, the question of the Palestinian Arabs loomed ever larger. It was forced into the headlines by a series of atrocities committed by Palestinian groups against innocent men, women and children. Palestinian propaganda became more skilful and their diplomatic efforts more effective. From the moment the Six-Day War ended, the *Jewish Chronicle* detected a shift of world opinion against Israel and began to comment anxiously on the need for effective pro-Israel propaganda. The paper engaged in several fierce exchanges with advocates of the Arab cause, notably Ian Gilmour, MP, Christopher Mayhew, MP, and Michael

Adams. The volume of anti-Israel propaganda was increased by the convergence between the New Left, the radical student movement and advocacy of the Palestinian cause. Israel and her Jewish supporters felt increasingly beleaguered. This mood was articulated in the *Jewish Chronicle* by the journalist Philip Kleinman, who began a regular column in March 1974, to survey the British press and media and report on anti-Jewish and anti-Israel bias.

The UN resolution in 1975 declaring Zionism to be a form of racism injected fresh venom into the propaganda war. From 1976, student unions in British universities were swept by a wave of anti-Zionism which embroiled students and academics in bitter debate. The *Jewish Chronicle* had always paid attention to Jewish student affairs, but its focus on the struggle being waged on campus was important in mobilising communal support for the Union of Jewish Students.[51]

Nevertheless, the *Jewish Chronicle* was prepared to test the apparent willingness of elements within the Palestine Liberation Organisation (PLO) to seek a peaceful solution to the Arab–Israel conflict. One of the moderates was Said Hammami, the PLO's first representative in London. In April 1974, Joseph Finklestone, the foreign editor, and later winner of the 1981 David Holden award for journalism, secured an interview with him. On the surface it was a barren encounter. Officially the PLO advocated as its panacea for the region's troubles the establishment of a unitary secular democratic state which would nullify Israel's existence. But Hammami suggested that two states, one Jewish and one Palestinian, might be acceptable, if only as an interim solution. He also distanced the PLO from the Black September Movement, which was responsible for some of the worst terrorist outrages. The assassination of Hammami in 1978 indicated how seriously the maximalists within the Palestinian camp regarded such overtures.[52]

Subsequently, the *Jewish Chronicle* was taken to task for publishing the interview. In reply to this criticism, an editorial on 26 April 1974 explained that 'Its purpose, clearly, was not to give spokesmen of the Arab cause an undeserved platform, but to examine the views – and the ambiguities which these disclose – of the Palestinians.' However, the leader continued that 'It is today beyond doubt that the Palestinians have developed a real sense of identity. They form an intrinsic part of the jig-saw puzzle of Middle East politics and they cannot be ignored or wished into silence.' At a time when much of Jewish opinion followed Golda Meir in rejecting the notion that the Palestinian Arabs existed as a distinct entity at all, it was significant that the *Jewish Chronicle* persisted in arguing that they could not be dismissed.

Under Frankel's guidance the paper ventured that the PLO represented the Palestinians and that King Hussein could not speak on their behalf at the negotiating table. On 19 July 1974 it took the even more advanced line of espousing a two-state solution to the conflict: 'Israel must – and has shown every indication of willingness to do so – negotiate with all those who will negotiate with her. And this may have to include talking to former murderers ... The long-term target should be peaceful co-existence between a State, however named and organised, in which Palestinians would constitute a majority and Israel, where Jews are a majority.'

The Yom Kippur War had a traumatic effect on Israeli politics. Golda Meir was replaced as Prime Minister by Yitzhak Rabin, a change welcomed by the *Jewish Chronicle* which commented that she had 'found it impossible to move with the spirit of the times'. Although the paper had done much to cultivate the image of 'Golda' that made her so beloved and admired throughout the diaspora, the war had been disillusioning. It now characterised her approach to problems as 'over simplistic' and criticised her 'tendency to sit back on an entrenched military as well as diplomatic position'.[53]

Rabin faced intense pressure from Israeli secular and religious nationalists to permit settlements on the West Bank. At first the settlers who came from the Gush Emunim Movement, Bloc of the Faithful, were evicted by the army. This policy was approved by the *Jewish Chronicle*, which saw the settlements as 'a possible death blow to any chance for peace talks with Jordan'. Gradually, however, Gush Emunim and its allies wore down the resolve of the Government and a string of new settlements were built. Small news items in the paper noted this process; editorially, Frankel continued to take a strong line against the Orthodox militants and condemned the settlements as obstacles to achieving peace.[54]

After the Six-Day War, news from Israel dominated the *Jewish Chronicle*. Domestic news paled, while items from regional centres were reduced in size and scope. Communal institutions, such as the Board of Deputies, now received only a cursory degree of attention. These trends in the paper's news values and editorial comment reflected changes in Anglo-Jewish society and identity. Jews in Britain were more affluent and travelled widely, many of them to Israel. They could afford to send their children to camps, kibbutzim and universities in Israel for the summer or for longer periods. Israel and Zionism became a central element of their identity and they wanted the *Jewish Chronicle* to quench their thirst for news, information and opinion on the relevant subjects.

The paper mirrored other developments in the socio-economic profile of Anglo-Jewry in the decade after the Six-Day War. A *Jewish Chronicle* readership survey late in 1967 produced 2,000 replies and indicated that 56 per cent of readers were Orthodox, 26 per cent Progressive and 2 per cent 'ultra-Orthodox' (8 per cent were unaffiliated and 6 per cent were 'other'). Over a quarter of readers were university educated, and nearly a third had attended a grammar school. Earlier indicators of occupational preference were confirmed: 26 per cent were engaged in the professions, 24 per cent owned their own businesses and 22 per cent were employees in executive or managerial roles. The vast majority read news about Israel avidly. Home news ranked second in the degree of interest, equal to the social and personal columns. Leader articles ranked fifth as a preference. The single most requested subject was religion.[55]

To meet this demand, in July 1969 'Ask the Rabbi', a weekly column, replaced an earlier innovation which presented short extracts from various sources on the 'Jewish Heritage'. Other changes reproduced trends in the wider society: for instance, the teen page mutated into the 'Inpage'. The regular supplements on property, furniture, banking and finance, menswear, and travel, as well as 'Frankly Feminine' and 'Brides and Homes', represented the suburbanisation and affluence of most of Anglo-Jewry. In June 1963, the paper carried its first supplement on north-west London. Thirteen years later, one was entirely devoted to Brent Cross, the shopping mall that served several of the residential districts most popular with Jews. The growth of Ilford Jewry, the largest single concentration of Jews in London, did not go unnoticed, either. In November 1973, a 'Redbridge Extra' section was introduced. By contrast, the East End was now the subject for elegiac essays and photo-features.

Other supplements were devoted to the changing character and work of communal institutions such as the Jewish Welfare Board and Jews' College. The Literary Supplement flourished in its own right. Through the Jewish Chronicle Literary Prize the paper stimulated Jewish writing and published new prose, poetry and drama in the supplement. The paper also became active in the sponsorship of the arts, drama, music, photography and archaeology. In 1967, William Frankel inaugurated a colour supplement as a device to boost circulation. These supplements, which eventually came out four times a year, soon became profitable. They stressed the visual angle on a particular story and were rich in photographs, particularly on themes in Jewish art. Features depicting contemporary Anglo-Jewish society and the up-market advertising both registered the extent to which the bulk of Anglo-Jewry had achieved a comfortable, middle-class existence.

Despite this affluence, the paper characterised the Jewish domestic scene in dismal terms. A rare editorial on Anglo-Jewry on 27 June 1975 was headed 'The Long Sleep' and suggested the 'danger is … that we shall quietly fade away through indifference'. Surveys of Jewish affiliation in Edgware in 1965, nationally in 1971, and in Wembley in 1975 all told a grim story. The *Jewish Chronicle* mounted inquiries into inter-marriage and published supplements devoted wholly to the question and how to deal with it.[56] Trends were not in one direction only; many young Jews became involved in the increasingly militant campaign for Soviet Jewry. The seventies saw a radicalisation and a broadening of such efforts, abetted by the widespread coverage which the paper gave to Soviet Jewish affairs and the campaign for emigration to Israel.

Tension between the Chief Rabbinate and Furnival Street, while much diminished since the 'Jacobs Affair', had not disappeared. The *Jewish Chronicle* continued to call for reform of the United Synagogue. It criticised Chief Rabbi Jakobovits for his refusal to join with Reform and Liberal rabbis on public occasions. After the Chief Rabbi declined to share a platform with Progressive rabbis on Israel's Independence Day in 1968, the paper accused him of throwing away a chance of bridging the divide between the different sections of Judaism.[57]

Contrary to the notion that a 'vendetta' existed between the *Jewish Chronicle* and the Chief Rabbi, the paper again made conciliatory overtures. In October 1968, the Chief Rabbi had lunch at its offices to discuss relations between the two institutions. Jakobovits told Kessler in a letter that 'I certainly hope that our frank exchanges helped to narrow the differences between the "letter" and the "spirit" of our community, if I may so describe Anglo-Jewry's leading literary and religious Establishments. Our instructive and yet by no means dull conversation, I trust, proved that likewise the image of a vibrant and forward-looking community need be no more dull than reports of dissension, decline and anti-religious provocation. We surely also agree that a growing Jewish commitment is ultimately the surest guarantee for a sustained readership of a Jewish paper no less than for a well-attended synagogue.' David Kessler replied that 'I believe that we are now set on the right road and have every confidence that if we continue along this path we shall together assist in the process of creating that degree of harmony in the community which all men of goodwill must desire.'[58]

Soon after the meeting, Frankel issued a memorandum to the senior editorial staff clarifying the paper's policy. The speeches and activity of the Chief Rabbi should be covered according to their importance. 'Editorial comment should be based on the facts as we know them. We know that the informed section of the community is aware that many generalisations and "declarations of intent" made during the past 18 months have remained unfulfilled in practice. We would lose our own authority if we appeared too gullible. So give the fullest credit to acts we think positive and even to words alone where you have reason to think they are necessary preliminaries to action. But where it is only a question of using fair-sounding words to cover up inaction or reaction, I would prefer that no editorial comment were made rather than a hostile one.'[59]

Whereas the first half of Frankel's editorship took place against a background of increasing material affluence, political confidence and youthful vigour, the circumstances of the second period were less happy. The British economy worsened, politics provided no solutions and the energy of some young people, on the Left and the Right, seemed to become nihilistic and violent.[60] The prominence of race and immigration in politics were indicators of the changing atmosphere. The *Jewish Chronicle* voiced alarm at Enoch Powell's 1968 'rivers of blood' speech, attacking non-white immigration, and thereafter followed his career with concern. When the extreme Right-wing National Front capitalised on anti-immigrant feeling, the paper warned Jews in Britain against the complacent belief that they were not as much the targets of organised racism as non-whites in British society.[61]

Between 1966 and 1974 there was a flurry of General Elections, and Frankel introduced important innovations in the paper's election coverage. In 1949, to emphasise the paper's independence of political parties, Shaftesley had decreed that the paper would no longer accept political advertising, and between 1950 and 1957 it barely commented on national political developments. Frankel was more adventurous. He asked each major party for its response to a series of questions on matters of Jewish interest. The replies were reviewed with an eye to what would concern Jewish voters. In October 1974 Frankel personally interviewed the leaders of the three main parties and printed their answers to his questions on a series of relevant topics.[62]

On at least two occasions, the *Jewish Chronicle* took a firm political stand. In January 1974 an editorial commented obliquely, but critically, on the incomes policy and confrontational politics of the 1970–4 Heath Government: 'In our long history we have had bitter experience of the danger of a divided society ... any government must try to ensure the maintenance of consensus by enunciating policies which are likely to be acceptable to the normally fair-minded working population.' At the time of the referendum on membership of the European Community the paper gave explicit advice as to how Jews should vote: 'from our own historic view as Jews we can perhaps see more clearly that in the British interest there are overwhelming reasons for a resounding "Yes"'.[63]

For a brief period, the National Front assumed threatening proportions, and during the tumultuous years in British politics between 1973 and 1977, it seemed to the *Jewish Chronicle* that racist and extreme Right-wing politics might gain broad support. The paper detected a 'moral crisis' in British society which, combined with inflation, mass unemployment and labour militancy, echoed the conditions in which Fascism had flourished in the 1930s. Some of the last editorials of Frankel's period at the *Jewish Chronicle* were filled with gloom and foreboding.[64]

By 1977, Frankel had been editor for nearly twenty years, and had been involved with the paper intimately for almost a quarter of a century. In the 1970 New Year Honours list he had been appointed a Commander of the Order of the British Empire. Having groomed Geoffrey Paul for the succession, in April 1976 he announced that he would retire as editor at the end of the year. The Trust approved the choice of Paul, while Frankel was invited to remain a director. The younger members of staff whom he had promoted and nurtured were about to take over.

9 The Jewish press in a divided community: Geoffrey Paul, 1977–1990

By the time he assumed the editorship of the *Jewish Chronicle* in 1977, Geoffrey Paul had held almost every senior editorial position, experience that would stand him in good stead as the paper entered a challenging phase of its history. Paul was born in Liverpool in 1929 into an Orthodox Jewish family of east European origin. His education was disrupted by the war, but the gripping events of those years instilled in him a passion for news and journalism. As soon as he could, he left home and took a job on the *Denbighshire Free Press* and later moved to the *Barnsley Chronicle*. Paul's background was strongly Zionist. Soon after the Arab attack on the nascent state of Israel, he contacted the people who were covertly sending Jewish volunteers from Britain. They told him to quit his job and get ready to leave. Just then, the fighting stopped and the influx of volunteers was halted. Paul was left stranded in London without a job.

He found work in the public relations department of the Jewish Agency, under Dr Selig Brodetsky and Dr Schneier Levenberg, and later with the Jewish Telegraphic Agency. For three years he was assistant editor of the *Jewish Observer and Middle East Review*, edited by Jon Kimche. In 1958, William Frankel invited him to join the *Jewish Chronicle*. Beginning as a sub-editor on the foreign news desk, he was subsequently appointed the Israel correspondent and was later sent to New York to cover the USA. Back in London, he took over from Joel Cang as foreign editor and moved on to become deputy editor.[1]

When he took over the editorial chair Paul had well-defined goals. He wanted to recover that section of the Jewish population which he felt had been alienated from the *Jewish Chronicle* by its role in the 'Jacobs Affair', and heal the wounds caused by the years of dissension. The paper's circulation, as always, was under keen scrutiny. The size of the Jewish population of the British Isles was falling, and the circulation of the *Jewish Chronicle* was declining slightly each year. From its peak of around 63,000 in 1968–9, circulation dropped to just over 50,000 in the 1970s, where it remained, with slight fluctuations, until 1989, when it dipped below this figure. Paul hoped to inject new life and vigour into the paper by recruiting younger journalists who were in tune with the changes that had occurred in Anglo-Jewish education and culture since the 1960s.

Before Paul could direct his attention fully to the wider problems of British Jewry, he had to tackle the production and labour problems which troubled the *Jewish Chronicle*, like the rest of the national press. Staff relations on the paper remained, on the whole, excellent. Journalists serving on it in the 1960s and 1970s had frequently been with the paper for thirty or forty years. The sense of camaraderie was fostered by regular social events, such as the annual cricket match in the grounds of Carmel College. However, the printing process was altogether different. During the 1970s, the paper was composed in the *Jewish Chronicle* building by means of a computerised type-setting system. The pages were made up on the 'stones', and the proofs were scrutinised by the editor, sub-editors and proof readers before they were finally sent to the printers in Guildford, Surrey. It was a cumbersome system with several bottlenecks and was vulnerable to industrial action. Production of a large issue, such as the New Year edition, had to be negotiated separately with the print unions and usually required an additional, hefty payment.[2]

These problems bulked large in the deliberations of the Board of Directors. The Board now comprised Leonard Stein, Phillip Zec, Ellis Birk, William Frankel, Sidney Moss, who was taken on to the Board in 1967 and was Managing Director from 1973 to 1991, Lionel Gordon, who joined in 1971, and Paul, who was appointed in 1977. Greville Janner, a Labour MP, was a director from 1973 to 1979, but resigned following his election to the presidency of the Board of Deputies. Under the chairmanship of David Kessler, who had been Managing Director until 1973, the Board carefully considered the options for converting to a new production process. In co-operation with the editor, the management decided to discontinue the paper's own, expensive composing operation in favour of outside computer type-setting. The first years of the new operation were not easy. Copy was sent to Edenbridge, Kent, to be set, the galleys were brought back to the paper for pasting up, and only then were the pages sent to the printers at Tonbridge, Kent, to be run off by the web offset lithographic process. At the last stage, editorial staff had to be present to assist the type-setters to make up the front and back pages. It was only later that the paper was able to go over to fax machines and, a still greater improvement, direct transmission of copy and proofs.[3]

As was the case for many editors at this time, industrial disputes and the reorganisation of production absorbed much of Paul's energy. But the new system brought with it refreshing changes in layout and other innovations. The women's page was transformed into 'Gallery', and a special London page was introduced in February 1977. 'London Line', covering the 'lighter side of London living', was an experiment in gearing the *Jewish Chronicle* to the fact that two-thirds of its readership were now in the Greater London area. In 1981 'London Line' became the longer-lasting 'London Extra' section. Paul boosted the paper's Middle Eastern coverage during 1982 with a 2–4-page section called 'Middle East Mirror'. In 1986, a link-up with the *Jerusalem Post* press service ensured rapid and high-quality input from Israel. At the start of 1989, the *Jewish Chronicle* went into colour. The redesigned front and back pages now carried poly-chromatic photographs, although the paper experienced the same vicissitudes with the use of colour as the national press.

The 'Open Forum' column, started under Frankel, was replaced in 1978 by Chaim Bermant's 'On the Other Hand', an idiosyncratic commentary on Jewish life and current events. Bermant, who had earlier contributed to the 'Personal Opinion' column under the pseudonym 'Ben Azai', was soon delighting or aggravating readers. His criticism of the Israeli Government and its supporters in the diaspora, in particular, enraged some readers and pleased others. For a while a petition circulated around London calling on the Board of Deputies to intervene and get him removed from the paper. Paul defended Bermant's right to express his point of view in his own column, but stressed that it did not reflect that of the paper itself. Indeed, one week, when Bermant delivered a scorching attack on the Joint Israel Appeal (JIA) and the Jewish Agency, the editor devoted his leading article to rebutting the piece. Bermant's popular column, with its humour, sagacity and irreverance, remained widely admired even while it caused uproar in certain quarters.[4]

In 1983 the Anglo-Jewish novelist Clive Sinclair took over from Tosco Fyvel, who had edited the Literary Supplements and book page with great distinction for ten years. Sinclair had achieved prominence as one of the ten best young British novelists after the publication of a book of short stories, *Hearts of Gold*. His interests and connections led to the arrival of a new wave of writers as book reviewers and a greater attention to Israeli authors whose influence on Jewish writing and culture in the diaspora had been steadily growing. Sinclair's tenure was brief and stormy. The termination of his engagement aroused a minor frisson in the Anglo-Jewish literary world, with claims of cultural philistinism on one side and literary incest on the other.[5]

The preferences of the readership were one element in the dispute over the literary editor. Sinclair was accused of being too 'high brow', but whether or not this claim was justified or relevant, the social composition of Anglo-Jewry had an ineluctable impact on the paper. The *Jewish Chronicle* now catered for the interests of an overwhelmingly London-based, middle-class suburban population. However, though Anglo-Jewry was more socially and economically homogeneous than ever before, it was no less fractured by religion and politics than it had been during the inter-war years. Throughout the 1980s, the paper acted as a lightning conductor on a series of issues that split British Jews. Its pages were filled, week after week, with reports and letters that testified to the existence of divided communities.[6]

By the mid 1980s, the Jewish population of Great Britain had fallen to approximately 330,000, of which two-thirds lived in Greater London, with a further 18,000 in the Home Counties. The main centres outside London were Manchester (30,000), Leeds (14,000), Glasgow (11,000), Brighton (10,000), Birmingham (6,000) and Liverpool (5,000). Within London, half of the total Jewish settlement was concentrated in five boroughs – Barnet, Brent, Harrow, Camden and Redbridge. While the mass of London Jewry was located in well-to-do suburbs, 10,000 lived in east London and nearly 25,000, mainly Chasidim, inhabited the north London boroughs of Hackney and Haringey.[7] In terms of occupation, a survey of Redbridge in 1978 revealed that over 40 per cent of Jews in work were employers and managers, professional people or in middle-ranking white-collar jobs. Under a quarter were engaged in skilled or unskilled manual labour, although a large proportion, about 15 per cent, were self-employed in non-professional jobs.[8]

These findings were confirmed by a 1985 readership survey for the *Jewish Chronicle*, based on over 700 questionnaires. It showed that 48 per cent of readers were in social classes A and B, although only 17 per cent of the total British adult population normally fell into these categories. A further 32 per cent were in social class C1 and only 13 per cent in the C2, and 7 per cent in the D and E categories. The terminal age of education was 'considerably higher' than the national average, and the percentage of home ownership, at 87 per cent, was 'far in excess' of nation-wide trends. Such a readership profile makes the *Jewish Chronicle* a highly attractive advertising medium. In the 1970s, 85 per cent of its revenue came from advertising and this department was, consequently, of central importance to the whole newspaper.[9]

If these surveys disclosed a measure of socio-economic uniformity that was good for the paper from a commercial angle, they also registered a disturbing polarisation of religious affiliation. Between 1970 and the mid 1980s, the proportion of strictly Orthodox Jews doubled, while at the other extreme, the percentage of Jews affiliated to the Liberal and Reform synagogues grew from just over 20 per cent to a little more than 25 per cent. As the total number of synagogue-affiliated Jews declined, the proportion within central Orthodoxy shrank from 72 per cent to 66 per cent.[10]

Paul saw a relationship between the two phenomena, as had Frankel, and warned that intensified Right-wing Orthodoxy was squeezing the adherents of the 'minhag Anglia' or tradition of broad-minded, central Orthodoxy. Protesting against the virtual ban on Progressive Jews pronounced by the Beth Din of the Union of Hebrew and Orthodox Congregations, Paul wrote: 'The negativism of ultra-Rightist Orthodoxy is forcing polarisation, not assisting ultimate unity.'[11] Yet the extreme Orthodox were acquiring a political strength that could not be ignored. Paul was taken aback by the volume, and vituperation, of mail that followed a critical article on Lubavitch Chasidism by Rabbi Dr Norman Solomon in 1982.[12]

Another sign of polarisation was 'phase three' of the 'Jacobs Affair' in 1983, which broke out after the Beth Din of the United Synagogue challenged the validity of marriages and conversions performed under Jacobs's auspices. Dismayed by inflexibility in the face of human needs, Paul pleaded for a compassionate approach to the difficult question of conversion under Jewish law: 'the letter is one thing, the spirit another'.[13] The paper not only encouraged compromise, it offered a platform for all sides to explore routes to co-operation. Paul felt that the 'Jacobs Affair' showed how a newspaper, at least one like the *Jewish Chronicle*, could not run ahead of its readership, crusading for one particular cause which they did not share. But he persistently denounced extremism and prodded religious leaders to seek the middle ground. He boldly called for a humane and sensitive handling of questions of conversion, notably in the drawn-out and perplexing case of Paula Cohen.[14]

British Jews were also divided over how best to support communal institutions and welfare bodies, and to what extent domestic needs took precedence over fundraising for Israel. The paper urged that, in order to combat the growing levels of disaffiliation and indifference, more resources ought to be ploughed into Jewish education and the provision of a highly qualified rabbinate.[15] This required proper funding, yet Anglo-Jewish institutions had to compete with each other for scarce resources against the background of an ageing community and the diminishing provision of welfare services by the state. The communal leadership seemed oblivious of the dangers inherent in this scissors-process. The *Jewish Chronicle* tried to stimulate public awareness of the impending crisis and consistently advocated a unified system of money raising and funding: a 'community chest' for educational and welfare services, similar to that which operated in the USA.[16]

With these competing demands in mind, the paper gave its backing to the first inquiry into the relative distribution between Israel and Anglo-Jewry of funds raised in Britain. This was a controversial idea, since it entailed challenging powerful Israel-orientated fundraising bodies, of which the JIA was foremost. The report, prepared under the supervision of Bernard Garbacz and a group of communal philanthropists, presented the choices facing Anglo-Jewry in uncompromising terms. The *Jewish Chronicle* endorsed its findings that 'our education system is under-funded and our welfare system in stark danger of becoming so'. It warned of a crisis unless the allocation of resources was readjusted. However, the report ran into a storm of criticism and was never acted upon.[17]

By the 1970s, the JIA had become the most powerful and efficient organisation in Anglo-Jewry, and some people, notably its own leadership, saw it as a model for organising other Jewish institutions. By comparison, the Board of Deputies was unwieldy, unruly and indecisive. Yet it was democratic, and the *Jewish Chronicle* defended it from business leaders who placed more faith in company-style directorates. The paper showed warm interest in the attempts which were made under the presidencies of Sir Samuel (later Lord) Fisher and Greville Janner, MP to reform the Board and engage the interest of youth and regional communities. 'We need more accountability in Anglo-Jewry, not less', it insisted in an editorial on 26 June 1981.[18]

The resurgence of the extreme Right during the mid 1970s triggered another 'defence debate' in Anglo-Jewry which was every bit as divisive as that of the 1930s. During 1974–7, the National Front won a significant level of support in local elections in the Midlands and London. The most dynamic and successful organisation resisting its advance was the Anti-Nazi League (ANL), which was, however, dominated by activists of the Trotskyite Socialist Workers' Party. Counter-measures by Jewish organisations in collaboration with the ANL and the black and Asian population were hugely complicated by the anti-Zionism which permeated the Left and sections of the black and Asian communities. The Board of Deputies spurned the ANL and sought other allies, but individuals and groups within Anglo-Jewry joined in its work. While they forcefully advocated the Anti-Nazi League's merits, the established leadership accused them of abetting enemies of Israel and Jewry.[19]

This dispute was fought out in representative Jewish institutions and, pre-eminently, in the Jewish press. The *Jewish Chronicle* commented on 27 October 1978 that 'Public debate and the correspondence columns of this newspaper suggest that no issue in recent years has so divided Jewish public opinion as the arguments for and against supporting the Anti-Nazi League campaign against the National Front.' The paper itself recommended the establishment of an umbrella body that would enable the Board of Deputies to co-operate with the Anti-Nazi League, which was, undoubtedly, an effective medium for anti-racist propaganda.[20]

When the discontent of Britain's black minority exploded into violence in the summer of 1981, the paper expressed grave fears for race relations in general and the position of the Jews in particular. 'Whatever tears at the fabric of our society must affect us', it warned on 17 April 1981 in the wake of the Brixton riots. This concern activated two more of its rare interventions in modern British electoral politics. Firstly, on 31 January 1981 the paper explicitly opposed the Conservative Government's Nationality Bill. Next, without specifying who Jews should vote for, a carefully worded editorial on 3 June 1983, on the eve of the General Election, suggested that: 'The thoughtful Jewish voter will recognise that his own status in British society, and that of other distinctive minorities, rests upon the stability of the nation at large.' Listed amongst the destabilising elements were the debilitation of the economy, unemployment, inadequate care for the sick and the aged and 'social divisions', all of which were blamed on the Tory Government by the Opposition parties.[21]

Mrs Margaret Thatcher's third election victory in 1987 returned to Parliament a record number of Jewish Tory MPs, of whom three were appointed to Cabinet posts. The prominence of Jews amongst the ideological progenitors and policy-makers of 'Thatcherism' gave rise to speculation that some intrinsic connection existed between Judaism and free-market Toryism or libertarian individualism.[22] This association of Jews with Tory politics had been long in the making, and the *Jewish Chronicle* had been part of the process.

During 1984 the Board of Deputies fought a running battle with the Labour leader of the Greater London Council (GLC), Ken Livingstone, in which the *Jewish Chronicle* was both a commentator and a participant. Jewish voting patterns in London in the 1987 General Election showed a notable shift to the Right. This trend had several causes, notably the identification of the Labour Party with anti-Israel policies, but the *Jewish Chronicle* may have contributed as a result of its long-running antagonism to Livingstone and his supporters in the Labour Group while they were in control of the GLC.[23]

The notion of an ideological affinity between Toryism and Judaism was reinforced by the Chief Rabbi's contribution to the debate on policy for the inner cities initiated by the Archbishop of Canterbury. He had sponsored a church inquiry, published as *Faith in the Cities* in 1985, which was sharply critical of the effect of Government policies on the poor, urban populations. The *Jewish Chronicle* had regretted the absence of a Jewish voice on this question, not least because of Anglo-Jewry's historical, immigrant experience and its stake in the stability of British society. But a reply was soon forthcoming. In January 1986 the paper published 'From Doom to Hope', in which the Chief Rabbi drew on his interpretation of the Jewish experience to suggest that only hard work and self-improvement would lift the inner-city population out of the trough of social despair. This perspective was welcomed by the Conservative Party. An Early Day Motion congratulating the Chief Rabbi was signed by 160 Tory MPs. But Anglo-Jewry was, yet again, intensely divided. Letters poured into the paper protesting against the apparently unsympathetic tone of the panaceas advocated by Dr Jakobovits and disclaiming his right to speak for all Jews in Britain.[24]

In contradistinction to his 'Right-wing' opinions on religious, moral and social matters, the Chief Rabbi was an outspoken 'dove' regarding Israel's occupation of the West Bank and its response to the claims made by the Palestinians. In this, he and Geoffrey Paul were in broad sympathy. Paul believed that a 'partnership' should exist between Israel and diaspora Jewry and rejected the argument that diaspora Jews had to abstain from comment on Israel's internal affairs and external policies.[25]

An editorial on 23 June 1978 declared that 'The Begin plan [for the West Bank] continues to equate territory with security, or if it does not, then it looks to the acquisition of territory as an end in itself. Neither course will bring Israel the peace she so desperately needs, unless one believes that the coming of the Messiah is imminent.' Paul had previously discussed the editorial with Dr Jakobovits, who heartily endorsed it in a subsequent letter to the paper. However, other voices denounced their utterances as a form of treachery. The correspondence columns had to be expanded to accommodate the volume of letters following the editorial and the Chief Rabbi's comments.[26]

Despite the indignation which met adverse comment on Israel's Government, expressed through letters to the editor and more informally, the *Jewish Chronicle* did not deviate from its path of constructive criticism. In a reply to a letter from a Likud supporter in England who argued that the paper should not speak out, a leading article on 13 July 1979 explained:

If this argument is to be persisted in, then the widely-proclaimed notion of an Israeli-diaspora 'partnership' is a hollow sham, and Israel's right to talk, as she does, in the name of the Jewish people is an arrogance which must be denied her. It must be accepted that every discussion of an Israeli issue must stem from a commitment of concern and devotion – short of political loyalty – to the Jewish State. But debate cannot be artificially concluded at the point where it begins to become critical by the suggestion that it 'aids the enemy'... There is a disquieting trend throughout organised Jewish life to stifle the questioning voice. But we need it. We require voices of thoughtful dissent for every voice of assent.

Indeed, between 1977 and 1981, the *Jewish Chronicle* provided an often excoriating commentary on the political behaviour of the first Begin Government.

Paul, naturally, ensured that the paper gave extensive coverage to the bold peace initiative by the Egyptian President, Anwar Sadat, in 1977. But the paper found Begin's response far from inspiring. It continually questioned the wisdom of the Israeli Government's policy of building settlements on the West Bank and urged Begin to rein in the 'hot heads' in his Cabinet. By 1980, editorials were arguing that Begin alienated Israel's friends by his rhetoric and his policies, such as the *de jure* annexation of east Jerusalem and the Golan Heights. These were 'incredible tactical errors' and examples of a 'policy of folly' that lost Israel friends while confirming the claims of its enemies.[27] When the Israeli economy plunged into crisis, emigration rose to alarming levels and corruption led to forced resignations from the Government, a leading article on Begin on 28 November 1980 announced baldly that it was 'Time to Go'.

Yet the Israeli Prime Minister confounded his critics. He won the 1981 Knesset elections after an ugly campaign in which ethnic tension between oriental Sephardi Israelis and European Ashkenazim was ruthlessly exploited, arousing fears of a new schism in Israeli society. Paul, who was familiar with the discontent amongst oriental Jews from his days covering the Black Panther Movement in 1969–70, regarded the ethnic divide as a 'frightening' development.[28] While the *Jewish Chronicle* lent its support to the Israeli Government through the difficult period of the evacuation from Sinai and praised it for fulfilling its obligations under the Camp David Accords, its commentary tended to remain critical. At the same time the paper was unequivocally hostile to any recognition of the Palestine Liberation Organisation. It justified Israeli attacks on PLO bases in southern Lebanon and chastised British officials for meeting with PLO representatives at any level.

The most strenuous phase in the propaganda war came with 'Operation Peace for Galilee', Israel's invasion of Lebanon in June 1982. For the first two weeks of the Operation, the *Jewish Chronicle* followed the explanation given by Israeli Defence Minister Ariel Sharon. Paul was amongst a delegation of Anglo-Jewish leaders flown out to southern Lebanon, in the wake of the Israeli advance, to be shown the mass of weaponry that had been captured from the retreating Palestinians. The paper anticipated an early withdrawal of Israeli forces and speculated on the aftermath. Even though the Israeli forces soon passed far beyond the vaunted 'forty-kilometre' limit to the incursion and closed in on Beirut, an editorial commented that 'it is the making of peace which is now the challenge which confronts Israel's Prime Minister and his cabinet colleagues'.[29] But instead of a rapid conclusion to the hostilities, the Israeli army besieged Beirut while the air force bombed the Palestinian forces and the civilians amongst whom they lived and operated.

Israeli policy and actions were now the subject of almost wholly adverse commentary in the media. During July, doubts began to surface in the *Jewish Chronicle*, too, in Chaim Bermant's column in particular. Editorials took a defensive posture: the space to vent reservations was severely cramped by the need to refute what was perceived as biased reporting in the British media. Nevertheless, on 13 August, a leading article commented that 'the real anger and deep concern about the changing nature of British media presentation of the unfolding tragedy of West Beirut cannot blind Jews to the truth that, even among the intensely committed of our community, there is a terrible unease, an anguish of soul, over the loss of civilian lives in West Beirut and the fact that, of whatever awful necessity, they were caused by the Israel Defence Forces.'[30]

Jews in Israel and the diaspora who believed that the conduct of policy in Lebanon was wrong began to organise protests. The *Jewish Chronicle* was an important forum for these views, as it was for those of the JIA and Board of Deputies delegations which travelled to Lebanon and returned with a sharply contrasting perspective. The divisions within Anglo-Jewry were manifested in the specially expanded letter columns, which brimmed to bursting. The paper made its own position clear when, on 10 September 1982, it supported the Reagan Peace Plan for the occupied territories, arguing that 'Continuing Israeli occupation and infiltration promises a long cycle of violence and counter-violence, such as has already been experienced, with brutalising consequences for both Arab and Jew. Even a Greater Israel cannot be worth the sacrifice of one more life, any life.'

The process of alienation was completed when Christian forces massacred Palestinians in the Sabra and Chatilla refugee camps, while Israeli troops stood outside. In an editorial on 24 September entitled 'End of the Line', Paul wrote that 'The last remnants of credibility attaching to the Prime Minister of Israel, Mr Menachem Begin, and his Defence Minister, Mr Ariel Sharon, disappeared somewhere into the rubble of the Palestinian refugee camps in Beirut over the Rosh Hashana [the Jewish New Year] weekend.' Reviewing the facts as they emerged from the press reports, subsequently borne out by the Israeli Government's own commission of inquiry, the editorial concluded that the Israeli Government 'bears indirect responsibility for what happened. No moralising can alter this fact, or that Mr Begin and Mr Sharon personally must carry the responsibility. The best service both can now perform for the State of Israel, the good name of the Israel Defence Forces and the stature of the Jewish people is to resign.'[31] This editorial provoked a massive response, with letters that were often vicious in their attacks on the paper and its editor.

Subsequently, Paul subscribed to the view of Israeli 'doves' that the occupation of the West Bank had brutalised Israeli society and aggravated social tensions.[32] But at the same time as commenting negatively on the lurch to the Right in Israeli politics, the *Jewish Chronicle* continued to berate the contacts between the British Foreign Office and the PLO. Its suspicions were not allayed by Yassir Arafat's 1988 declarations in Algiers or Geneva, accepting UN Resolutions 242 and 338, which the paper considered 'falls far short of open and unequivocal recognition of Israel'. In spite of urgings from 'the younger and more politically-minded reporters' on the staff, until the day he left the editorship of the paper Paul refused to allow them to interview PLO representatives. He explained to an audience in Oxford in 1989 that 'I believe that the PLO has said all that it has to say for the moment and that – unless we know in advance that there will be more straight answers to straight questions, on territorial issues, on refugees, on Jerusalem, on the viability of a Palestinian state – a majority of our readers would misinterpret our intentions.'[33]

In its coverage and commentary on the Intifada, the sustained unrest amongst Palestinians on the West Bank and the Gaza Strip that began at the end of 1987, the paper represented Israel sympathetically as the 'unwilling policeman' waiting on a permanent settlement. The *Jewish Chronicle* empathised with the dilemma that divided Israeli Jews: fear that surrendering the occupied territories would endanger Israel's security, balanced with an awareness that the status quo was equally fraught with dangers. The suppression of the uprising strengthened the image of an 'ugly Israel', but the censorious attitude of the British press and television again led the paper to take up a defensive posture. While it stood firm on its earlier position concerning the settlements, the rights of the Palestinian Arabs and the brutalising effect of the occupation on Israeli society, it rounded on the application of double standards to Israel. It complained that although other regimes in the world conducted brutal policies against their own citizens or subject peoples, they were never held up to such exacting standards of behaviour.[34]

The *Jewish Chronicle*'s coverage of Israel was by no means concerned solely with political or economic problems. The immigration, *aliyah*, of Soviet Jews preoccupied many editorials between 1978, when Ida Nudel, Vladimir Slepak, Yuri Orlov and Anatoly Sharansky were all imprisoned in the USSR as refuseniks, and February 1986, when Sharansky was freed and arrived triumphantly in Israel. During the long period when détente was frozen the Soviet authorities regarded the paper as a staunch enemy. The then foreign editor, Joseph Finklestone, was refused a visa to cover the Moscow Olympics and the situation of Russian Jews. William Frankel, one of the directors, was also denied entry to the country.[35]

The importance of Israel as a haven for Jews was reinforced by 'Operation Moses', the evacuation of the Beta Israel or Falashas from Ethiopia to Israel in the midst of the great famine in 1984–5. David Kessler had long been interested in the Falashas and had written widely about their history and current plight. He emphasised the urgency of their situation and helped to ensure that the paper kept the subject in the public eye. As a result of his inspiration, at the time of the airlift, the *Jewish Chronicle* collaborated with the Central British Fund to launch an appeal which raised nearly £200,000 to assist in the settlement of the Beta Israel in their new homes.[36]

Kessler was also a prime-mover in several major changes that occurred in the structure and management of the *Jewish Chronicle* in the mid 1980s. The Board had come to the conclusion that the Jewish Chronicle Trust left the paper vulnerable to a hostile take-over by a predator who purchased sufficient shares in Jewish Chronicle Ltd to gain control. In order to bolster the paper's defences, a means was found to protect the financial interests of the existing shareholders while controlling their voting rights. This was achieved through the creation of a scheme which divided the company's share capital into an equal number of voting shares of 1p each and non-voting shares of £1 each. The scheme was submitted to an extraordinary general meeting of the shareholders on 22 November 1984. By an arrangement with the Inland Revenue, at the same time they were given the opportunity to sell as many shares as they desired to the company at a price of £2.50 each. Seven shareholders took up the offer to sell all or part of their shares. In a remarkable manifestation of their concern for the *Jewish Chronicle*, members of the Kessler family, who held 80 per cent of the ordinary shares, voluntarily surrendered their sovereignty over the paper. By consent, 84 per cent of the newly issued 1p voting shares were then assigned gratis to the Kessler Foundation, giving it complete control over the paper and its assets.

The Articles of Association of the Kessler Foundation stipulated that the original members of the Council should be constituted by the managing director and editor of the *Jewish Chronicle*, ex officio, one non-independent family member and three independent members. The latter were Judge Israel Finestein, Peter Oppenheimer and Alex Rosenzweig. In accordance with the Articles, the chairman must be an independent member and is granted a casting vote.[37]

In April 1986, Geoffrey Paul informed the Board that he wished to retire early, for personal reasons. The following year, David Kessler retired as chairman of the Board and was succeeded by Ellis Birk. After extensive consultations, the Board of Directors chose Ned Temko, an American-born journalist, as Paul's successor. When he eventually took over in September 1990, he became the first foreign-born editor since Abraham Benisch. One hundred and fifty years after its foundation the *Jewish Chronicle* entered on a new, exciting phase of its history.

Conclusion

The Jewish press in England took root during the 1840s and 1850s, when the Jewish population was becoming more geographically dispersed and heterogeneous than ever before. British Jewry was divided spatially as well as socially, and sundered by controversy over the Reform congregation and conduct of the emancipation campaign. These developments, which had their parallel throughout the Jewish centres of western and central Europe, resulted from the dissolution of the traditional Jewish community. But the ending of the *kehillah* did not lead to the disappearance of the Jews as a distinct group. The emancipation and post-emancipation periods saw the reformulation of Jewish identity and the creation of new institutions by which it could be maintained and transmitted.[1]

In Germany, France and Russia in the years during and after emancipation, the Jewish press was born and flourished as a central component of the new Jewish communities. In England, and later throughout the United Kingdom, the *Jewish Chronicle* provided an essential medium through which a new Jewish identity could be constructed. By creating a 'public sphere' in which the Jews could interact, define and share a set of common concerns, it was part of the process by which they constituted themselves as a modern, abstract community as against one that was founded on face-to-face relations as well as shared values.[2]

After emancipation, in the 1860s and 1870s, the paper had a key role in working out the identity of British Jews as citizens. It helped to delineate the relationship between Jews and the state, and explored ways to combine the obligations of citizenship with the preservation of Judaism and Jewish tradition. At the same time it sought to integrate Jews into English culture without jeopardising their Jewishness. This difficult task was continued, with added urgency, during the 1880s and 1890s under the impact of mass immigration and anti-Semitism, both at home and abroad. It is almost impossible to understand the emergence of a modern Jewish identity in Britain without appreciating the paper's contribution. Not only did it provide an arena for debating and defining what it meant to be Jewish, but its mere existence was a unifying factor. The *Jewish Chronicle* was one thing shared by the vast majority of British Jews, whatever their social status, geographical origin or religious outlook. Purchasing and reading it was an act of affirming Jewishness that was uniquely modern.

In the course of the emancipation struggle, from 1841 to 1858, the paper acted like its Continental equivalents as an arm of the public campaign and a vehicle for promoting self-improvement within the Jewish population. Its attention alighted on communal governance, welfare bodies, education and the practice of Judaism. Once established, the Jewish press became a powerful motor driving forward the creation of communal organisations and the reform of those already in existence. The coming into being of a Jewish public opinion, for which the Jewish press was a fundamental prerequisite, was vital to the inauguration of Sussex Hall, the Board of Guardians, the United Synagogue, Jews' College, the Anglo-Jewish Association, the Federation of Synagogues, The Maccabaeans, the Jewish Historical Society and many other communal bodies.

After identifying the need for these institutions and campaigning for their establishment, the *Jewish Chronicle* acted as watchdog over them. It was virtually the only communal forum in which unfettered debate could take place concerning their operation. Nor was it slavish towards office-holders. Thanks to its independent position, the paper was able to get away with criticising Sir Moses Montefiore for his conduct of domestic affairs in the 1850s and his handling of matters connected with Palestine in the 1860s. Articles, features and supplements in the paper were also important as a 'booster' to raise the profile of organisations which depended on philanthropy for their survival. In fact, fundraising created an organic connection between the paper and the institutions which it fostered. As a medium for publicity and advertising it was indispensable, so communal bodies paid for notices and lists of donors to be published. The paper derived revenue by this means and provided an essential service at the same time.

The international dimension to the *Jewish Chronicle* was no less crucial than its influence on domestic affairs. Just as it contributed to the construction of modern Jewish communities in the British Isles, it became part of the information network that was responsible for the evolution of a new international identity for the Jewish people. Despite emancipation, Jewish solidarity across national frontiers persisted. New forms of co-operation and the definition of shared interests were first explored at the time of the Damascus Affair. The Jewish press was a direct outcome of the affair and was deliberately intended to foster ties between Jews around the world. Thenceforward, Jewish newspapers gave their readers a means of staying in touch with the affairs of Jews in other countries, far away. In times of crisis, papers could also mobilise Jewish support and put pressure on national governments to assist Jews in plight.

The *Jewish Chronicle* was prominent in the international campaign at the time of the Mortara Affair and added its prestigious voice to those raised against the Romanian Government over the treatment of its Jewish subjects. Finally, the paper offered Jews in Britain a rare glimpse of Jews in exotic places and sustained coverage of the 'old *Yishuv*' in Palestine. This international reportage fortified the sense of solidarity amongst Jews worldwide and fostered a notion of 'peoplehood' well before the Zionist Movement pronounced that the Jews formed one nation. It was a complex identity and was not without problems, as demonstrated in the polemics in 1878–81 between the paper and Gladstone during and after the Bulgarian Agitation. The question of patriotism, loyalty and identity which then figured so heavily in the paper foreshadowed the more familiar debates over Zionism.

In the 1880s and 1890s, the internationalisation of Jewish identity through the Jewish press was demonstrated again in the campaign on behalf of persecuted Russian Jewry. Pressure on the Tsarist Government failed to ameliorate the situation of Russian Jews and over 150,000 migrated to Britain. This influx created tensions within the Jewish population and between Jews and English society. The *Jewish Chronicle* now assumed a vital mediating role. Initially, the paper reacted harshly to the immigrants and advocated a policy of rapid acculturation. This expressed the prejudices of its Anglo-Jewish readership and also reflected the apprehension caused by anti-Jewish currents in Europe and closer to home, where they took the form of anti-alienism. By the 1900s, the paper viewed the immigrants with greater sympathy and was committed to the defence of free immigration, although it still supported the practice of voluntary repatriation operated by Jewish communal bodies.

The strength and numbers of the immigrant population meant that it was possible for the new community to sustain a number of Yiddish publications. Their existence graphically expressed the cleavage of the Jewish population. This was a period in which the Anglo-Jewish press represented only a section, possibly even a minority, of Jewish opinion. However, during the twentieth century the paper was, once again, central to the process of community building, knitting together the 'new' and the old communities. By the 1910s, it was read by immigrant as well as native Jews and spoke to all. It remained virtually the only forum open to members of every subdivision within the fissiparous Jewish communities in Britain until the expansion of the Board of Deputies in the 1940s. During the inter-war years, it was a unique safety-valve for dissension in a Jewish population riven by generational and ideological conflicts.

The paper's single most decisive intervention in the sphere of communal politics and institution building came with its support for the Zionist Movement from 1907 onwards. The ability of the *Jewish Chronicle* to influence opinion in the Jewish world was critical to the development of the movement in the face of communal opposition and powerful ideological objections. Its capacity to mobilise Jewish people was essential to the success of the Zionists in 1917 and the defence of the Mandate from the 1920s to the 1940s. Yet the paper had a somewhat quixotic approach. Under both Greenbergs it was unrelentingly hostile towards Chaim Weizmann and his stewardship of the Zionist Organisation. While the paper was the strongest advocate of Zionism in Britain and throughout the world, it was also one of the most painful thorns in the side of the Zionist leadership.

Since 1945, the *Jewish Chronicle* has served the needs of an increasingly suburban and middle-class Jewish population. It has combined, in a singular fashion, a detailed attention to local issues with coverage of the Jewish world and Israel. Its editorial policy on subjects such as Jewish defence work, the Board of Deputies, the Chief Rabbinate and the United Synagogue has showed a remarkable continuity from the 1910s to the last quarter of the twentieth century. The arguments over the response to Fascist and anti-Semitic agitation in the late 1940s, the 1960s and the mid 1970s virtually replicate the claims and counter-claims made during the 1930s. The friction between the paper and Chief Rabbis Brodie and Jakobovits, and the 'Jacobs Affair', has a feel of *déjà vu* in the light of the continuous debates with Chief Rabbis Nathan Hermann Adler and Herman Adler over modernisation of the forms of Jewish worship and the Morris Joseph episode in the 1890s.

This continuity of editorial policy is a testimony to the tenacity with which the paper has held to the centre-ground in Anglo-Jewry. While it has consistently supported the authority of communal institutions, no president of the Board of Deputies or Chief Rabbi has escaped its censure at one time or another. Every communal institution has been subjected to critical scrutiny, often with damning results. Of course, the tone of the paper has varied. It was most forthright under Leopold Greenberg and in the first period of William Frankel's editorship. Otherwise it has tended to be more restrained, although persistence has proved just as effective as stridency.

Today the *Jewish Chronicle* is a pivotal institution in Anglo-Jewry, crucial to any communal campaign, an independent watchdog, an arbiter of disputes and a showcase for all aspects of Jewish culture. In this sense it is, pre-eminently, a 'community newspaper'. It has the benefit of a well-defined, interested readership, but suffers from all the limitations of a local paper or one that serves a relatively small population. Such a paper has an obligation to report community or local news. It functions as a 'watchdog' over institutions, bestowing honour where it is merited, boosting good causes or simply offering a neutral perspective. Stories and features inevitably reflect a narrow range of concerns, sometimes branded 'parochial'. This criticism is misplaced, since it is one of the functions of such newspapers to foster the sense of community and to address the shared agenda of its readers.

The *Jewish Chronicle* has also been criticised for being too establishment-oriented. This is ill-founded in fact and, in any case, ignores the necessary position of a community newspaper. To carry weight it must be 'responsible', and so unavoidably tends to echo the values of communal institutions and leaders. Yet it is also subject to pressure from minority groups or interests and has an obligation to provide them with a platform. A community newspaper can never afford to ignore its readers' preferences. Their views are made known in the correspondence columns, which are a vital part of a community organ, providing feedback for the editorial staff and contributing to communal debate in a wider context. A community newspaper inevitably reflects the opinions of a majority of its readership or it does not sell and withers away.[3]

By virtue of being a community newspaper as well as a commercial enterprise, the *Jewish Chronicle* has always striven to satisfy a majority of the Jewish public. But it has regularly veered away from a centrist position in order to carry out a newspaper's function to probe and evaluate, as well as to explain and support. Because it was a modern institution which grew out of pluralism or heterodoxy, it has consistently been at odds with monolithic interpretations of Judaism. It has never been the mouthpiece of 'the Jewish establishment' or any particular institution. Even when it was orientated towards Zionism it remained independent of all Zionist organisations and actually took an intensely critical view of the Zionist leadership.

It has also made enormous non-journalistic contributions to Anglo-Jewry. From 1959 to 1974 Jewish Chronicle Publications took over, and so kept alive, the *Journal of Jewish Studies*. For many years the paper sponsored a lectureship in Medieval Hebrew at Oxford University and in 1989 established the Jewish Chronicle Chair in Jewish Studies at University College London. It has funded numerous large and small projects, such as the religious adviser for small Jewish communities and, in 1976, the journey of two Jewish athletes to compete in the Maccabi Games in Israel. In spite of the difficulties it faced, the paper supported the publishing house of Vallentine, Mitchell to ensure that Anglo-Jewry would be supplied with Jewish works of quality and significance. Jewish Chronicle Publications itself brings out each year the *Jewish Year Book* and the *Jewish Travel*

Guide, both valuable accessories to Jewish life, and publishes the indispensable *Florence Greenberg Jewish Cookery Book*.

Above all, the *Jewish Chronicle* is a medium through which Jews in Britain interact with, argue amongst and amuse each other. Over 150 years, it has become established as part of the ritual and rhythm of Jewish communal life. The social and personal columns are the adjunct to every major turning point in the life of a Jew – birth, bar mitzvah, engagement, marriage, parenthood, death. Its features on Judaism are an auxiliary to the religious calender, and it fosters the observance and celebration of Jewish festivals and fasts throughout the Jewish year. These perennial, ubiquitous aspects of the paper, which have contributed so much to the loyalty of its readership, have been justly celebrated.[4]

In the unstable and often ephemeral world of the press, a century and a half of publishing history marks a huge achievement for any newspaper or periodical. In the context of religious and communal newspapers, it is almost unknown. The Jews of Britain were fortunate to escape the devastation which befell Jewish communities in Europe, but the continuity of the *Jewish Chronicle* cannot be ascribed only to providence. The massive Jewish population in the United States of America has proven unable to sustain an independent publication of similar quality or scope. By virtue of its unique blend of the local and the international, the particular and the universal, the mundane and the profound, the *Jewish Chronicle* has ensured its place in Jewish life, not to mention its function for non-Jews concerned to follow Jewish affairs. In its role as chronicle of a community, it has become part of the elaborate fabric of that community itself. Anglo-Jewry and the *Jewish Chronicle* entered the era of modern Jewish life simultaneously: in the synthesis that developed lay the secret of the paper's resilience, liveliness and durability.

Notes

INTRODUCTION

1 Ivon Asquith, 'The Structure, Ownership and Control of the Press, 1780–1855', in George Boyce, James Curran and Pauline Wingate (eds.), *Newspaper History – from the Seventeenth Century to the Present Day* (London, 1978), pp. 98–116; Alan J. Lee, *The Origins of the Popular Press, 1855–1914*, paperback edition (London, 1980), pp. 67–72.

2 T. Nevett, *Advertising in Britain* (London, 1982), pp. 15–40.

3 Asquith, 'The Structure, Ownership and Control of the Press', pp. 99–102, 108–9; Lee, *Origins of the Popular Press*, pp. 54–67; Lucy Brown, *Victorian News and Newspapers* (Oxford, 1985), chaps. 1 and 2. The *Jewish Chronicle* is the owner of one of the few remaining Stanhope presses.

4 Asquith, 'The Structure, Ownership and Control of the Press', pp. 112–13; Brown, *Victorian News and Newspapers*, pp. 11–15; Nevett, *Advertising in Britain*, pp. 26–31 and T. Nevett, 'Advertising and Editorial Integrity in the Nineteenth Century', in Michael Harris and Alan Lee (eds.), *The Press in English Society from the Seventeenth to the Nineteenth Centuries* (London, 1986), pp. 149–52.

5 A. Aspinall, *Politics and the Press c. 1780–1850. Opinion in Three English Cities* (London,1949); Donald Read, *Press and People 1730–1850* (London, 1961); Lee, *Origins of the Popular Press*, chap. 5; James Curran, 'The Press as an Agency of Social Control: An Historical Perspective', in George Boyce, James Curran and Pauline Wingate (eds.), *Newspaper History – from the Seventeenth Century to the Present Day* (London, 1978), pp. 51–61; Brown, *Victorian News and Newspapers*, pp. 54–60.

6 Brian Harrison, 'Press and Pressure Groups in Modern Britain', in Joanne Shattock and Michael Wolff (eds.), *The Victorian Press: Samplings and Soundings* (Leicester, 1982), pp. 161–295; Louis Billington, 'The Religious Periodical and Newspaper Press, 1770–1870', in Harris and Lee (eds.), *The Press in English Society*, p. 113. Although Billington's survey is an indispensable guide to the Christian press in this period, he omits any mention of the Jewish press.

7 P. G. Scott, 'Richard Cope Morgan, Religious Periodicals and the Pontifex Factor', *Victorian Periodicals Newsletter* (later, *Victorian Periodicals Review* (*VPR*)) (*VPN*), 16 (1972), 1–14.

8 Billington, 'The Religious Periodical and Newspaper Press', pp. 121–32;

Joseph L. Altholz, 'The Redaction of Catholic Periodicals', in Joel H. Wiener (ed.), *Innovators and Preachers. The Role of the Editor in Victorian England* (Westport, CT, 1985), pp. 144–6, 148–9. H. R. Fox Bourne, *English Newspapers*, 2 vols. (London, 1887), vol. 2, pp. 126–31 and J. Grant, *The Newspaper Press*, 3 vols. (London, 1871–2), vol. 3, pp. 101–6, 134–57 comment on the religious press and hint at the degree of partisan feeling.

9   Billington, 'The Religious Periodical and Newspaper Press', in Harris and Lee (eds.), *The Press in English Society*, pp. 123–4.

10   *The Jewish Chronicle 1841–1941. A Century of Newspaper History* (London, 1949), pp. 1–2; David Sorkin, *The Transformation of German Jewry, 1780–1840* (Oxford, 1987), pp. 58–9; Meyer Waxman, *A History of Jewish Literature*, 5 vols. (New York, 1945), vol. 3, pp. 120–1.

11   Sorkin, *The Transformation of German Jewry*, pp. 81–6; David Paul Nord, 'The Public Community. The Urbanization of Journalism in Chicago', *Journal of Urban History*, 11:4 (1985), 411–13 and 436–8.

12   Sorkin, *The Transformation of German Jewry*, p. 138; Johanna Philippson, 'Ludwig Philippson und die Allgemeine Zeitung des Judentums', in Hans Liebeschutz und Arnold Paucker (eds.), *Das Judentum in der Deutschen Umwelt, 1800–1850* (Tübingen, 1977), pp. 246–7.

13   Phyllis Cohen Albert, 'Ethnicity and Jewish Solidarity in Nineteenth Century France', in Jehuda Reinharz and Daniel Swetschinski (eds.), *Mystics, Philosophers and Politicians: Essays in Honor of Alexander Altmann* (Burban, NC, 1982), pp. 261, 267–9; Shmuel Ettinger, 'The Modern Period', in H. H. Ben-Sasson (ed.), *History of the Jewish People* (London, 1976), p. 849.

14   *The Jewish Chronicle 1841–1941*, pp. 3–7.

15   Ibid. and James Picciotto, *Sketches of Anglo-Jewish History*, ed. I. Finestein (London, 1956), pp. 396–9.

16   V. D. Lipman, 'The Rise of Jewish Suburbia', *Transactions of the Jewish Historical Society of England (TJHSE)*, 21 (1968), 80–90 and V. D. Lipman,'The Development of London Jewry', in S. S. Levin (ed.), *A Century of Anglo-Jewish Life 1870–1970* (London, 1971), pp. 44–7.

17   V. D. Lipman, 'The Anglo-Jewish Community in Victorian Society', in D. Noy and I. Ben Ami (eds.), *Folklore Research Centre Studies 5: Studies in the Cultural Life of the Jews in England* (Jerusalem, 1975), pp. 151–64; H. Pollins, *Economic History of the Jews in England* (East Brunswick, NJ, 1982), pp. 87–115; B. Williams, *The Making of Manchester Jewry, 1774–1875*, paperback edition (Manchester, 1985), pp. 111–31.

18   Pollins, *Economic History of the Jews in England*, pp. 116–29; Cecil Roth, *A History of the Jews in England*, paperback edition (Oxford, 1978), pp. 241–7.

19   Williams, *Making of Manchester Jewry*, pp. 118–20; Pollins, *Economic History of the Jews in England*, pp. 107–15; P. S. Lachs, 'A Study of a Professional Elite: Anglo-Jewish Barristers in the Nineteenth Century', *Jewish Social Studies (JSS)*, 44:2 (1982), 125–34.

20   H. S. Q. Henriques, *The Jews and the English Law* (Oxford, 1908), pp. 248–53; Roth, *A History of the Jews in England*, pp. 247–53; M. C. N. Salbstein, *The Emancipation of the Jews in Britain: The Question of the Admission of the Jews to Parliament, 1828–60* (East Brunswick, NJ, 1982) and A. Gillam, *The Emancipation of the Jews in England, 1830–1860* (New York, 1982).

21 J. Garrard, *Leadership and Power in Victorian Industrial Towns, 1830–80* (Leicester, 1983), pp. 13–23; R. Trainor, 'Urban Elites in Victorian Britain', *Urban History Yearbook, 1985* (Leicester, 1985), pp. 3–4.
22 U. R. Q. Henriques, 'The Jewish Emancipation Controversy in Nineteenth Century Britain', *Past and Present*, 40 (1968), 126–46.
23 Salbstein, *The Emancipation of the Jews in Britain*, pp. 210–18; I. Finestein, 'Anglo-Jewish Opinion during the Struggle for Emancipation (1828–1858)', *TJHSE*, 20 (1959–61), 126–30.
24 Roth, *A History of the Jews in England*, pp. 256–9; Salbstein, *The Emancipation of the Jews in Britain*, pp. 78–94; Finestein, 'Anglo-Jewish Opinion', pp. 131–4; V. D. Lipman, 'The Age of Emancipation', in V. D. Lipman (ed.), *Three Centuries of Anglo-Jewish History* (London, 1961), pp. 82–5; R. Liberles, 'The Origins of the Jewish Reform Movement in England', *Association of Jewish Studies Review (AJSR)*, 1 (1976), 121–50.
25 Lipman, 'The Age of Emancipation', pp. 84–5; Liberles, 'The Origins of the Jewish Reform Movement in England', pp. 135–43.

1 ORIGINS AND PIONEERS, 1841–1855

1 Memoir by Asher Myers: *JC*, 13 November 1891, 28–9.
2 *Voice of Jacob (VJ)*, 11 September 1846, 197–9.
3 See obituaries, Samuel, *JC*, 13 November 1868, 5; Raphall, *JC*, 12 July 1868, 6.
4 *VJ*, 11 September 1846, 197–9. Subscribers were listed at the start of each bound volume. At the end of the first year, excluding multiple purchasers such as Sir Moses Montefiore, who bought ten copies, the *VJ* had 180 subscribers in London and England, 100 in the West Indies and under a dozen elsewhere in the world. London accounted for 80 regular subscribers.
5 *VJ*, 16 September 1841, 3–6. On Theodores see Bill Williams, *The Making of Manchester Jewry, 1740–1875* (Manchester, 1985), p. 100.
6 *VJ*, 26 November 1841, 34; 10 December 1841, 43–4; 29 April 1842, 121–2.
7 *The Jewish Chronicle 1841–1941. A Century of Newspaper History* (London, 1949), p. 13; obituary and memoir by Benisch, *JC*, 18 September 1868, 7.
8 *The Jewish Chronicle 1841–1941*, pp. 13–14; obituary of Angel and leader comment, *JC*, 9 September 1898, 8–11.
9 The first issue of the *JC*, 12 November 1841, 1, reprints the prospectus. Angel gave his recollections to Asher Myers for the Jubilee edition, 13 November 1891, 25.
10 *JC*, 14 January 1842, 56; 18 March 1842, 105.
11 *JC*, 24 December 1841, 38 and 18 March 1842, 105. J. Picciotto, *Sketches of Anglo-Jewish History*, ed. I. Finestein (London, 1956), p. 400; I. Asquith, 'Advertising and the Press in the Late Eighteenth and Early Nineteenth Centuries', *Historical Journal*, 18 (1975), 703–19.
12 *JC*, 12 November 1841, 2; 26 November 1841, 10.
13 *JC*, 24 December 1841, 35–6. See also 15 April 1842, 131.
14 Hyman Symons, *Forty Years a Chief Rabbi. The Life and Times of Solomon Hirschell* (London, 1980), pp. 92–101 and Liberles, ' The Origins of the Jewish Reform Movement in England', *AJSR*, 1 (1976).

15 *JC*, 4 February 1842, 70.
16 *JC*, 25 February 1842, 89–90.
17 *JC*, 6 May 1842, 5; 13 May 1842, 135; 22 May 1842, 36. See Arthur Ellis Franklin, *Records of the Franklin Family and Collaterals* (London, 1915), p. 27.
18 Comments on circulation and finances, *VJ*, 5 August 1842, 117–84 and 14 October 1842, 48.
19 *VJ*, 30 August 1844, 216.
20 *The Jewish Chronicle 1841–1941*, p. 30.
21 This description of Mitchell was recorded in the fiftieth anniversary account of the *Jewish Chronicle* written by the then editor, Asher Myers: *JC*, 13 November 1891, 35.
22 On Mitchell's charitable activities, see, for example, *JC*, 20 December 1844, 62; 28 November 1845, 29–30; 6 February 1846, 75.
23 See the letter from Lionel de Rothschild declining to attend a public gathering, interpreted by a correspondent as showing disfavour for continued agitation: *JC*, 8 October 1847, 261. The fact that Mitchell printed this communication suggests a spirit of irreverence.
24 *JC*, 13 November 1891, 35. The United Synagogue burial records confirm that he was interred 'by the wall' of the Great Synagogue in June 1854. I gratefully acknowledge the assistance or Mr Charles Tucker, archivist of the United Synagogue, in confirming this detail.
25 *JC*, 9 July 1847, 179–80; 16 July 1847, 188–92; 17 December 1847, 355; 4 February 1848, 415–21.
26 *JC*, 5 April 1850, 201 and 8 November 1850, 33–4 for the dismal response.
27 *JC*, 6 December 1844, 48; criticism of Chief Rabbi for not subscribing, 5 September 1845, 235; 11 October 1848, 9–10.
28 *VJ*, 4 August 1843, 210–12; 30 January 1846, 66–7.
29 *VJ*, 30 August 1844, 216; 30 January 1846, 66–7. Franklin called the *JC* the 'fortnightly organ' of the Reform Synagogue, 27 March 1846, 103. For objections to these attacks, see, *JC*, 6 February 1846, 71–2.
30 Obituary, *JC*, 20 May 1864, 5; *The Jewish Chronicle 1841–1941*, pp. 42–4.
31 *JC*, 21 July 1848, 609 announcing Bresslau's departure and 22 September 1848, 681, signalling his return; 10 October 1851, 2.
32 Alan J. Lee, *The Origins of the Popular Press 1855–1914*, paperback edition (London, 1980), pp. 21–6.
33 *JC*, 18 October 1844, 1; 1 November 1844, 1–2; 6 December 1844, 52. It was printed by Isaac Vallentine, as before, and published like its predecessor by W. Brittain.
34 M. Goulston, 'The Status of the Anglo-Jewish Rabbinate, 1840–1914', *Jewish Journal of Sociology* (*JJS*), 10:2 (1968), 55–83.
35 *JC*, 18 October 1844, 3–5; 1 November 1844, 2–3 and 15 November 1844, 29. C. Roth, 'The Chief Rabbinate in England', in I. Epstein, E. Levine and C. Roth (eds.), *Essays Presented to J. H. Hertz* (London, 1942), pp. 381–2; R. Apple, 'Nathan Marcus Adler's Installation as Chief Rabbi in 1845', *Jewish Review*, 21:6 (1967), 9.
36 R. Apple, 'United Synagogue: Religious Founders and Leaders', in S. S. Levin (ed.), *A Century of Anglo-Jewish Life 1870–1970* (London, 1971), pp. 13–16.

37 *JC*, 20 December 1844, 53. D. Philipson, *The Reform Movement in Judaism* (New York, 1931), chap. 5.
38 *JC*, 23 January 1846, 62.
39 *JC*, 26 June 1846, 161; 10 July 1846, 173; 24 July 1846, 181.
40 *JC*, 17 October 1845, 1–2; 31 October 1845, 9–10; 21 August 1846, 197–8. As well as carrying the resolutions of the 1846 Breslau assembly, the paper also printed full reports of the debates and voting, *JC*, 4 September 1846, 210. David Rudavsky, *Modern Jewish Religious Movements* (New York, 1979), pp. 156–85, 192–215.
41 *JC*, 16 September 1846, 1–2. See also: 'The Fatal Effects of Non-Reform', *JC*, 18 August 1848, 641–2 and 'The Veneration of Antiquity', *JC*, 25 August 1848, 649–50. On 6 December 1850, the paper reprinted the Address of the Religious Society of the Jews of Frankfurt-am-Main to their Co-religionists, the chief statement of the Neo-Orthodox position championed by Frankel and S. R. Hirsch.
42 *JC*, 4 September 1846, 205–6; 18 September 1846, 213–14 and 'What Reform Does Judaism in England Mostly Require?', *JC*, 2 November 1849, 25–6 and 9 November 1849, 33–4; 20 May 1853, 257.
43 *JC*, 19 December 1851, 84–5; 26 December 1851, 89. Albert Hyamson, *Jews' College, London, 1855–1955* (London, 1955).
44 'What Will Become of our College?', *JC*, 18 February 1853, 153.
45 See, for example, 'Remarks on the Civil Disabilities of the Jews', *JC*, 8 November 1844, 21; Tobias Theodores, 'The Christian Country', *JC*, 6 December 1844, 47.
46 *JC*, 30 June 1848, 590. On Crooll, see M. C. N. Salbstein, *The Emancipation of the Jews in Britain: The Question of the Admission of the Jews to Parliament, 1828–60* (East Brunswick, NJ, 1982), pp. 78–84 and I. Finestein, 'Anglo-Jewish Opinion during the Struggle for Emancipation (1828–1858)', *TJHSE*, 20 (1959–61), 113–43.
47 *JC*, 3 December 1847, 336–7; 31 December 1847, 373–6.
48 *JC*, 7 February 1845, 93; 7 March 1845, 109–10.
49 *JC*, 9 July 1847, 173–4; 16 July 1847, 185–6; 30 July 1847, 205–6. Salbstein, *Emancipation of the Jews*, chap. 8.
50 *JC*, 17 December 1847, 361–2. It was the same as the Friday edition, apart from the first page, which carried the results of the vote. Salbstein, *Emancipation of the Jews*, pp. 154–5.
51 *JC*, 8 October 1847, 261; 4 February 1848, 415–21.
52 *JC*, 2 June 1848, 553–4.
53 *JC*, 28 July 1848, 617–18.
54 O. Chadwick, *The Victorian Church*, vol. 1 (London, 1966), pp. 291–303; E. R. Norman, *Anti-Catholicism in Victorian England* (London, 1968), pp. 52–79 and E. R. Norman, *The English Catholic Church in the Nineteenth Century* (Oxford, 1984), pp. 112–14; Salbstein, *Emancipation of the Jews*, p. 194.
55 *JC*, 3 January 1851, 97; 24 January 1851, 121–2; 21 February 1851, 153; on the ghetto: *JC*, 7 February 1851, 138. Several editorials developed the idea of a Jewish–Protestant alliance, such as, 'What does the Pope Want?', *JC*, 7 February 1851, 137–8. The Anglo-Jewish experience foreshadowed in miniature the situation in Germany during the *Kulturkampf* in the 1870s: U. Tal,

Christians and Jews in Germany: Religion, Politics and Ideology in the Second Reich, 1870–1914 (Ithaca, NY, 1975).

56 *JC*, 2 July 1852, 305. Cf. Geoffrey Alderman, *The Jewish Community in British Politics* (Oxford, 1983), pp. 25–26.

57 *JC*, 9 July 1852, 313; 16 July 1852, 321; 25 October 1852, 9; 7 January 1853, 105; 6 May 1853, 240.

58 Because of the loss of momentum and interest another bill failed in the House of Commons, *JC*, 1 June 1854, 297–8. Salbstein, *Emancipation of the Jews*, pp. 193–7.

59 I. Finestein, 'Some Modern Themes in the Emancipation Debate in Early Victorian England', in Jonathan Sacks (ed.), *Tradition and Transition: Essays Presented to Chief Rabbi Sir Immanuel Jakobovits to Celebrate Twenty Years in Office* (London, 1986), pp. 131–46.

60 *JC*, 31 March 1847, 105.

61 *JC*, 18 May 1845, 141–2. Arthur Barnett, 'Sussex Hall – The First Anglo-Jewish Venture in Popular Education', *TJHSE*, 19 (1960), 65–79.

62 *JC*, 17 November 1848, 53–4. See also *JC*, 28 April 1848, 513–14; 12 May 1848, 529–30; 14 February 1851, 148–9; 17 March 1854, 206–7.

63 *JC*, 28 December 1849, 89–90.

64 *JC*, 30 October 1846, 9. See also *JC*, 29 October 1847, 285–6. On the impact of migration see 'The Jew as he Was. Pt. 1', by Anon., *JC*, 22 December 1854, 7. V. D. Lipman, 'Social Topography of a London Congregation. The Bayswater Synagogue 1863–1963', *JJS*, 6:1 (1964), 69–75, V. D. Lipman, 'The Rise of Jewish Suburbia', *TJHSE*, 21 (1968), 78–103 and V. D. Lipman, 'The Anglo-Jewish Community in Victorian Society', in D. Noy and I. Ben Ami (eds.), *Folklore Research Centre Studies*, vol. 5, *Studies in the Cultural Life of the Jews in England* (Jerusalem, 1975), pp. 151–64.

65 See article by 'An Israelite', *JC*, 12 December 1845, 42; 17 December 1847, 349–50. See also *JC*, 26 December 1845, 47 for Mitchell at a discussion of a workhouse for the foreign poor.

66 For example, the exchange of letters, *JC*, 13 May 1853, 253 and 20 May 1853, 262 and editorials, 17 March 1848, 465–6 and 18 January 1850, 113–14.

67 *JC*, 18 October 1848, 17–18; 29 October 1847, 285–6; 10 May 1850, 241–2. V. D. Lipman, *A Century of Social Service 1859–1959: The Jewish Board of Guardians* (London, 1959), p. 21.

68 Residential segregation: *JC*, 30 October 1846, 9 and 22 December 1854, 7. Visiting: *JC*, 31 October 1851, 25. G. M. Young, *Portrait of an Age: Victorian England*, paperback edition (Oxford, 1986), pp. 19–22.

69 *JC*, 27 August 1852, 369–70; 14 January 1853, 113–14; 11 November 1853, 44.

70 *JC*, 20 December 1844, 54–5. On Aguilar: *JC*, 5 September 1845, 239–40; 1 October 1847, 254; 8 October 1847, 263.

71 *JC*, 31 March 1848, 481–2. V. D. Lipman, 'Synagogal Organisation in Anglo-Jewry', *JJS*, 1:1 (1959), 80–93.

72 *JC*, 29 October 1847, 286. See also the four-part serial letter by 'A. Subscriber', 'What is the Vocation of the Board of Deputies?', commencing 30 April 1847, 123–4.

73 *JC*, 7 March 1845, 109–10.

74 *JC*, 22 October 1852, 17–18. The dispute rumbled on for months. Salbstein, *Emancipation of the Jews*, p. 120.
75 *JC*, 21 April 1848, 505–6 and 5 May 1848, 511–12.
76 *JC*, 11 March 1853, 177–8; 28 April 1853, 233; 24 June 1853, 298; 8 July 1853, 315, 316–17, 318. I. Finestein, 'The Anglo-Jewish Revolt of 1853', *Jewish Quarterly* (winter 1978), 103–13.
77 *JC*, 26 August 1853, 371–3; 2 September 1853, 377; special issue 5 September 1853. On the admission of the press: *JC*, 16 September 1853, 293.
78 *JC*, 2 December 1853, 71; supplement, 9 December 1853; 17 December 1853, 89–90. Finestein, 'The Anglo-Jewish Revolt of 1853', 112.
79 I. Finestein, 'The Uneasy Victorian: Montefiore as Communal Leader', in S. and V. D. Lipman (eds.), *The Century of Moses Montefiore* (Oxford, 1985), pp. 46–50.
80 For example, on *Punch*, *JC*, 15 November 1844, 35; *Standard*, *JC*, 31 December 1847, 376–7; *Morning Herald*, *JC*, 7 January 1848, 381–2. On Mayhew: *JC*, 14 December 1849, 73–4 and Dickens, 7 March 1851, 169–70.
81 *JC*, 13 June 1845, 179–80.
82 *JC*, 11 June 1847, 153–4; 1 June 1849, 269–70; 5 July 1850, 305–6; open letter to Lord Shaftesbury in four parts, beginning 20 May 1853, 260. On Palestine: *JC*, 30 May 1845, 176; 8 February 1850, 137–8.
83 *JC* Supp., 13 January 1854, 136.
84 Lucy Brown, *Victorian News and Newspapers* (Oxford, 1985), pp. 210–25, 233–40; Michael Palmer, 'The British Press and International News: Of Agencies and Newspapers, 1851–99', in G. Boyce, J. Curran and P. Wingate (eds.), *Newspaper History – from the Seventeenth Century to the Present Day* (London, 1978), pp. 205–15; Louis Billington, 'The Religious Periodical and Newspaper Press, 1770–1870', in M. Harris and A. J. Lee (eds.), *The Press in English Society from the Seventeenth to the Nineteenth Centuries* (London, 1986), p. 122.
85 *JC*, 17 October 1845, 7–8; 12 December 1845, 37–8; 28 February 1846, 93 and 26 June 1846, 129. M. Stanislawski, *Tsar Nicholas I and the Jews* (Philadelphia, 1983), pp. 5–11; C. Abramsky, 'The Visits to Russia (1846, 1872)', in S. and V. D. Lipman (eds.), *Century of Moses Montefiore*, pp. 257–63.
86 *JC*, 23 June 1848, 581–2; 17 November 1848, 55–6.
87 *JC*, 7 April 1848, 489–90. S. W. Baron, 'The Impact of the Revolution of 1848 on Jewish Emancipation', *JSS*, 11 (1949), 195–248; Jacob Katz, *Out of the Ghetto. The Social Background of Jewish Emancipation 1770–1870* (New York, 1978), pp. 196–8.
88 *JC*, 27 July 1849, 333–5 and 3 August 1849, 341–2; William O. McCagg Jr, *A History of Habsburg Jews, 1670–1918* (Bloomington, 1989), pp. 134–5. On English and Anglo-Jewish reponses to the Hungarian rising, see Williams, *Making of Manchester Jewry*, pp. 168–9.
89 *JC*, 1 January 1850, 114; 24 May 1850, 263, 21 June 1850, 289–90.
90 For example, *JC*, 17 March 1854, 203–4 on the Crimean War.
91 *JC*, 8 November 1844, 25; 12 June 1846, 156–7
92 *JC*, 16 May 1845, 161; 27 June 1845, 90, 18 May 1849, 255–6. Tudor Parfitt, 'Sir Moses Montefiore and Palestine', in V. D. Lipman (ed.), *Sir Moses Montefiore* (London, 1982), pp. 35–6.

93 *JC*, 26 January 1849, 125–6.
94 For example, *JC*, 26 January 1848, 126 and n. 82. Naomi Shepherd, *The Zealous Intruders. The Western Rediscovery of Palestine* (London, 1987), pp. 228–34, 240–3, 246–51.
95 *JC*, 16 November 1849, 43–4; 4 April 1851, 202–3; 30 May 1856, 603 and later issues for the first series on the Falashas. David Kessler, *The Falashas* (London, 1982), pp. 115–25.
96 Cf. Phyllis Cohen Albert, 'Ethnicity and Jewish Solidarity in Nineteenth Century France', in Jehuda Reinharz and Daniel Swetschinski (eds.), *Mystics, Philosophers and Politicians: Essays in Honor of Alexander Altmann* (Burban, NC, 1982), pp. 267–9; Katz, *Out of the Ghetto*, pp. 213–14.

2 DEFINING AN IDENTITY

1 Letters by Bresslau appeared in the *Hebrew Observer* (*HO*) from 4 February 1853. On 18 March 1853 he published his first signed articles, and by May 1853 his involvement was so great that the *Morning Advertiser* mistook him for the editor: *HO*, 13 May 1853, 147. Bresslau was also involved in the Association for the Promotion of Jewish Settlements in Palestine, of which Benisch was the moving force, *HO*, 6 May 1853. *The Jewish Chronicle 1841–1941. A Century of Newspaper History* (London, 1949), pp. 59–63; cf. J. M. Shaftesley, 'Dr Abraham Benisch as Newspaper Editor', *TJHSE*, 21 (1968), 214 and n. 1, 230.
2 *JC*, 22 December 1854, 5. Bresslau died alone and all but forgotten in the German Hospital in Dalston in 1864. One of his last publications in the paper he once owned was a Hebrew translation of 'God Save the Queen'. Obituary, *JC*, 20 May 1864, 5.
3 Adolf Boehm, *Die Zionistische Bewegung*, pt 1 (Berlin, 1921), p. 49; entry on Benisch by Natan Gelber, *Encyclopedia Judaica*, vol. 4 (Berlin, 1929); Shaftesley, 'Dr Abraham Benisch', 215–18.
4 Nahum Sokolow, *Geschichte Des Zionismus* (Berlin, 1921), pp. 138–59, 181–6; Norman B. Bentwich and John M. Shaftesley, 'Forerunners of Zionism in the Victorian Era', in J. M. Shaftesley (ed.), *Remember the Days: Essays on Anglo-Jewish History presented to Cecil Roth* (London, 1966), pp. 221–3; *The Jewish Chronicle 1841–1941*, p. 60.
5 *JC*, 30 March 1855, 116; 11 January 1856, 444–5.
6 *JC*, 2 May 1856, 374. See also 14 September 1855, 309; 1 October 1858, 4.
7 *JC*, 1 January 1858, 20–1; 13 January 1860, 4.
8 *JC*, 1 June 1855, 188–9. The debates over the constitution were fully reported between June 1855 and February 1856. The paper also carried correspondence from the various parties. Benisch made occasional editorial comments: *JC*, 2 November 1855, 364–5; 25 April 1856, 564–5.
9 *JC*, 24 April 1857, 980–1. I. Finestein, 'The Uneasy Victorian: Montefiore as Communal Leader', in S. and V. D. Lipman (eds.), *The Century of Moses Montefiore* (Oxford, 1985), pp. 45–8.
10 For example, *JC*, 19 April 1861, 4. 2. V. D. Lipman, 'Social Topography of a London Congregation. The Bayswater Synagogue 1863–1963', *JJS*, 6:1 (1964), 69–73; V. D. Lipman, 'The Rise of Jewish Suburbia', *TJHSE*, 21 (1968), 83–8.
11 *JC*, 26 June 1857, 1052–3; 18 September 1857, 1148–9; correspondence

December 1858–January 1859 on illegal Jewish hawkers and leading article, 17 December 1858, 6 and editorial note, 21 January 1859, 1. Correspondence concerning striking cigar makers, 8 January 1858, 29 and 15 January 1858, 38.

12 *JC*, 5 September 1856, 716. V. D. Lipman, *A Century of Social Service 1859–1959. The Jewish Board of Guardians* (London, 1959), pp. 5–20.

13 See, for instance, 'Political Economy versus the Soup Kitchen', *JC*, 13 February 1857, 908–9. Lipman, *Century of Social Service*, pp. 21–2.

14 Lipman, *Century of Social Service*, pp. 21–4. For correspondence, see *JC*, 19 March 1858, 110; 26 March 1858, 118 and subsequent issues. Editorial support: *JC*, 29 January 1858, 52; 12 March 1858, 100–1; 30 April 1858, 156–7; 1 July 1859, 4.

15 *JC*, 9 March 1860, 4. On Victorian theories of poverty, see M. E. Rose, *The Relief of Poverty 1834–1914* (London, 1972), pp. 22–7, 34–8 and D. Fraser, *The Evolution of the British Welfare State*, second edition (London, 1973), pp. 124–32.

16 *JC*, 18 April 1856, 556–7. M. C. N. Salbstein, *The Emancipation of the Jews in Britain: The Question of the Admission of the Jews to Parliament, 1828–60* (East Brunswick, NJ, 1982), pp. 197–8.

17 *JC*, 27 March 1857, 948–9 and election notice by the City Liberals, ibid., 947.

18 *JC*, 3 April 1857, 956–7; 19 June 1857, 1044–5; 17 July 1857, 1074; 24 July 1857, 1084.

19 One correspondent was so incensed that he asked: 'Will Rothschild take his seat with this insult to his faith thrown in his teeth?', *JC*, 23 July 1858, 253. For Benisch's reflections, *JC*, 27 April 1860, 4. Salbstein, *Emancipation of the Jews*, pp. 239–41.

20 'Gossip', *JC*, 18 November 1859, 7 and subsequent correspondence; 29 June 1860, 6; 13 July 1860, 7; 21 September 1860, 2. Harold Pollins, *A History of the Jewish Working Men's Club and Institute, 1874–1912* (Oxford, 1981), p. 5.

21 *JC*, 4 February 1859, 4. G. I. T. Machin, *Politics and the Churches in Great Britain 1842–1868* (Oxford, 1977), pp. 299–301, 306–8 and passim.

22 *JC*, 22 February 1867, 4–5; 10 July 1868, 4. Machin, *Politics and the Churches in Great Britain*, pp. 272–3, 294, 439.

23 *JC*, 11 May 1855, 164 and 13 July 1855, 236–7. O. Chadwick, *The Victorian Church*, vol. 1 (London, 1966), pp. 455–68; J. Wigley, *The Rise and Fall of the Victorian Sunday* (Manchester, 1980), pp. 68–9; B. Harrison, 'The Sunday Trading Riots of 1855', *Historical Journal*, 8: 2 (1965), 219–45.

24 *JC*, 3 May 1867, 6. Wigley, *Rise and Fall of the Victorian Sunday*, pp. 110–21.

25 *JC*, 1 March 1867, 4–5. See also 5 August 1864, 4.

26 For example, during the 1859 General Election, see: *JC*, 8 April 1859, 1; 15 April 1859, 1 and 4. Candidates for election recognised its influence among Jewish voters and paid for the insertion of their manifestos or arranged for the publication of letters of endorsement from influential Jews.

27 *JC*, 11 August 1865, 5. Geoffrey Alderman, *The Jewish Community in British Politics* (Oxford, 1983), pp. 34–5, 41.

28 *JC*, 9 October 1868, 5.

29 *JC*, 24 July 1868, 5; 31 July 1868, 7. Benisch was obliged to write to the Liberal *Daily News* denying the rumours: *JC*, 2 October 1868, 5. Cf. Marjorie Lamberti, *Jewish Activism in Imperial Germany – The Struggle for Civil Equality*

(New Haven, CT, 1978), pp. 94–104, on the 'Mugdan Affair', 1908–9, a similar issue in which the German Liberals thoughtlessly endorsed a Jewish convert.

30 Alderman, *Jewish Community in British Politics*, pp. 35–6. *JC*, 16 October 1868, 4. The result was due to other factors, too. Amongst these was the complicated voting technique intended to ensure an even spread of votes across the slate in a multi-member constituency. In this case, the system inadvertently operated against Rothschild because, while many Jews 'plumped' for the Liberals, not enough of the total vote cast ended up on his pile. See correspondence, *JC*, 20 November 1868, 5 and 27 November 1868, 7. He was re-elected in February 1869.

31 For samples of his polemic, see: *JC*, 4 May 1855, 156; 9 July 1858, 235; 30 May 1856, 604–5; 2 May 1862, 4; 9 May 1862, 4.

32 Examples of protests: *JC*, 6 June 1856, 612–13; 5 December 1856, 820; 6 December 1861, 4–5; 25 January 1861, 4.

33 *JC*, 28 August 1868, 4–5. On the blood libel: *JC*, 25 October 1861, 4; 14 February 1862, 4. M. H. Spielmann, *The History of Punch* (London, 1895), pp. 103–4, 197–200.

34 *JC*, 5 December 1856, 820.

35 On Alexander II and his reforms: *JC*, 16 March 1855, 100–1; 14 May 1858, 172; 8 July 1859, 4.

36 On *Razsvet*: *JC*, 22 February 1861, 2. A. Orbach, *New Voices of Russian Jewry: A Study of the Russian Jewish Press of Odessa in the Era of the Great Reforms, 1860–71* (Leiden, 1980), pp. 22–3 and S. Zipperstein, *The Jews of Odessa. A Cultural History, 1794–1881* (Stanford, 1985), pp. 76–83.

37 *JC*, 1 May 1863, 4. Cf. John Klier, 'The Polish Revolt of 1863 and the Birth of Russification: Bad for the Jews?', *Polin*, vol. 1 (Oxford, 1986), pp. 96–110.

38 C. T. MacIntyre, *England against the Papacy, 1858–61* (Cambridge, 1963), pp. 30–8; G. F. A. Best, 'Popular Protestantism in Victorian Britain', in R. Robson (ed.), *Ideas and Institutions of Victorian Britain* (London, 1964), pp. 115–42; W. Ralls, 'The Papal Aggression of 1850: A Study in Victorian Anti-Catholicism', in Gerald Parsons (ed.), *Religion in Victorian Britain*, vol. 2, *Controversies* (Manchester, 1988), pp. 116–34; E. R. Norman, *Anti-Catholicism in Victorian England* (London, 1968).

39 MacIntyre, *England against the Papacy*, pp. 36–7; cf. E. R. Norman, *The English Catholic Church in the Nineteenth Century* (Oxford, 1984), p. 187: 'The case of Edgar Mortara soon became a European scandal, in a campaign of carefully contrived vilification got up by Liberal and Protestant newspapers.'

40 *JC*, 3 September 1858, 300; 17 September 1858, 316; 8 October 1858, 2. C. H. L. Emanuel, *A Century and a Half of Jewish History* (London, 1910), p. 73.

41 *JC*, 28 October 1859, 4.

42 *JC*, 12 October 1860, 4. MacIntyre, *England against the Papacy*, pp. 199–203.

43 For example, Benisch took the side of Protestant Prussia against Catholic Austria in the war of 1866: *JC*, 20 July 1866, 4–5; 31 August 1866, 4–5.

44 Carol Ioancu, *Les Juifs en Roumanie, 1866–1919* (Aix-en-Provence, 1978), pp. 35–7, 58–9, 68–73, 75–98.

45 Michael Graetz, *Les Juifs en France au XIXe siècle* (Evreux, 1989), pp. 11–15, 393–6.

46 *JC*, 10 August 1860, 4; 16 November 1860, 5; 4 January 1861, 5; 18 January 1861, 4. Graetz, *Juifs en France au XIXe siècle*, p. 14.

47 Cf. Bentwich and Shaftesley, 'Forerunners of Zionism in the Victorian Era', pp. 221–8.

48 *JC*, 5 October 1855, 332. Tudor Parfitt, 'Sir Moses Montefiore and Palestine', in V. D. Lipman (ed.), *Sir Moses Montefiore* (Oxford, 1982), pp. 36–8.

49 *JC*, 11 April 1862, 4. See Naomi Shepherd, *The Zealous Intruders. The Western Rediscovery of Palestine* (London, 1987), pp. 118–19.

50 *JC*, 14 October 1864, 2; 21 October 1864, 2.

51 Chadwick, *Victorian Church*, vol. 1, passim; Elisabeth Jay, *Faith and Doubt in Victorian Britain* (London, 1986); Gerald Parsons, 'Reform, Revival and Realignment: The Experience of Victorian Anglicanism', in Gerald Parsons (ed.), *Religion in Victorian Britain*, vol. 1, *Traditions* (Manchester, 1988), pp. 13–66.

52 O. Chadwick, *The Victorian Church*, vol. 2 (London, 1970), pp. 75–90; J. L. Altholz, 'The Mind of Victorian Orthodoxy: Anglican Responses to "Essays and Reviews"', in Gerald Parsons (ed.), *Religion in Victorian Britain*, vol. 4, *Interpretations* (Manchester, 1988) pp. 28–40.

53 A. Hertzberg, *The French Enlightenment and the Jews* (New York, 1970).

54 Chadwick, *Victorian Church*, vol. 2, pp. 90–7; Gerald Parsons, 'Biblical Criticism in Victorian Britain: From Controversy to Acceptance?', in Gerald Parsons (ed.), *Religion in Victorian Britain*, vol. 2, *Controversies* (Manchester, 1988), pp. 239–57.

55 *JC*, 28 November 1862, 4; 5 December 1862, 4–5 to 27 February 1863, 4–5 except 9 January 1863 and 20 February 1863.

56 For example, his two editorials on the origin and development of Christianity: *JC*, 3 November 1865, 4–5; 10 November 1865, 4–5.

57 For instance, *JC*, 18 November 1864, 4–5. Cf. Todd Endelman, *Radical Assimilation in English Jewish History, 1656–1945* (Bloomington, IN, 1990), pp. 78–98.

58 *JC*, 10 July 1857, 1068.

59 *JC*, 7 September 1855, 300. On Jewish working-class women: *JC*, 5 October 1860, 4; 26 April 1861, 7; 8 November 1861, 2.

60 *JC*, 8 January 1858, 28. When Holdheim, the German reformer, died, 'Gossip' scolded the decision to honour his memory since he was 'the man who literally reduced Judaism to *nil*': *JC*, 21 September 1860, 2.

61 *JC*, 27 April 1866, 3. On Farjoen, see Bryan Cheyette, 'From Apology to Revolt: Benjamin Farjoen, Amy Levy and the Post-emancipation Anglo-Jewish Novel, 1880–1900', *TJHSE*, 29 (1982–6), 257–60.

62 A. J. Lee, 'The Structure, Ownership and Control of the Press, 1855–1914', in George Boyce, James Curran and Pauline Wingate (eds.), *Newspaper History – from the Seventeenth Century to the Present Day* (London, 1978), pp. 123–4.

63 Examples of 'puffs', *JC*, 16 October 1863, 5; 27 May 1864, 7; 3 June 1864, 7. Israel Davis on Benisch's investments, *JC*, 17 November 1911, 28.

64 *JC*, 26 March 1869, 1; *The Jewish Chronicle 1841–1941*, p. 81.

65 *JC*, 5 April 1872, 8. Obituary of Lionel Van Oven, *JC*, 13 January 1905, 11–13.

66 Collection of obituaries compiled by Richard L. Henry, *Michael Henry*

(London, 1875), pp. 16–49; see also the memoir by Lionel Van Oven, *JC*, 13 November 1891, 31.

67 Henry, *Michael Henry*, pp. 16–49; on singing, see *JC*, 5 June 1868, 4–5 and 17 July 1868, 4–5.

68 Gerald Parsons, 'Reform, Revival and Realignment: The Experience of Victorian Anglicanism', in Parsons (ed.), *Religion in Victorian Britain*, vol. 1, *Traditions*, pp. 47–51; Rose, *The Relief of Poverty*, pp. 26–7; Fraser, *The Evolution of the British Welfare State*, pp. 130–2.

69 The first letter appeared soon after Henry had taken over: *JC*, 30 April 1869, 3. Obituary: *JC*, 1 July 1887, 7–9.

70 *JC*, 10 January 1873, 572. Cf. James Grant, *The Newspaper Press*, 3 vols. (London, 1871–2), vol. 1, p. vi, 'Its mission is to Enlighten, to Civilize, and to Morally Transform the world ... The Press has before it one of the most glorious Missions in which human agencies were ever employed.' George Boyce, 'The Fourth Estate: The Reappraisal of a Concept', in Boyce, Curran and Wingate (eds.), *Newspaper History*, pp. 20–4.

71 T. Nevett, *Advertising in Britain* (London, 1982), pp. 67–86. The first full column of social and personal notices occurs in late 1871; three years later this had doubled.

72 *JC*, 29 March 1878, 4; 31 May 1878, 2. Women were the weak link Henry noted over the apostacy of Esther Mocatta, who became a Unitarian, *JC*, 28 September 1877, 3.

73 *JC*, 20 December 1867, 5. See also *JC*, 27 March 1868, 4.

74 The ambivalent position of minorities in a liberal society is discussed lucidly in Geoff Dench, *Minorities in the Open Society* (London, 1986). See also Bill Williams, 'The Anti-Semitism of Tolerance: Middle-class Manchester and the Jews, 1870–1900', in A. J. Kidd and K. W. Roberts (eds.), *City, Class and Culture* (Manchester, 1985), pp. 74–102.

75 *JC*, 15 April 1870, 6–7. Henry upheld a separatist position in the debate over whether the Jews' Deaf and Dumb Home should take Christian children into its special school: *JC*, 9 July 1869, 6.

76 *JC*, 15 October 1869, 2 and 7. The Act was amended in 1871 after the intervention of Sir David Salomons, MP.

77 Norbert C. Soldon, 'Individualist Periodicals. The Crisis of Late Victorian Liberalism', *VPN*, 6:3–4 (1973), 17–26. G. M. Young, *Portrait of an Age: Victorian England*, paperback edition (Oxford, 1986), pp. 117–19.

78 *JC*, 30 January 1874 , 730, 732–3.

79 A. Newman, *The United Synagogue 1870–1970* (London, 1977), pp. 7–14.

80 *JC*, 7 February 1868, 4–5; 17 April 1868, 4.

81 *JC*, 2 December 1870, 8; 24 April 1874, 56–7. On improvements see editorials from *JC*, 4 November 1870, 6–7 to 16 December 1870, 7.

82 *JC*, 31 March 1871, 9–10; four-part editorial from 1 August 1873, 301 to 22 August 1873, 348–9. See Michael Goulston, 'The Status of the Anglo-Jewish Rabbinate, 1840–1914', *JJS*, 10:1 (1968), 55–65.

83 *JC*, 5 November 1869, 8–9; 13 November 1874, 528–9. Parsons, 'Reform, Revival and Realignment', in Parsons (ed.), *Religion in Victorian Britain*, vol. 1, *Traditions*, pp. 47–56; J. M. Shaftesley, 'Religious Controversies', in S. S. Levin (ed.), *A Century of Anglo-Jewish Life* (London, 1971), pp. 97–8.

84 Shaftesley, 'Dr Abraham Benisch', pp. 220–1.
85 *JC*, 25 August 1871, 3–4, 8–9; 15 September 1871, 2. Charles H. L. Emanuel, *A Century and a Half of Jewish History* (London, 1910), pp. 93–4, 103, 107–8.
86 *JC*, 19 January 1872, 7–8; 21 June 1872, 168–9; 28 February 1873, 692–3.
87 *JC*, 5 September 1873, 376.
88 *JC*, 18 September 1874, 401.
89 *JC*, 18 February 1870, 8; 2 September 1870, 3 and editorial comment, 7.
90 *JC*, 21 June 1872, 169; 25 April 1873, 65–7.
91 *JC*, 26 January, 1872, 8–9. Pollins, *History of the Jewish Working Men's Club*, pp. 5–11, 27–31. See Henry, *Michael Henry* for details of his pedagogic activities.
92 *JC*, 2 February 1872, 12; 16 February 1872, 9; 1 March 1872, 5. Lloyd Gartner, *The Jewish Immigrant in England, 1870–1914* (London, 1960), pp. 222–4.
93 For an early example of Henry's thought on poverty, see *JC*, 3 August 1866, 4–5. Gareth Stedman Jones, *Outcast London. A Study in the Relationship between Classes in Victorian Society* (London, 1976), pp. 241–61; Lipman, *Century of Social Service*, pp. 48–9.
94 Lipman, *Century of Social Service*, pp. 68–9.
95 *JC*, 6 August 1869, 6; 13 August 1869, 8; 19 November 1869, 7; 8 July 1870, 9. For readers' reactions: *JC*, 3 February 1871, 6–7. Cf. Ursula Henriques, 'Lyons versus Thomas: The Jewish Abduction Case', *TJHSE*, 29 (1982–6), 267–80.
96 *JC*, 29 October 1869, 6–7; 6 December 1872, 492–3. Endelman, *Radical Assimilation in English Jewish History*, p. 124. Benisch was friendly with Voysey and delivered a lecture in his church.
97 *JC*, 15 December 1871, 8–9.
98 *JC*, 15 August 1873, 330–1 to 1 January 1875, 637–8 and editorial comment, 641. At Henry's further request Picciotto later went beyond his initial brief, which was to begin with the Readmission of the Jews under Cromwell, and added important chapters on the earliest history of the Jews in England. The essays were later published in book form. For the most recent edition, see J. Picciotto, *Sketches of Anglo-Jewish History*, ed. I. Finestein (London, 1956).
99 *JC*, 25 December 1874, 624–5. This was mild compared to the tirades in the English Protestant press and the pamphlet war. See G. Parsons, 'Victorian Roman Catholicism: Emancipation, Expansion and Achievement', in Parsons (ed.), *Religion in Victorian Britain*, vol. 1, *Traditions*, pp. 175–6; Norman, *The English Catholic Church*, pp. 308–12.
100 *JC*, 2 August 1872, 251–2; 22 August 1873, 349–50.
101 *JC*, 30 July 1869, 7. On the Suez Canal: *JC*, 26 November 1869, 9. On Mikveh Israel: *JC*, 29 October 1869, 10; 1 November 1872, 421–2.
102 Obituary and reminiscences in Henry, *Michael Henry*, pp. 16–49.
103 On the Bulgarian Agitation and the Jews, see Colin Holmes, *Anti-Semitism in British Society 1876–1939* (London, 1979), pp. 10–12. Cf. *The Jewish Chronicle 1841–1941*, p. 89 – 'three not very eventful years'.
104 See, for example, *JC*, 18 December 1868, 4: 'As matters now stand, the Turks are the real protectors of the Jews in the East.'
105 *JC*, 22 October 1875, 476. Justin McCarthy, MP and Sir John Robinson, *The*

'*Daily News' Jubilee* (London, 1896), pp. xv–xvi; R. Shannon, *Gladstone and the Bulgarian Agitation* (London, 1964).

106 E. J. Feuchtwanger, *Gladstone*, revised edition (London, 1989), pp. 181–4. Alderman, *Jewish Community in British Politics*, pp. 36–40.

107 H. C. G. Matthew (ed.), *The Gladstone Diaries*, vol. 9, *January 1875–December 1880* (Oxford, 1986), p. 161; Shannon, *Gladstone and the Bulgarian Agitation*, pp. 202–11; Lord Burnham, *Peterborough Court. The Story of 'The Daily Telegraph'* (London, 1955), pp. 20–3; Wilfred Hindle, *The Morning Post 1772–1837* (London, 1937), pp. 220, 225–6.

108 *JC*, 3 November 1876, 486. Matthew (ed.), *The Gladstone Diaries*, vol. 9, entry for 20 October 1876, p. 164 and 25 October 1876, p. 165. The following week, Benisch distinguished the Bulgarians from the other Slavs and argued that, in fact, they did deserve Jewish sympathy. The *Jewish Chronicle* even went so far as to sponsor a fund for the victims. *JC*, 10 November 1876, 498.

109 *JC*, 11 May 1877, 10; 18 May 1877, 3–4. Matthew (ed.), *The Gladstone Diaries*, vol. 9, entry for 3 May 1877, p. 216.

110 *JC*, 10 August 1877, 9–10.

111 *JC*, 7 December 1877, 3; 1 February 1878, 4. Alderman, *Jewish Community in British Politics*, pp. 37–8. Cf. Matthew, introduction to *The Gladstone Diaries*, vol. 9, pp. lxxxxviii–lxxxix.

112 See *JC*, 15 February 1878, 3–4; 22 February 1878, 12.

113 On Smith: *JC*, 22 February 1878, 9–11 and 1 March 1878, 9–10. Criticism of Gladstone: *JC*, 15 March 1878, 3; 5 April 1878, 3.

114 *JC*, 22 December 1876, 595; 12 January 1877, 4–5. Shaftesley, 'Dr Abraham Benisch', pp. 220–1.

115 *JC*, 13 July 1877, 6. Emanuel, *Century and a Half of Jewish History*, pp. 104–7.

116 *JC*, 31 March 1876, 844, 848–9; 4 August 1876, 275; 11 August 1876, 296–7.

117 On *Daniel Deronda*: *JC*, 15 December 1876, 585. On *Solomon Isaac*: *JC*, 23 November 1877, 12.

3 THE ERA OF ASHER MYERS AND ISRAEL DAVIS, 1878–1906

1 Obituary, *JC*, 16 May 1902, 7–8; 17 November 1911, 28; *The Jewish Chronicle 1841–1941. A Century of Newspaper History* (London, 1949), pp. 91–2.

2 A. J. Lee, 'The Structure, Ownership and Control of the Press, 1855–1914', in George Boyce, James Curran and Pauline Wingate (eds.), *Newspaper History – from the Seventeenth Century to the Present Day* (London, 1978), p. 127; Alan J. Lee, *The Origins of the Popular Press, 1855–1914*, paperback edition (London, 1980), pp. 114–15.

3 Valedictory by Davis, *JC*, 28 December 1906, 8; *The Jewish Chronicle 1841–1941*, p. 92; J. M. Shaftesley, 'Religious Controversies', in S. S. Levin (ed.), *A Century of Anglo-Jewish Life* (London, 1971), pp. 110–11.

4 Lucy Brown, *Victorian News and Newspapers* (Oxford, 1985), pp. 86–7, 168, 260, 268–9; T. Nevett, *Advertising in Britain* (London, 1982), pp. 67–70; Keith Robbins, *Nineteenth Century Britain. England, Scotland and Wales. The Making of a Nation* (Oxford, 1989), pp. 159–60; Diana Dixon, 'Children and the Press, 1866–1914', in Michael Harris and Alan Lee (eds.), *The Press in English Society from the Seventeenth to the Nineteenth Centuries* (London, 1986), pp. 133–44.

5 Lee, *Origins of the Popular Press*, pp. 117–30; G. A. Cranfield, *The Press and Society. From Caxton to Northcliffe* (London, 1978), pp. 207–8; Lee, 'The Structure, Ownership and Control of the Press, 1855–1914', pp. 119–24; Louis Billington, 'The Religious Periodical and Newspaper Press, 1770–1870', in Harris and Lee (eds.), *The Press in English Society*, pp. 130–2.

6 *The Jewish Chronicle 1841–1941*, pp. 157–60; Cecil Roth, 'Lucien Wolf. A Memoir', in Lucien Wolf, *Essays in Jewish History*, ed. C. Roth (London, 1934), pp. 4–7; Stephen Bayme, 'Jewish Leadership and Anti-Semitism in Britain, 1898–1918', Ph.D. thesis, Columbia University, 1977, pp. 53, 253, 270–1.

7 Jamie Camplin, *The Rise of the Plutocrats. Wealth and Power in Edwardian England* (London, 1978), chap. 6.

8 *JC*, 28 October 1881, 13; *Mitchell's* (later) *The Newspaper Press Directory*, (London), 1874, p. 148; 1878, p. 147; 1886, p. 181; 1896, p. 251. No detailed information about the *Jewish Chronicle*'s circulation appears to have survived.

9 V. D. Lipman, *A History of the Jews in Britain Since 1858* (Leicester, 1990), chaps. 2–5; Eugene C. Black, *The Social Politics of Anglo-Jewry, 1880–1920* (Oxford, 1989); I. Finestein, 'The New Community, 1880–1914', in V. D. Lipman (ed.), *Three Centuries of Anglo-Jewish History* (London, 1961); Lloyd P. Gartner, *The Jewish Immigrant in England, 1870–1914* (London, 1960).

10 For Myers's comments prior to the deluge: *JC*, 12 September 1879, 9; 7 November 1879, 9–10; 20 August 1880, 9–10. A. R. Rollin, 'Russo-Jewish Immigrants in England before 1881', *TJHSE*, 21 (1968), 202–13.

11 *JC*, 12 August 1881, 3; 6 January 1882, 4–5, 9–10; 13 January 1882, 4; 20 January 1882, 10–12. Michael Aaronson, 'The Anti-Jewish Pogroms in Russia in 1881', in John D. Klier and Shlomo Lambroza (eds.), *Pogroms: Anti-Jewish Violence in Modern Russian History* (Cambridge, 1992), pp. 44–61.

12 Jonathen Frankel, 'The Crisis of 1881–82', in David Berger (ed.), *The Legacy of Jewish Migration: 1881 and its Impact* (New York, 1983), pp. 13–14; Gartner, *The Jewish Immigrant*, pp. 42–3; Anne Taylor, *Laurence Oliphant, 1829–1888* (Oxford, 1982), pp. 205–8.

13 *JC*, 2 December 1881, 9; 21 April 1882, 8–9; 14 July 1882, 11–12. Black, *Social Politics of Anglo-Jewry*, pp. 243–8; Gartner, *The Jewish Immigrant*, pp. 49–53.

14 *JC*, 15 May 1885, 9. Gartner, *The Jewish Immigrant*, pp. 52–4; Geoffrey Alderman, *The Federation of Synagogues 1887–1987* (London, 1987), pp. 7–9.

15 For the arguments and the campaign, see John Garrard, *The English and Immigration: A Comparative Study of the Jewish Influx 1880–1910* (London, 1971) and Bernard Gainer, *The Alien Invasion. The Origins of the Alien Act of 1905* (London, 1972).

16 *In Darkest Russia* was financed by the Russo-Jewish Committee: *JC*, 17 July 1891, 5. On Madame Novikoff, W. T. Stead and the *Pall Mall Gazette*, see Brown, *Victorian Newspapers*, pp. 236–7.

17 Public meeting of the Association for the Prevention of the Immigration of Destitute Aliens, *JC*, 31 July 1891, 11; election: 17 June 1892, 7, 11; election notices: 24 June 1892, 4–5. Garrard, *The English and Immigration*, p. 30; David Feldman, 'The Importance of Being English. Jewish immigration and the Decay of Liberal England', in David Feldman and Gareth Stedman Jones

(eds.), *Metropolis London. Histories and Representations Since 1800* (London, 1989), pp. 68–9.

18 V. D. Lipman, *A Century of Social Service 1859–1959. The Jewish Board of Guardians* (London, 1959), pp. 92–7, 100–2, 111–12.

19 *JC*, 17 June 1892, 7; 16 December 1892, 5–6; 23 December 1892, 13–14.

20 *JC*, 10 November 1893, 13–14. Lipman, *Century of Social Service*, pp. 111–13. Myers served on the Board of Guardians until 1902.

21 *JC*, 6 April 1894, 5–6, correspondence in subsequent issues.

22 Compare *JC*, 12 July 1895, 7–8 to 19 July 1895, 11.

23 *JC*, 7 December 1894, 11; 9 October 1896, 13–14.

24 See special supplements, *JC*, 11 July 1902, etc. Almost every issue of the paper during 1902 carried editorial comment on the plight of Romanian Jewry.

25 *JC*, 22 June 1900, 15; 6 July 1900, 17; 20 July 1900, 10. Black, *Social Politics of Anglo-Jewry*, pp. 257–60.

26 Geoffrey Alderman, *The Jewish Community in British Politics* (Oxford, 1983), p. 68; Feldman, 'The Importance of Being English', pp. 69–70.

27 *JC*, 17 May 1901, 17; 2 August 1901, 8; 9 August 1901, 13.

28 *JC*, 12 July 1901, 16–17; 19 July 1901, 15.

29 For a general account of Anglo-Jewish responses, see Gartner, *Jewish Immigrant*, pp. 49–56; Black, *Social Politics of Anglo-Jewry*, pp. 243–67, 285–92.

30 Paula Hyman, *From Dreyfus to Vichy: The Remaking of French Jewry, 1906–1939* (New York, 1979); Steven Aschheim, *Brothers and Strangers: The East European Jew in German and German Jewish Consciousness, 1800–1923* (Madison, WI, 1982); Jack Wertheimer, *Unwelcome Strangers. East European Jews in Imperial Germany* (Oxford, 1987); Robert Wistrich, *The Jews of Vienna in the Age of Franz Ferdinand* (Oxford, 1990).

31 *JC*, 25 February 1881, 9–10; 11 February 1887, 11.

32 *JC*, 21 October 1887, 9; 3 August 1888, 6 and riposte 10 August 1888, 9. Alderman, *The Federation of Synagogues*, pp. 1–18.

33 *JC*, 6 July 1894, 13–14. Gartner, *Jewish Immigrant*, pp. 207–8; A. Newman, *The United Synagogue 1870–1970* (London, 1977), pp. 71–2.

34 Jerry White, *The Rothschild Buildings* (London, 1982); Black, *Social Politics of Anglo-Jewry*, pp. 167–72.

35 *JC*, 9 February 1883, 9–10; 14 September 1883, 9; 9 May 1884, 11–12. Suzanne Kirsch Greenberg, 'Anglicization and the Education of Jewish Immigrant Children in the East End of London', in Ada Rapoport-Albert and Steven Zipperstein (eds.), *Jewish History. Essays in Honour of Chimen Abramsky* (London, 1988), pp. 111–26.

36 On the flowering of Yiddish culture, see Gartner, *Jewish Immigrant*, pp. 255–61; Jacob Hodess, 'The History of the Jewish Press in England', in *The Jews in England. Studies and Sources, 1880–1940* (Yiddish) (New York, 1966), pp. 53–69; Leonard Prager, 'The Beginnings of Yiddish Fiction in England', in D. Noy and I. Ben Ami (eds.), *Folklore Research Centre Studies*, vol. 5, *Studies in the Cultural Life of the Jews in England* (Jerusalem, 1975), pp. 245–55; Lulla Rosenfeld, *Bright Star of Exile. Jacob Adler and the Yiddish Theatre* (New York, 1977), pp. 161–204; David Mazower, *Yiddish Theatre in London*

(London, 1987), pp. 9–27. The paper did not carry an advert in Yiddish until 1898.

37 *JC*, 18 Feburuary 1887, 5. Cf. Rosenfeld, *Bright Star of Exile*, pp. 199–201.

38 *JC*, 6 December 1895, 6.

39 For example: *JC*, 24 June 1898, 14; 13 October 1899, 21; 22 December 1899, 19.

40 Harold Pollins, *A History of the Jewish Working Men's Club and Institute, 1874–1912* (Oxford, 1981), p. 10; Richard A. Voelz, '"…A Good Jew and a Good Englishman": The Jewish Lads' Brigade, 1894–1922', *Journal of Contemporary History (JCH)*, 23:1 (1988), 119–27.

41 Dieter Schonebohm, *Ostjuden in London: Der Jewish Chronicle und die Arbeiterbewegung der jüdischen Immigranten im Londoner East End, 1881–1900* (Frankfurt-on-Main, 1987).

42 William J. Fishman, *Morris Winshevsky's London Yiddish Newspaper. One Hundred Years in Retrospect* (Oxford, 1985) and William J. Fishman, *East End Jewish Radicals, 1875–1914* (London, 1975), chap. 5; Gartner, *The Jewish Immigrant*, pp. 106–10.

43 See Fishman, *East End Jewish Radicals*, pp. 164–9.

44 Gartner, *The Jewish Immigrant*, pp. 122–6; Fishman, *East End Jewish Radicals*, pp. 163–84.

45 Anne Kershen, 'Jewish Trades Unionism in Leeds and London, 1870–1914', in David Cesarani (ed.), *The Making of Modern Anglo-Jewry* (Oxford, 1990), pp. 34–52; Haia Shpayer-Macov, 'Anarchism in British Public Opinion, 1880–1914', *Victorian Studies (VS)* (summer 1988), 487–515.

46 *JC*, 5 August 1887, 5; 19 August 1887, 5. Martin L. Friedland, *The Trials of Israel Lipski* (London, 1984), pp. 118, 125–30, 139–44, 161–3, 183–6; Colin Holmes, 'East End Crime and the Jewish Community, 1887–1911', in A. Newman (ed.), *The Jewish East End* (London, 1981), pp. 109–14.

47 *JC*, 14 September 1888, 5; 5 October 1888, 5; 12 October 1888, 4. Chaim Bermant, *London's East End. Point of Arrival* (London, 1975), pp. 111–21; William J. Fishman, *East End 1888* (London, 1988), pp. 213–25; Holmes, 'East End Crime and the Jewish Community, 1887–1911', pp. 114–15.

48 Colin Holmes, *Anti-Semitism in British Society, 1876–1939* (London, 1979), pt 1; Bayme, 'Jewish Leadership and Anti-Semitism in Britain', passim.

49 *JC*, 18 October 1895, 11.

50 Quoted in Michael Palmer, 'The British Press and International News: Of Agencies and Newspapers, 1851–99', in George Boyce, James Curran and Pauline Wingate (eds.), *Newspaper History – from the Seventeenth Century to the Present Day* (London, 1978), p. 218; Ann Parry, 'The *National Review* and the Dreyfus Affair: "The Conscience of the Civilized World"', *VPR*, 25:1 (1992), 6–15.

51 *JC*, 24 November 1899, 17; P. G. J. Pulzer, *The Rise of Political Anti-Semitism in Germany and Austria*, revised edition (London, 1988); Richard S. Levy, *The Downfall of the Anti-Semitic Political Parties in Imperial Germany* (New Haven, CT, 1975), pp. 195–253.

52 *JC*, 16 November 1883, 6; 23 November 1883, 9–10.

53 Cf. Pulzer, *Rise of Political Anti-Semitism*, pp. 156–63, 171–83; Walter R. Weitzmann, 'The Politics of the Viennese Jewish Community, 1890–1914', in

Ivor Oxaal, Michael Pollak and Gerhard Botz (eds.), *Jews, Anti-Semitism and Culture in Vienna* (London, 1987), pp. 127–30.

54 The most recent study of the Dreyfus Affair is Jean-Denis Bredin, *The Affair. The Case of Alfred Dreyfus* (New York, 1986).

55 *JC*, 21 August 1896, 11; 27 November 1896, 15. Deborah Yellin Bacharach, 'The Impact of the Dreyfus Affair on Great Britain', Ph.D. thesis, University of Minnesota, 1978.

56 *JC*, 30 September 1898, 15–16.

57 Richard I. Cohen, 'The Dreyfus Affair and the Jews', in S. Almog (ed.), *Anti-Semitism Through the Ages* (Oxford, 1988), pp. 291–310; Michael Marrus, *The Politics of Assimilation* (Oxford, 1980), pp. 196–242. Cf. Bachrach, 'Impact of the Dreyfus Affair', pp. 80–96.

58 *JC*, 6 January 1899, 16–17; 10 February 1899, 20. Bacharach, 'Impact of the Dreyfus Affair', pp. 161–87.

59 Interview with Oliphant by Sydney Samuel recorded in a letter: *JC*, 2 January 1880, 5 and editorial, 9 January 1880, 9–10. For comments by Myers, see *JC*, 11 June 1880, 9–10; 24 December 1880, 9–10. Taylor, *Laurence Oliphant*, p. 199.

60 David Vital, *The Origins of Zionism* (Oxford, 1980), pp. 49–108; Jonathan Frankel, *Prophecy and Politics. Socialism, Nationalism and the Russian Jews, 1862–1917* (Cambridge, 1981), pp. 49–90.

61 For example *JC*, 12 May 1882, 8–9.

62 Stuart A. Cohen, *English Zionists and British Jews. The Communal Poltics of Anglo-Jewry, 1895–1920* (Princeton, NJ, 1982), pp. 7–12.

63 Raphael Patai (ed.), *The Complete Diaries of Theodore Herzl* (New York, 1960), vol. 1, pp. 272–9, esp. entry for 26 November 1895. Josef Fraenkel, 'The *Jewish Chronicle* and the Launching of Political Zionism', in Raphael Patai (ed.), *Herzl Year Book*, vol. 2 (New York, 1959), pp. 217–27.

64 *JC*, 9 July 1897, 13.

65 *JC*, 21 May 1897, 15–16. Cohen, *English Zionists and British Jews*, pp. 155–214 and Stuart A. Cohen, 'Ideological Components in Anglo-Jewish Opposition to Zionism before and during the First World War: A Restatement', *TJHSE*, 30 (1987–8), 149–62.

66 *JC*, 20 December 1901, 16. Cohen, *English Zionists and British Jews*, pp. 34–46, 155–214; Virginia H. Hein, *The British Followers of Herzl: English Zionist Leaders 1896–1904* (New York, 1987).

67 *JC*, 3 January 1902, 33. Israel Cohen, *A Jewish Pilgrimage. The Autobiography of Israel Cohen* (London, 1956), p. 76; Paul Goodman, *Zionism in England 1899–1949* (London, 1949), pp. 16.

68 See I. Finestein, *Post-Emancipation Jewry: The Anglo-Jewish Experience* (Oxford, 1980).

69 *JC*, 27 September 1878, 9–10; 17 January 1879, 4. Alderman, *Jewish Community in British Politics*, pp. 39–41.

70 *JC*, 19 December 1879, 6; 26 December 1879, 4, 6–7, 9–10.

71 H. G. C. Matthew (ed.), *The Gladstone Diaries*, vol. 10, *January 1881–June 1883* (Oxford, 1990), pp. 197–8.

72 Ibid., pp. 201, 206. See H. G. C. Matthew, introduction to volume 10, p. lxiii: it was 'a very weak argument'.

73 *JC*, 3 February 1882, 9. See obituary, 20 May 1898, 10–12 and leading article, 17.

74 Hugh McLeod, *Class and Religion in the Late Victorian City* (London, 1974); James R. Moore, 'The Crisis of Faith: Reformation versus Revolution', in Gerald Parsons (ed.), *Religion in Victorian Britain*, vol. 2, *Controversies*, pp. 220–37; Todd M. Endelman, 'The Social and Political Context of Conversion in Germany and England, 1870, 1914', in Todd M. Endelman (ed.), *Jewish Apostasy in the Modern World* (New York, 1987), pp. 97–8 and Todd M. Endelman, *Radical Assimilation in English Jewish History, 1656–1945* (Bloomington, IN, 1990), pp. 81–92.

75 For example, *JC*, 3 September 1886, 9; 24 September 1886, 9–10. Peter Bailey, '"A Mingled Mass of Perfectly Legitimate Pleasures": The Victorian Middle Classes and the Problem of Leisure', *VS*, 21:1 (1977), 7–8; John Springhall, *Coming of Age: Adolescence in Britain 1860–1960* (London, 1986), pp. 113–20.

76 On the 'Wanderers', see Norman Bentwich, *Solomon Schechter. A Biography* (Cambridge, 1938), pp. 59–61; Margery and Norman Bentwich, *Herbert Bentwich. The Pilgrim Father* (London, 1940), pp. 67–73; Herbert Loewe, *Israel Abrahams. A Biographical Sketch* (London, 1944), pp. 21–2; Norman Bentwich, 'The Wanderers and Other Jewish Scholars of my Youth', *TJHSE*, 20 (1959–61), 51–62.

77 *JC*, 27 November 1891, 13. *The Jewish Chronicle 1841–1941*, p. 93; Margery and Norman Bentwich, *Herbert Bentwich*, p. 100; Loewe, *Israel Abrahams*, p. 22; Endelman, *Radical Assimilation*, pp. 112–13.

78 David Cesarani, 'Dual Heritage or Duel of Heritages? Englishness and Jewishness in the Heritage Industry', *Immigrants and Minorities*, 10:1/2 (1991), 30–1.

79 Sir Isidore Spielmann, Presidential Address, 9 February 1903, *TJHSE*, 5 (1902–5), 52; Lucien Wolf, Presidential Address, 15 January 1912, *TJHSE*, 7 (1911–14), 214.

80 *JC*, 18 April 1884, 9. G. Parsons, 'Reform, Revival and Realignment: The Experience of Victorian Anglicanism', in G. Parsons (ed.), *Religion in Victorian Britain*, vol. 1, *Traditions* (Manchester, 1988), pp. 220–37.

81 J. M. Shaftesley, 'Religious Controversies', in S. S. Levin (ed.), *A Century of Anglo-Jewish Life* (London, 1971), pp. 98–9; Wolf, 'The Queen's Jewry', in Lucien Wolf, *Essays in Jewish History*, ed. C. Roth, pp. 348–9.

82 *JC*, 24 January 1890, 13–14. Shaftesley, 'Religious Controversies', pp. 100–1 and Newman, *United Synagogue*, pp. 90–4.

83 *JC*, 3 June 1892, 5; 8 July 1892, 11. See Shaftesley, 'Religious Controversies', pp. 101–4; Raymond Apple, *The Hampstead Synagogue, 1892–1967* (London, 1967), pp. 10–34.

84 Raymond Apple, 'United Synagogue: Religious Founders and Leaders', in Levin (ed.), *Century of Anglo-Jewish Life*, pp. 18–19; Stephen Sharot, 'Religious Change in Native Orthodoxy in London, 1870–1914: Rabbinate and Clergy', *JJS*, 15:2 (1973), 176–80.

85 For example, *JC*, 23 July 1880, 9; 25 September 1891, 9.

86 Article by 'A Jewess', *JC*, 17 September 1886, 7; for an early letter: 14 February 1879, 5.

87 *JC*, 7 February 1896, 6; 21 February 1902, 10–11.

88 *JC*, 29 July 1887, 8–9; 17 May 1889, 10–11. Edward Kessler (ed.), *An English*

Jew. The Life and Writings of Claude Montefiore (London, 1989); Bentwich, *Solomon Schechter*; Loewe, *Israel Abrahams*.

89 *JC*, 25 January 1889, 11. Bryan Cheyette, 'From Apology to Revolt: Benjamin Farjoen, Amy Levy and the Post-Emancipation Anglo-Jewish Novel, 1880–1900', *TJHSE*, 29 (1982–6), 253–65.

90 *JC*, 20 May 1892, 9; 30 September 1892, 15–16; 12 April 1895, 17. Cf. Bryan Cheyette, 'The Other Self: Anglo-Jewish Fiction and the Representation of the Jews in England, 1875–1905', in Cesarani (ed.), *The Making of Modern Anglo-Jewry*, pp. 106–9.

91 *JC*, 2 November 1900, 19. Cf. Cheyette, 'From Apology to Revolt', 256–7.

92 Martin S. Looker, '"God Save the Queen". Victoria's Jubilees and the Religious Press', *VPR*, 21:3 (1988), 115–19.

93 Bayme, 'Jewish Leadership and Anti-Semitism', chap. 3 and Holmes, *Anti-Semitism in British Society*, pp. 66–70.

94 *JC*, 13 February 1932, 18.

95 The *Jewish Chronicle* had acquired a telephone in March 1889. For Davis's methods see his reminiscences, *JC*, 17 November 1911, 28.

96 Obituary, *JC*, 28 January 1927, 7; *The Jewish Chronicle 1841–1941*, pp. 112–13.

97 Graham Maddock and Peter Golding, 'The Structure, Ownership and Control of the Press, 1914–1950', in George Boyce, James Curran and Pauline Wingate (eds.), *Newspaper History – from the Seventeenth Century to the Present Day* (London, 1978), pp. 130–5; Lee, *The Origins of the Popular Press*, pp. 121–30.

98 Gartner, *The Jewish Immigrant*, pp. 258–61; Leonard Prager, 'A Bibliography of Yiddish Periodicals in Great Britain (1867–1967)', *Studies in Bibliography and Booklore*, 9 (1969), 3–32 and Leonard Prager, *Yiddish Culture in Great Britain* (Frankfurt-on-Main, 1990), pp. 38–41 and passim.

99 *JC*, 24 November 1905, 12. T. Nevett, *Advertising in Britain* (London, 1982), pp. 82–3.

100 *JC*, 13 June 1902, 7. L. J. Greenberg to Jacobus Kann, 16 December 1906, Kann Papers, Central Zionist Archive, Jerusalem (CZA), A121/108; *The Jewish Chronicle 1841–1941*, pp. 120, 122.

101 Advertisements for leaflets, *JC*, 5 February 1904, 22 and full list, 11 March 1904, 18.

102 *JC*, 14 August 1903, 17–18 and supplement. Lipman, *History of the Jews in Britain*, pp. 70–2.

103 *JC*, 5 June 1903, 17; 19 June 1903, 11, 21. The Russian correspondent of *The Times* was actually expelled.

104 *JC*, 5 February 1904, 21–2; 8 April 1904, 7–8.

105 Geoffrey Alderman, 'The Jew as Scapegoat? The Settlement and Reception of Jews in South Wales before 1914', *TJHSE*, 26 (1979), 62–70; Bayme, 'Jewish Leadership and Anti-Semitism', pp. 240–50.

106 *JC*, 26 May 1905, 8. The *Jewish Chronicle* was more robust in its response to the hostile Admiralty Committee report on *shechita*. It gave a good deal of space to the issue, including a special supplement, in August and October 1904.

107 *JC*, 15 July 1904, 7–8. Cf. Bayme, 'Jewish Leadership and Anti-Semitism', pp. 240–50.

108 *JC*, 27 January 1905, 8–9. For the background, see Frankel, *Prophecy and Politics*.
109 Shlomo Lambroza, 'The Pogroms of 1903–1906', in Klier and Lambroza (eds.), *Pogroms*, pp. 195–247.
110 *JC*, 28 April 1905, 7–9; 5 May 1905, 7–8 and almost every subsequent issue. Alderman, *Jewish Community in British Politics*, pp. 71–2.
111 *JC*, 19 January 1906, 9–10. Cf. Alderman, *Jewish Community in British Politics*, pp. 74–6.
112 Correspondence between Duparc and Sokolow, Sokolow Papers, CZA, A18/630.
113 *JC*, 9 February 1906, 7. *The Jewish Chronicle 1841–1941*, p. 120.
114 *JC*, 23 November 1906, 13. Black, *Social Politics of Anglo-Jewry*, pp. 309–16.
115 Hein, *British Followers of Theodor Herzl*, pp. 204–31; Cohen, *English Zionists and British Jews*, pp. 81–4, 85–90, 111–13.
116 *JC*, 4 August 1905, 7–8; 2 February 1906, 7. David Vital, *Zionism: The Formative Years* (Oxford, 1982), pp. 237–367 and 435–43. Davis had an ambiguous attitude towards Zionism. In his will, he left a large sum of money for the teaching of English in Palestine. A generous interpretation of the bequest helped save the English Zionist Federation from financial crisis in the late 1920s: *JC*, 11 March 1927, 10.
117 L. J. Greenberg to Jacobus Kann, 16 December 1906; Greenberg to Sokolow, 4 January 1907, CZA, A121/108.

4 THE HEGEMONY OF LEOPOLD GREENBERG, 1907–1931

1 L. J. Greenberg to Jacobus Kann, 4 December 1906, Kann Papers, CZA, A121/108.
2 Greenberg to Kann, 9 December 1906, CZA, A121/108.
3 Executive Committee of the JCT to the JCT Office, London, 17 December 1906, CZA, A121/108; Greenberg to Kann, 21 December 1906, CZA, A121/108. The legal work was conducted by Lloyd George, Roberts & Co.
4 Nahum Sokolow to Kann, 21 December 1906, CZA, A121/108.
5 Kann to Sokolow, 24 December 1906; Kann to Greenberg, 24 December 1906; Cowan to Kann, 27 December 1906; Greenberg telegram to Sokolow, 26 December 1906; Greenberg to Kann, 26 December 1906, CZA, A121/108.
6 *Tagblatt*, 2 January 1907, CZA, A121/108; Sokolow to Zionist Central Bureau, 4 February 1907, CZA, A121/108. David Freeman, 'Jacobus H. Kann of the Hague', in Raphael Patai (ed.), *The Herzl Yearbook*, vol. 7 (New York, 1971), pp. 63–4; *The Jewish Chronicle 1841–1941. A Century of Newspaper History* (London, 1949), pp. 124–8.
7 Katzenelson to Zionist Central Bureau, 21 January 1907; Theodore Hirsch to Kann, 12 February 1907; Hirsch to Kann, 19 June 1907; Greenberg to Kann, 3 July 1907; Greenberg to Kann, 26 July 1907; Hirsch to Kann, 7 November 1907, CZA, A121/108. The widow of Asher Myers was also made a shareholder. *The Jewish Chronicle 1841–1941*, p. 127.
8 Weizmann to Ussishkin, 29 March 1905, *Chaim Weizmann Letters and Papers*, Series A, vol. 4, *January 1905–December 1906*, ed. Camillo Dresner and Barnett

Litvinoff (Jerusalem, 1973) (hereafter, *CWLP* and volume number), p. 63; *The Jewish Chronicle 1841–1941*, p. 134.

9 Entries for 4 March 1901, 28 March 1901, 1 August 1901, 2 December 1901, 24 April 1902, Charity Account Ledger December 1900–July 1903, Rothschild Archive, I/101/1. T. H. S. Escott, a well-known Fleet Street personality, was also in receipt of substantial payments.

10 Stephen Koss, *The Rise and Fall of the Political Press in Britain*, vol. 1, *The Twentieth Century* (London, 1981), pp. 409–35; Virginia H. Hein, *The British Followers of Herzl: English Zionist Leaders 1896–1904* (New York, 1987), pp. 103–7, 217; Freeman, 'Jacobus H. Kann of the Hague', pp. 51–70. Soon after the sale, rumours circulated among other Jewish papers, notably the *Jewish World*, that Horatio Bottomley, the editor of *John Bull*, a Conservative paper in the stable of Odhams Press (which was owned by Julius Salter Elias, later Lord Southwood), had obtained a stake in it: *The Jewish Chronicle 1841–1941*, p. 164.

11 Weizmann to Sokolow, 12 February 1910, *CWLP*, vol. 5, p. 186. Stuart A. Cohen, *English Zionists and British Jews. The Communal Politics of Anglo-Jewry, 1895–1920* (Princeton, NJ, 1982), pp. 114–15, 121–5, 298 and passim; J. Reinharz, *Chaim Weizmann. The Making of a Zionist Leader* (Oxford, 1985), p. 335 and n. 125, p. 505; *The Jewish Chronicle 1841–1941*, p. 164. The *Zionist Banner*, edited by S. Massel and Joseph L. Cohen, transmuted into *The Zionist* and continued until 1914 under the editorship of Harry Sacher, Leon Simon and Samuel Landman.

12 In 1906 two members of staff threatened to leave if Greenberg made the paper into a Zionist organ: Greenberg to Kann, 26 December 1906, CZA, A121/108.

13 Birmingham Jewish Research Group, *Birmingham Jewry 1749–1914*, vol. 1 (Birmingham, 1980), p. 94; Zoe Josephs (ed.), *Birmingham Jewry 1740–1930*, vol. 2 (Birmingham, 1984), p. 125; Hein, *British Followers of Theodor Herzl*, pp. 91–102. In 1885 he seconded a resolution in support of the Liberal candidate for Whitechapel, Samuel Montagu, at an election meeting in London: *JC*, 13 November 1885, 10.

14 *JC*, 19 February 1886, 6–7, 11. Bentwich, 'Wanderers'. p. 55; Raymond Apple, *The Hampstead Synagogue, 1892–1967* (London, 1967), p. 95.

15 Letters, *JC*, 26 June 1891, 7; 8 April 1894, 10 and 15 December 1895, 9.

16 *JC*, 3 October 1902, 23.

17 *Young Israel (YI)*, 1:1 (March 1897), 1–2; *The Jewish Chronicle 1841–1941*, p. 165. Cf. Diana Dixon, 'Children and the Press, 1866–1914', in Michael Harris and Alan Lee (eds.), *The Press in English Society from the Seventeenth to the Nineteenth Centuries* (London, 1986), pp. 133–48, esp. 141–3 on the religious youth press.

18 Alan J. Lee, *The Origins of the Popular Press, 1855–1914*, paperback edition (London, 1980), pp. 117–30; John Goodbody, 'The Star: Its Role in the New Journalism', *VPR*, 20:4 (1987), 141–50.

19 *JC*, 5 May 1911, 12; 9 February 1912, 25. See self-promotion of Greenberg & Co: *JC*, 26 July 1907, 5. It was common for advertising agents to own newspapers: T. Nevett, *Advertising in Britain* (London, 1982), p. 104.

20 The 'wine-wars' between Chaikin and Palwin, both claiming the exclusive importation of kosher wines from Palestine, were the longest-running example

of this tendency. Cf. Andrew R. Heinze, *Adapting to Abundance. Jewish Immigrants, Mass Consumption and the Search for American Identity* (New York, 1990), pp. 147–60.

21 Greenberg to Kann, 9 April 1913, CZA, A121/108. Exact circulation figures are not known. Greenberg to Kann, 22 March 1912 and Kann to Greenberg, 25 March 1912, CZA, A121/151.

22 *JC*, 4 April 1913, 15; Greenberg to Kann, 27 April 1913, CZA, A121/151. *Jewish Chronicle* writing paper started using the phrase 'Organ of Anglo-Jewry' around 1910.

23 For example: *JC*, 4 June 1886, 7; 20 July 1888, 5; 26 May 1899, 18. Edward J. Bristow, *Prostitution and Prejudice. The Jewish Fight Against White Slavery, 1870–1939* (Oxford, 1982).

24 See also *JC*, 1 April 1910, pp. 5–6; Lloyd P. Gartner, 'Anglo-Jewry and the Jewish International Traffic in Prostitution, 1885–1914', *AJSR*, 7–8 (1982–3), 129–78.

25 Jewish Research Group of the Edmonton Hundred Historical Society, *Heritage. An Historical Series on the Jewish Inhabitants of North London*, no. 1 (London, 1982), pp. 22–4. On the 'Siege of Sidney Street', D. Rumbelow, *The Houndsditch Murders and the Siege of Sidney Street* (London, 1973); Colin Holmes, 'East End Crime and the Jewish Community, 1887–1911', in A. Newman (ed.), *The Jewish East End, 1840–1939* (London, 1981), pp. 109–24.

26 *JC*, 19 November 1909, 6; 17 March 1911, 7. Kenneth E. Collins (ed.), *Aspects of Scottish Jewry* (Glasgow, 1987), p. 30; Andrew Rose, *Stinie. Murder on the Common* (London, 1985); Holmes, 'East End Crime and the Jewish Community', pp. 111, 117.

27 For example, *JC*, 14 February 1908, 6; 22 September 1911, 10; 23 August 1912, 9–10.

28 *JC*, 25 August 1911, 5–6, 8–12; 1 September 1911, 5–6. Geoffrey Alderman, 'The Jew as Scapegoat? The Settlement and Reception of Jews in South Wales before 1914', *TJHSE*, vol. 26 (1974–8), 65–8; Geoffrey Alderman, 'The Anti-Jewish Riots of August 1911 in South Wales', *Welsh History Review*, 6:2 (1972–3), 190–200; cf. A. M. Wiener, 'Tredegar Riots', *CAJEX*, 26:1 (1976), 17–26 and correspondence, 29–31. See also Kenneth Lunn, 'Political Anti-Semitism before 1914: Fascism's Heritage?', in Kenneth Lunn and Richard C. Thurlow (eds.), *British Fascism* (London, 1980), pp. 20–40; C. Holmes, *Anti-Semitism in British Society 1876–1939* (London, 1979), pp. 63–88.

29 The *Jewish Chronicle* did a similar interview with Chesterton: *JC*, 28 April 1911, 18. Lunn, 'Political Anti-Semitism Before 1914: Fascism's Heritage?', in Lunn and Thurlow (eds.), *British Fascism*, pp. 22–5.

30 Frances Donaldson, *The Marconi Scandal* (London, 1962); G. R. Searle, *Corruption in British Politics 1895–1930* (Oxford, 1987), pp. 172–212; Bryan Cheyette, 'Hilaire Belloc and the "Marconi Scandal" 1900–1914: A Reassessment of the Interactionist Model of Racial Hatred', in Tony Kushner and Kenneth Lunn (eds.), *The Politics of Marginality. Race, the Radical Right and Minorities in Twentieth Century Britain* (London, 1990), pp. 131–42.

31 *JC*, 18 October 1912, 7–8. See also *JC*, 15 November 1912, 9; 20 June 1913, 9. For 'Greenberg's campaign against the Chestertons', see Dean Rapp, 'The

Jewish Response to G. K. Chesterton's Antisemitism, 1911–33', *Patterns of Prejudice*, 24: 2–4 (1990), 77–9.

32 *JC*, 11 October 1907, 14–15 and intervening issues until 8 November 1907, 19.

33 *JC*, 1 May 1908, 5. Also, defence of 'Jewish vote', *JC*, 20 November 1908, 7; cf. 3 December 1909, 7. Geoffrey Alderman, *The Jewish Community in British Politics* (Oxford, 1983), pp. 80–3.

34 *JC*, 5 August 1910, 5, 7–8; 13 September 1912, 13.

35 *JC*, 20 May 1910, 6; 18 November 1910, 7–8.

36 *JC*, 9 February 1912, 10; 12 April 1912, 8 and 19–20; 20 February 1914, 11–12; letter, 27 February 1914, 22. Cohen, *English Zionists and British Jews*, pp. 134–7.

37 *JC*, 8 January 1909, 10. See Gerry Black, 'Health and Medical Care of the Jewish Poor in the East End of London 1880–1919', Ph.D. thesis, Leicester University, 1987.

38 *JC*, 15 May 1914, 10.

39 *JC*, 17 March 1911, 7–8. B. Homa, *A Fortress in Anglo-Jewry. The Story of the Machzike Hadath* (London, 1953), pp. 75–6; Lloyd P. Gartner, *The Jewish Immigrant in England, 1870–1914* (London, 1960), pp. 217–18.

40 Cf. *JC*, 8 October 1909, 5 to 4 March 1910, 5.

41 *JC*, 25 December 1908, 5; 5 February 1909, 7; 29 July 1910, 6.

42 *JC*, 21 July 1911, 5. Cf. *JC*, 22 December 1911, 7 and 28 June 1912, 11–12. Kann to Greenberg, 10 October 1911, CZA, A121/151. A. Newman, *The United Synagogue 1870–1970* (London, 1977), pp. 97–102; Geoffrey Alderman, *The Federation of Synagogues 1887–1987* (London, 1987), pp. 44–6.

43 *JC*, 7 June 1907, 7–8; 27 September 1907, 5. See Max Beloff, 'Lucien Wolf and the Anglo-Russian Entente 1907–1914', in his *The Intellectual in Politics and Other Essays* (London, 1970), pp. 111–42.

44 *JC*, 19 January 1912, 8; 12 June 1914, 9–10.

45 *JC*, 24 July 1908, 7–8. Anthony Allfrey, *Edward VII and his Jewish Court* (London, 1991); Cecil Roth, 'The Court Jews of Edwardian England', *JSS*, 5 (1943), 365–6.

46 D. Cesarani, 'An Embattled Minority: The Jews in Britain During World War One', in T. Kushner and K. Lunn (eds.), *The Politics of Marginality. Race, the Radical Right and Minorities in Twentieth Century Britain* (London, 1990), pp. 61–81.

47 *JC*, 4 September 1914, 7; 16 October 1914, 7–8. Cf. *The Jewish Chronicle 1841–1941*, pp. 141–2. David Vital, *Zionism: The Crucial Phase* (Oxford, 1986), pp. 109–19, 171–5, 182–90; M. Levene, 'Anglo-Jewish Foreign Policy in Crisis – Lucien Wolf, the Conjoint Foreign Committee and the War, 1914–1919', *TJHSE*, 30 (1987–8), 179–98.

48 *JC*, 25 June 1915, 9. Weizmann to Sokolow, 28 June 1915, *CWLP*, vol. 7, p. 215.

49 For example, *JC*, 26 March 1915, 11; 23 April 1915, 7, 9. On DORA, reprimand, *JC*, 2 December 1921, 31.

50 See Sharman Kadish, *Bolsheviks and British Jews. The Anglo-Jewish Community, Britain and the Bolshevik Revolution* (London, 1992), chap. 2.

51 *JC*, 20 November 1914, 5. Cesarani, 'An Embattled Minority', pp. 61–81.

52 For example, *JC*, 23 October 1914, 7. C. C. Aaronsfeld, 'Jewish Enemy Aliens

in England during the First World War', *JSS*, 18 (1956), 275–83; S. Yarrow, 'The Impact of Hostility on Germans in Britain, 1914–1918', in Kushner and Lunn (eds.), *The Politics of Marginality*, pp. 97–130.

53 *JC*, 18 June 1915, 7; Board of Deputies Minutes (BD), vol. 16, 13 June 1915, Board of Deputies Archive (BDA). Yarrow, 'The Impact of Hostility on Germans', pp. 100–9.

54 *JC*, 28 August 1914, 5; Mentor on aliens and alleged shirking, 16 October 1914, 7; 17 December 1915, 7–8; on discrimination, 26 November 1915, 9.

55 *JC*, 6 November 1914, 5–6; 27 November 1914, 5.

56 *JC*, 11 December 1914, 20–1 and see 8 January 1915, 7. Leonard Stein later attributed to Greenberg the impetus behind the Jewish regiment idea and asserted that he was prompted by Zionist objectives. L. Stein, 'Eder as Zionist', in J. B. Hobman (ed.), *David Eder. Memoirs of a Modern Pioneer* (London, 1945), p. 135.

57 *JC*, 28 January 1916, 11; 10 March 1916, 7; 4 February 1916, 13. Jews formed little more than a short footnote in the debate on conscription. Of the 16,500 objectors, Quakers and Seventh-day Adventists formed the largest groups of those motivated by religious conviction: John Rae, *Conscience and Politics. The British Government and the Conscientious Objectors to Military Service 1916–19* (Cambridge, 1970), chaps. 5–6.

58 *JC*, 16 June 1916, 7; 23 June 1916, 7; 14 July 1916, 7. J. Bush, *Behind the Lines. East London Labour, 1914–1919* (London, 1984), pp. 181–6.

59 *JC*, 9 March 1917, 7. Kadish, *Bolsheviks and British Jew*, pp. 197–220.

60 J. H. Patterson, *With the Judaeans in the Palestine Campaign* (London, 1922), pp. 13–29; Leonard Stein, *The Balfour Declaration* (London, 1961), pp. 484–96.

61 Cesarani, 'An Embattled Minority', pp. 72–4.

62 Greenberg to Jacobus Kann, 20 November 1915; Greenberg to Kann, 18 April 1917, CZA, A121/151.

63 On peace proposals, *JC*, 20 September 1918, 3; 27 September 1918, 5. Greenberg to Zangwill, 11 October 1918, CZA, A120/364.

64 David Vital, *Zionism: The Crucial Phase* (Oxford, 1987), pp. 6–85.

65 *JC*, 8 February 1907, 7; 1 January 1909, 6. Cohen, *English Zionists and British Jews*, pp. 105–23; Paul Goodman, *Zionism in England, 1899–1949* (London, 1949), pp. 29–33.

66 Greenberg to Kann, 1 August 1913; Greenberg to Kann, 10 September 1914, A121/151.

67 Leonard Stein, *The Balfour Declaration* (London, 1961), pt 2; I. Friedmann, *Germany, Turkey, Zionism* (Oxford, 1977), pt 3; Vital, *Zionism: The Crucial Phase*, pts 2–3.

68 Greenberg to Kann, 29 December 1914; Greenberg to Kann, 22 January 1915, CZA, A121/151.

69 *JC*, 1 January 1915, 7; 8 January 1915, 10; 18 June 1915, 8. Weizmann to Gaster, 16 December 1914 and Weizmann to Sacher, 29 December 1914, *CWLP*, vol. 7, p. 63; Weizmann to Magnes, 29 January 1915, *CWLP*, vol. 7, pp. 126–8.

70 Stein, *The Balfour Declaration*, chaps. 10, 20–37; Vital, *Zionism: The Crucial Phase*, chaps. 5–9.

71 Weizmann to Sokolow, 4 February 1917, *CWLP*, vol. 7, p. 327; Stein, *The Balfour Declaration*, pp. 362–8.
72 Mark Levene, 'The Balfour Declaration: A Case of Mistaken Identity', *English Historical Review*, 107 (1991), 54–77.
73 Stein, *The Balfour Declaration*, chap. 30; Cohen, *English Zionists and British Jews*, pp. 223–39; Eugene C. Black, *The Social Politics of Anglo-Jewry, 1880–1920* (Oxford, 1989), pp. 364–72.
74 Cohen, *English Zionists and British Jews*, pp. 243–76.
75 *JC*, 15 June 1917, 5. According to one source Greenberg was approached with a request to give a regular column to an anti-Zionist writer: *The Jewish Chronicle 1841–1941*, pp. 149–50.
76 Stein, *The Balfour Declaration*, pp. 559–60.
77 M. L. Saunders and P. M. Taylor, *British Propaganda during the First World War, 1914–18* (London, 1982), p. 200; Ran Marom, 'The Bolsheviks and the Balfour Declaration, 1917–20', *Wiener Library Bulletin (WLB)*, 29 (1976), 20–2.
78 *JC*, 15 February 1918, 12. Cohen, *English Zionists and British Jews*, pp. 303–12.
79 League of British Jews Literary Sub-Committee, minutes, 25 March 1918, BDA, E3/208/1 and 2; Asher to Wolf, 28 July 1918, BDA, E3/208/1.
80 Spielmann to Zangwill, n.d., Zangwill Papers, CZA, A120/63. Cited in Cohen, *English Zionists and British Jews*, p. 309.
81 Greenberg to Zangwill, 17 October 1918, Zangwill Papers, CZA, A120/364. Weizmann believed that Greenberg had a vendetta against him dating back to the 1900s: *Trial and Error. The Autobiography of Chaim Weizmann* (London, 1949), pp. 117, 150, 209 and Norman Rose, *Chaim Weizmann: A Biography* (New York, 1986), p. 24.
82 Greenberg to Zangwill, 31 January 1919, CZA, A120/364.
83 Greenberg to Kann, 10 January 1919, CZA, A121/147.
84 'Scheme for Carrying into Effect the Government Declaration in Reference to Palestine', n.d., CZA, K11/86/2. In a letter to Sokolow in 1922, he said: 'I think you recollect my telling you at the time when the Balfour Declaration was made that I thought it was all right with a slight exception; that ... I did not trust the Government': Greenberg to Sokolow, 13 June 1922, CZA, A18/348.
85 Greenberg to Kann, 3 March 1919, CZA, A121/147.
86 *JC*, 3 October 1919, 7, 14–15. Neil Caplan, *Futile Diplomacy*, vol. 1, *Early Arab-Zionist Negotiation Attempts 1913–1931* (London, 1983), pp. 38–46.
87 Weizmann to Sokolow, 27 November 1920, *CWLP*, vol. 10, pp. 98–9; *Zionist Review (ZR)*, 11:10 (February 1919), 170; 3:7 (November 1919), 105; 4:8 (December 1920), 137–8.
88 *JC*, 11 November 1921, 7–8, 20–2, 27–8, 30–4. Weizmann to Wyndham Deedes, 13 December 1921, *CWLP*, vol. 10, p. 332.
89 *JC*, 28 October 1921, 5. David Cesarani, 'Anti-Zionist Politics and Political Anti-Semitism in Britain 1920–24', *Patterns of Prejudice*, 23:1 (1989), 28–43; Bernard Wasserstein, *The British in Palestine: The Mandatory Government and the Arab–Jewish Conflict 1917–1929* (London, 1978), pp. 113–19; Martin Gilbert, *Winston S. Churchill*, vol. 4, *The Stricken World 1916–1922* (Boston, 1975), pp. 615–51.

90 Cesarani, 'Anti-Zionist Politics and Political Anti-Semitism', 29–40.
91 Greenberg to Weizmann, 28 June 1921, Weizmann Archive (WA), Rehovot; Greenberg to N. S. Burstein, 13 November 1922, Burstein Papers, CZA, A298/7.
92 Rose, *Chaim Weizmann*, pp. 214–22; Wasserstein, *British in Palestine*, pp. 113–21; Gilbert, *Churchill*, vol. 4, pp. 650–62.
93 *JC*, 10 August 1923, 5–6; 13 August 1928, 7; 5 October 1928, 7–8; 26 October 1928, 7–8. Greenberg to Weizmann, 7 June 1928, WA. W. Laqueur, *History of Zionism*, second edition (New York, 1978), pp. 462–3; Rose, *Weizmann*, pp. 223–34, 241–2.
94 Weizmann to Sokolow, 27 November 1920, *CWLP*, vol. 10, pp. 98–9; Weizmann to *Jewish Chronicle*, 20 February 1922, *CWLP*, vol. 11, pp. 154–53; Weizmann to Berthold Feiwel, 23 February 1923, *CWLP*, vol. 11, pp. 317–18; Weizmann to Vera Weizmann, 6 January 1927, *CWLP*, vol. 13, pp. 181–2. *ZR*, 5:6 (November 1921), 108; 8:5 (September 1924), 49. For public protests: *JC*, 25 September 1925, 8; 2 October 1925, 21.
95 Weizmann to Greenberg, 27 February 1922, *CWLP*, vol. 11, 567 and resolution of Zionist Executive, 28 February 1922, *CWLP*, vol. 11, 567.
96 Weizmann to Greenberg, 8 February 1923, *CWLP*, vol. 11, p. 247. Weizmann to Greenberg, 16 February 1923, *CWLP*, vol. 11, p. 263.
97 Kann to Greenberg, 15 March 1927, Greenberg to Kann, 19 April 1927, CZA, A121/109.
98 Kann to Greenberg, 26 September 1929, CZA, A121/109; Greenberg to Kann, 30 September 1929, CZA, A121/109.
99 Greenberg to Kann, 9 January 1929, CZA, A121/109.
100 *JC*, 24 October 1930, 7. Laqueur, *History of Zionism*, pp. 490–3; Rose, *Weizmann*, pp. 275–94.
101 *JC*, 31 October 1930, 7–8; 7 November 1930, 5–6. Alderman, *Jewish Community in British Politics*, pp. 111–14; Norman Rose, *The Gentile Zionists* (London, 1973), pp. 37–40.
102 *JC*, 20 February 1931, 7–8; 27 March 1931, 9–10 on 'Micky Mouse Zionism'. Joseph Gorny, *The British Labour Movement and Zionism 1917–1948* (London, 1983), pp. 88–107.
103 *Monthly Pioneer*, 1:10 (April 1929), 3; 1:12 (June 1929), 9; 3:3 (October 1930), 3. *JC*, 21 November 1930, 30; 27 March 1931, 9–10 and 18–20.
104 For the social background to the inter-war years, see V. D. Lipman, *A History of the Jews in Britain Since 1858* (Leicester, 1990), chap. 9.
105 Greenberg to Kann, 14 February 1929, CZA, A121/109.
106 *JC*, 28 March 1919, 7 and almost every subsequent issue during 1919–20. D. Cesarani, 'Anti-Alienism in England after the First World War', *Immigrants and Minorities*, 6:1 (March 1987), 9–14.
107 *JC*, 21 November 1924, 5; 26 December 1924, 5–6. D. Cesarani, 'William Joynson-Hicks and the Radical Right in England after the First World War', in Tony Kushner and Kenneth Lunn (eds.), *Traditions of Intolerance* (Manchester, 1989), pp. 118–39.
108 *JC*, 21 March 1919, 5–6. Kadish, *Bolsheviks and British Jews*, chap. 1.
109 Kadish, *Bolsheviks and British Jews*, pp. 120–1. The signatories were: Lionel de Rothschild, Lord Swaythling, Sir Philip Magnus, MP, Marcus Samuel,

Harry Samuel, Leonard L. Cohen, Israel Gollancz, John Monash, Claude Montefiore and Isidore Spielman.
110 *JC*, 25 April 1919, 5; 2 May 1919, 5, 7 and issues during the following weeks. Kadish, *Bolsheviks and British Jews*, pp. 120–34 and passim.
111 Norman Cohn, *Warrent for Genocide: The Myth of the Jewish World Conspiracy and the Protocols of the Elders of Zion* (London, 1967); Holmes, *Anti-Semitism in British Society*, pp. 141–60.
112 See Keith M. Wilson, '"The Protocols of Zion" and the "Morning Post", 1919–1920', *Patterns of Prejudice*, 19:3 (1985), 5–14; Wilfred Hindle, *The Morning Post, 1772–1937* (London, 1937), pp. 235–6.
113 *JC*, 22 October 1920, 5–6.
114 *JC*, 22 January 1926, 7, 15. BD, 17 January 1926, vol. 20, BDA.
115 For example, *JC*, 4 May 1923, 7. See correspondence between Greenberg and the solicitor of the Board of Deputies, BDA, E3/208/3.
116 JC, 26 August 1927, 8 and subsequent issues. Collins, *Aspects of Scottish Jewry*, p. 30.
117 *JC*, 9 February 1923, 7–8; 9 January 1925, 13; Supplement, 30 August 1929, v–viii; 26 December 1930, 5; 24 April 1931, 5. Rosalyn Livshin, 'The Acculturation of the Children of Immigrant Jews in Manchester, 1890–1920', in D. Cesarani (ed.), *The Making of Modern Anglo-Jewry* (Oxford, 1990), pp. 90–4.
118 *JC*, 13 July 1923, 17–39; 2 August 1929, 5–6. On 'Liberal Judaism' (Greenberg's contemptuous apostrophes): *JC*, 9 January 1920, 10; 15 December 1922, 9; 18 December 1925, 7.
119 On Hitler: *JC*, 9 November 1923, 5; 16 November 1923, 7; 4 April 1924, 11. Donald Niewyk, *The Jews in Weimar Germany* (Baton Rouge, 1980), chaps. 3–4.
120 *JC*, 3 October 1930, 6; 10 October 1930, 6; 6 February 1931, 6. On the German Foreign Office and the *Jewish Chronicle*, see *JC*, 4 December 1959, 25.
121 *JC*, 23 May 1919, 5; 30 May 1919, 5–6 and in subsequent issues. Pogroms in the Ukraine: *JC*, 6 June 1919, 5; 13 June 1919, 5; 20 June 1919, 5. Norman Davis, *Heart of Europe: A Short History of Poland*, paperback edition (Oxford, 1987), pp. 110–21; Celia Heller, *On the Edge of Destruction. Jews of Poland between the Two World Wars* (New York, 1977), pp. 47–57; Joseph Marcus, *Social and Political History of the Jews of Poland 1919–1939* (New York, 1983), pp. 300–2.
122 *JC*, 7 February 1930, 7. Zvi Gitelman, *Jewish Nationality and Soviet Politics: The Jewish Sections of the CPSU, 1917–1930* (Princeton, NJ, 1972).
123 *JC*, 3 October 1919, 7–8; 18 June 1920, 7; 25 May 1923, 6; 7 May 1926, seven-page cyclostyled emergency number posted to subscribers and 14 May 1926, four-page issue. Greenberg to Kann, 13 May 1921, CZA, A121/151.
124 Greenberg to Kann, 12 December 1924, CZA, A121/151; Greenberg to Kann, 29 December 1927; Greenberg to Kann, 11 February 1929, CZA, A121/109. Intermittent copies of the annual balance sheet are in CZA, A121/151.
125 *Jewish Guardian*, 3 October 1919. Lucy Cohen, *Some Recollections of Claude G. Montefiore* (London, 1941), p. 123. Josef Fraenkel, 'The Jewish Press in

Great Britain 1823–1963', in *Exhibition of the Jewish Press in Great Britain 1823–1963* (London, 1963).

126 *London Advertising Register*, second edition (London, 1927). On Magnus, see Ruth Sebag-Montefiore, *A Family Patchwork* (London, 1987), pp. 71–89.

127 Goodman, *Zionism in England*, p. 63; Chaim Bermant, *The Cousinhood* (London, 1971), p. 263. But Greenberg took the threat seriously. He sent a young staffer out to buy two copies of the *Jewish Guardian* when it appeared every Thursday morning and did his best to catch any story appearing in it which the *Jewish Chronicle* had so far missed: recollections of Sam Klein, *JC*, London Extra, 13 November 1981, 3.

128 *JC*, 27 November 1931, 11–13.

129 The burial saga is recorded in a Jewish Agency file: CZA, S25/779.

5 DISCORDANT INTERLUDE: J. M. RICH AND MORTIMER EPSTEIN, 1932–1936

1 Ivan Greenberg to Jacobus Kann, 20 November 1931; Kann to Greenberg, 23 November 1931; Greenberg to Kann, 25 November 1931, CZA, A121/109.

2 Obituary, *JC*, 28 June 1946, 6.

3 Obituary, *JC*, 20 November 1987, 43.

4 Laski to Rich, 6 November 1935; Laski to Rich, 12 August 1935, BDA, E3/208/3. For the regular correspondence between Rich and Laksi, see BDA, E3/208/3.

5 *JC*, 16 December 1932, 11; Obituary: *JC*, 18 October 1946, 13.

6 This analysis draws on the work of Deborah Dash Moore, *At Home in America: Second Generation New York Jews* (New York, 1981), pp. 24–53. See also Bill Williams, *Manchester Jewry: A Pictorial History 1788–1988* (Manchester, 1988), pp. 81–2; Ernest Krausz, *Leeds Jewry: Its History and Social Structure* (Cambridge, 1964), pp. 22–6; Kenneth Collins, *Second City Jewry* (Glasgow, 1989), pp. 210–20.

7 John Stevenson and Chris Cook, *The Slump* (London, 1979), pp. 8–30; H. Pollins, *Economic History of the Jews in England* (East Brunswick, NJ, 1982), pp. 183–6; Williams, *Manchester Jewry 1788–1988*, p. 97; Louis Saipe, *A Century of Care: The History of the Leeds Jewish Welfare Board 1878–1978* (Leeds, 1978), pp. 30–4.

8 *JC*, 8 June 1934, 10–11. 'Izzy' Bernstein was the first reporter who was permitted to cover a boxing match. In addition, the paper gave more and more attention to other sports in which Jews took a leading part, such as billiards and table-tennis. John Harding with Jack Berg, *Jack Kid Berg: The Whitechapel Windmill* (London, 1987).

9 Deirdre Beddoe, *Back to Home and Duty. Women between the Wars, 1918–1939* (London, 1989), pp. 14–19 and 103.

10 David Cesarani, 'The East End of Simon Blumenfeld's "Jew Boy"', *London Journal*, 13:1 (1987–8), 46–53.

11 David Cesarani, 'The Transformation of Communal Authority in Anglo-Jewry, 1914–1940', in D. Cesarani (ed.), *The Making of Modern Anglo-Jewry* (Oxford, 1990), pp. 126–32.

12 *JC*, 3 February 1933, 7–8 and 24 February 1933, 8. Nana Sagi and Malcolm

Lowe, 'Research Report: Pre-War Reactions to Nazi Anti-Jewish Policies in the Jewish Press', *Yad Vashem Studies*, vol. 13 (Jerusalem, 1979), pp. 388–93; Brigitte Granzow, *A Mirror of Nazism. British Opinion and the Emergence of Hitler 1929–1933* (London, 1964); Andrew Sharf, *The British Press and the Jews under Nazi Rule* (London, 1964), pp. 6–41; Benny Morris, *The Roots of Appeasement. The British Weekly Press and Nazi Germany during the 1930s* (London, 1991), pp. 2–10.

13 Sharon Gewirtz, 'Anglo-Jewish Responses to Nazi Germany 1933–39: The Anti-Nazi Boycott and the Board of Deputies of British Jews', *JCH*, 26:2 (1991), 259–60.

14 *JC*, 28 July 1933, 16; 1 September 1933, 30. See Rich to Laski, 19 October 1933 and Laski to Gilbert/Rich, 26 July 1934, BDA, E3/208/3.

15 Bernard Krikler, 'Boycotting Nazi Germany', *WLB*, 23:4 (1969), 32–6.

16 Sharf, *The British Press and the Jews under Nazi Rule*, chaps. 2–3. See also Richard Griffiths, *Fellow Travellers of the Right. British Enthusiasts for Nazi Germany 1933–39* (Oxford, 1983), pts 1–2; Tony Kushner, 'Beyond the Pale? British Reactions to Nazi Anti-Semitism, 1933–39', in T. Kushner and K. Lunn (eds.), *The Politics of Marginality. Race, the Radical Right and Minorities in Twentieth Century Britain* (London, 1990), pp. 143–60; Morris, *The Roots of Appeasement*, chaps 3–5.

17 *JC*, 24 March 1933, 10. Louise London, 'Jewish Refugees, Anglo-Jewry and British Government Policy, 1930–1940', in Cesarani (ed.), *Making of Modern Anglo-Jewry*, pp. 164–74; A. J. Sherman, *Island Refuge: Britain and Refugees from the Third Reich, 1933–1939* (London, 1973), passim.

18 Correspondence concerning the 1933 Palestine supplement: J. M. Rich to Nahum Sokolow, 30 May 1933, CZA, A18/630.

19 *JC*, 8 January 1932, 5; 13 September 1935, 10. W. Laqueur, *History of Zionism*, second edition (New York, 1978), pp. 357–69.

20 *JC*, 12 May 1933, 8; 27 October 1933, 8. Legislative council: *JC*, 26 October 1934, 7; 20 December 1935, 9; 10 January 1936, 7. David Cesarani, 'Zionism in England, 1917–1939', D.Phil. thesis, University of Oxford, 1986, pp. 267–72; Rose, *Gentile Zionists*, pp. 55–62.

21 *JC*, 24 April 1936, 9 and thereafter. Cesarani, 'Zionism in England', pp. 429–32. Yehuda Porath, *The Palestinian Arab National Movement*, vol. 2, *From Riots to Rebellion, 1929–1939* (London, 1977).

22 *JC*, 16 February 1934, 7; 9 March 1934, 9; 27 July 1934, 29. G. R. Geddye, *Fallen Bastions* (London, 1938). On Myers, obituary, *JC*: 27 September 1940, 12.

23 Compare *JC*, 8 September 1933, 11; 8 June 1934, 13–14; 24 August 1934, 11 with *JC*, 5 May 1933, 8–9; 24 November 1933, 9.

24 *JC*, 30 September 1932, 12; 7 October 1932, 8. Robert Skidelsky, *Oswald Mosley* (London, 1981), chaps. 12–14.

25 On this contested question, see Skidelsky, *Oswald Mosley*, chaps. 19–20; Richard Thurlow, *Fascism in Britain: A History, 1918–1985* (Oxford, 1987), pp. 101–11; Colin Holmes, 'Anti-Semitism and the BUF', in K. Lunn and R. Thurlow (eds.), *British Fascism* (London, 1980), pp. 114–34.

26 Skidelsky, *Oswald Mosley*, chap. 21; Thurlow, *Fascism in Britain*, pp. 106–11; Robert Benewick, *Political Violence and Public Order: A Study of British*

Fascism (London, 1969), pp. 217–32; C. T. Husband, 'East End Racism, 1900–1980: Geographical Continuities in Vigilantist and Extreme Right-wing Political Behaviour', *London Journal*, 8 (1982), 3–26. On the defence debate, see G. Lebzelter, *Political Anti-Semitism in England, 1918–1939* (London, 1978), chap. 7; David Rosenberg, *Facing up to Antisemitism* (London 1985), pp. 46–60; Elaine R. Smith, 'Jewish Responses to Political Antisemitism and Fascism in the East End of London, 1920–1939', in Kushner and Lunn (eds.), *Traditions of Intolerance*, pp. 53–71.

27 *JC*, 15 May 1936, 9; 5 June 1936, 13–14.

28 J. M. Rich to Joseph Leftwich, 14 September 1936, Leftwich Papers, CZA, A330/624.

29 *JC*, 31 July 1936, 7. Lebzelter, *Political Anti-Semitism in England*, pp. 139–43; Smith, 'Jewish Responses to Political Antisemitism and Fascism', pp. 63–7.

30 *JC*, 21 August 1936, 14–18; 28 August 1936, 14–17; 11 September 1936, 12, 12–16. Telephone interview with Maurice Goldsmith, London, 30 January 1992.

31 William J. Fishman, 'A People's Journée: The Battle of Cable Street (4 October 1936)', in Philip Kranz (ed.), *History from Below* (Madison WI, 1980), pp. 157–83.

32 *JC*, 27 November 1936, 11–12; 11 December 1936, 11–12; 25 December 1936, 6. For the continuing row with the JPC, see: *JC*, 6 November 1936, 8; 13 November 1936, 11, 18–19.

33 Kann to Kessler and exchange of letters, 2 June, 3 June, 6 June, 9 June, 13 June, 16 June 1932. Correspondence files of Leopold Kessler in the possession of Mr David Kessler and papers of Mr David Kessler (hereafter cited as Kessler Papers (KP)).

34 Kann to Kessler, 2 June 1932 and reply, 3 June and 9 June 1932, KP.

35 Kessler to Kann, 9 June 1932 and reply, 13 June 1932; Kessler to Peacock and Goddard, 20 September 1927; Kessler to Epstein, 10 March 1933; Kessler to Albert Oppenheimer, solicitor, 22 April 1933, KP.

36 Kann to Kessler, 30 January 1933 and reply, 1 February 1933, KP.

37 Epstein to Kessler, 3 October 1933 and 10 October 1933; Kessler to Kann, 24 October 1933 and exchange of letters, 26 October, 28 October, 2 November and 7 November 1933, KP.

38 Kann to Kessler, 16 January 1934, 25 May, 7 June 1934 and 13 June 1934; Kessler to Kann, 9 June 1934 and 15 June 1934, Kessler to M. Kann, 26 October 1934, KP.

39 M. Kann to Kessler, 3 November 1934 and reply, 7 November 1934; Kessler to Kann, 15 December 1934 and exchange of letters, 25 December 1934, 4 January and 22 January, 24 January 1935, KP.

40 Kann to Kessler, 15 February 1935 and 1 March 1935; M. Kann to Kessler, 5 March 1935 and 8 May 1935; Kann to Kessler, enclosing motion, 15 May 1935; Kessler to Kann, 5 June 1935 and 3 July 1935, KP.

41 Kessler to Kann, 5 June 1935; Kessler to Epstein, 5 June 1935 and reply, 6 June 1935; Kessler to Epstein, 9 June 1935; Kann to Kessler, 14 June 1935, KP.

42 Ruth Kessler to David Kessler, 2 June 1935; correspondence between Kann and Kessler, 14 June 1935–29 July 1935, KP.

43 Chairman's statement to the Board of Directors, 31 January 1936, KP.

44 Kessler to Oppenheimer, 30 December 1935; David Kessler to Jack Kessler, 23 January 1936; Kann to Kessler, 27 January 1936; Leon Fischer to Kessler, 7 February 1936 and 22 February 1936. On Stein, see *Encyclopedia Judaica*.

45 Kessler to Rich, 8 May 1936; Oppenheimer to Epstein, 4 December 1936; Epstein to Directors of the *Jewish Chronicle*, 10 December 1936, KP.

46 Interview with David Kessler, Stoke Hammond, 10 September 1990.

6 IVAN GREENBERG AND THE CRISIS YEARS, 1937–1946

1 Greenberg obituary: *JC*, 18 March 1966, 29; Shaftesley obituary: *JC*, 14 August 1981, 22.

2 Obituary: *JC*, 3 April 1959, 11.

3 The series ran intermittently from 22 January 1937 to 26 February 1937. BD, vol. 27, 21 February 1937, BDA. Goldsmith's articles were so powerful that Greenberg hired him as a sub-editor.

4 See Laski's *Jewish Rights and Jewish Wrongs* (London, 1938); H. Pollins, *Economic History of the Jews in England* (East Brunswick, NJ, 1982), p. 190.

5 *JC*, 24 June 1938, 10; 1 July 1938, 9–10; 26 August 1938, 8. On press responses to the refugees, see Andrew Sharf, *The British Press and Jews under Nazi Rule* (London, 1963), pp. 158–71.

6 *JC*, 17 December 1937, 8; 16 June 1939, 10.

7 Michael J. Cohen, *Palestine: The Retreat from the Mandate. The Making of British Policy, 1936–1945* (London, 1979), chaps. 1–3; Nicholas Bethell, *The Palestine Triangle* (London, 1979), pp. 39–48; M. Gilbert, *Exile and Return. The Emergence of Jewish Statehood* (London, 1978), pp. 195–215; David Cesarani, 'The Transformation of Communal Authority in Anglo-Jewry, 1914–1940', in D. Cesarani (ed.), *The Making of Modern Anglo-Jewry* (Oxford, 1990), pp. 126–37.

8 See D. Cesarani, 'Zionism in England, 1917–1939', D.Phil. thesis, University of Oxford, 1986, pp. 323–31; Norman Rose, *The Gentile Zionists* (London, 1973), pp. 123–43.

9 Churchill: *JC*, 3 September 1937, 24–5; 3; Marchioness of Reading, 8 October 1937, 24.

10 Henry Mond to Weizmann, 20 December 1937, WA; Norman Rose (ed.), *Baffy. The Diaries of Blanche Dugdale 1936–1947* (London, 1973), p. 73.

11 *JC*, 7 January 1938, 9; 21 January 1938, 8. Cesarani, 'Zionism in England', pp. 211–34, 276–83; Rose, *Gentile Zionists*, pp. 151–72.

12 *JC*, 4 February 1938, 8; 11 February 1938, 13; 18 February 9–10; 25 February 1938, 8. Cesarani, 'Transformation of Communal Authority', pp. 132–7.

13 *ZR*, 5:1 (January 1938), 7–8; New Series, 10 November 1938, 3–4 and 13 July 1939, 2–3; *JC*, 1 April 1938, 38–9; 8 April 1938, 29.

14 Stein to Kessler, 15 February 1938 and reply, 2 March 1938; Leopold Kessler to David Kessler, 27 February 1938; Stein to Leopold Kessler, 13 April 1938 and reply, 14 April 1938, KP. The identity of the diplomatic editor is unknown.

15 Stein to Leopold Kessler, 17 June 1938 and reply, 21 June 1938, KP.

16 *JC*, 11 November 1938, 7; 3 February 1939, 7–8; 10 February 1939, 7. Cohen, *Retreat from Mandate*, chap. 5; Gilbert, *Exile and Return*, pp. 217–26; Bethell, *Palestine Triangle*, pp. 56–67.

17 For example, 'Facing the Bullies': *JC*, 14 April 1939, 7–8 and 5 May 1939, 7. Cohen, *Retreat from Mandate*, pp. 69–86.
18 Rose, *Gentile Zionists*, pp. 207–10; Bethell, *Palestine Triangle*, pp. 69–71.
19 Cf. *JC*, 27 May 1938, 9 to 23 June 1939, 10. Y. Bauer, *From Diplomacy to Resistance. A History of Jewish Palestine 1939–1945* (New York, 1973), pp. 11–15; Bethell, *Palestine Triangle*, pp. 40–1.
20 *JC*, 18 March 1938, 9–10. A. J. Sherman, *Island Refuge: Britain and Refugees from the Third Reich, 1933–1939* (London, 1973), pp. 85–93. Information on Heilig supplied by David Kessler.
21 *JC*, 24 June 1938, 9–10 and following weeks. On Evian see Sherman, *Island Refuge*, pp. 95–119; David Wyman, *Paper Walls. America and the Refugee Crisis, 1938–1941* (New York, 1985), pp. 43–51; Richard Breitman and Alan M. Kraut, *American Refugee Policy and European Jewry, 1933–1945* (Blooomington, IN, 1987), pp. 56–62.
22 Cf. *JC*, 16 September 1938, 9–10 and 23 September 1938, 9–10. Richard Cockett, *Twilight of Truth: Chamberlain, Appeasement and the Manipulation of the Press* (London, 1989), pp. 66–83; Benny Morris, *The Roots of Appeasement. The British Weekly Press and Nazi Germany during the 1930s* (London, 1991), pp. 121–52.
23 *JC*, 18 November 1938, 7–8, and following weeks. Lionel Kochan, *Pogrom 10 November 1938* (London, 1957), passim; Sherman, *Island Refuge*, pp. 166–71. Cf. F. R. Gannon, *The British Press and Germany 1936–1939* (Oxford, 1971), pp. 226–8; Morris, *The Roots of Appeasement*, p. 153.
24 For example, *JC*, 25 November 1938, 2 and 2 December 1938, 3. Louise London, 'British Immigration Control Procedures and Jewish Refugees, 1933–1939', in Werner E. Mosse *et al.* (eds.), *Second Chance. Two Centuries of German-speaking Jews in the United Kingdom* (Tübingen, 1991), pp. 506–15 and Tony Kushner, 'An Alien Occupation – Jewish Refuges and Domestic Service in Britain, 1933–1948', in Mosse *et al.* (eds.), *Second Chance*, pp. 559–63; Sherman, *Island Refuge*, pp. 137–65.
25 *JC*, 9 June 1939, 7–8 and subsequent issues. Tony Kushner, 'Beyond the Pale? British Reactions to Nazi Anti-Semitism, 1933–39', in T. Kushner and K. Lunn (eds.), *The Politics of Marginality. Race, the Radical Right and Minorities in Twentieth Century Britain* (London, 1990), pp. 143–60.
26 For a vignette of this period, see the memoirs of 'a reporter': *JC*, 6 May 1949, 11. On the background, see Angus Calder, *The People's War: Britain 1939–45* (London, 1971), pp. 35–48.
27 *JC*, 22 September 1939, 18; 6 December 1940, 16.
28 Greenberg to John M. Shaftesley, n.d., probably 1939, CZA, A330/116. See, for example, *JC*, 5 January 1940, 16; 12 January 1940, 1; 12 April 1940, 8; 12 June 1940, 1.
29 *JC*, 20 August 1943, 5; 15 October 1943, 8; 19 October 1955, 6. The paper was prevented from reporting until after the war the drowning of dozens of people, mainly Jews, in a flooded East London bomb shelter during 1940, the Bethnal Green tube station disaster in 1943, and the destruction of Hughes Mansions in Vallance Road on 27 March 1945, a block which was inhabited largely by Jewish people: *JC*, 17 September 1948, 6.

30 T. Nevett, *Advertising in Britain* (London, 1982), pp. 172–3; *The Newspaper Press Directory* (London, 1945), pp. 59–61.

31 *The Newspaper Press Directory* (1945), pp. 48–9; David Kessler to Ivan Greenberg, 13 December 1940, Ivan Greenberg Papers, Anglo-Jewish Archives, Parkes Library, Southampton University (AJ), AJ110/2.

32 *JC*, 20 February 1942, 10; 20 March 1942, 1; 26 June 1942, 8; 26 January 1945, 10. *Newspaper Press Directory* (1945), pp. 48–51; Calder, *The People's War*, pp. 504–5; Iverach McDonald, *The History of The Times*, vol. 5, *Struggles in War and Peace 1939–1966* (London, 1984), pp. 54–64.

33 *JC*, 6 October 1939, 6.

34 *JC*, 17 May 1940, 1. His dramatic account of the fall of Holland was the front-page story on 24 May 1940.

35 *JC*, 22 August 1947, 13. On the Kann family: *JC*, 27 June 1947, 6. David Freeman, 'Jacobus H. Kann of The Hague', in Raphael Patai (ed.), *The Herzl Yearbook*, vol. 7 (New York, 1971), p. 69.

36 *JC*, 21 September 1945, 5.

37 David Kessler to Greenberg, 13 December 1940; Greenberg to Kessler, 19 December 1940; Kessler to Greenberg, 5 January 1940, AJ110/2.

38 Jewish Chronicle Ltd Minute Book, vol. 1, 1 August 1941, Jewish Chronicle Archive (hereafter, JCMB). The first recorded entry in the Minute Book, taking up from the point at which enemy action had destroyed the company's offices, was August 1940.

39 David Kessler to Greenberg, 13 December 1940; Greenberg to David Kessler, 19 December 1940, AJ110/2. The centenary history, amended by several hands and attributed to no one author in particular, eventually appeared as *The Jewish Chronicle 1841–1941. A Century of Newspaper History* in 1949.

40 JCMB, vol. 1, 10 July 1941; 2 January 1942.

41 *JC*, 6 October 1939, 12; BD, vol. 27, 1 October 1939, BDA. Cesarani, 'Transformation of Communal Authority', pp. 135–6.

42 Laski to Greenberg, 7 November 1939, AJ/110/4/10.

43 Cf. *ZR*, 23 November 1939, 8.

44 *JC*, 24 November 1939, 14; BD, vol. 27, 19 November 1939, BDA.

45 *JC*, 1 December 1939, 16; 15 December 1939, 16. Gideon Shimoni, 'Selig Brodetsky and the Ascendency of Zionism in Anglo-Jewry (1939–1945)', *JJS*, 22:2 (1980), 132–4.

46 *JC*, 20 October 1939, 14–15. By-elections: *JC*, 1 March 1940, 1 and 24 May 1940, 8–9. Tony Kushner, *The Persistence of Prejudice. Antisemitism in British Society during the Second World War* (Manchester, 1989), pp. 16–22.

47 *JC*, 24 May 1940, 12. Richard Thurlow, *Fascism in Britain: A History, 1918–1985* (Oxford, 1987), pp. 181–2; Kushner, *Persistence of Prejudice*, pp. 78–105.

48 Bernard Wasserstein, *Britain and the Jews of Europe 1939–1945* (Oxford, 1979), pp. 83–108; Peter and Leni Gillman, *Collar the Lot!* (London, 1980) and Kushner, *The Persistence of Prejudice*, pp. 142–52.

49 *JC*, 17 May 1940, 12; 24 May 1940, 12; 31 May 1940, 12; 21 June 1940, 12. Wasserstein, *Britain and the Jews of Europe*, pp. 92–3.

50 *Jewish Standard*, 5 July 1940, 4; 12 July 1940, 2, 3.

51 Bernard Wasserstein, 'Patterns of Jewish Leadership in Great Britain during

the Nazi Era', in Randolph L. Braham (ed.), *Jewish Leadership during the Nazi Era: Patterns of Behaviour in the Free World* (New York, 1985), p. 37.

52 *JC*, 11 October 1940, 10; 25 October 1940, 11; 1 November 1940, 1, 19; 15 November 1940, 1, 14; 29 November 1940, 10. See Wasserstein, *Britain and the Jews of Europe*, pp. 116–20; Kushner, *The Persistence of Prejudice*, pp. 54–8, 65–77.

53 Reports and debate on black marketeers: *JC*, 6 March 1942, 1, 10; 17 July 1942, 8. On anti-Semitism : *JC*, 27 February 1942, 10; 18 September 1942, 8; 26 February 1943, 8; 9 April 1943, 8. Wasserstein, *Britain and the Jews of Europe*, pp. 119–20; Kushner, *The Persistence of Prejudice*, pp. 102–3, 119–22.

54 Wasserstein, *Britain and the Jews of Europe*, 163–5; Michael Balfour, *Propaganda in War 1939–45* (London, 1979), pp. 31–2, 299–304; Ian McLaine, *Ministry of Morale. Home Front Morale and the Ministry of Information in World War Two* (London, 1979), pp. 166–8; K. R. M. Short, 'Hollywood Fights Anti-Semitism, 1940–5', in K. R. M. Short (ed.), *Film and Radio Propaganda in World War II* (London, 1983), pp. 147–8.

55 Kushner, *The Persistence of Prejudice*, pp. 167–70, 177–80; Wasserstein, *Britain and the Jews of Europe*, pp. 51–80, esp. 65–7; Richard Bolchover, *British Jewry and the Holocaust* (Cambridge, Cambridge University Press, 1993); cf. Wasserstein, 'Patterns of Jewish Leadership in Great Britain during the Nazi Era', pp. 29–43 and Yoav Gelber, 'Moralist and Realistic Approaches in the Study of the Allies' Attitude to the Holocaust', in Asher Cohen, Yoav Gelber and Charlotte Wardi (eds.), *Comprehending the Holocaust* (Frankfurt-on-Main, 1988), pp. 107–23.

56 For examples of reports, see *JC*, 1 March 1940, 14; 5 April 1940, 20; 7 March 1941, 10 and following issues. Editorial comment: 26 January 1940, 14; 5 April 1940, 20; 26 April 1940, 14–15; 27 September 1940, 24; 8 November 1940, 10. The accuracy of *Jewish Chronicle* reports can be appreciated when set against the surviving ghetto diaries such as L. Dobroszycki (ed.), *The Chronicle of the Lodz Ghetto* (London, 1984) and Abraham Lewin, *A Cup of Tears. A Diary of the Warsaw Ghetto*, ed. Antony Polonsky (London, 1988). Bolchover, *British Jewry and the Holocaust*, pp. 7–12.

57 *JC*, 31 May 1940, 1, 10; 25 October 1940, 1; 7 March 1941, 1; 1 November 1940, 1; 26 July 1940, 1.

58 R. Hilberg, *The Destruction of the European Jews*, 3 vols. (New York, 1985), vol. 1, pp. 188–269. For an overview, see Martin Gilbert, *Holocaust. The Jewish Tragedy* (London, 1989).

59 *JC*, 4 July 1941, 1; 18 July 1941, 1; 25 July 1941, 12; 15 August 1941, 1; 29 August 1941, 8, 10.

60 *JC*, 24 October 1941, 1; 31 October 1941, 12; 7 November 1941, 1; 21 November 1941, 1; 19 December 1941, 12.

61 See Bolchover, *British Jewry and the Holocaust*, pp. 97–102; cf. Wasserstein, 'Patterns of Jewish Leadership in Great Britain during the Nazi Era', pp. 31–2.

62 Hilberg, *Destruction of European Jewry*, vol. 2; Yitzkak Arad, *Belzec, Sobibor, Treblinka: The Operation Reinhard Death Camps* (Bloomington, IN, 1987).

63 See Wasserstein, *Britain and the Jews of Europe*, pp. 166–71; Martin Gilbert, *Auschwitz and the Allies* (London, 1981), chaps. 2–7; Walter Laqueur, *The Terrible Secret* (London, 1982), chaps. 2–4.

64 Dina Porat, *The Blue and the Yellow Stars of David. The Zionist Leadership in Palestine and the Holocaust, 1939–1945* (Cambridge, MA, 1990), p. 23.

65 See Laqueur, *The Terrible Secret*, pp. 73–5; Gilbert, *Auschwitz and the Allies*, pp. 42–3.

66 Bolchover, *British Jewry and the Holocaust*, pp. 42–53, 104–20; cf. Wasserstein, 'Patterns of Jewish Leadership in Great Britain during the Nazi Era', pp. 31–2.

67 Cf. the similarly muted response in the *Yishuv*, Porat, *The Blue and the Yellow Stars of David*, pp. 34–40.

68 For aspects of the general press response, see Sharf, *The British Press*, pp. 90–100 and Ernest Hearst, 'The British and the Slaughter of the Jews – (1)', *WLB*, 21 (1966/7), 32–8 and Ernest Hearst, 'The British and the Slaughter of the Jews – (2)', *WLB*, 22 (1967), 30–40.

69 *JC*, 18 December 1942, 1, 5, 8; 25 December 1942, 8. John P. Fox, 'The Jewish Factor in British War Crimes Policy in 1942', *English Historical Review*, 92 (1977), 82–106; Wasserstein, *Britain and the Jews of Europe*, pp. 170–7; Gilbert, *Auschwitz and the Allies*, pp. 94–105; Bolchover, *British Jewry and the Holocaust*, pp. 66–9.

70 On the deportation of Dutch Jews: *JC*, 1 January 1943, 1 and 12 November 1943, 1; on Auschwitz: *JC*, 12 February 1943, 1 and 25 June 1943, 1; on the Warsaw Ghetto uprising: *JC*, 7 May 1943, 1, 14 May 1943, 1, 28 May 1943, 1 and 5 November 1943, 1, 9; on Salonika: *JC*, 28 May 1943, 1 and 17 December 1943, 9; on Belgian Jewry: *JC*, 13 August 1943, 7; on Vilna Ghetto and Sobibor: *JC*, 12 November 1943, 1.

71 *JC*, 7 May 1943, 8 and the subsequent weeks. On Zygielbojm: *JC*, 14 May 1943, 1; 21 May 1943, 11. Sharf, *The British Press*, pp. 113–14. For general responses: Sharf, *The British Press*, pp. 111–13 and Porat, *The Blue and the Yellow Stars of David*, pp. 41–5.

72 Wasserstein, *Britain and the Jews of Europe*, pp. 179–88; Kushner, *The Persistence of Prejudice*, pp. 176–80; Bolchover, *British Jewry and the Holocaust*, pp. 31–42; David Wyman, *The Abandonment of the Jews. America and the Holocaust 1941–1945* (New York, 1985), pp. 61–104.

73 See Wasserstein, *Britain and the Jews of Europe*, pp. 188–205; Wyman, *The Abandonment of the Jews*, pp. 104–23.

74 *JC*, 3 September 1943, 8. See also *JC*, 26 November 1943, 10. Wasserstein, *Britain and the Jews of Europe*, pp. 168–9, 171, 178, 295–7.

75 *JC*, 26 November 1943, 10. On the campaign for a Jewish army, see Wasserstein, *Britain and the Jews of Europe*, pp. 273–87 and as a therapy, Bolchover, *British Jewry and the Holocaust*, pp. 126–32.

76 *JC*, 30 June 1944, 8. Martin Gilbert, *Auschwitz and the Allies* (London, 1981), pp. 207–30; Wasserstein, *Britain and the Jews of Europe*, pp. 249–70; Tony Kushner, 'Rules of the Game: Britain, America and the Holocaust in 1944', *Holocaust and Genocide Studies*, 5:4 (1990), 382–402.

77 *JC*, 18 August 1944, 1, 7; 1 September 1944, 10; 22 September 1944, 10. Jon Bridgman, *The End of the Holocaust: The Liberation of the Camps* (London, 1990), pp. 20–1.

78 *Illustrated London News*, 28 April 1945, 445, 447; 5 May 1945, 471. Bridgman, *The End of the Holocaust*, pp. 20–1, 33–4, 82–3; Wasserstein, *Britain and the Jews of Europe*, pp. 343–4; Kushner, *The Persistence of Prejudice*, pp. 199–200

and 'The Impact of the Holocaust on British Society and Culture', *Contemporary Record*, 5:2 (1991), pp. 356–61.

79 On the A-bombs: *JC*, 17 August 1945, 10. For general press reactions, see Sharf, *The British Press*, pp. 143–54; cf. Bridgman, *The End of the Holocaust*, pp. 103–14.

80 *JC*, 10 January 1941, 10; 4 December 1942, 8; 29 January 1943, 8; 9 June 1944, 8 and 23 June 1944, 10. On aid to the USSR: *JC*, 29 May 1942, 1; 26 June 1942, 8; 8 September 1944, 8. Reflections on peace: *JC*, 9 March 1945, 10.

81 *JC*, 25 May 1945, 8; on *The Times*, 7 September 1945, 12; on the Hampstead petition, 19 October 1945, 10.

82 Abraham Abrahams to Greenberg, 4 August 1943; Abrahams to Greenberg, 24 August 1943; correspondence between Greenberg and H. Hurwitz, 1945–9, papers of I. M. Greenberg, Jabotinsky Institute, Tel Aviv (JI), 2–265P.

83 Abrahams to Greenberg, 8 November 1943, JI, 2–265P; Joseph Leftwich to Greenberg, 22 June 1944, JI, 3–265P; Lord Strabolgi to Greenberg, 23 January 1945, JI, 8–265P.

84 *JC*, 1 December 1939, 16; 8 March 1940, 16. On refugee ships: *JC*, 29 November 1940, 10; 27 February 1942, 1; 6 March 1942, 10. Ronald W. Zweig, *Britain and Palestine during the Second World War* (London, 1986), pp. 153–4; Bethell, *Palestine Triangle*, pp. 86–100, 113–20; Wasserstein, *Britain and the Jews of Europe*, pp. 51–80, 141–54.

85 *JC*, 7 June 1940, 12 and 29 August 1941, 10, for example. Cohen, *Retreat from Mandate*, pp. 98–117; Bauer, *From Diplomacy to Resistance*, pp. 86–92, 100–1, 124–9, 153–62; Zweig, *Britain and Palestine*, pp. 20–40.

86 *JC*, 3 April 1942, 10; 24 April 1942, 8, 10 and almost every week thereafter. Wyman, *Abandonment of the Jews*, pp. 84–6; Bolchover, *British Jewry and the Holocaust*, pp. 38–9.

87 For example, *JC*, 14 August 1942, 8 and n. 86. See file 3–4, Papers of Samuel Landman, JI, 247P; Papers of Joseph Leftwich, CZA, A330/116.

88 *JC*, 1 November 1940, 10; 15 November 1940, 10; 30 May 1941, 14.

89 Weizmann to Weisgal, 29 March 1940, *CWLP*, vol. 19, pp. 264–5.

90 Shimoni, 'Selig Brodetsky and the Ascendency of Zionism', 136–7.

91 *ZR*, 12 March 1943, 8. On the TAC during the war, see M. Orbach, 'Noah Barou and the TAC', in H. Infield (ed.), *Essays in Jewish Sociology. Labour Co-operation in Memory of Dr Noah Barou* (London, 1962), pp. 31–3.

92 *JC*, 28 May 1943, 7; 9 July 1943, 1. Cf. *ZR*, 21 May 1943, 1; 28 May 1943, 5; 18 June 1943, 3; 16 July 1943, 1.

93 Shimoni, 'Selig Brodetsky and the Ascendency of Zionism', 137–40, 144–6.

94 *JC*, 20 August 1943, 8; 8 October 1943, 10; 3 December 1943, 8, 9. Bauer, *From Diplomacy to Resistance*, pp. 265–72. On censorship: *JC*, 20 August 1943, 5; 15 October 1943, 8; 19 October 1945, 6.

95 Bauer, *From Diplomacy to Resistance*, pp. 312–20; Bethell, *Palestine Triangle*, pp. 155–62.

96 JCMB, vol. 1, 16 January 1942 and 29 October 1943. Stein to Greenberg, 4 April 1944; Stein to Greenberg, 20 January 1945, JI, 5–265P.

97 Oppenheimer to Greenberg, 14 October 1944, JI, 5–265P.

98 *JC*, 10 November 1944, 10. Cohen, *Retreat from Mandate*, pp. 179–82; Bauer, *From Diplomacy to Resistance*, pp. 332–40.

99 Cohen, *Retreat from Mandate*, pp. 150–82; J. Gorny, *The British Labour Movement and Zionism 1917–1948* (London, 1983), pp. 202–21; Zweig, *Britain and Palestine*, pp. 148–76; Bethell, *Palestine Triangle*, pp. 194–202.

100 *JC*, 9 November 1945, 10 and 16 November 1945, 10. Bethell, *Palestine Triangle*, pp. 214–19; Michael J. Cohen, *Palestine and the Great Powers 1945–1948* (Princeton, NJ, 1982), pp. 67–90.

101 *Anglo-American Committee of Inquiry on Palestine Report* (London, 1946) and transcript of hearings in London, 25 and 28–31 January 1946.

102 *JC*, 1 February 1946, 10; 1 March 1946, 1 and 12 April 1946, 1; 28 June 1946, 10. Bethell, *Palestine Triangle*, pp. 226–7, 232–4; Cohen, *Palestine and the Great Powers*, pp. 96–115. *AJR Information* (*AJRI*), 6:11 (November 1951), 3.

103 Laski to Kessler, 1 January 1946, KP; interview with David Kessler, 10 September 1990. See David Leitch, 'Explosion at the King David Hotel', in M. Sissons and P. French (eds.), *The Age of Austerity* (London, 1963), pp. 60–6.

104 JCMB, vol. 1, 24 May 1946.

105 JCMB, vol. 1, 26 June 1946.

106 JCMB, vol. 1, 2 July 1946.

107 *JC*, 5 July 1946, 10. Interview with David Kessler, 10 September 1990 and *JC*, 13 November 1981, p. 24.

108 This uncorroborated claim was made in a letter from Doris Greenberg to Joseph Leftwich, 8 August 1946, CZA, A330/116.

109 Greenberg to E. Hoofien, 21 September 1946, Archives of the Anglo-Palestine Bank, CZA, L51/734.

110 Memorandum, n.d., probably November 1946, CZA, L51/734.

111 Greenberg to Hoofien, 18 October 1946; Berl Locker to Hoofien, 23 October 1946, CZA, L51/734. Correspondence concerning share purchases, CZA, L51/734. A short time later, David Kessler was able to purchase the Wolffsohn and Kann shares for his family by direct negotiation.

7 THE POST-WAR ERA: J. M. SHAFTESLEY AND DAVID KESSLER, 1946–1958

1 Obituary: *JC*, 14 August 1981, 22. Shaftesley's first appearance in the *Jewish Chronicle* was a letter to the editor on the decline of Jewish literary societies: *JC*, 20 November 1925.

2 *JC*, 26 July 1946, 1, 10. Nicholas Bethell, *The Palestine Triangle* (London, 1979), pp. 253–67; Michael J. Cohen, *Palestine and the Great Powers 1945–1948* (Princeton, NJ, 1982), pp. 90–3. For British press coverage, see David Leitch, 'Explosion at the King David Hotel', in M. Sissons and P. French (eds.), *The Age of Austerity* (London, 1963), pp. 59–60.

3 Cohen, *Palestine and the Great Powers*, pp. 177–83; Colin Cross, *The Fascists in Britain* (London, 1964), pp. 199–202; Leitch, 'Explosion at the King David Hotel', pp. 60–6; Tony Kushner, *The Persistence of Prejudice. Antisemitism in British Society during the Second World War* (Manchester, 1989), pp. 199–200.

4 *JC*, 3 January 1947, 8, 12; 17 January 1947, 12.

5 *JC*, 25 July 1947, 12 and successive weeks. Cohen, *Palestine and the Great Powers*, pp. 203–38, 250–7.

6 *JC*, 1 August 1947, 1, 6, 12. Bethell, *Palestine Triangle*, pp. 337–40; Cohen, *Palestine and the Great Powers*, pp. 242–7; Leitch, 'Explosion at the King David Hotel', pp. 70–2.

7 *JC*, 8 August 1947, 1–2, 6, 10; 15 August 1947, 1.

8 *JC*, 5 December 1947, 1, 12. Cohen, *Palestine and the Great Powers*, pp. 276–300.

9 *JC*, 14 May 1948, 10; 22 October 1948, 12. On Bevin: *JC*, 7 April 1950, 12; 16 March 1951, 12. Cohen, *Palestine and the Great Powers*, pp. 301–79.

10 *JC*, 30 August 1946, 11; 4 October 1946, 1; 14 February 1947, 10. *Newspaper Press Directory* (1947), pp. 48–52 and (1948), pp. 49–54.

11 *Newspaper Press Directory* (1948), p. 52. Shaftesley to Brodetsky, 27 February 1947 and Brodetsky to Attlee and to Shinwell, 17 February 1947, BDA, C15/3/11/2.

12 *JC*, 14 February 1947, 10; 7 March 1947, 10. For the effect on the periodical press, see Edward Hyams, *The New Statesman: The History of the First Fifty Years 1913–1963* (London, 1963), p. 253.

13 *JC*, 31 December 1948, 10 and circulation figures provided by Mr S. N. Moss. Controls were finally abolished in 1956: Iverach McDonald, *The History of The Times*, vol. 5, *Struggles in War and Peace 1939–1966* (London, 1984), pp. 295–8.

14 Colin Seymour-Ure, *The British Press and Broadcasting since 1945* (London, 1991), pp. 16–33; Graham Murdock and Peter Golding, 'Structure and Ownership of the Press, 1914–1976', in George Boyce, James Curran, Pauline Wingate (eds.), *Newspaper History – from the Seventeenth Century to the Present Day* (London, 1978), pp. 130–48; McDonald, *Struggles in War and Peace*, pp. 194–6.

15 For background, Arthur Marwick, *British Society Since 1945*, second edition (London, 1990), pt 1; Alan Sked and Chris Cook, *Post-War Britain: A Political History*, second edition (London, 1986), chaps. 1–5.

16 JCMB, vol. 1, 5 May 1951; 30 November 1956. On Samuel, see Edwin Samuel, *A Lifetime in Jerusalem* (London, 1970).

17 *JC*, 17 February 1956, 1; JCMB, vol. 1, 9 April 1956. The cost of one ton of newsprint rose from £11 in 1939 to £28 in 1945, to £53 in 1955 and to £250 in 1977. On labour troubles in the industry, McDonald, *Struggles in War and Peace*, pp. 299–303; Francis Williams, *Dangerous Estate. The Anatomy of Newspapers* (London, 1959), pp. 238–40.

18 *JC*, 9 January 1948, 10 and following issues. The articles were later published by Vallentine, Mitchell as *East End Story* (London, n.d.).

19 *JC*, 18 April 1952, 11. See also Noah Barou, *The Jews in Work and Trade: A World Survey* (London, 1948); on the contraction of the clothing industry in the East End, Gillian Lonsdale, 'The Changing Character of the East London Industry', *East London Papers*, 5:2 (1962), 93–9.

20 *JC*, 29 July 1955, 16. Maurice Freedman (ed.), *A Minority in Britain. Social Studies of the Anglo-Jewish Community* (London, 1955). For a critique of some of the findings, see Harold Pollins, *Economic History of the Jews in England* (East Brunswick, NJ, 1982), pp. 210–12.

21 *JC*, 6 November 1946, 12; 14 March 1947, 10; 18 April 1947, 12; 2 May 1947, 10; 13 February 1948, 12; 4 June 1948, 12. Geoffrey Alderman, *Federation of Synagogues 1887–1987* (London, 1987), p. 71; A. Newman, *The United Synagogue 1870–1970* (London, 1977), pp. 180–1.

22 *JC*, 2 December 1949, 13; 9 December 1949, 5. *AJRI*, 5:1 (January 1950), 3.

23 *JC*, 9 June 1950, 14; 12 September 1952, 5.

24 *JC*, 21 November 1952, 7, 12.

25 *AJRI*, 10:6 (June 1955), 3.

26 *JC*, 22 November 1946, 12; 26 December 1947, 10; 12 March 1948, 12. Aubrey Newman, *The Board of Deputies of British Jews 1760–1985. A Brief Survey* (London, 1987), pp. 32–5. Interview with David Kessler, Stoke Hammond, 3 April 1991.

27 For example, *JC*, 4 February 1949, 12.

28 Sidney Solomons to Shaftesley, 13 May 1947; Solomons to Shaftesley, 24 December 1947; Solomons to Shaftesley, 13 September 1948, BDA, C15/3/11/2. C. H. Rolph, *Further Particulars* (London, 1987), pp. 112–15.

29 *JC*, 7 May 1954, 18; Finchley Golf Club: *JC*, 10 May 1957, 18; 28 June 1957, 18; on Notting Hill: *JC*, 12 September 1958, 8; 10 October 1958, 16. Colin Holmes, *John Bull's Island. Immigration and British Society, 1871–1971* (London, 1988), pp. 256–61; Geoffrey Alderman, *London Jewry and London Politics 1889–1986* (London, 1989), pp. 108–9.

30 Seretse Khama: *JC*, 17 March 1950, 12; on South Africa: *JC*, 3 December 1948, 10; 21 January 1949, 10; desegregation and anti-Semitism in the southern USA: *JC*, 24 October 1958, 20.

31 *JC*, 11 November 1949, 6; 2 December 1949, 9; 23 December 1949, 13. For an assessment of Stencl, see S. S. Prawer, *A. N. Stencl: Poet of Whitechapel* (Oxford, 1984).

32 The *Jewish Chronicle* and the Tercentenary Council together produced a commemorative volume published by Vallentine, Mitchell, *Three Hundred Years. A Volume to Commemorate the Tercentenary of the Resettlement of the Jews in Great Britain 1656–1956* (London, 1957).

33 *JC*, 13 September 1946, 11; 4 October 1946, 10.

34 *JC*, 20 May 1949, 12; 19 August 1949, 12; 7 July 1950, 12; 11 May 1951, 12; 24 May 1957, 16.

35 *JC*, 24 November 1950, 12; 22 December 1950, 12.

36 *JC*, 13 June 1947, 12; 14 January 1949, 12; 4 August 1950, 12. See Benjamin Pinkus, *The Jews of the Soviet Union* (Cambridge, 1988), pp. 145–54 and 161–2.

37 *JC*, 17 March 1950, 1 and 24 March 1950, 14; 7 July 1950, 12. Bernard Weinryb, 'Poland', in Peter Meyer *et al.* (eds.), *The Jews in the Soviet Satellites* (New York, 1953), pp. 230–326.

38 *JC*, 23 March 1956, 16; 17 August 1956, 10. Pinkus, *The Jews in the Soviet Union*, pp. 216–44.

39 Edward Luttwak and Dan Horowitz, *The Israeli Army* (London, 1975), pp. 105–11; Noah Lucas, *The Modern History of Israel* (London, 1975), pp. 367–74.

40 *JC*, 23 October 1953, 16. It remained the policy of the paper to express disquiet at the practice of reprisal raids, even though it accepted that condemnation by

other countries very often resulted from the use of double standards: see, for example, *JC*: 23 December 1955, 14; 5 October 1956, 16.

41 *JC*, 30 October 1953, 20; 6 November 1953, 20. Interview with David Kessler, Stoke Hammond, 10 September 1990.

42 *JC*, 13 August 1948, 10; 20 August 1948, 10; 1 April 1949, 12; 5 August 1949, 10. Benny Morris, *The Birth of the Palestinian Refugee Problem, 1947–49* (Cambridge, 1987), pp. 254–85 and passim.

43 *JC*, 11 December 1953, 16; 22 June 1956, 16. Lucas, *Modern History of Israel*, pp. 298–323 and 374–9.

44 *JC*, 18 November 1955, 18. See David Carlton, *Britain and the Suez Crisis* (London, 1988), pp. 1–55. The Israeli Embassy was unhappy with this intervention by the *Jewish Chronicle* in an area which it considered was its exclusive domain.

45 *JC*, 30 July 1954, 12; 4 March 1955, 18; 3 August 1956, 12.

46 *JC*, 2 November 1956, 14; 9 November 1956, 16 and subsequent weeks. Carlton, *Britain and the Suez Crisis*, pp. 56–80; Lucas, *Modern History of Israel*, pp. 380–90.

47 *JC*, 9 November 1956, 23; 16 November 1956, 16; 23 November 1956, 16. Gershon Levi (ed.), *Barnett Janner: A Personal Portrait by Elsie Janner* (London, 1984), pp. 135–7; Geoffrey Alderman, *The Jewish Community in British Politics* (Oxford, 1983), pp. 131–3.

48 *JC*, 25 April 1958, 16.

8 THE *JEWISH CHRONICLE* UNDER WILLIAM FRANKEL, 1958–1977

1 JCMB, vol. 1, 1 April 1955 and 17 November 1958. *JC*, 31 October 1958, 1.

2 *JC* Supplement, 14 January 1966, iv, and Colour Magazine, 26 June 1987, pp. 21, 24. Interview with William Frankel, London, 28 September 1990.

3 Chaim Bermant, *Troubled Eden* (London, 1969), p. 162.

4 JCMB, vol. 1, 17 November 1958. On Zec, see Maurice Edelman, *The Mirror. A Political History* (London, 1966), pp. 110–30.

5 Frankel presided over a further redesign in October 1970.

6 E. Krausz, 'The Economic and Social Structure of Anglo-Jewry', in Julius Gould and Shaul Esh (eds.), *Jewish Life in Modern Britain* (London, 1964), pp. 30–3; Harold Pollins, *Economic History of the Jews in England* (East Brunswick, NJ, 1982), pp. 209–17, 219–21.

7 A. Marwick, *British Society since 1945*, second edition (London, 1990), pp. 110–40; Norman Cohen, 'Trends in Anglo-Jewish Religious Life', in Gould and Esh (eds.), *Jewish Life in Modern Britain*, pp. 42–3, and Isidor Fishman and Harold Levy, 'Jewish Education in Great Britain', in *Jewish Life in Modern Britain*, pp. 67–74.

8 *JC*, 19 December 1958, 19 to 16 January 1959, 19.

9 Shaftesley to Leftwich, 16 January 1963, CZA, A330/487.

10 For example, *JC*, 13 May 1960, 20; 27 August 1965, 6; 25 March 1960, 24; 10 March 1961, 26.

11 *JC*, 22 May 1959, 16; 20 October 1961, 20; 7 May 1965, 7; 5 May 1967, 6.

12 *JC*, 21 October 1966, 6; 23 December 1966, 6.

13 *JC*, 15 January 1960, 18; 29 January 1960, 18.

14 A. Newman, *The United Synagogue 1870–1970* (London, 1977), pp. 170–3. On militant orthodoxy: *JC*, 1 April 1960, 12.

15 Kopul Rosen to William Frankel, 21 December 1960, Editor's Correspondence, File 1961–2: O–Z, Jewish Chronicle Archive (JCA).

16 *JC*, 13 January 1961, 8.

17 Frankel to Rosen, 27 December 1960, Editor's Correspondence, File 1961–2: O–Z, JCA. See also *AJRI*, 16:3 (March 1961), 3 for a sympathetic account of the affair.

18 Louis Jacobs, *Helping with Inquiries* (London, 1989), pp. 118–19, 121–2. Interview with William Frankel, London, 28 September 1990.

19 *JC*, 22 July 1960, 16; letters of protest: 29 July 1960, 14. Jacobs, *Helping with Inquiries*, pp. 124–33; Bermant, *Troubled Eden*, pp. 239–47.

20 For the Chief Rabbi's point of view, see Israel Brodie, *The Strength of my Heart* (London, 1969), pp. 343–55.

21 *JC*, 2 February 1962, 1, 8. Jacobs, *Helping with Inquiries*, pp. 134–43; Chaim Bermant, *Lord Jakobovits. The Authorized Biography of the Chief Rabbi* (London, 1990), p. 71.

22 *JC*, 19 January 1962, 12; 2 March 1962, 8; 9 March 1962, 10–12; 30 March 1962, 17. Norman Cohen, 'Trends in Anglo-Jewish Religious Life', pp. 47–8.

23 *JC*, 6 April 1962, 11. William Frankel to Wolf Kelman, 15 January 1962. See also Frankel to Kelman, 12 January and 20 January 1962, Editor's Correspondence, File 1962, A–M, JCA.

24 Raphael Loewe to William Frankel, 11 February 1962; Frankel to Loewe, 15 February 1962; Loewe to Frankel, 20 March 1962, Editor's Correspondence, File 1962, N–Z, JCA.

25 William Frankel to Louis Rabinowitz, 27 April 1962, Editor's Correspondence, File 1962, A–M, JCA.

26 *JC*, 11 May 1962, 20; 18 May 1962, 8.

27 Memorandum, received 23 April 1963, David Kessler Correspondence File, 1963, A–Z, JCA.

28 Kessler to Brodie, 8 October 1963, David Kessler Correspondence File, 1963, A–Z, JCA.

29 Brodie to Kessler, 15 October 1963, David Kessler Correspondence File, 1963, A–Z, JCA.

30 Jacobs, *Helping with Inquiries*, pp. 159–86; Newman, *United Synagogue*, pp. 184–7; Bermant, *Troubled Eden*, pp. 248–50; Bermant, *Lord Jakobovits*, pp. 70–1.

31 *JC*, 13 March 1964, 7; 1 May 1964, 7.

32 *JC*, 8 May 1964, 1, 7, 12–15; see also 15 May 1964, 7, 13, 14. The *Yorkshire Post* commented on the paper's stand that 'It does not appear to have suffered from its independence ... Its editor has a cool eye and a calm air.'

33 William Frankel to Richard Yaffe, 4 June 1964 and 8 June 1964, Editor's File, American Series, JCA.

34 Frankel to Yaffe, 18 August 1964, Editor's File, American Series, JCA. *JC*, 2 April 1965, 7. Interview with William Frankel, London, 28 September 1990.

35 *JC*, 10 July 1964, 7 and 27 November 1964, 7. Bermant, *Lord Jakobovits*, p. 88.

36 Frankel to Rabinowitz, 13 November 1962, Editor's Correspondence, File 1962, N–Z, JCA.

37 *JC*, 14 May 1965, 7; 21 May 1965, 7; 28 May 1965, 7. Frankel to Yaacov Herzog, 26 May 1965, Editor's Correspondence, File 1964–5, A–Z, JCA.

38 *JC*, 10 September 1965, 6; 19 November 1965, 6; 25 February 1966, 6. Frankel to Jakobovits, 1 November 1966, David Kessler General File, 1966–8, J–Z, JCA. See William Frankel, 'The Authorized Biography of the Chief Rabbi', *Jewish Quarterly*, 37:4 (winter 1990–1), 18–20.

39 *JC*, 16 September 1966, 6; 14 April 1967, 6. Bermant, *Lord Jakobovits*, pp. 88, 90–1.

40 Shaftesley to Leon [Feldberg], 12 March 1962; Shaftesley to Leftwich, 27 July 1962; Shaftesley to Leftwich, 20 February 1968, CZA, A330/487. Interview with David Kessler, Stoke Hammond, 10 September 1990.

41 H. L. Nathan to Leopold Kessler, 5 November 1936; Nathan to Kessler, 11 November 1936; Kessler to Nathan, 16 November 1936, KP. On the existence of the undertaking, Kessler to Kann, 24 October 1933, KP.

42 Kessler to Waley Cohen, 1 January 1937; Waley Cohen to Kessler, 7 January 1937; Kessler to Waley Cohen, 13 January 1937; Henry Snowman to David Kessler, 31 March 1939, KP.

43 *JC*, 10 October 1969, 19 and Chairman's speech, 2 October 1969, JCA.

44 Such as that at Samu in November 1966: *JC*, 14 October 1966, 6; 18 November 1966, 6; 2 December 1966, 6.

45 Noah Lucas, *The Modern History of Israel* (London, 1975), pp. 407–10; Edward Luttwak and Dan Horowitz, *The Israeli Army* (London, 1975), pp. 209–81; Chaim Herzog, *The Arab–Israeli Wars* (London, 1984).

46 Bermant, *Lord Jakobovits*, p. 146.

47 *JC*, 31 May 1968, 7; 29 August 1969, 7 and following weeks; 2 January 1970, 6; 1 May 1970, 7.

48 Kessler to Bentwich *et al.*, 29 March 1968, David Kessler Correspondence File, 1966–8, A–H, JCA. *JC*, 7 June 1968, 6. Epilogue to Lucas, *Modern History of Israel*.

49 For example, 9 July 1971, 20; 17 December 1971, 18; 23 June 1972, 24.

50 Luttwak and Horowitz, *The Israeli Army*, pp. 337–97 and Chaim Herzog, *The War of Atonement* (London, 1977), passim.

51 *JC*, 30 January 1976, 18; 12 March 1976, 1; 2 April 1976, 24.

52 *JC*, 5 April 1974, 2. There were no further interviews with PLO personnel in the *Jewish Chronicle* for over ten years. Uri Avnery, *My Friend, the Enemy* (London, 1986), pp. 40–114, esp. 51–5.

53 *JC*, 19 April 1974, 22; 26 April 1974, 22.

54 *JC*, 2 August 1974, 18; 6 August 1976, 14.

55 *JC*, 19 January 1968, 7. Percentages have been rounded up or down.

56 E. Krausz, 'The Edgeware Survey: Factors in Jewish Identification', *JJS*, 11 (1969), 151–64; G. Cromer, 'Intermarriage and Communal Survival in a London Suburb', *JJS*, 16: 2 (1974), 155–69.

57 *JC*, 23 February 1968, 6; 19 April 1968, 6. See also 24 July 1970, 6 and 23 October 1970, 6. Bermant, *Lord Jakobovits*, pp. 90–2.

58 Jakobovits to Kessler, 10 October 1968 and Kessler to Jakobovits, 18 October 1968, David Kessler Correspondence File, 1966–8, A–H, JCA.

59 William Frankel to David Pela and Joseph Finklestone, 9 October 1968, David Kessler General Correspondence File, 1964–8, JCA.

60 Marwick, *British Society since 1945*, chaps. 11–12; A. Sked and C. Cook, *Post-War Britain: A Political History*, second edition (London, 1986), chaps. 9–10.
61 On Powell: *JC*, 3 May 1968, 6; 22 November 1968, 6. On the NF: *JC*, 11 April 1969, 6; 30 May 1969, 6. See Martin Walker, *The National Front* (London, 1977).
62 *JC*, 21 January 1949, 12; 25 September 1964, 7; 2 October 1964, 7; 8 April 1966, 6; 12 June 1970, 8–9; 15 February 1974, 22; 4 October 1974, 12–13.
63 *JC*, 18 January 1974, 22; 30 May 1975, 14. See Sked and Cook, *Post-War Britain*, pp. 285–99, 303–5.
64 *JC*, 21 June 1974, 22; 21 May 1976, 20; 9 July 1976, 18. Marwick, *British Society since 1945*, chaps. 13, 16; Sked and Cook, *Post-War Britain*, chap. 11.

9 THE JEWISH PRESS IN A DIVIDED COMMUNITY: GEOFFREY PAUL, 1977–1990

1 Interview with Geoffrey Paul, London, 4 September 1990.
2 For the background, see Royal Commission on the Press 1974–7, *Industrial Relations in the Newspaper Industry* (London, 1976); Colin Seymour-Ure, *The British Press and Broadcasting since 1945* (Oxford, 1991), pp. 21–6; Linda Melvern, *The End of the Street* (London, 1986).
3 *JC*, 13 November 1981, 25.
4 *JC*, 20 February 1981, 20; 5 October 1984, 18 and 20.
5 *JC*, 15 April 1983, 1; 16 October 1987, 23.
6 Stephen Brook, *The Club. The Jews of Modern Britain* (London, 1989), pp. 155–70, 198–201, 206–10, 365–81.
7 Stanley Waterman and Barry Kosmin, *British Jewry in the Eighties: A Statistical and Geographical Study* (London, 1986), p. 23.
8 Ibid., p. 45; Barry A. Kosmin and Caren Levy, *The work and Employment of Suburban Jews* (London, 1981); Harold Pollins, *Economic History of the Jews in England* (East Brunswick, NJ, 1982), pp. 213–17, 233–5.
9 *1985 Jewish Chronicle Readership Survey*, pp. 2–3.
10 Ibid., pp. 30–1. Brook, *The Club* pp. 77–90.
11 *JC*, 6 April 1979, 26 and 28 December 1979, 16. Brook, *The Club*, pp. 155–70.
12 *JC*, 14 May 1982, 20. For the article, see 16 April 1982, 21.
13 *JC*, 30 September 1983, 14. Louis Jacobs, *Helping with Inquiries* (London, 1989), pp. 211–22.
14 *JC*, 8 February 1985, 16; 15 November 1985, 22. On Paula Cohen, see Chaim Bermant, *Lord Jakobovits. The Authorized Biography of the Chief Rabbi* (London, 1990), pp. 106–7.
15 *JC*, 1 June 1979, 14; 14 September 1979, 24.
16 *JC*, 12 January 1978, 20; 4 January 1980, 18.
17 *JC*, 2 September 1983, 30; 4 January 1985, 18.
18 Brook, *The Club*, pp. 217–25.
19 *JC*, 4 March 1977, 20. Stan Taylor, *The National Front in English Politics* (London, 1982), chaps. 5–6; Geoffrey Alderman, *London Jewry and London Politics, 1889–1986* (London, 1989), pp. 121–2.

20 *JC*, 6 October 1978, 25. Taylor, *The National Front in English Politics*, pp. 131–40; Alderman, *London Jewry and London Politics*, pp. 120–4.
21 A. Sked and C. Cook, *Post-War Britain: A Political History*, second edition (London, 1986), pp. 333–57, 422–3, 430–2.
22 *JC*, 17 June 1983, 18. See, for example, Peter Jenkins, *Mrs Thatcher's Revolution. The Ending of the Socialist Era* (London, 1987), pp. 61–5; Hugo Young, *One of Us* (London, 1989), pp. 422–4.
23 *JC*, 24 August 1984, 16; 14 September 1984, 20; 21 December 1984, 14. Alderman, *London Jewry and London Politics*, pp. 127–38; Geoffrey Alderman, 'London Jews and the 1987 General Election', *Jewish Quarterly*, 34:3 (1987), 13–16.
24 *JC*, 20 December 1985, 18; 24 January 1986, 26–8 for the Chief Rabbi's statement. Bermant, *Lord Jakobovits*, pp. 175–8; Alderman, *London Jewry and London Politics*, pp. 138–9.
25 *JC*, 4 February 1977, 16.
26 Bermant, *Lord Jakobovits*, pp. 146–7.
27 Cf. *JC*, 11 July 1980, 22; 8 August 1980, 16; 29 August 1980, 18.
28 *JC*, 26 June 1981, 22; 3 July 1981, 20.
29 *JC*, 11 June 1982, 22 and subsequent issues. Ze'ev Schiff, *Operation Peace for Galilee* (New York, 1983).
30 *JC*, 2 July 1982, 22 and following weeks. Thomas Friedman, *From Beirut to Jerusalem* (London, 1990) pp. 129–55.
31 See Friedman, *From Beirut to Jerusalem*, pp. 156–66.
32 *JC*, 24 December 1982, 16; 18 February 1983, 18; 11 May 1984, 18.
33 *JC*, 29 April 1983, 16; 18 October 1985, 20; 14 November 1988, 24 and 26. Lecture by Geoffrey Paul, Yarnaton Manor, Oxford, 1989.
34 For example, *JC*, 15 January 1988, 24; 5 February 1988, 20; 11 March 1988, 24. Friedman, *From Beirut to Jerusalem*, pp. 366–94.
35 *JC*, 25 July 1980, 1.
36 *JC*, 7 December 1979, 28; 9 November 1984, 20; 11 January 1985, 18.
37 Notice to Shareholders, 31 October 1984 and *Jewish Chronicle* memorandum, January 1989. It is hoped that, in addition, the Foundation will acquire by gift a substantial holding of non-voting shares.

CONCLUSION

1 Jacob Katz, *Out of the Ghetto. The Social Background of Jewish Emancipation 1770–1870*, paperback edition (New York, 1978), pp. 191–219; Jacob Katz (ed.), *Toward Modernity: The European Jewish Model* (New Brunswick, NJ, 1986).
2 D. P. Nord, 'The Public Community. The Urbanisation of Journalism in Chicago', *Journal of Urban History*, 11:4 (1985), 436–8; D. Sorkin, *The Transformation of German Jewry, 1780–1840* (Oxford, 1987), pp. 81–5; P. Cohen Albert, 'Ethnicity and Jewish Solidarity in Nineteenth Century France', in J. Reinharz and D. Swetschinski (eds.), *Mystics, Philosophers and Politicians* (Burban, NC, 1982), pp. 267–9; Steve Zipperstein, *The Jews of Odessa. A Cultural History, 1794–1881* (Stanford, 1985), pp. 74–83.
3 See Ian Jackson, *The Provincial Press and the Community* (London, 1971).
4 Chiefly in *Friday Nights. A Jewish Chronicle Anthology 1841–1971*, selected by A. B. Levy, edited and introduced by William Frankel (London, 1973).

Bibliography

Aaronsfeld, C. C., 'Jewish Enemy Aliens in England During the First World War', *JSS*, 18 (1956).

Aaronson, I. M., 'The Anti-Jewish Pogroms in Russia in 1881', in Klier and Lambroza (eds.), *Pogroms: Anti-Jewish Violence in Modern Russian History*.

Abraham, L., *A Cup of Tears. A Diary of the Warsaw Ghetto*, ed. A. Polonsky, London, 1988.

Abramsky, C., 'The Visits to Russia (1846, 1872)', in S. and V. D. Lipman (eds.), *Century of Moses Montefiore*.

Alderman, G., 'The Anti-Jewish Riots of August 1911 In South Wales', *Welsh History Review*, 6:2 (1972–3).

'The Jew as Scapegoat? The Settlement and Reception of Jews in South Wales before 1914', *TJHSE*, 26 (1974–8).

The Jewish Community in British Politics, Oxford, 1983.

The Federation of Synagogues 1887–1987, London, 1987.

'London Jews and the 1987 General Election', *Jewish Quarterly*, 34:3 (1987).

London Jewry and London Politics 1889–1986, London, 1989.

Allfrey, A., *Edward VII and his Jewish Court*, London, 1991.

Almog, S. (ed.), *Anti-Semitism through the Ages*, Oxford, 1988.

Altholz, J. L., 'The Redaction of Catholic Periodicals', in Wiener (ed.), *Innovators and Preachers. The Role of the Editor in Victorian England*.

'The Mind of Victorian Orthodoxy: Anglican Responses to "Essays and Reviews"' in Parsons (ed.), *Religion in Victorian Britain*, vol. 4, *Interpretations*.

Andrews, A., *The History of British Journalism*, 2 vols., London, 1859.

Anglo-American Committee of Inquiry on Palestine, *Report*, London, 1946.

Apple, R., *The Hampstead Synagogue, 1892–1967*, London, 1967.

'Nathan Marcus Adler's Installation as Chief Rabbi in 1845', *Jewish Review*, 21:6 (1967).

'United Synagogue: Religious Founders and Leaders', in Levin (ed.), *A Century of Anglo-Jewish Life 1870–1970*.

Arad, Y., *Belzec, Sobibor, Treblinka: The Operation Reinhard Death Camps*, Bloomington, IN, 1987.

Aschheim, S., *Brothers and Strangers: The East European Jew in German and German Jewish Consciousness, 1800–1923*, Madison, WI, 1982.

Aspinall, A., *Politics and the Press c1780–1850*, London, 1949.

Asquith, I., 'Advertising and the Press in the Late Eighteenth and Early Nineteenth Centuries', *Historical Journal*, 18 (1975).
'The Structure, Ownership and Control of the Press, 1780–1855', in Boyce, Curran and Wingate (eds.), *Newspaper History*.
Avnery, U., *My Friend, the Enemy*, London, 1986.
Ayerst, D., *Guardian. Biography of a Newspaper*, London, 1971.
Bailey, P., '"A Mingled Mass of Perfectly Legitimate Pleasures": The Victorian Middle Classes and the Problem of Leisure', *Victorian Studies*, 21: 1 (1977).
Balfour, M., *Propaganda in War 1939–45*, London, 1979.
Barnett, A., 'Sussex Hall – The First Anglo-Jewish Venture in Popular Education', *TJHSE*, 19 (1960).
Baron, S. W., 'The Impact of the Revolution of 1848 on Jewish Emancipation', *JSS*, 11 (1949).
Barou, N., *The Jews in Work and Trade: A World Survey*, London, 1948.
Bauer, Y., *From Diplomacy to Resistance. A History of Jewish Palestine 1939–1945*, New York, 1973.
Bayme, S., 'Jewish Leadership and Anti-Semitism in Britain, 1898–1918', Ph.D. thesis, Columbia University, 1977.
Beddoe, D., *Back to Home and Duty. Women between the Wars, 1918–1939*, London, 1989.
Beloff, M., 'Lucien Wolf and the Anglo-Russian Entente 1907–1914', in his *The Intellectual in Politics and Other Essays*, London, 1970.
Ben-Sasson, H. H. (ed.), *History of the Jewish People*, London, 1976.
Benewick, R., *Political Violence and Public Order: A Study of British Fascism*, London, 1969.
Bentwich, M. and N., *Herbert Bentwich. The Pilgrim Father*, London, 1940.
Bentwich, N., *Solomon Schechter. A Biography*, Cambridge, 1938.
'The Wanderers and Other Jewish Scholars of my Youth', *TJHSE*, 20 (1959–61).
Bentwich, N. and J. M. Shaftesley, 'Forerunners of Zionism in the Victorian Era', in J. M. Shaftesley (ed.), *Remember the Days*.
Berger, D. (ed.), *The Legacy of Jewish Migration: 1881 and its Impact*, New York, 1983.
Bermant, C., *Troubled Eden. An Anatomy of British Jewry*, London, 1969.
The Cousinhood, London, 1971.
London's East End. Point of Arrival, London, 1975.
Lord Jakobovits. The Authorized Biography of the Chief Rabbi, London, 1990.
Best, G. A., 'Popular Protestantism in Victorian Britain', in Robson (ed.), *Ideas and Institutions of Victorian Britain*.
Bethell, N., *The Palestine Triangle*, London, 1979.
Billington, L., 'The Religious Periodical and Newspaper Press, 1770–1870', in Harris and Lee (eds.), *The Press in English Society*.
Birmingham Jewish Research Group, *Birmingham Jewry 1749–1914*, vol. 1, Birmingham, 1980.
Black, E. C., *The Social Politics of Anglo-Jewry, 1880–1920*, Oxford, 1989.
Black, G., 'Health and Medical Care of the Jewish Poor in the East End of London 1880–1919', Ph.D. thesis, Leicester University, 1987.
Blumenfeld, R. D., *The Press in my Time*, London, 1933.
Boehm, A., *Die Zionistische Bewegung*, pt. 1, Berlin, 1921.

Bolchover, R., *British Jewry and the Holocaust*, Cambridge, 1993.

Boyce, G., 'The Fourth Estate: The Reappraisal of a Concept', in Boyce, Curran and Wingate (eds.), *Newspaper History*.

Boyce, G., J. Curran and P. Wingate (eds.), *Newspaper History – From the Seventeenth Century to the Present Day*, London, 1978.

Boyd-Barrett, O., C. Seymour-Ure and J. Tunstall, *Studies on the Press*, Royal Commission on the Press (1974–7), Working Paper 3, London, 1977.

Braham, R. L. (ed.), *Jewish Leadership during the Nazi Era: Patterns of Behaviour in the Free World*, New York, 1985.

Bredin, J.-D., *The Affair. The Case of Alfred Dreyfus*, New York, 1986.

Breitman, R., and A. M. Kraut, *American Refugee Policy and European Jewry, 1933–1945*, Bloomington, IN, 1987.

Brendon, P., *The Life and Death of the Press Barons*, London, 1982.

Bridgman, J., *The End of the Holocaust: The Liberation of the Camps*, London, 1990.

Bristow, E. J., *Prostitution and Prejudice. The Jewish Fight against White Slavery, 1870–1939*, Oxford, 1982.

Brodie, I., *The Strength of my Heart*, London, 1969.

Brook, S., *The Club. The Jews of Modern Britain*, London, 1989.

Brown, L., *Victorian News and Newspapers*, Oxford, 1985.

Brown, P. A. H., *London Publishers and Printers*, London, 1982.

Burnham, Lord, *Peterborough Court. The Story of 'The Daily Telegraph'*, London, 1955.

Bush, J., *Behind the Lines. East London Labour, 1914–1919*, London, 1984.

Calder, A., *The People's War: Britain 1939–45*, London, 1971.

Camplin, J., *The Rise of the Plutocrats. Wealth and Power in Edwardian England*, London, 1978.

Caplan, N., *Futile Diplomacy*, vol. 1, *Early Arab–Zionist Negotiation Attempts 1913–1931*, London, 1983.

Carlton, D., *Britain and the Suez Crisis*, London, 1988.

Cesarani, D., 'Zionism in England, 1917–1939', D.Phil. thesis, University of Oxford, 1986.

   'Anti-Alienism in England after the First World War', *Immigrants and Minorities*, 6:1 (March 1987).

   'The East End of Simon Blumenfeld's "Jew Boy"', *London Journal*, 13:1 (1987–8).

   'William Joynson-Hicks and the Radical Right in England after the First World War', in Kushner and Lunn (eds.), *Traditions of Intolerance*.

   'Anti-Zionist Politics and Political Anti-Semitism in Britain 1920–24', *Patterns of Prejudice*, 23:1 (1989).

   'The Transformation of Communal Authority in Anglo-Jewry, 1914–1940', in Cesarani (ed.), *The Making of Modern Anglo-Jewry*.

   'An Embattled Minority: The Jews in Britain during World War One', in Kushner and Lunn (eds.), *The Politics of Marginality*.

   'Dual Heritage or Duel of Heritages? Englishness and Jewishness in the Heritage Industry', in Kushner (ed.), *The Jewish Heritage in British History: Englishness and Jewishness*.

   (ed.) *The Making of Modern Anglo-Jewry*, Oxford, 1990.

Chadwick, O., *The Victorian Church*, vol. 1, London, 1966.
  The Victorian Church, vol. 2, London, 1970.
Cheyette B., 'From Apology to Revolt: Benjamin Farjoen, Amy Levy and the Post-emancipation Anglo-Jewish Novel, 1880–1900', *TJHSE*, 29 (1982–6).
  'The Other Self: Anglo-Jewish Fiction and the Representation of the Jews in England, 1875–1905', in Cesarani (ed.), *The Making of Modern Anglo-Jewry*.
  'Hilaire Belloc and the "Marconi Scandal" 1900–1914: A Reassessment of the Interactionist Model of Racial Hatred', in Kushner and Lunn (eds.), *The Politics of Marginality*.
Cockett, R., *Twilight of Truth: Chamberlain, Appeasement and the Manipulation of the Press*, London, 1989.
Cohen, A., Y. Gelber, and C. Wardi (eds.), *Comprehending the Holocaust*, Frankfurt-on-Main, 1988.
Cohen, I., *A Jewish Pilgrimage. The Autobiography of Israel Cohen*, London, 1956.
Cohen, L., *Some Recollections of Claude G. Montefiore*, London, 1941.
Cohen, M. J., *Palestine: The Retreat from the Mandate. The Making of British Policy, 1936–1945*, London, 1979.
  Palestine and the Great Powers 1945–1948, Princeton, NJ, 1982.
Cohen, N., 'Trends in Anglo-Jewish Religious Life', in Gould and Esh (eds.), *Jewish Life in Modern Britain*.
Cohen, R. I., 'The Dreyfus Affair and the Jews', in Almog (ed.), *Anti-Semitism through the Ages*.
Cohen, S. A., *English Zionists and British Jews. The Communal Politics of Anglo-Jewry, 1895–1920*, Princeton, NJ, 1982.
  'Ideological Components in Anglo-Jewish Opposition to Zionism before and during the First World War: A Restatement', *TJHSE*, 30 (1987–8).
Cohen Albert, P., 'Ethnicity and Jewish Solidarity in Nineteenth Century France', in Reinharz and Swetschinski (eds.), *Mystics, Philosophers and Politicians*.
Cohn, N., *Warrant for Genocide: The Myth of the Jewish World Conspiracy and the Protocols of the Elders of Zion*, London, 1967.
Collins, K. E. *Second City Jewry*, Glasgow, 1989.
Collins, K. E. (ed.), *Aspects of Scottish Jewry*, Glasgow, 1987.
Cranfield, G. A., *Press and Society. From Caxton to Northcliffe*, London, 1978.
Cromer, G., 'Intermarriage and Communal Survival in a London Suburb', *JJS*, 16:2 (1974).
Cross, C., *The Fascists in Britain*, London, 1964.
Curran, J. 'The Press as an Agency of Social Control: An Historical Perspective', in Boyce, Curran and Wingate (eds.), *Newspaper History*.
Dash Moore, D., *At Home in America: Second Generation New York Jews*, New York, 1981.
Davis, N., *Heart of Europe: A Short History of Poland*, paperback edition, Oxford, 1987.
Dench, G., *Minorities in the Open Society*, London, 1986.
Dibblee, G. B., *The Newspaper*, London, 1913.
Dixon, D., 'Children and the Press 1866–1914', in Harris and Lee (eds.), *The Press in English Society*.
Dobroszycki, L. (ed.), *The Chronicle of the Lodz Ghetto*, London, 1984.
Dodgson Bowman, W., *The Story of "The Times"*, London, 1931.

Donaldson, F., *The Marconi Scandal*, London, 1962.

Economist, The, The Economist, 1843–1943. A Centenary Volume, Oxford, 1943.

Edelman, M., *The Mirror. A Political History*, London, 1966.

Emanuel, C. H. L., *A Century and a Half of Jewish History*, London, 1910.

Encyclopedia Judaica, vol. 4, Berlin, 1929.

Endelman, T. M., 'The Social and Political Context of Conversion in Germany and England, 1870–1914', in Endelman (ed.), *Jewish Apostasy in the Modern World*.

Radical Assimilation in English Jewish History, 1656–1945, Bloomington, IN, 1990.

Endelman, T. M. (ed.), *Jewish Apostasy in the Modern World*, New York, 1987.

Epstein I., E. Levine and C. Roth (eds.), *Essays Presented to J. H. Hertz*, London, 1942.

Escott, T. H. S., *Masters of English Journalism*, London, 1911.

Ettinger, S., 'The Modern Period', in Ben-Sasson (ed.), *History of the Jewish People*.

Feldman, D., 'The Importance of Being English. Jewish Immigration and the Decay of Liberal England', in Feldman and Stedman Jones (eds.), *Metropolis London*.

Feldman, D., and G. Stedman Jones (eds.), *Metropolis London. Histories and Representations since 1800*, London, 1989.

Feuchtwanger, E. J., *Gladstone*, revised edition, London, 1989.

Finestein, I., 'Anglo-Jewish Opinion during the Struggle for Emancipation, (1828–1858)', *TJHSE*, 20 (1959–61).

'The New Community, 1880–1914', in Lipman (ed.), *Three Centuries of Anglo-Jewish History*.

'The Anglo-Jewish Revolt of 1853', *Jewish Quarterly* (winter 1978).

Post-Emancipation Jewry: The Anglo-Jewish Experience, Oxford, 1980.

'The Uneasy Victorian: Montefiore as Communal Leader', in S. and V. D. Lipman (eds.), *Century of Moses Montefiore*.

'Some Modern Themes in the Emancipation Debate in Early Victorian England', in Sacks (ed.), *Tradition and Transition: Essays Presented to Chief Rabbi Sir Immanuel Jakobovits to Celebrate Twenty Years in Office*.

Fishman, I., and H. Levy, 'Jewish Education in Great Britain', in Gould and Esh (eds.), *Jewish Life in Modern Britain*.

Fishman, W. J., *East End Jewish Radicals, 1875–1914*, London, 1975.

'A People's Journée: The Battle of Cable Street (4 October 1936)', in Kranz (ed.), *History from Below*.

Morris Winshevsky's London Yiddish Newspaper. One Hundred Years in Retrospect, Oxford, 1985.

East End 1888, London, 1988.

Fox, J. P., 'The Jewish Factor in British War Crimes Policy in 1942', *English Historical Review*, 92 (1977).

Fox Bourne, H. R., *English Newspapers*, 2 vols., London, 1887.

Fraenkel, J., 'The *Jewish Chronicle* and the Launching of Political Zionism', in Patai (ed.), *Herzl Year Book*, vol. 2.

The Jewish Press of the Diaspora, Leiden, 1961.

'The Jewish Press In Great Britain 1823–1963' in Fraenkel (ed.), *Exhibition of the Jewish Press in Great Britain 1823–1963*.

The Jewish Press of the World, seventh edition, London, 1972.

Frankel, J., *Prophecy and Politics. Socialism, Nationalism and the Russian Jews, 1862–1917*, Cambridge, 1981.

'The Crisis of 1881–82', in Berger (ed.), *The Legacy of Jewish Migration: 1881 and its Impact*.

Fraenkel, J. (ed.), *Exhibition of the Jewish Press in Great Britain* 1823–1963, London, 1963.

Frankel, W. 'The Authorized Biography of the Chief Rabbi', *Jewish Quarterly*, 37:4 (winter 1990–1).

Frankel, W. (ed.), *Friday Nights. A Jewish Chronicle Anthology 1841–1971*, London, 1973.

Franklin, A. E., *Records of the Franklin Family and Collaterals*, London,1915.

Fraser, D., *The Evolution of the British Welfare State*, second edition, London, 1973.

Freedman, M. (ed.), *A Minority in Britain. Social Studies of the Anglo-Jewish Community*, London, 1955.

Freeman, D., 'Jacobus H. Kann of the Hague', in Patai (ed.), *The Herzl Yearbook*, vol. 7.

Friedland, M. L., *The Trials of Israel Lipski*, London, 1984.

Friedman, T., *From Beirut to Jerusalem*, London, 1990.

Friedmann, I., *Germany, Turkey, Zionism*, Oxford, 1977.

Fyfe, H., *Sixty Years of Fleet Street*, London, 1949.

Gainer, B., *The Alien Invasion. The Origins of the Alien Act of 1905*, London, 1972.

Gannon, F. R., *The British Press and Germany 1936–1939*, Oxford, 1971.

Garrard, J., *The English and Immigration: A Comparative Study of the Jewish Influx 1880–1910*, London, 1971.

Leadership and Power in Victorian Industrial Towns, 1830–80, Leicester, 1983.

Gartner, L. P., *The Jewish Immigrant in England, 1870–1914*, London, 1960.

'Anglo-Jewry and the Jewish International Traffic in Prostitution, 1885–1914', *AJSR*, 7–8 (1982–3).

Geddye, G. R., *Fallen Bastions*, London, 1938.

Gelber, Y., 'Moralist and Realistic Approaches in the Study of the Allies' Attitude to the Holocaust', in Cohen, Gelber and Wardi (eds.), *Comprehending the Holocaust*.

Gewirtz, S., 'Anglo-Jewish Responses to Nazi Germany 1933–39: The Anti-Nazi Boycott and the Board of Deputies of British Jews', *JCH*, 26:2 (1991), 255–76.

Gilbert, M., *Winston S. Churchill*, vol. 4, *The Stricken World 1916–1922*, Boston, 1975.

Exile and Return. The Emergence of Jewish Statehood, London, 1978.

Auschwitz and the Allies, London, 1981.

Holocaust. The Jewish Tragedy, London, 1989.

Gillam, A., *The Emancipation of the Jews in England, 1830–1860*, New York, 1982.

Gillman, P. and L., *Collar the Lot!*, London,1980.

Gitelman, Z., *Jewish Nationality and Soviet Politics: The Jewish Sections of the CPSU, 1917–1930*, Princeton, NJ, 1972.

Goodbody, J., 'The Star: Its Role in the New Journalism', VPR, 20:4 (1987).

Goodman, P., Zionism in England, 1899–1949, London, 1949.

Gorny, J., The British Labour Movement and Zionism 1917–1948, London, 1983.

Gould, J., and S. Esh (eds.), Jewish Life in Modern Britain, London, 1964.

Goulston, M., 'The Status of the Anglo-Jewish Rabbinate, 1840–1914', JJS, 10:2 (1968).

Graetz, M., Les Juifs en France au XIXe siècle, Evreux, 1989.

Grant, J., The Newspaper Press, 3 vols., London, 1871–2.

Granzow, B., A Mirror of Nazism. British Opinion and the Emergence of Hitler 1929–1933, London, 1964.

Griffiths, R., Fellow Travellers of the Right. British Enthusiasts for Nazi Germany 1933–39, paperback edition, Oxford, 1983.

Harding, J., with J. Berg, Jack Kid Berg: The Whitechapel Windmill, London, 1987.

Harris, M., and A. J. Lee (eds.), The Press in English Society from the Seventeenth to the Nineteenth Centuries, London, 1986.

Harrison, B., 'Press and Pressure Groups in Modern Britain', in Shattock and Wolff (eds.), The Victorian Press.

'The Sunday Trading Riots of 1855', Historical Journal, 8:2 (1965).

Hart-Davis, D., The House the Berrys Built. Inside 'The Telegraph', paperback edition, London, 1991.

Hearst, E., 'The British and the Slaughter of the Jews. Pt. 1', WLB, 21 (1966/7).

'The British and the Slaughter of the Jews. Pt. 2', WLB, 22 (1967).

Hein, V. H., The British Followers of Herzl: English Zionist Leaders 1896–1904, New York, 1987.

Heinze, A., Adapting to Abundance. Jewish Immigrants, Mass Consumption and the Search for American Identity, New York, 1990.

Heller, C., On the Edge of Destruction. Jews of Poland between the Two World Wars, New York, 1977.

Henriques, H. S. Q., The Jews and the English Law, Oxford, 1908.

Henriques, U. R. Q., 'The Jewish Emancipation Controversy in Nineteenth Century Britain', Past and Present, 40 (1968).

'Lyons versus Thomas: The Jewish Abduction Case', TJHSE, 29 (1982–6).

Henry, Richard L., Michael Henry, London, 1875.

Hertzberg A., The French Enlightenment and the Jews, New York, 1970.

Herzog, C., The War of Atonement, London, 1977.

The Arab–Israeli Wars, London, 1984.

Hetherington, A., Guardian Years, London, 1981.

Hilberg, R., The Destruction of the European Jews, 3 vols., New York, 1985.

Hindle, W., The Morning Post 1772–1937, London, 1937.

Hobman, J. B. (ed.), David Eder. Memoirs of a Modern Pioneer, London, 1945.

Hobson, H., P. Knightly and L. Russell, The Pearl of Days. An Intimate Memoir of the Sunday Times 1822–1972, London, 1972.

Hodess, J., 'The History of the Jewish Press in England', in The Jews in England. Studies and Sources, 1880–1940, [Yiddish] New York, 1966.

Holmes, C., Anti-Semitism in British Society 1876–1939, London, 1979.

'Anti-Semitism and the BUF', in Lunn and Thurlow (eds.), British Fascism.

'East End Crime and the Jewish Community, 1887–1911', in Newman (ed.), The Jewish East End.

John Bull's Island. Immigration and British Society, 1871–1971, London, 1988.

Homa, B., *A Fortress in Anglo-Jewry. The Story of the Machzike Hadath*, London, 1953.

Houghton, W. E., *The Wellesley Index to Victorian Periodicals*, 2 vols., London, 1966–72.

Husband, C. T., 'East End Racism, 1900–1980: Geographical Continuities in Vigilantist and Extreme Right-Wing Political Behaviour', *London Journal*, 8 (1982).

Hyams, E., *The New Statesman: The History of the First Fifty Years 1913–1963*, London, 1963.

Hyamson, A., *Jews' College, London, 1855–1955*, London, 1955.

Hyman, P., *From Dreyfus to Vichy: The Remaking of French Jewry, 1906–1939*, New York, 1979.

Infield, H. (ed.), *Essays in Jewish Sociology. Labour Co-operation in Memory of Dr Noah Barou*, London, 1962.

Ioancu, C., *Les Juifs en Roumanie, 1866–1919*, Aix-en-Provence, 1978.

Jackson, I., *The Provincial Press and the Community*, London, 1971.

Jacobs, L., *Helping with Inquiries*, London, 1989.

Jay, E., *Faith and Doubt in Victorian Britain*, London, 1986.

Jenkins, P., *Mrs Thatcher's Revolution. The Ending of the Socialist Era*, London, 1987.

Jewish Chronicle and the Tercentenary Council, *Three Hundred Years: A Volume to Commemorate the Tercentenary of the Resettlement of the Jews in Great Britain 1656–1956*, London, 1957.

The Jewish Chronicle 1841–1941. A Century of Newspaper History, London, 1949.

Jewish Research Group of the Edmonton Hundred Historical Society, *Heritage. An Historical Series on the Jewish Inhabitants of North London*, no. 1, London, 1982.

Jones, G. S., *Outcast London. A Study in the Relationship between Classes in Victorian Society*, London, 1976.

Josephs, Z. (ed.), *Birmingham Jewry 1740–1930*, vol. 2, Birmingham, 1984.

Journalist, A., *Bohemian Days in Fleet Street*, London, 1913.

Kadish, S., *Bolsheviks and British Jews. The Anglo-Jewish Community, Britain and the Bolshevik Revolution*, London, 1992.

Katz, J., *Out of the Ghetto. The Social Background of Jewish Emancipation 1770–1870*, paperback edition, New York, 1978.

Katz, J. (ed.) *Toward Modernity: The European Jewish Model*, New Brunswick, NJ, 1986.

Kershen, A., 'Jewish Trades Unionism in Leeds and London, 1870–1914', in Cesarani (ed.), *The Making of Modern Anglo-Jewry*.

Kessler, D., *The Falashas*, London, 1982.

Kessler, E. (ed.), *An English Jew. The Life and Writings of Claude Montefiore*, London, 1989.

Kidd, A. J., and K. W. Roberts (eds.), *City, Class and Culture*, Manchester, 1985.

Kirsch Greenberg, S., 'Anglicization and the Education of Jewish Immigrant Children in the East End of London', in Rapoport-Albert and Zipperstein (eds.), *Jewish History. Essays in Honour of Chimen Abramsky*.

Klier, J. D., 'The Polish Revolt of 1863 and the Birth of Russification: Bad for the Jews?', *Polin*, vol. 1, Oxford, 1986.

Klier, J. D. and S. Lambroza (eds.), *Pogroms: Anti-Jewish Violence in Modern Russian History*, Cambridge, 1992.

Knight Hunt, F., *The Fourth Estate*, 2 vols., London, 1850.

Kochan, K., *Pogrom 10 November 1938*, London, 1957.

Kosmin, B., and C. Levy, *The Work and Employment of Suburban Jews*, London, 1981.

Koss, S., *The Rise and Fall of the Political Press in Britain*, vol. 1, *The Nineteenth Century*, London, 1981.

  The Rise and Fall of the Political Press in Britain, vol. 2, *The Twentieth Century*, London, 1984.

Kranz, P. (ed.), *History from Below*, Madison, WI, 1980.

Krausz, E., 'The Economic and Social Structure of Anglo-Jewry', in Gould and Esh (eds.), *Jewish Life in Modern Britain*.

  Leeds Jewry: Its History and Social Structure, Cambridge, 1964.

  'The Edgware Survey: Factors in Jewish Identification', *JJS*, 11 (1969).

Krikler, B., 'Boycotting Nazi Germany', *WLB*, 23:4 (1969).

Kushner, T., *The Persistence of Prejudice. Antisemitism in British Society during the Second World War*, Manchester, 1989.

  'Beyond the Pale? British Reactions to Nazi Anti-Semitism, 1933–39', in Kushner and Lunn (eds.), *The Politics of Marginality*.

  'Rules of the Game: Britain, America and the Holocaust in 1944', *Holocaust and Genocide Studies*, 5:4 (1990).

  'An Alien Occupation – Jewish Refuges and Domestic Service in Britain, 1933–1948', in Mosse *et al.* (eds.), *Second Chance*.

  'The Impact of the Holocaust on British Society and Culture', *Contemporary Record*, 5:2 (1991).

Kushner, T. (ed.), *The Jewish Heritage in British History: Englishness and Jewishness*, London, 1992.

Kushner, T. and K. Lunn (eds.), *Traditions of Intolerance. Historical Perspectives on Fascism and Race Discourse in Britain*, Manchester, 1989.

  The Politics of Marginality. Race, the Radical Right and Minorities in Twentieth Century Britain, London, 1990.

Kynaston, D., *The Financial Times. A Centenary History*, London, 1988.

Lachs, P. S., 'A Study of a Professional Elite: Anglo-Jewish Barristers in the Nineteenth Century', *JSS*, 44:2 (1982).

Lamberti, M., *Jewish Activism in Imperial Germany – The Struggle for Civil Equality*, New Haven, CT, 1978.

Laqueur, W., *History of Zionism*, paperback edition, New York, 1978.

  The Terrible Secret, London, 1982.

Laski, N., *Jewish Rights and Jewish Wrongs*, London, 1938.

Lebzelter, G., *Political Anti-Semitism in England, 1918–1939*, London, 1978.

Lee, A. J., 'The Structure, Ownership and Control of the Press, 1855–1914', in Boyce, Curran and Wingate, *Newspaper History*.

  The Origins of the Popular Press 1855–1914, paperback edition, London, 1980.

Leitch, D., 'Explosion at the King David Hotel', in Sissons and French (eds.), *The Age of Austerity*.

Levene, M., 'Anglo-Jewish Foreign Policy in Crisis – Lucien Wolf, the Conjoint Foreign Committee and the War, 1914–1919', *TJHSE*, 30 (1987–88).
'The Balfour Declaration: A Case of Mistaken Identity', *English Historical Review*, 107 (1991).
Levi, G. (ed.), *Barnett Janner: A Personal Portrait by Elsie Janner*, London, 1984.
Levin, S. S. (ed.), *A Century of Anglo-Jewish Life 1870–1970*, London, 1970.
Levy, A. B., *East End Story*, London, n.d.
Levy, R. S., *The Downfall of the Anti-Semitic Political Parties in Imperial Germany*, New Haven, CT, 1975.
Liberles, R., 'The Origins of the Jewish Reform Movement in England', *AJSR*, 1 (1976).
Liebeschutz, H. and A. Paucker (eds.), *Das Judentum in der Deutschen Umwelt, 1800–1850*, Tübingen, 1977.
Lipman, S. and V. D. (eds.), *The Century of Moses Montefiore*, Oxford, 1985.
Lipman, V. D., *A Century of Social Service 1859–1959: The Jewish Board of Guardians*, London, 1959.
'Synagogal Organisation in Anglo-Jewry', *JJS*, 1:1 (1959).
'The Age of Emancipation', in Lipman (ed.), *Three Centuries of Anglo-Jewish History*.
'Social Topography of a London Congregation: The Bayswater Synagogue 1863–1963', *JJS*, 6:1 (1964).
'The Rise of Jewish Suburbia', *TJHSE*, 21 (1968).
'The Development of London Jewry', in Levin (ed.), *A Century of Anglo-Jewish Life*.
'The Anglo-Jewish Community in Victorian Society', in Noy and Ben Ami (eds.), *Folklore Research Centre Studies 5, Studies in the Cultural Life of the Jews in England*.
A History of the Jews in Britain Since 1858, Leicester, 1990.
Lipman, V. D. (ed.), *Three Centuries of Anglo-Jewish History*, London, 1961.
Livshin, R., 'The Acculturation of the Children of Immigrant Jews in Manchester, 1890–1920', in Cesarani (ed.), *The Making of Modern Anglo-Jewry*.
Loewe, H., *Israel Abrahams. A Biographical Sketch*, London, 1944.
Lambroza, S., 'The Pogroms of 1903–1906', in Klier and Lambroza (eds.), *Pogroms: Anti-Jewish Violence in Modern Russian History*.
London Advertising Register, second edition, London, 1927.
London, L., 'Jewish Refugees, Anglo-Jewry and British Government Policy, 1930–1940', in Cesarani (ed.), *The Making of Modern Anglo-Jewry*.
'British Immigration Control Procedures and Jewish Refugees, 1933–1939', in Mosse *et al.* (eds.), *Second Chance*.
Lonsdale, G., 'The Changing Character of the East London Industry', *East London Papers*, 5:2 (1962).
Looker, M. S., '"God Save the Queen": Victoria's Jubilees and the Religious Press', *VPR*, 21:3 (1988).
Lucas, N., *The Modern History of Israel*, London, 1975.
Lunn, K., 'Political Anti-semitism before 1914: Fascism's Heritage?' in Lunn and Thurlow (eds.), *British Fascism*.
Lunn, K. and R. C. Thurlow (eds.), *British Fascism*, London, 1980.
Luttwak, E., and D. Horowitz, *The Israeli Army*, London, 1975.

McCagg, W. O., Jr, *A History of Habsburg Jews, 1670–1918*, Bloomington, 1989.

McCarthy, J., and Sir J. Robinson, *The 'Daily News' Jubilee*, London, 1896.

McDonald, I., *The History of 'The Times'*, vol. 5, *Struggles in War and Peace 1939–1966*, London, 1984.

MacIntyre, C. T., *England against the Papacy, 1858–61*, Cambridge, 1963.

McLaine, I., *Ministry of Morale. Home Front Morale and the Ministry of Information in World War Two*, London, 1979.

McLeod, H., *Class and Religion in the Late Victorian City*, London, 1974.

McQuail, D., *Analysis of Newspaper Content*, Royal Commission on the Press (1974–7), Research section 4, London, 1977.

Machin, G. I. T., *Politics and the Churches in Great Britain 1832–1868*, Oxford, 1977.

Maddock, G. and P. Golding, 'The Structure, Ownership and Control of the Press, 1780–1850', in Boyce, Curran and Wingate (eds.), *Newspaper History*.

Marcus, J., *Social and Political History of the Jews of Poland 1919–1939*, New York, 1983.

Marom, R., 'The Bolsheviks and the Balfour Declaration, 1917–20', *WLB*, 29 (1976).

Marrus, M., *The Politics of Assimilation*, Oxford, 1980.

Marwick, A. *British Society since 1945*, second edition, London, 1990.

Matthew, H. G. C. (ed.), *The Gladstone Diaries*, vol. 9, *January 1875–December 1880*, Oxford, 1986.

The Gladstone Diaries, vol. 10, *January 1881–June 1883*, Oxford, 1990.

Mazower, D., *Yiddish Theatre in London*, London, 1987.

Melvern, L., *The End of the Street*, London, 1986.

Meyer, P., *et al.* (eds.), *The Jews in the Soviet Satellites*, New York, 1953.

Mitchell's (later) *The Newspaper Press Directory*.

Moore, J. R., 'The Crisis of Faith: Reformation versus Revolution', in Parsons (ed.), *Religion in Victorian Britain*, vol. 2, *Controversies*.

Morris, B., *The Birth of the Palestinian Refugee Problem, 1947–49*, Cambridge, 1987.

The Roots of Appeasement. The British Weekly Press and Nazi Germany during the 1930s, London, 1991.

Mosse, W. E., *et al.* (eds.), *Second Chance. Two Centuries of German-speaking Jews in the United Kingdom*, Tübingen, 1991.

Murdock, G., and P. Golding, 'Structure and Ownership of the Press, 1914–1976', in Boyce, Curran and Wingate (eds.), *Newspaper History*.

Neuberg, V. E., *Popular Literature. A History and Guide from the Beginning of Printing to the Year 1897*, London, 1977.

Nevett, T. *Advertising in Britain*, London, 1982.

'Advertising and Editorial Integrity in the Nineteenth Century', in Harris and Lee (eds.), *The Press in English Society*.

Newman, A., *The United Synagogue 1870–1970*, London, 1977.

The Board of Deputies of British Jews 1760–1985. A Brief Survey, London, 1987.

Newman, A. (ed.), *The Jewish East End, 1840–1939*, London, 1981.

Newspaper Press Directory, London, 1945.

Newspaper Press Directory, London, 1947.

Newspaper Press Directory, London, 1948.

Niewyk, D., *The Jews in Weimar Germany*, Baton Rouge, 1980.

Nord, D. P., 'The Public Community. The Urbanization of Journalism in Chicago', *Journal of Urban History*, 11:4 (1985).

Norman, E. R., *Anti-Catholicism in Victorian England*, London, 1968.

The English Catholic Church in the Nineteenth Century, Oxford, 1984.

Noy, D., and I. Ben Ami (eds.), *Folklore Research Centre Studies 5, Studies in the Cultural Life of the Jews in England*, Jerusalem, 1975.

Orbach, A., *New Voices of Russian Jewry: A Study of the Russian Jewish Press of Odessa in the Era of the Great Reforms, 1860–71*, Leiden, 1980.

Orbach, M., 'Noah Barou and the TAC', in Infield (ed.), *Essays in Jewish Sociology. Labour Co-operation in Memory of Dr Noah Barou*.

Oxaal, I., M. Pollak and G. Botz (eds.), *Jews, Anti-Semitism and Culture in Vienna*, London, 1987.

PEP, *Report on the British Press*, London, April 1938.

Palmer, M., 'The British Press and International News: Of Agencies and Newspapers, 1851–99' in Boyce, Curran and Wingate (eds.), *Newspaper History*.

Parfitt, T., 'Sir Moses Montefiore and Palestine', in Lipman (ed.), *Sir Moses Montefiore*.

Parry, A., 'The *National Review* and the Dreyfus Affair: "The Conscience of the Civilized World"', *VPR*, 25:1 (1992).

Parsons, G., 'Reform, Revival and Realignment: The Experience of Victorian Anglicanism', in Parsons (ed.), *Religion in Victorian Britain*, vol. 1, *Traditions*.

'Victorian Roman Catholicism', in Parsons (ed.), *Religion in Victorian Britain*, vol. 1, *Traditions*.

'Biblical Criticism in Victorian Britain: From Controversy to Acceptance?', in Parsons (ed.), *Religion in Victorian Britain*, vol. 2, *Controversies*.

(ed.), *Religion in Victorian Britain*, vol. 1, *Traditions*, Manchester, 1988.

(ed.), *Religion in Victorian Britain*, vol. 2, *Controversies*, Manchester, 1988.

(ed.), *Religion in Victorian Britain*, vol. 4, *Interpretations*, Manchester, 1988.

Patai, R. (ed.), *Herzl Year Book*, vol. 2, New York, 1959.

(ed.), *The Complete Diaries of Theodore Herzl*, vol. 1, New York, 1960.

(ed.), *The Herzl Yearbook*, vol. 7, New York, 1971.

Patterson, J. H., *With the Judaeans in the Palestine Campaign*, London, 1922.

Philippson, J., 'Ludwig Philippson und die Allgemeine Zeitung des Judentums', in Liebeschutz and Paucker (eds.), *Das Judentum in der Deutschen Umwelt, 1800–1850*.

Philipson, D., *The Reform Movement in Judaism*, New York, 1931.

Picciotto, J., *Sketches of Anglo-Jewish History*, ed. I. Finestein, London, 1956.

Pinkus, B., *The Jews in the Soviet Union*, Cambridge, 1988.

Pollins, H., *A History of the Jewish Working Men's Club and Institute, 1874–1912*, Oxford, 1981.

Economic History of the Jews in England, East Brunswick, NJ, 1982.

Porat, D., *The Blue and the Yellow Stars of David. The Zionist Leadership in Palestine and the Holocaust, 1939–1945*, Cambridge, MA, 1990.

Porath, Y., *The Palestinian Arab National Movement*, vol. 2, *From Riots to Rebellion, 1929–1939*, London, 1977.

Prager, L., 'A Bibliography of Yiddish Periodicals in Great Britain (1867–1967)', *Studies in Bibliography and Booklore*, 9 (1969).
'The Beginnings of Yiddish Fiction in England', in Noy and Ben Ami (eds.), *Folklore Research Centre Studies 5, Studies in the Cultural Life of the Jews in England*.
Yiddish Culture in Great Britain, Frankfurt-on-Main, 1990.
Prawer, S. S., *A. N. Stencl: Poet of Whitechapel*, Oxford, 1984.
Pulzer, P. G. J., *The Rise of Political Anti-Semitism in Germany and Austria*, revised edition, London, 1988.
Rae, J., *Conscience and Politics. The British Government and the Conscientious Objectors to Military Service 1916–19*, Cambridge, 1970.
Ralls, W., 'The Papal Aggression of 1850: A Study in Victorian Anti-Catholicism', in Parsons (ed.), *Religion in Victorian Britain*, vol. 2, *Controversies*.
Rapoport-Albert, A. and S. Zipperstein (eds.), *Jewish History. Essays in Honour of Chimen Abramsky*, London, 1988.
Rapp, D., 'The Jewish Response to G. K. Chesterton's Antisemitism, 1911–33', *Patterns of Prejudice*, 24: 2–4 (1990).
Read, D. *Press and People 1730–1850. Opinion in Three English Cities*, London, 1961.
Reinharz, J., *Chaim Weizmann. The Making of a Zionist Leader*, Oxford, 1985.
Reinharz, J., and D. Swetschinski (eds.), *Mystics, Philosophers and Politicians: Essays in Honor of Alexander Altmann*, Burban, NC, 1982.
Robbins, K., *Nineteenth Century Britain. England, Scotland and Wales. The Making of a Nation*, Oxford, 1989.
Robertson Scott, J. W., *The Story of the Pall Mall Gazette*, Oxford, 1950.
Robson, R. (ed.), *Ideas and Institutions of Victorian Britain*, London, 1964.
Rollin, A. R., 'Russo-Jewish Immigrants in England before 1881', *TJHSE*, 21 (1968).
Rolph, C. H., *Further Particulars*, London, 1987.
Rose, A., *Stinie. Murder on the Common*, London, 1985.
Rose, M. E., *The Relief of Poverty 1834–1914*, London, 1972.
Rose, N. *The Gentile Zionists*, London, 1973.
Chaim Weizmann: A Biography, New York, 1986.
Rose, N. (ed.), *Baffy. The Diaries of Blanche Dugdale 1936–1947*, London, 1973.
Rosenberg, D., *Facing up to Antisemitism*, London, 1985.
Rosenfeld, L., *Bright Star of Exile. Jacob Adler and the Yiddish Theatre*, New York, 1977.
Roth, C., 'Lucien Wolf. A Memoir', in Wolf, *Essays in Jewish History*.
'The Chief Rabbinate in England', in Epstein, Levine and Roth (eds.), *Essays Presented to J. H. Hertz*.
'The Court Jews of Edwardian England', *JSS*, 5 (1943).
A History of the Jews in England, paperback edition, Oxford, 1978.
Royal Commission on the Press (1947–9), *Report*, Cmd 7700, London, 1949.
Royal Commission on the Press (1961–2), *Report*, Cmd 1811, London, 1962.
Royal Commission on the Press (1974–7), *Industrial Relations in the Newspaper Industry*, London, 1976.
Rudavsky, D., *Modern Jewish Religious Movements*, New York, 1979.

Rumbelow, D., *The Houndsditch Murders and the Siege of Sidney Street*, London, 1973.

Sacks, J. (ed.), *Tradition and Transition: Essays Presented to Chief Rabbi Sir Immanuel Jakobovits to Celebrate Twenty Years in Office*, London, 1986.

Sagi, N., and M. Lowe, 'Research Report: Pre-War Reactions to Nazi Anti-Jewish Policies in the Jewish Press', *Yad Vashem Studies*, vol. 13 (Jerusalem, 1979).

Saipe, L., *A Century of Care: The History of the Leeds Jewish Welfare Board 1878–1978*, Leeds, 1978.

Salbstein, M. C. N., *The Emancipation of the Jews in Britain: The Question of the Admission of the Jews to Parliament, 1828–60*, East Brunswick, NJ, 1982.

Samuel, E., *A Lifetime in Jerusalem*, London, 1970.

Saunders, M. L., and P. M. Taylor, *British Propaganda during the First World War, 1914–18*, London, 1982.

Schiff, Z., *Operation Peace for Galilee*, New York, 1983.

Schonebohm, D., *Ostjuden in London: Der Jewish Chronicle und die Arbeiterbewegung der jüdischen Immigranten im Londoner East End, 1881–1900*, Franfkurt-on-Main, 1987.

Scott, G., *Reporter Anonymous. The Story of the Press Association*, London, 1968.

Scott, P. G., 'Richard Cope Morgan, Religious Periodicals and the Pontifex Factor', *VPN*, 16 (1972).

Searle, G. R., *Corruption in British Politics 1895–1930*, Oxford, 1987.

Sebag-Montefiore, R., *A Family Patchwork*, London, 1987.

Seymour-Ure, C., *The British Press and Broadcasting since 1945*, Oxford, 1991.

Shaftesley, J. M. (ed.), *Remember the Days: Essays on Anglo-Jewish History presented to Cecil Roth*, London, 1966.

'Dr Abraham Benisch as Newspaper Editor', *TJHSE*, 21 (1968).

'Religious Controversies', in Levin (ed.), *A Century of Anglo-Jewish Life*.

Shannon, R., *Gladstone and the Bulgarian Agitation*, London, 1964.

Sharf, A., *The British Press and the Jews under Nazi Rule*, London, 1964.

Sharot, S., 'Religious Change in Native Orthodoxy in London, 1870–1914: Rabbinate and Clergy', *JJS*, 15:2 (1973).

Shattock, J., and M. Wolff (eds.), *The Victorian Press: Samplings and Soundings*, Leicester, 1982.

Shepherd, N., *The Zealous Intruders. The Western Rediscovery of Palestine*, London, 1987.

Sherman, A. J., *Island Refuge: Britain and Refugees from the Third Reich, 1933–1939*, London, 1973.

Shimoni, G., 'Selig Brodetsky and the Ascendency of Zionism in Anglo-Jewry (1939–1945)', *JJS*, 22:2 (1980).

Short, K. R. M., 'Hollywood fights Anti-Semitism, 1940–5', in Short (ed.), *Film and Radio Propaganda in World War II*.

Short, K. R. M. (ed.), *Film and Radio Propaganda in World War II*, London, 1983.

Shpayer-Macov, H., 'Anarchism in British Public Opinion, 1880–1914', *VS*, 20 (1988).

Sissons, M., and P. French (eds.), *The Age of Austerity*, London, 1963.

Sked, A., and C. Cook, *Post-War Britain A Political History*, second edition, London, 1986.

Skidelsky, R., *Oswald Mosley*, London, 1981.

Smith, A., *The British Press Since the War*, London, 1974.

Smith, E. R., 'Jewish Responses to Political Antisemitism and Fascism in the East End of London, 1920–1939', in Kushner and Lunn (eds.), *Traditions of Intolerance*.

Sokolow, N., *Geschichte des Zionismus*, Berlin, 1921.

Soldon, N. C., 'Individualist Periodicals. The Crisis of Late Victorian Liberalism', *VPN*, 6:3–4 (1973).

Sorkin, D., *The Transformation of German Jewry, 1780–1840*, Oxford, 1987.

Spielman, Sir I., Presidential Address, 9 February 1903, *TJHSE*, 5 (1902–5).

Spielmann, M. H., *The History of 'Punch'*, London, 1895.

Springhall, J., *Coming of Age: Adolescence in Britain 1860–1960*, London, 1986.

Stanislawski, M., *Tsar Nicholas I and the Jews*, Philadelphia, 1983.

Stein, L., 'Eder as Zionist', in Hobman (ed.), *David Eder. Memoirs of a Modern Pioneer*.

The Balfour Declaration, London, 1961.

Stevenson, J., and C. Cook, *The Slump*, London, 1979.

Symons, H. *Forty Years a Chief Rabbi. The Life and Times of Solomon Hirschell*, London, 1980.

Tal, U., *Christians and Jews in Germany: Religion, Politics and Ideology in the Second Reich, 1870–1914*, Ithaca, NY, 1975.

Taylor, A., *Laurence Oliphant, 1829–1888*, Oxford, 1982.

Taylor, H. A., *The British Press. A Critical Survey*, London, 1961.

Taylor, S., *The National Front in English Politics*, London, 1982.

Thurlow, R., *Fascism in Britain: A History, 1918–1985*, Oxford, 1987.

Trainor, R., 'Urban Elites in Victorian Britain', *Urban History Yearbook, 1985*, Leicester, 1985.

Tunstall, J., *Journalists at Work*, London, 1971.

Vital D., *The Origins of Zionism*, Oxford, 1980.

Zionism: The Formative Years, Oxford, 1982.

Zionism: The Crucial Phase, Oxford, 1987.

Voelz, R. A., '"... A Good Jew and a Good Englishman": The Jewish Lads' Brigade, 1894–1922', *JCH*, 23:1 (1988).

Walker, M., *The National Front*, London, 1977.

Wasserstein, B., *The British in Palestine: The Mandatory Government and the Arab-Jewish Conflict 1917–1929*, London, 1978.

Britain and the Jews of Europe 1939–1945, Oxford, 1979.

'Patterns of Jewish Leadership in Great Britain during the Nazi Era', in Braham (ed.), *Jewish Leadership during the Nazi Era: Patterns of Behaviour in the Free World*.

Waterman, S., and B. Kosmin, *British Jewry in the Eighties. A Statistical and Geographical Study*, London, 1986.

Waxman, M., *A History of Jewish Literature*, 5 vols., New York, 1945.

Weinryb, B., 'Poland', in Meyer *et al.* (eds.), *The Jews in the Soviet Satellites*.

Weitzmann, W. R., 'The Politics of the Viennese Jewish Community, 1890–1914', in Oxaal, Pollak and Botz (eds.), *Jews, Anti-Semitism and Culture in Vienna*.

Weizmann, Chaim, *Letters and Papers*, Series A, vol. 4, *January 1905–December 1906*, ed. Camillo Dresner and Barnett Litvinoff, Jerusalem, 1973.

Letters and Papers, Series A, vol. 5, *January 1907–February 1913*, ed. Hannah Weiner and Barnett Litvinoff, Jerusalem, 1973.

Letters and Papers, Series A, vol. 7, *August 1914–November 1917*, ed. Leonard Stein, Jerusalem, 1975.

Letters and Papers, Series A, vol. 10, *July 1920–December 1921*, ed. Bernard Wasserstein, Jerusalem, 1977.

Letters and Papers, Series A, vol. 11, *January 1922–July 1923*, ed. Bernard Wasserstein, New Brunswick, NJ, 1977.

Letters and Papers, Series A, vol. 13, *March 1926–October 1930*, ed. P. Ofer, Jerusalem, 1978.

Letters and Papers, Series A, vol. 19, *July 1939–October 1940*, ed. Norman Rose, Jerusalem, 1979.

Trial and Error. The Autobiography of Chaim Weizmann, London, 1949.

Wertheimer, J., *Unwelcome Strangers: East European Jews in Imperial Germany*, Oxford, 1987.

Whates, H. R. G., *The Birmingham Post 1857–1957. A Centenary Retrospect*, Birmingham, 1957.

White, J., *The Rothschild Buildings. Life in an East End Tenement Block, 1887–1920*, London, 1982.

Wiener, A. M., 'Tredegar Riots', *CAJEX*, 26:1 (1976).

Wiener, J. H. (ed.), *Innovators and Preachers. The Role of the Editor in Victorian England*, Westport, CT, 1985.

Wigley, J., *The Rise and Fall of the Victorian Sunday*, Manchester, 1980.

Williams, B. 'The Anti-Semitism of Tolerance: Middle-class Manchester and the Jews, 1870–1900', in Kidd and Roberts (eds.), *City, Class and Culture*.

The Making of Manchester Jewry, 1740–1875, paperback edition, Manchester, 1985.

Manchester Jewry: A Pictorial History 1788–1988, Manchester, 1988.

Williams, F., *Dangerous Estate. The Anatomy of Newspapers*, London, 1959.

Wilson, K. M., '"The Protocols of Zion" and the "Morning Post", 1919–1920', *Patterns of Prejudice*, 19:3 (1985).

Wistrich, R., *The Jews of Vienna in the Age of Franz Ferdinand*, Oxford, 1990.

Wolf, L., Presidential Address, 15 January 1912, *TJHSE*, 7 (1911–14).

Essays in Jewish History, ed. C. Roth, London, 1934.

'The Queen's Jewry', in Wolf, *Essays in Jewish History*.

Wyman, D., *Paper Walls. America and the Refugee Crisis, 1938–1941*, New York, 1985.

The Abandonment of the Jews. America and the Holocaust 1941–1945, New York, 1985.

Yarrow, S., 'The Impact of Hostility on Germans in Britain, 1914–1918', in Kushner and Lunn (eds.), *The Politics of Marginality*.

Yellin Bacharach, D., 'The Impact of the Dreyfus Affair on Great Britain', Ph.D. thesis, University of Minnesota, 1978.

Young, G. M., *Portrait of an Age: Victorian England*, Oxford, 1986.

Young, H., *One of Us*, London, 1989.

Zipperstein, S., *The Jews of Odessa. A Cultural History, 1794–1881*, Stanford, 1985.

Zweig, R. W., *Britain and Palestine during the Second World War*, London, 1986.

Index

Frankel, David   3
Frankel, William   210, 246, fig. 13
 Board of *JC* member   237
 CBE   235
 editor *JC*   211–35
Franklin, Ellis   9
Franklin, Jacob   8–14, 15, 49
'Frankly Feminine'   232
Franks, Maurice   168
Freedman, Maurice   198, 199–200
Freeman, A. E.   62
French Jewish press   4
Freud, Lucien   203
Friedberg, Barnett   140
From Doom to Hope   242–3
Fyvel, Tosco   197, 238

Galicia, Jews in   29
'Gallery'   237
Garbacz, Bernard   241
gas chambers   176
 reports of   179
Gaster, Moses   90, 106, 122, 123, 124, 127
Gates, Marion   113, 158
Gelberg, Simon (Simon Gilbert)   74–5, 97
 disagreement with editor   99–100
General Elections (1847)   19–20; (1852)
  21; (1857)   35–6; (1865)   38; (1868)
  39; (1885)   50; (1892)   72, 73; (1895)
  73; (1900)   74; (1905)   99; (1945)
  188; (1966–74)   234; (1983)   242;
  (1987)   242
General Strike   139
German Jewish press   3–4
Germany
 anti-Semitism in   82–3
 emancipation of Jews   29
 Jews in   29, 59, 115–16, 174
 Nazism in   145–6, 147, 148, 164–5, 180
 post-war   204–5
 Reform Movement   17–18
 refugees from   147, 159–60
 Weimar Republic   82–3
Gertler, Mark   112, 203
Gilbert, Simon (Simon Gelberg)   74–5,
  143–4, 145, 146, 148–9, 193
 associate editor *JC*   158
 beliefs   147, 149–50
 on Nazi blacklist   168
 'Watchman'   153
Gilmour, Ian   229
Gladstone, William Ewart   x, 55, 88–9,
  250
 views on Jews and the Eastern Question
  62–4
Glanville, Brian   203, 213

Glasgow Evening News   93–4
Glasgow, Jews in   144, 239
 anti-Jewish riots in, 1947   195
Gluckstein, Leopold   62
Golding, Louis   138, 197, 203
Goldman, William   203
Goldmann, Nahum   208
Goldsmid, Col. Albert   78
Goldsmid, Sir Francis   41, 60
Goldsmith, Maurice   xii, 151, 159
Gollancz, Victor   204
Goodman, Harry   201
Goodman, Lord   226
Gordon, David   70
Gordon, Lionel   237
Gordon, Samuel   94
'Gossip'   44
Gould, Julius   215
Graetz, Heinrich   32, 49
Great Depression   144
Great Synagogue   56, 79
Green, A.A.   94, 95, 109
Green, Revd Aaron Levy   52, 92
'Green Flag'   197
Greenberg, Florence   138
 Jewish Cookery Book   198, 253
Greenberg, Ivan   141, 142, 156, fig. 10
 beliefs   159–60, 180, 183–90
 editor of *JC*   158–91
 on Nazi blacklist   168
 sacked   190–2, 198
Greenberg, Leopold   158, fig. 1
 beliefs   105–7, 110, 122–33, 136
 death and burial   140–1
 editor of *JC*   105–41
 'Mentor'   109, 112, 115, 116, 119, 120,
  121, 124, 134–5
 proprietor of *JC*   103–5
Gross, John   212
Grunfeld, Dayan Isidor   200
Grynszpan, Herschel   165
Guardian (Church of England)   166
Guedalla, Philip   136
Gumb, Alex   169, 189, 190
Gush Emunim Movement   231
Guthrie, Alfred Brown   158, 166
Gwynne, H.A.   136

Ha-measef   3
Haas, Jacob de   69, 88
Habsburg Empire, Jewish emancipation in
  29
Hackney   202
Haganah   188, 194
'Halitvak'   112
Halpern, Capt. Joshua   184

proprietors
  Abraham Benisch; Lionel Louis
    Cohen; Israel Davis; Leopold
    Greenberg; Joseph Mitchell; Samuel
    Montagu; Sidney Montagu Samuel;
    Isaac Vallentine; Lionel van Oven *see*
    individual entries
purchase of *Jewish Gazette* 197–8
readership survey 231–2, 239
regional coverage 101, 197
relaunch 16
revitalisation 211–12
role in creation of Board of Guardians
    35
role in Jewish identity 45, 248–53
strike 96–7
supplements 197, 232
support for Jewish projects 252–3
technical improvements 96–7, 154–5,
    156
and Yiddish culture 100, 112, 203
and Yiddish press 96
Jewish Chronicle and Hebrew Observer 32
*Jewish Chronicle and Working Man's
    Friend* 14
Jewish Chronicle Chair in Jewish Studies
    252
Jewish Chronicle Company 198
Jewish Chronicle Ltd 225, 247
Jewish Chronicle Literary Prize 232
Jewish Chronicle Newspaper Ltd 225
Jewish Chronicle Publications 252
Jewish Chronicle Travel Guide 198
Jewish Chronicle Trust Ltd 224–6, 247
Jewish Chronicle Year Book 198
Jewish Colonial Trust 103, 154
Jewish Commonwealth 129
Jewish crime 40, 109
  causes of 136–7
Jewish Daily Post 154
Jewish defence 149, 150, 151, 159–60,
    202, 215, 241
Jewish displaced persons 183, 188, 204
Jewish emancipation 5–7, 18–23, 35–6
  in Europe 29–30
  threats to 63–4
Jewish employment practices 159
Jewish Gazette 197–8, 210, 225
Jewish Graphic 140
Jewish Guardian 127, 139–40
Jewish Historical Society of England x,
    91, 96, 100, 249
Jewish immigrants 23, 30, 57–8, 70–5,
    75–82
  conscription 119

cultural and religious differences 57–8,
    75–8
socialist activities 79
Jewish labour movement 79, 80
Jewish Ladies' Society for Preventative and
    Rescue Work 109
Jewish Lads' Brigade 78
Jewish Leader 115
Jewish Memorial Council 137
Jewish military service 94–5, 117–20, 166
Jewish National Fund 132
Jewish National Home 128, 130, 164,
    184, 188
Jewish Observer and Middle East Review
    236
Jewish Opinion 127
Jewish People's Council Against Fascism
    and Anti-Semitism 151, 152
Jewish Peril 135
Jewish poor 5, 23–4, 34–5, 57–9, 64–5, 76,
    77–8, 137 *see also* East End
Jewish press
  American 28–9, 43, 115–16
  Anglo-Jewish *see* separate entry
  Continental 3–4, 10, 21, 28–9, 248, 249
  Russian 41
  Yiddish *see* separate entry
Jewish Recorder 49, 67, 68
Jewish refugees 164–5, 180, 182
  from Austria 159–60
  from Nazi Germany 147, 159–60
Jewish Regiment 119–20
Jewish Religious Education Board 91
Jewish Religious Union 113
Jewish Representative Council 146
Jewish Review 200–1
Jewish Soup Kitchen 24
Jewish Standard 171, 180, 183
Jewish stereotypes 27, 39–40, 110–11,
    148–9
  see also images and myths
Jewish Synod 91–2
Jewish tailors' strike (1889) 80
Jewish Telegraph 197
Jewish Telegraphic Agency 236
Jewish Territorial Organisation 101, 103
Jewish terrorism 109, 186–9, 193–5
Jewish trades directory 65
Jewish trade unions 80
Jewish Travel Guide 252–3
Jewish vote 35, 38–9, 55, 150, 242
Jewish Weekly 140
Jewish Welfare Board 226, 232
Jewish women 24–5, 92–3
  conscription of Israeli 207

Lightning Source UK Ltd.
Milton Keynes UK
UKOW03f0611250614

234016UK00007B/136/P